To my sons Zoltán and Tibor

Language and Translation in International Commercial Arbitration

From the Constitution of the Arbitral Tribunal through Recognition and Enforcement Proceedings

by

Tibor Várady

T•M•C• Asser Press
The Hague

Published by T·M·C·ASSER PRESS
P.O. Box 16163, 2500 BD The Hague, The Netherlands
<www.asserpress.nl>

T·M·C·ASSER PRESS' English language books are distributed exclusively by:

Cambridge University Press, The Edinburgh Building, Shaftesbury Road,
Cambridge CB2 2RU, UK,
or
for customers in the USA, Canada and Mexico:
Cambridge University Press, 100 Brook Hill Drive, West Nyack, NY 10994-2133, USA
<www.cambridge.org>

ISBN 978-90-6704-233-8

Foreword

Anyone who has acted as arbitrator or counsel in an arbitration in which more than one language was used, sat as judge on an international court that had more than one working language, or served on a drafting committee of a multi-language treaty knows how many unexpected complications, both procedural and substantive, the 'language issue' can create. And the problems that arise in that context are not limited to those that relate to the choice of the most appropriate translation of a particular word or that arise from a later discovered translation error. Although finding the most appropriate translation for a given word or phrase to be used when drafting legal documents intended to be equally authentic, for example, is by no means always an easy matter. Language issues can present innumerable more serious types of problems depending on a particular legal setting; they can also have unforeseen and costly consequences.

In this thoroughly researched and carefully structured book, Professor Tibor Várady focuses on the variety of language issues that can arise at different stages of international commercial arbitration proceedings. He also proposes sound and creative solutions designed to help the parties to the proceedings, their arbitrators and counsel to anticipate and resolve these problems. The result is, to my knowledge, the first book-length monograph on the subject that addresses all language issues likely to arise in international commercial arbitrations. What is more, it is a work of high scholarly quality. Although such a combination of the practical and theoretical is rare, Professor Várady has managed to achieve it.

This book could probably only have been written by a person of Professor Várady's rather unique linguistic background and his extensive practical experience as a commercial arbitrator who also happens to be an eminent scholar. He was born an ethnic Hungarian in the former Yugoslavia, which at the time was a multi-language country in which Serbo-Croat predominated; he is married to an ethnic Serb; he studied law in Belgrade where the language of instruction was Serbian, although his first language was Hungarian; and he wrote his Master of Laws thesis and Doctor of Juridical Science dissertation in English at the Harvard Law School. He has conducted arbitrations in five different languages and has taught in English at a number of American law schools, including the University of California at Berkeley, Emory University and Cornell University. He was a professor of law at the University of Novi Sad in Serbia, where the language of instruction is Serbian. Professor Várady now lives in Hungary and teaches at the Central European University in Budapest. There he lectures in English. He is also the co-author, with two American legal scholars, of *International Commercial Arbitration*, a leading American law school course book, now in its third edition.

What makes Professor Várady's present book so valuable, particularly as a text for practitioners, is the systematic manner in which he deals with the multitude of language issues that can arise in arbitration proceedings, beginning with language-related issues that should be addressed prior to the constitution of an arbitral tribunal and concluding with those likely to arise in judicial proceedings following the arbitral award. Also analyzed are the various considerations relating to the determination of the language of the arbitration, problems of translation and interpretation in international arbitration proceedings, and many other matters in which language issues can play an important role in the arbitral context. What is more, the book provides the reader with strategies for the avoidance of language problems and with an overview of the language regulations that different national and international arbitration facilities have promulgated. Relevant arbitral and judicial jurisprudence is also analyzed. All in all, this book provides the reader with a comprehensive and insightful study of a subject that until the publication of Professor Várady's impressive work had been largely neglected in the literature.

The Hague, September 2006

Judge Thomas BUERGENTHAL
International Court of Justice

Preface and Acknowledgements

Plurality of languages is certainly one of the hallmarks of international dispute resolution – and of international commercial arbitration in particular. The parties typically belong to different linguistic and cultural backgrounds; communication within the arbitration process is an interaction with anchors in different cultures. Interface between languages and choices between languages are charted by rules, there are sanctions for infringements of these rules – and there are controversies regarding the rules and their application. This book endeavors to follow issues linked to language and translation through various stages of the process: starting with problems and logistic dilemmas which appear in the pre-arbitration phase, continuing with a focus on the arbitration proceedings proper, and concluding with an analysis of the issues in post-award court proceedings.

One of the reasons prompting this book (just as a number of other books) is the spectacular expansion of international commercial arbitration during the past decades. It is important to note that what has changed is not only the number of cases submitted to arbitration, or the number of legislative acts devoted to arbitration. We have also witnessed an impressive growth in complexity, and a diversification of cases and problem-patterns. A considerable number of issues have gained relevance only recently. Practice has produced more ideas (and dilemmas) than theoretical anticipation. Within recent years, issues linked to language and translation have become the subject matter of a newly shaped and quite significant practice (both arbitration and court practice), and this development has brought to the surface a growing variety of questions, distinctions, and challenges. This new reality has not yet received a fitting conceptualization; this is still very much a task ahead of us. Another task is the articulation of appropriate guidance for participants in the arbitration process. This book was inspired by these tasks.

Within these introductory sentences, I would like to express my sincere appreciation to all those who lent support, and offered valuable information and suggestions. I would particularly like to mention the help I received from arbitral institutions, and notably from Dr. Éva Horváth, President of the Budapest Court of Arbitration, Dr. Davor Babić, Secretary of the Zagreb Court of Arbitration, Mr. Detlev Kühner, Counsel of the ICC International Court of Arbitration, Dr. Manfred Heider, Counsel of the Vienna International Court of Arbitration and Ms. Mirjana Čukavac, Secretary of the Belgrade Court of Arbitration. I also owe gratitude to colleagues, practitioners, law teachers, and students, including Professor Harold Berman, Professor Krešimir Sajko, Dr. Pierre Karrer, Dr. Hans

Kopp, Professor Arsen Janevski, Dr. János Burai-Kovács, and Lucja Nowak LL.M. I am indebted to Mr. Alan McConnel Duff, the only non-lawyer on this list, an author of books on translation, for his ideas, and suggestions.

I owe special gratitude to my research assistant Ms. Dalma Demeter LL.M, for her most thorough research, for her valuable comments and assistance in editing.

Tibor Várady

Contents

Abbreviations

AAA	American Arbitration Association
ABGB	German Act on General Conditions
ACICA	Australian Centre for International Commercial Arbitration
AIA	Italian Arbitration Association
ASA Bulletin	Swiss Arbitration Association Bulletin
BANI	Indonesian National Board of Arbitration
Basel Rules	Arbitration Rules of the Basel Chamber of Commerce
BCCI	Court of Arbitration at the Bulgarian Chamber of Commerce and Industry
Belgrade Rules	Foreign Trade Court of Arbitration at the Serbian Chamber of Commerce, Rules of Arbitration
BGB	the German Civil Code
BGH	Bundesgerictshof
Budapest Court of Arbitration	Court of Arbitration at the Hungarian Chamber of Commerce and Industry
Budapest Rules	Rules of Arbitration
Bulgarian Rules / BCCI Rules	Rules of Arbitration of the Court of Arbitration at the Bulgarian Chamber of Commerce and Industry (BCCI)
CAMCA	Commercial Arbitration and Mediation Center for the Americas
CEPANI	Belgian Center for the Study and Practice of National and International Arbitration
CIETAC	China International Economic and Trade Arbitration Commission
CIETAC Rules	Rules of Arbitration of 2005
CRCICA	Cairo Regional Center for International Commercial Arbitration
CSD	Claims Settlement Declaration
DIS	German Arbitration Institute
DIS Rules	Rules of Arbitration of 1998
English Arbitration Act / UK Arbitration Act	Arbitration Act for England, Northern Ireland and Wales, 1996
GAFTA	Grain and Feed Trade Association
German Arbitration Act	German Code of Civil Procedure, Book Ten on Arbitration Procedure, 1998
Hague Convention / 1965 Hague Convention	Hague Convention on Service Abroad of Judicial and Extrajudicial Documents in Civil or Commercial Matters, 1965
HKIAC	Hong Kong International Arbitration Centre
Hong Kong Rules	Hong Kong International Arbitration Centre, Procedures for the Administration of International Arbitration, 2005
I.C.J.	International Court of Justice
IBA	International Bar Association

ICAC	International Commercial Arbitration Court at the Chamber of Commerce and Industry of the Russian Federation (or Russian Rules)
ICC Bulletin	ICC International Court of Arbitration Bulletin
ICC Court of Arbitration	International Court of Arbitration at the International Chamber of Commerce
ICC Rules	ICC Rules of Arbitration of 1998
ICSID	International Centre for Settlement of Investment Disputes
ICTY	International Criminal Tribunal for the former Yugoslavia
LCIA	London Court of International Arbitration
LCIA Rules	Rules of Arbitration of 1998
LICA	Bulgarian Law on International Commercial Arbitration, 1988
LMAA	London Maritime Arbitrators Association
MERCOSUR Agreement	MERCOSUR Agreement on International Commercial Arbitration, 1998
MIGA	Multilateral Investment Guarantee Agency
Milano Rules	Milan Chamber of National and International Arbitration, International Arbitration Rules, 2004
Model Law / UNCITRAL Model Law	UNCITRAL Model Law on International Commercial Arbitration, 1985
Model Rules / UNCITRAL Model Rules	UNCITRAL Arbitration Rules, 1976
NAI	Netherlands Arbitration Institute
New York Convention	New York Convention on Recognition and Enforcement of Foreign Arbitral Awards, 1958
OHADA	Organisation pour l'Harmonisation en Afrique du Droit des Affaires
PCA	The Hague Permanent Court of Arbitration
Prague Rules	Court of Arbitration at the Czech Chamber of Commerce, Rules of Arbitration
Russian Rules	International Commercial Arbitration Court at the Chamber of Commerce and Industry of the Russian Federation (or ICAC)
SFRY	Socialist Federal Republic of Yugoslavia
SIAC	Singapore International Arbitration Center
Stockholm Rules	Stockholm Chamber of Commerce Arbitration Institute, Arbitration Rules of 1999
Swiss Rules	Swiss Rules of International Arbitration, 2004
UNCITRAL Notes	UNCITRAL Notes on Organizing Arbitral Proceedings, 1996
US Arbitration Act	United States Federal Arbitration Act, 1925
Vienna Arbitral Center	International Arbitration Center of the Austrian Federal Economic Chamber
Vienna Rules	Rules of Arbitration and Conciliation
Warsaw Rules	Rules of the Court of Arbitration at the Polish Chamber of Commerce, 2003
WIPO	World Intellectual Property Organization
Zagreb Rules	Court of Arbitration at the Croatian Chamber of Commerce, Rules of Arbitration
Zürich Rules	International Arbitration Rules of the Zurich Chamber of Commerce

Chapter I

Notions and Concepts

A. Introduction

A.1. **Prologue – A case which stumbled for reasons of language**

I would like to start this introductory chapter with recollections of a case in which the issue of language was not heeded in due time, and the arbitrators were eventually confronted with an intractable problem. I received an invitation to act as third arbitrator in an *ad hoc* case. The invitation was sent by an Italian arbitrator chosen by the Italian respondent. The invitation was written in French. I also received a copy of the contract which was written in Italian and another copy in the language of a former Soviet republic. I was more or less able to understand the arbitration clause in Italian, and I asked a friend to help me to be sure I got it right. The other language was not a Slavic language – it was a language which I did not understand at all. It was stated in the Italian text of the contract that the two versions of the contract were equally valid. (I guess this was stated in both versions.) The arbitrator appointed by the Claimant wrote me to confirm my nomination as third arbitrator. This letter was in Russian. I do not really speak Russian, but I have spent most of my life in Yugoslavia, and I studied and taught in a language then called Serbo-Croatian (today Serbian, Croatian and Bosnian are considered as separate languages in the constitutions of the new States which emerged after the dissolution of Yugoslavia). Given a certain proximity between Serbian and Russian, I was able to understand the letter. (It would not have been difficult to guess its content anyway.)

The arbitration clause stated that each party will nominate its arbitrator, and the party-nominated arbitrators will choose the third arbitrator. (There was no fallback provision for the case the two arbitrators would not agree on the third one – and this is probably the only potential problem which did not become a real one.) The arbitration clause also stated that after the tribunal was constituted, the arbitrators should meet in the city where the third arbitrator has his domicile. It was further specified that during their initial meeting, the arbitrators should agree on the language of the arbitration proceedings, on the applicable procedural rules, and on the applicable substantive law.

My first dilemma was in which language should I communicate with my fellow arbitrators before we met to agree on the language of the proceedings.

I eventually wrote in the languages in which I received the letters: in French to the arbitrator appointed by the Respondent, and in Russian to the arbitrator appointed by the Claimant. (For the Russian letter I needed help. I drafted the letter in English, and a student of mine from Russia translated it.) I was hoping that this problem was of a transitory nature, and that we shall come up with a language we all speak when we get together in Budapest. This was not the case. It turned out that the arbitrator appointed by the Claimant spoke only his native language and Russian, while the arbitrator appointed by the Respondent spoke Italian and French – and some English, which was about as dubious as my Russian. We had no language in common. I tried to translate between Russian and French. I can read a legal text in Russian with a chance to understand maybe 60 or possibly 70 percent of it, and with some luck, I can handle some simple conversation. This is, of course, way short of being able to conduct an arbitration case in Russian. The Italian colleague did not speak any Russian, and the other colleague did not speak any of the languages spoken by the Italian colleague. I have to add, of course, that neither the Italian colleague nor myself spoke a word of the native language of the arbitrator appointed by the Claimant. Thus, we had no language in common.

At that point, my only consolation was the thought that this episode could serve as a convincing example with which I could demonstrate to my students why is it advisable to include in the arbitration agreement a provision on the language of the arbitral proceedings. Had this been the case, different arbitrators would have been chosen, since both the parties and the arbitrators would have been mindful of the language requirement at the time when their decisions – to appoint or to accept the appointment – were made.

As we discussed – or tried to discuss – possible steps towards organizing the case, we were aware of the circumstance that according to the arbitration clause, one of our duties during the initial meeting was to determine the language of the arbitral proceedings. Normally, the language of the proceedings is determined by the parties themselves or, in the absence of party agreement, by the arbitrators. Here we had a party agreement which explicitly deferred the decision to the arbitrators. The question arose on what grounds and according to what principles we should choose a language. The Italian colleague argued that as a rule, the language of the contract serves as a foothold for making the proper choice. He referred to Article 15(3) of the 1988 Rules of the International Court of Arbitration at the International Chamber of Commerce (hereinafter 'ICC Rules').[1] The language of the contract typically does not mandate a solution –

[1] According to Art. 15(3) of the 1988 Rules, in the absence of party agreement the Arbitral Tribunal shall determine the language (or languages) of the arbitration '[d]ue regard being paid to all relevant circumstances and in particular to the language of the contract'. (The 1998 Rules

actually it does not even represent a presumption – but it is, unquestionably a consequential indicator. Not in our case, however, because the contract was drafted in two languages, and the two versions were declared to be equal.

Could we have chosen a language just because it would have been the language spoken by all three arbitrators? In other words, can the choice of the language of arbitration be based on considerations of convenience for the arbitrators themselves, rather than on links with the parties and their contract? I suppose yes – although this is certainly not an ideal solution. The parties clearly have the first shot at determining a suitable language of arbitration. If they fail to make use of this opportunity, the choice falls to the arbitrators. It is certainly desirable for the arbitrators to choose a language which is tied to the parties and to their contract, but the arbitrators also have to be mindful of the decision-making process and of the conditions of their own participation in it.

Yet in our case, none of the above considerations could have yielded a solution. We did not have a language in common. Whichever language would have been chosen, at least one of us would have had to rely on translation. It is not uncommon for a party – or an attorney for a party – to communicate through a translator. Could this apply to the arbitrators themselves? Would this be professionally acceptable? There may be no norm preventing such practice, and there have indeed been some cases in which one of the arbitrators did not speak the language of the arbitral proceedings, and had to rely on translation. The question is whether this is a desirable practice. Also, I am not aware of any case in which the arbitrators needed a translator in order to communicate between themselves.

After some discussion we decided that our composition would impede decision making in line with good practices. We informed the parties that each of us was individually willing to act as an arbitrator – but a different composition was needed. We also suggested to the parties to agree on the language of the proceedings before re-starting the process of nomination.

This case is – fortunately – not typical. I have used it as an introduction because it highlights with almost brutal emphasis the issue of language, and the need to make timely arrangements regarding the language of arbitration. Such timely arrangements are often missing. This rarely creates an impasse, but may very well give rise to serious difficulties. Problems related to language and translation are, of course, not restricted to the stage of choosing a language; they may emerge – and often do emerge – during the arbitration proceedings, and also during subsequent court proceedings dealing with arbitral awards. Let

---

have somewhat de-emphasized the role of the language of the contract. It is still the only point of support mentioned, but Art. 16 of the 1998 Rules refers to all relevant circumstances 'including the language of the contract'.)

me mention just a few of the many emerging questions. The question has, for example, arisen, what considerations and what strategies guide the choice of the language of arbitration – and how the participants in the proceedings should adapt to the chosen language. The language of communication between the parties and the arbitral institution may become an issue – just as the language of communication between the parties themselves and with the arbitrators – before the language of arbitration was determined. The question also arises what the language of arbitration actually encompasses, and what are the procedural consequences of omissions or shortcomings regarding language and translation. The relationship between use of languages (or failure to use some languages) and due process is often an issue both during arbitral proceedings and in court proceedings controlling the award. This book will endeavor to identify and to analyze these and similar issues following the sequence of arbitral proceedings from its inception through the rendering of the award, and it will also follow issues linked to language and translation in post-award court proceedings.

This first chapter will endeavor to clarify notions and concepts pertaining to the language of arbitration.

A.2. **Does globalization extend to language?**

The emergence of language-related issues and problems in arbitration is not unusual or surprising. International commercial arbitration is a transcultural venture. The parties typically belong to different linguistic and cultural backgrounds; the contract is sometimes drafted in a third language. Communication is typically an interaction with anchors in different cultures. The applicable substantive law may add to the cultural variety, since the parties frequently opt for a 'neutral law'. Furthermore, quite often, the language of correspondence changes during the development of an international business transaction; moreover, documents which become relevant during the dispute are frequently drafted in different languages.

The question may arise, whether diversity with regard to language will at some point be superseded by a *lingua franca* of international commercial arbitration – and of international trade in general. A similar process has already taken place with regard to the **law** of international commercial arbitration. A strong trend of **unification** was propelled by the 1958 New York Convention on Recognition and Enforcement of Foreign Arbitral Awards (hereinafter 'New York Convention'), and by some other conventions. At the same time, an equally strong trend of **convergence** has been fostered by the 1985 UNCITRAL Model Law on International Commercial Arbitration (hereinafter 'Model Law' or 'UNCITRAL Model Law'). Moreover, extensive room for maneuver – practically independent from municipal legislators – was created by the universally accepted broad concept of party autonomy. Within this maneuvering room, institutional rule making followed the same patterns, and became increasingly harmonized worldwide. Thus, it has become possible to speak of a 'world law of international commercial arbitration'. In part this may still only be a metaphor, but to a considerable extent the world law of international commercial arbitration has already become reality.[2]

Of course, it is most important to point out that the world law of international commercial arbitration has not been created by way of giving extended world wide recognition to **one** national set of norms and solutions. What took place is not a worldwide reception of, say, the English, or French, or German, or US, or Chinese law. The norms which have become universal – or quasi universal – have emerged by way of a compromise, or as a result of spontaneous harmonization. With regard to language, this is simply not an option; and this is an important reason why the establishment of one language as the language of international commercial arbitration is not likely to occur in the foreseeable future.

The multilingual reality is not always readily perceived. I would like to mention here a somewhat baffling case in which the Commercial Court of Tashkent City (Uzbekistan) refused to enforce a GAFTA award[3] in favor of Romak S. A. from Geneva because the award presented to the Uzbek court was not translated into Uzbek, the official language of Uzbekistan. Describing the efforts to obtain recognition, Mealey's Report states that: 'A source told Mealey's International Arbitration Report that Romak officials have been in touch with Uzbek government officials here and in Tashkent.' It was even mentioned that during the contacts with Uzbek officials the question was raised whether '[U]zbekistan's military cooperation with the US military campaign in neighboring Afghanistan might affect Romak's efforts to collect the award…'.[4] This strategy may have reminded Uzbek authorities of the atmosphere during previous decades, when political interventions and references to the ideological priorities of the day had a chance to trump observance of legal rules. It would have been simpler to take another course of action, to heed the fact that newly independent States have a sense of national pride – which is perfectly compatible with international law. This sense of national pride led to the decision to adopt Uzbek as the official language – and it may have also contributed to decisions to join interna-

---

[2] See Várady-Barcelo-Von Mehren, *International Commercial Arbitration – A Transnational Perspective*, 3rd edn. (Thomson &West 2006) pp. v-vi.

[3] Award of the Grain and Feed Trade Association, London, between Romak S. A. Geneva, and FTC Uzdon Tashkent, reported in 16-10 *Mealey's International Arbitration Report* (2001) 2.

[4] Ibidem.

tional agreements (including the New York Convention) as a new State. For the party seeking recognition to have heeded this fact would simply have meant respecting Article IV(2) of the New York Convention.[5] Only the submission of the award in an Uzbek translation – as required by Article IV(2) – could have represented a true test for the Uzbek judiciary.

One has to mention that, in the course of history, there have been endeavors to establish a uniform international legal language. Pliny the Younger went even so far as to predict the establishment of a universal language without restriction to some specific field of human activity. In his words:

> 'Italy has been selected by God to collect dispersed power, to soften customs and to unite, by the communion of one language, the diverse and barbarous dialects of so many peoples, so that all the races of mankind should have one fatherland.'[6]

The language that was supposed to supersede the various barbarous dialects was, of course, Latin. No field of human activity provided as much support for the prediction of Pliny as the realm of law. Within Europe at least, Latin was the language of the law over centuries. Nevertheless, it is clear today that Pliny was wrong. The 'barbarous' languages prevailed.

There have been other relatively short episodes of dominance of a language in the domain of law within a geographic region. An interesting example is the emergence of 'Law French' in England in the Middle Ages.[7] In his book *The Language of the Law* Mellinkoff devotes a chapter to the 'Rise and Fall of Law French'.[8] He states that '[f]rom mid-thirteenth century on, at least through the Middle English period, French predominates as the language of the law'.[9]

The question arises whether after Latin, another language will get a chance on a global level. At this moment – at least in our field – English is inching towards a position similar to that held by Latin several centuries ago. Nowadays, English has become the most widely used language in the areas of international trade and international commercial arbitration. Yet the variety of

---

[5] According to Art. 4(2) 'If the said award ... is not made in an official language of the country in which the award is relied upon, the party applying for recognition and enforcement of the award shall produce a translation of these documents into such language... .' After the dissolution of the USSR, the Uzbek language became the only official language of Uzbekistan.

[6] See Macartney, *National States and National Minorities, Russel and Russel* (New York 1986) p. 27.

[7] Pollock and Maitland (*The History of English Law*, 2nd edn. 1898, p. 205) note that law French became the language of the courts.

[8] David Mellinkoff, *The Language of the Law* (Boston-Toronto, Little, Brown and Comp. 1963) Chapter IX starts at p. 95.

[9] Mellinkoff, op. cit. p. 99.

languages is still a fact of life. The future will tell whether this variety will ever be superseded by English as a *lingua franca*, or whether some other language – say Chinese – will get a similar chance at some point.

For the time being – and in the foreseeable future – the language issue is unlikely to be resolved by the adoption of one of the many languages of the world as the only language of international commercial arbitration. It is much more rational to expect a different type of synchronization: a worldwide harmonization of standards, which will guide us how to choose between different languages, or how to combine different languages.

A.3. Language and the market value of arbitral institutions

Openness towards the use of more than one language is more consanguine with a transnational approach – and it is also an important element of the market value of arbitral institutions. The designation of one language as the only possible ('official') language of an arbitral institution would certainly screen (and reduce) the cases submitted to this institution. The losses might be quite considerable, particularly if the given sole language was not among the widely spoken languages.

The market value of the arbitral institution would in all likelihood decrease if, say, Czech were posited to be the only possible language of arbitral proceedings at the Prague Court of Arbitration, or if Hungarian were the only possible language before the Budapest Court of Arbitration – but negative consequences would probably also arise if French or English were the only possible language of ICC arbitrations. Even arbitral institutions anchored in English-speaking countries (like the London Court of International Arbitration, hereinafter 'LCIA', or the American Arbitration Association, hereinafter 'AAA') allow in their rules a free choice of other languages.

In ICC arbitrations, English is clearly the dominant, but not the sole language. In their commentary on the ICC Rules, Schäfer, Verbist and Imhoos state that the ICC Rules are 'language neutral' and allow arbitral proceedings in any imaginable language.[10] The ICC does not publish exact statistics about the languages used, but the ICC International Court of Arbitration Bulletin (hereinafter: '*ICC Bulletin*') gives data[11] which provide orientation. Here are some figures from recent years:

---

10 Schäfer, Verbist, Imhoos, *Die ICC Schiedsgerichtsordnung in der Praxis* (Bonn 2000). It is stated at p. 110: ‚Die ICC SchO ist „sprachneutral", d.h. sie lässt es zu, daß Schiedsverfahren in jeder denkbaren Sprache geführt werden.'

11 These data consider the language of the *award*. The language of the award normally coincides with the language of the proceedings. There are cases, however, where the award is rendered in one language, while more languages are used during the proceedings.

2000 – awards were rendered in English, French, German, Spanish, Italian and Portuguese. About three-quarters of the awards were rendered in English, two thirds of the remainder were in French.[12]
2001 – awards were rendered in English (72%), French (17%), German (5%), Spanish (4%), Italian and Portuguese.[13]
2002 – awards were rendered in English (72%), French (16%), Spanish (6%), German (3%), Italian, Polish, Portuguese, and Russian.[14]
2003 – about three quarters of the awards were rendered in English, the second most frequently used language was French, followed by Spanish, German, Portuguese, Russian and Hungarian.[15]

These figures show a dominance of English, but also offer support for the assumption that openness towards more languages may be an important marketing asset of the arbitral institution.

At this point, it is interesting to investigate a possible correlation between the language of the proceedings and the value of the dispute. We shall focus on institutional environments where the language of the seat of arbitration does not belong to one of the 'world languages'. It is logical that in cases in which the value of the dispute is more substantial, the foreign party is inclined to choose an attorney from his/her own country, and might very well want to designate an arbitrator from his/her own country. For a US party, for example, it might be difficult to find an attorney and arbitrator of his/her country who could speak say Albanian (or Czech, Slovak, Danish, Dutch, Hungarian, Serbian, Polish, Croatian, etc.) as a second language; accordingly, it becomes a fact of considerable importance whether the, say, Polish (or Czech, Hungarian, Danish, Dutch, Croatian, Slovak, Serbian, etc.) court of arbitration is open and ready to conduct arbitral proceedings in other languages. If such an opportunity exists, it is likely to be relied upon more frequently in cases in which the disputed value is higher. (Which also means that parties will more easily confide disputes of a higher value to an institution which provides for such an opportunity.)

I tried to examine the possible correlation between the value of the dispute and the language of the proceedings on a few examples from Central-Eastern Europe. From the Court of Arbitration at the Hungarian Chamber of Commerce and Industry hereinafter 'Budapest Court of Arbitration'), I received the following data:[16]

---

[12] 12/1 *ICC Bulletin* (Spring 2001) p. 12.
[13] 13/1 *ICC Bulletin* (Spring 2002) p. 13.
[14] 14/1 *ICC Bulletin* (Spring 2003) p. 16.
[15] 15/1 *ICC Bulletin* (Spring 2004) p. 15.
[16] Information kindly provided by Dr. Éva Horváth, President of the Budapest Court of Arbitration.

Hungarian Court of Arbitration – Cases involving a foreign party:

2001		
Total number of cases	49; cases conducted in a foreign language	10 = 20.4%
All cases above € 100.000	8; cases conducted in a foreign language	5 = 62.5%
2002		
Total number of cases	30; cases conducted in a foreign language	8 = 26.7%
All cases above € 100.000	9; cases conducted in a foreign language	5 = 55.6%
2003		
Total number of cases	137; cases conducted in a foreign language	18 = 13 %
All cases above € 100.000	47; cases conducted in a foreign language	12 = 26 %

With regard to the Court of Arbitration at the Croatian Chamber of Commerce[17] the figures are similar – although less indicative, given the smaller number of cases:

Croatian Court of Arbitration – Cases involving a foreign party:

2002		
Total number of cases	22; cases conducted in a foreign language	2 = 9%
All cases above € 100.000	3; cases conducted in a foreign language	1 = 33%
2003		
Total number of cases	13; cases conducted in a foreign language	1 = 8%
All cases above € 100.000	4; cases conducted in a foreign language	1 = 25%

One may conclude first of all, that it is very much a fact of life that international commercial arbitration is conducted world-wide in line with the same principles and according to the same (or similar) rules – but in different languages. At the same time, readiness and ability to entertain cases in another language than that of the seat of the institution is always a clear comparative advantage. This advantage may gain a particular importance when the language of the seat is not one of the widely spoken languages, and if the institution has ambitions to attract disputes about considerable value.

B. What Does the Language of Arbitration Encompass?

In the introduction above – and for the purposes of introductory considerations – I was talking about the 'language of international commercial arbitration'. This is probably adequate to indicate the area of the problem. More precision is needed, however, when particular issues are being faced. Language problems

---

[17] Information kindly provided by Dr. Davor Babić, Secretary of the Zagreb Court of Arbitration.

are emerging – and getting resolved – in great many arbitration cases. This often takes place without conceptualizing the problem. The number of scholarly studies devoted to the language of international commercial arbitration is surprisingly small. During the past decades some changes have taken place. Theory has still not devoted much attention to the problem, but there has been a considerable increase in the number of arbitration acts and institutional rules that contain norms dedicated to the issue of language. There are also more cases emerging in both arbitral and judicial practice in which language-related problems have been explicitly raised as a contested issue. The emerging rules and cases demonstrate the need for more precision and conceptual clarity. Questions are surfacing regarding notions, definitions, distinctions, and also regarding the consequences of non-observance of the designated language. In this chapter, I would like to investigate various definitions and inferences from definitions (or inferences from the lack of definition), focusing on questions, which might (hopefully) facilitate a better understanding of the **notion itself**.

Let me start by raising the question what kind of communication are we actually talking about, when we speak of the issue of language in international commercial arbitration. The answer is not obvious – not even in model norms, which have guided the process of harmonization of the law of international commercial arbitration during the past decades. Article 22 (1) of the UNCITRAL Model Law, after stating how the 'language or languages to be used in arbitral proceedings' will be chosen or determined, also explains what such a designation will encompass:

> 'This agreement or determination, unless otherwise specified therein, shall apply to any written statement by a party, any hearing and any award, decision or other communication by the arbitral tribunal.'

The definition given by the 1976 UNCITRAL Arbitration Rules (hereinafter: 'Model Rules' or 'UNCITRAL Model Rules') is similar but not identical. According to Article 17(1):

> 'This determination shall apply to the statement of claim, the statement of defense, and any further written statements and, if oral hearing takes place, to the language or languages to be used in such hearings.'

The comparison shows an obvious difference. The definition used by the Model Rules does not mention 'award, decision or other communication by the arbitral tribunal'. This could have been remedied, say, by Article 32 of the Model Rules, which speaks of the form of the award, and thus, it could contain (but does not contain) rules on the language of the award. Is this omission intentional? I am inclined to say that it is not. Normally, the language of the proceedings is the same as the language of the award and the language of communication by the arbitral tribunal. There are no apparent reasons for divorcing the two. Moreover, if it were a matter of deliberate choice to adopt in the Model Rules a definition which does not cover the award and the language of communication by the arbitral tribunal, it would then have been logical to devote a special provision to these omitted elements, rather than leaving unresolved the question of the language of such important elements of the proceedings.

Even if some differences in formulations may not have been intentional, the question nevertheless arises: To what exactly does a language extend, once it was determined by the parties or by the arbitrators? More often than not, arbitration acts and rules of arbitral institutions do not define to what segments of the arbitral procedure the language of the arbitration proceedings extends. The terminology of the basic designation also varies. Unlike the Model Law and the Model Rules which deal with the 'language or languages to be used in the proceedings', the ICC Rules speak of 'the language or languages of arbitration' (Art. 16). The same term is used by some other institutional rules, such as Article 14 of the 2003 AAA International Arbitration Rules amended in 2006 and Article 17 of the 1998 London Court of International Arbitration Rules (hereinafter 'LCIA Rules'). Neither of these rules defines what the term 'language or languages of arbitration' encompasses. Article 17(1) of the LCIA Rules points out, however, as a distinct matter 'communications to and from the Registrar'.

The number of legislative acts and institutional rules that contain more precise definitions has increased during the past decades. To quote just a few examples, the 1987 Republic of Cyprus Act on International Commercial Arbitration (Art. 22), the 1993 Russian Arbitration Act (Art. 2), the 1994 Hungarian Act on Arbitration (Art. 30), the 1997 Iran Act on International Commercial Arbitration (Art. 21), the 1998 German Arbitration Act[18] (Art. 1045), the 2001 Croatian Arbitration Act (Art. 21), the 2003 Spanish Arbitration Act[19] (Art. 28), the 2004 Chile Arbitration Act (Art. 22), and the 2005 Polish Arbitration Act (Art. 1187)[20] have adopted the wording of Article 22(1) of the Model Law. A number of institutional rules adopted the wording of the Model Rules. This is the definition adopted for example in the Rules of the Hague Permanent Court of Arbitration (hereinafter 'PCA'),[21] Article 17 of the 2002 Rules of the

---

[18] Chapter Ten of the German Code of Civil Procedure (*Zivilprozessordnung*).

[19] In force since March 26, 2004.

[20] Part Five of the 1964 Polish Code of Civil Procedure as amended on October 17, 2005.

[21] The Permanent Court of Arbitration has several sets of rules: the 1992 Optional Rules for Arbitrating Disputes between Two States, the 1993 Optional Rules for Arbitrating Disputes between Two Parties of Which Only One Is a State, the 1996 Optional Rules for Arbitration Involv-

Cairo Regional Center for International Commercial Arbitration (hereinafter: 'CRCICA'), Article 14 of the 2002 Rules of Procedure of the Inter-American Commercial Arbitration Association, Article 20 of the 1997 Rules of the Singapore International Arbitration Center (SIAC), Article 17 of the 2004 Swiss Rules of International Arbitration (hereinafter: 'Swiss Rules'),[22] or Article 20 of the 2005 Rules of the Australian Centre for International Commercial Arbitration (ACICA). Other rules have espoused somewhat different formulations. To cite an example, according to 1998 the Rules of the German Arbitration Institute (hereinafter: 'DIS Rules'), the language of arbitration proceedings extends to 'any written statement by a party, any hearing and any award, decision or other communication by the arbitral tribunal' (Art. 22).

One could venture to say that differences in wordings do not stem from considered choices, but rather from a varying degree of precision (or imprecision) in referring to an area which has not been put into question by the drafters. It is probably safe to assume that it is generally understood that the language of arbitration proceedings should and does encompass all written and oral communications to and from the arbitral tribunal, including the award. There may be more, but I found only one example in which the language of proceedings ('the process of case examination') is explicitly divorced from the language of the award. This is Article 14 of the 2003 Procedural Rules of the Indonesian National Board of Arbitration (hereinafter 'BANI') in which Section 1 deals with language of the 'the process of case examination', while Section 4 deals with the language of the award.

I would like now to turn to a distinction that has been purposefully made by some recent institutional rules and which deserves special attention. According to the Rules of Arbitration and Conciliation of the International Arbitration Center of the Austrian Federal Economic Chamber (hereinafter: 'Vienna Rules'), for example, a clear distinction has been drawn between the language of arbitral proceedings and the language of communication between the arbitral institution and the parties. The language of arbitral proceedings is determined in the usual way – either by the parties, or by the arbitral tribunal (and – at least in principle – they could opt for any language). On the other hand, the language of

---

ing International Organizations and States, the 1996 Optional Rules for Arbitration between International Organizations and Private Parties. In all of these rules, language issues are regulated by Art. 17, which adopts the wording of the Model Rules.

22 The Swiss Rules are the first joint rules of various Swiss arbitral institutions. As it is stated in the Introduction of these Rules: '(b) In order to promote institutional arbitration in Switzerland and to harmonise the existing rules of arbitration, the Chambers of Commerce and Industry of Basel, Bern, Geneva, Ticino, Vaud and Zurich... have adopted the present uniform rules, the Swiss Rules of International Arbitration... which replace the Chambers' former rules of international arbitration.' These new uniform rules are in force since January 1, 2004.

communication with the institution is set by the Rules, which provide for two alternative administrative languages: German and English.[23]

As mentioned earlier, the concept of a separate language of communication with the institution has been recognized by Article 17(1) of the LCIA Rules. Some other rules have also adopted this concept.

The distinction between the language of arbitral proceedings and the language of communication with the arbitral institution may still be debatable, but it has gained some ground, and it deserves attention.

In the subsequent parts of this chapter, I shall focus separately on questions arising in connection with the language of arbitral proceedings, and questions arising in connection with the language of communication with the institution. Questions concerning the desirability of the separation of the two will also be addressed.

C. Determination of the Language of Arbitration – The Standard Answer and a Number of Questions and Distinctions

C.1. (Lack of) influence of courts and of municipal law on the language of arbitral proceedings

The language of arbitral proceedings and of awards is normally established by the parties (or by the arbitrators) without court interference, and without influence of norms of municipal laws. In international commercial arbitration the designation of the language of the proceedings belongs to the sphere of autonomy. Codes and statutes dealing with international commercial arbitration would typically only confirm this principle. A model of this legislative approach is Article 22 of the UNCITRAL Model Law. According to this Article:

> '1) The parties are free to agree on the language or languages to be used in the arbitral proceedings. Failing such agreement, the arbitral tribunal shall determine the language or languages to be used in the proceedings. This agreement or determination, unless otherwise specified therein, shall apply to any written statement by a party, any hearing and any award, decision or other communication by the arbitral tribunal.
> 2) The arbitral tribunal may order that any documentary evidence shall be accompanied by a translation into the language or languages agreed upon by the parties or determined by the arbitral tribunal.'

---

[23] This solution was introduced by Art. 4/a of the 2001 Vienna Rules. The new, June 2006 Vienna Rules have confirmed this provision in Art. 6.

This approach of giving complete freedom to the parties (or to the arbitrators) is accepted world-wide. There are very few legislative acts which try to influence in any way the choice made by the parties or by the arbitrators. One of the few (and not really consequential) examples is the 2001 Turkish Act on International Arbitration,[24] which states in Article 10/C that the language of the arbitral proceeding may be the Turkish language or 'the official language of a State recognized by Turkey'. The parties (or the arbitrators) are free to choose one of such languages. The restriction to official languages 'of a State recognized by Turkey' does not rule out many options, but it certainly rules out the possible use of the Kurdish language. The 1993 Romanian Act[25] also contains a formulation which endeavors to define and limit the range of possible languages, but only in the case when it is determined by the arbitrators, rather than by the parties. According to Article 369(4), the language may be freely chosen in the arbitration agreement, but in the absence of such an agreement, the arbitral tribunal may opt for '[t]he language of the contract from which the dispute has arisen or...another language used in international communication...'. It is not entirely clear whether the reference to 'another language used in international communication' is actually a reference to communication between the parties in the given dispute, or in international communication in general. If one were to adopt the latter understanding, very few languages – if any – would be excluded. In a number of Arabic countries the law provides that the language of the arbitral proceedings shall be Arabic, unless another language is chosen by the parties or determined by the arbitral tribunal. This is the solution in Egypt,[26] in Jordan,[27] and in Oman[28] (but not in other Arab countries like in Algeria, Bahrain, or Tunisia where the laws contain no such provision).[29] The essence of the solution in the arbitration acts of Egypt, Jordan and Oman is that both the parties and the arbitrators are free to choose any language, but a fallback solution is provided for cases in which no choice was made (or for the time until a choice was made). Such provisions, like the respective provisions in the Turk-

---

[24] Act No. 4686 of June 20, 2001 on International Arbitration.

[25] Book IV of the Code of Civil Procedure, as amended by Act No. 59 of July 23, 1993.

[26] Act No. 27/1994 Promulgating the Act Concerning Arbitration in Civil and Commercial Matters – as last amended by Act No. 8/2000 (13 *Official Gazette* April 4 (2000)) – Art. 29.

[27] Act No. 31/2001 June 14, 2001 – Art. 28.

[28] The Law of Arbitration in Civil and Commercial Matters – Sultani Decree No. 47/1997 Promulgating the Law on Arbitration in Civil and Commercial Disputes – Art. 29.

[29] See the Algerian Legislative Decree No. 93-09 of April 25, 1993 modifying and supplementing Ordinance No. 66-154 of June 8, 1966 on the Code of Civil Procedure; Decree Law No. 9 of Bahrain of 1994 with respect to Promulgation of International Commercial Arbitration (adopted on August 16, 1994); the 1993 Tunisian Arbitration Code, Promulgated by Act No. 93-42 of April 16, 1993 (Art. 67)

ish and Romanian arbitration acts, represent little or practically no impairment of the principle of autonomy of the parties and of the arbitrators. The only serious exception we found is that contained in Section 25 of the 1985 Saudi Arabian Arbitration Regulation[30] which simply states that 'The Arabic language shall be the official language to be used before the arbitration panel.' One has to bear in mind, however, that the Saudi Regulation contemplates arbitration which is in many respects different from the dominant world-wide model. One of its features is that arbitrators can only be 'Saudi nationals or Muslim expatriates'.[31]

At this point I would also like to mention the solution adopted in the 1998 MERCOSUR Agreement on International Commercial Arbitration (hereinafter 'MERCOSUR Agreement').[32] According to Article 13(2) of this Agreement: 'Failing an explicit determination by the parties, the language shall be that of the seat of the arbitral tribunal.' This solution does not restrict the autonomy of the parties, but it appears to eliminate a possible determination by the arbitrators. It offers a solution which is practically identical with that contained in a number of institutional rules which have set a default language.[33]

Thus, according to the mainstream and almost universally accepted solution, the designation of the language of arbitral proceedings belongs to the domain of autonomy. An answer shall be provided by the parties themselves, or by the institutional rules chosen by the parties, or possibly by the arbitrators who were appointed following party agreement. In a case which reached the Supreme Court of Austria,[34] the principle of autonomy was tested from an interesting angle. In this case the language of arbitration proceedings was not agreed upon between the parties, and in a procedural order, the arbitrators determined English as the language of the proceedings. The place of arbitration was Vienna. One of the parties was dissatisfied with the solution, and asked a Vienna court to overrule this procedural order. The Vienna court did so, and issued an injunction which established English **and German** as the languages of the arbitral proceedings. Had it remained unchallenged, this would have been as a quite consequential decision, since it would have extended court control to the arbitration process itself, rather than to its result. The arbitrators appealed against the vacatur of their procedural order, and the Vienna Court of Appeal repealed the injunction, stating that the court cannot review procedural orders

---

30 Regulation of May 27, 1985.

31 Section 3 of the 1985 Regulation.

32 Adopted on July 23, 1998 in Buenos Aires.

33 See on the concept of default language set by institutional rules in Section C.4 of this chapter.

34 *Oberster Gerichtshof*, Decision of December 4, 1994, 4 Ob 1542/94 – Reported in *Yearbook Commercial Arbitration*, Vol. XXII (1997) pp. 263-265.

(*prozessleitende Verfügungen*) of the arbitrators. This decision was appealed to the Supreme Court of Austria, but the Supreme Court rejected reconsideration. It became thus clear that a procedural order of the arbitrators regarding language (or any other procedural order) cannot be subject to court scrutiny before an award has been rendered. Courts may control the result of arbitral proceedings, but in principle cannot interfere with the proceedings proper, which belongs to the sphere of autonomy.[35]

C.2. **The standard answer**

Within the sphere of autonomy (of the parties and of the arbitrators) there is one pattern in the determination of the language of arbitral proceedings which has become clearly dominant worldwide: the parties choose the language(s) of arbitral proceedings, and if they fail to do so, the arbitrators make the choice. This is the standard adopted by the UNCITRAL Model Law (Art. 22) and Model Rules (Art. 17), and by most modern arbitration acts; this is also the standard adopted by most institutional rules.[36] Having identified the prevailing pattern, let us mention that it leaves some open questions.

The most important open question is that of the **initial language**. In institutional arbitration, a possible answer to this question is sometimes offered by way of a departure from the basic pattern, i.e., by the introduction of a **default language.** The question has also been raised whether the freedom of choice extends to **any language**, and whether **more than one language** may be chosen

[35] See a comment on the Austrian decision by W. Melis, Secretary of the Vienna Court of Arbitration, in *Yearbook Commercial Arbitration*, Vol. XXII (1997) 264; See on the broader issue of court review of procedural decisions S. Jarvin, 'To What Extent Are Procedural Decisions of Arbitrators Subject to Court Review?' in *Improving the Efficiency of Arbitration Agreements and Awards: 40 Years of Application of the New York Convention, ICCA* (Kluwer 1999) pp. 366-382.

[36] To cite a few examples, this is the solution adopted by the 1998 ICC Rules – Art. 16; the LCIA Rules – Art. 17; the 2003 AAA International Arbitration Rules (as amended and effective May 1, 2006) – Art. 14; the 2005 Rules of the Court of Arbitration at the Hungarian Chamber of Commerce and Industry (hereinafter 'Budapest Rules'), Art. 9; the 1994 Rules of the Italian Arbitration Association (hereinafter 'AIA') – Art. 21; the 1999 Arbitration Rules of the Stockholm Chamber of Commerce (hereinafter 'Stockholm Rules') – Art. 23; the 2001 Rules of the Netherlands Arbitration Institute (hereinafter 'NAI') – Art. 40; the 1997 Mexican Center of Arbitration Rules – Art. 22; the DIS Rules – Art. 22; the 2004 International Arbitration Rules of the Milan Chamber of National and International Arbitration (hereinafter 'Milano Rules') – Art. 12; the 1999 Rules of the Estonian Chamber of Commerce and Industry – Art. 20; the 2002 CRCICA Rules – Art. 17; the 1999 Rules of the Arbitration Tribunal of the State of Rio de Janeiro – Art.13; the 2000 General Rules of the Caracas Chamber of Commerce Arbitration Center – Art. 46; the 2004 Swiss Rules – Art. 17; the 2005 Rules of the Belgian Center for the Study and Practice of National and International Arbitration (hereinafter 'CEPANI') – Art. 14.

as the language of arbitral proceedings. I shall turn now to these open questions, and to the most important departure from the basic pattern.

C.3. The issue of the 'initial language'

The basic and prevailing solution works perfectly if the choice has already been made by the parties. More often than not, however, the parties do not choose a language. The fallback solution is given: the choice will be made by a ruling of the arbitrators. The problem is that this solution may not arrive soon enough. There is bound to be communication before the arbitral tribunal is constituted. In what language should that 'early' communication occur? In what language should the claimant address the arbitral institution? In what language should the institution invite the respondent to submit a statement of defense, and to choose its arbitrator? Or, in case of *ad hoc* arbitration, in what language will the claimant first address the respondent?

The issue is also important from the point of view of party strategies. Parties choose arbitrators and attorneys keeping in mind the language in which these actors will have to perform. Difficulties will obviously arise if choices have to be made before the language of the proceedings becomes known.

A further dilemma belongs to the arbitrator. If someone is approached with the request to be one of the arbitrators in a given case, (s)he will naturally first consider, whether (s)he is capable of handling the case. Language is an obvious element of such considerations.[37] But the language may be unknown at the time a prospective arbitrator is being approached (unless the parties agreed in advance on the language of the arbitral proceedings). As is illustrated by our introductory example[38] these dilemmas and difficulties may present an impasse if the arbitrators chosen without the guidance of a predetermined language do not happen to have a language in common.

It is not inconceivable to act as arbitrator via interpreter, but this is certainly an imperfect solution: it is time consuming, the arbitrator would not get the full flavor of the arguments presented, and the proceedings would certainly lack the flair of sophisticated and efficient proceedings. In his article devoted to the language of institutional arbitration Lazareff argues:

[37] According to Art. 2.2 of the 1986 International Bar Association Rules of Ethics for International Arbitrators: 'A prospective arbitrator shall accept an appointment only if he is fully satisfied that he is competent to determine the issues in dispute**, and has an adequate knowledge of the language of the arbitration**.' [emphasis added].

[38] See subsection A.1 in this chapter.

> 'Accordingly, in our view, when he is asked to act, a prospective arbitrator should only accept if he speaks, reads and writes fluently in what any professional would consider ought to be the language or one of the languages of arbitration.'[39]

This is quite convincing, but in the absence of an early choice made by the parties which would clarify what **is** the language of arbitration, professionals may reasonably differ in considering what **ought to be** the language of the proceedings in a given case. Professionals can only make educated guesses – and this is probably the best one can do in the given situation.

If we have *ad hoc* arbitration, there is practically no remedy. The prospective arbitrators will make educated guesses, and the moving party will submit the statement of claim or notice of arbitration in a language that is likely to become the language of the proceedings. Often, this will not turn out to be a stumbling block. Yet problems might emerge, and the ensuing situation may be used and abused by the party which has an interest in stalling the proceedings.

In institutional arbitration, the institution and its rules may provide for a remedy. Unfortunately, not many institutional rules do so. Among the emerging solutions one may distinguish two types of answer to the question of initial language: a) the institution will either set in its rules an initial language, or b) it will endeavor to work out a solution without a designated initial language.

C.3.1. *Setting an initial language*

Among those rules that have identified an initial language, further ramifications and options have emerged. According to one option, the rules will set a **criterion**, which will yield a given initial language. In most cases, this criterion is the language of the contract (or of the arbitration agreement). This is normally sufficient to close the gap, but sometimes the criterion does not yield a solution. The language of the contract (or of the arbitration agreement) will not represent reliable guidance and will not lead to an unequivocal result when the contract is drafted in two languages. Another option is the identification of a **named language** (usually the official language of the country of the seat of the arbitral institution). A combination of these two solutions is also possible.

To take an example, according to Article 17(1) of the LCIA Rules: 'The initial language of the arbitration shall be the language of the Arbitration Agreement, unless the parties have agreed in writing otherwise...'. Section 3 of Article 17 explains that this initial language will govern until the formation of the

[39] S. Lazareff, 'The Language of Institutional Arbitration', 8/1 *The ICC International Court of Arbitration Bulletin* (May 1997) 18 at p. 24.

arbitral tribunal, at which point the tribunal will (in the absence of party agreement) determine the language of the proceedings.

At the same time, Article 17 of the LCIA Rules has also accorded certain relevance to a named language (English). Contemplating those special situations in which there is a 'non-participating or defaulting party', Article 17(1) states a rule according to which, such party '[s]hall have no cause for complaint if communications to and from the Registrar and the arbitration proceedings are conducted in English'.

The Budapest Rules opted for a named language – or rather named languages – instead of a neutral criterion. According to Article 8(3) of the Budapest Rules, if the parties did not choose a language of arbitral proceedings, documents shall

> '[u]ntil the arbitral tribunal determines the language of the proceedings ... be submitted either in the Hungarian, the German or the English language depending on the decision of the Arbitration Court'.[40]

The named language (or languages) is sometimes designated in combination with the language of the arbitration agreement, and/or the language of the contract. For example, according to Article 5(2) of the 1998 Rules on the Organization and Operation of the Court of Arbitration at the Chamber of Commerce of Bosnia and Herzegovina:

> 'Until the language or languages of the proceedings is determined, all statements may be submitted in one of the languages of Bosnia and Herzegovina, or in the language of the main agreement, or in the language of the arbitration agreement.'[41]

Essentially the same solution was adopted by the 1992 Rules of the Court of Arbitration at the Croatian Chamber of Commerce (hereinafter 'Zagreb Rules') The present (2002) Zagreb Rules have omitted the provision on the initial language – but only because the rule was included into Article 21 of the 2001 Croatian Arbitration Act.[42] According to Article 21(3) of this Act:

---

[40] The term 'Arbitration Court' refers to the institution, rather than to the arbitrators acting in a case. In other words, the initial language is either Hungarian, or German, or English; the choice will be made by the institution, considering the circumstances of the case.

[41] The languages of Bosnia and Herzegovina are Bosnian, Serbian and Croatian. (Until about ten years ago, these languages were considered to be one: Serbo-Croatian.)

[42] As a matter of general policy, the Zagreb Rules are avoiding to repeat provisions of the Croatian Arbitration Act which applies to arbitration which takes place in Croatia.

> 'Until the language of the proceedings had been determined, a claim, a defense and other deeds can be submitted in the language of the main contract, of the arbitration agreement, or in the Croatian language.'[43]

Let us mention in connection with the Croatian Act that while initial languages are typically set in institutional rules, they may also be established by national legislation. Another of the rather rare examples is the 2006 Serbian Act of Arbitration,[44] which accepts the same solution as that of the Croatian Act, and states in Article 35 that until the language of arbitration is established, parties may present written submissions in the language of the contract, or in the language of the arbitration agreement, or in Serbian (the Serbian Arbitration Act applies if the arbitration takes place in Serbia).

C.3.2. *Working out a solution without an identified initial language*

Another possible approach to the problem is not to set any initial language in the rules, but rather to leave it to the arbitral institution to sort this out together with the parties. This is the approach adopted by the 1998 Rules of the Netherlands Arbitration Institute (hereinafter: 'NAI'). According to Article 40(2):

> 'Until such time as the arbitral tribunal has determined the language or languages as referred to in paragraph (1), the Administrator may, at the request of the other party or on his own motion, require a party to provide translations of his submissions and documents in a language which the other party understands and in such form and within such period of time as the Administrator shall determine.'

Essentially the same solution was adopted by the new 2004 Milano Rules. Article 5 of the Milano Rules first states the generally accepted rule according to which the language of the arbitral proceedings shall be determined by the parties, or by the arbitrator. A provision is, however, added to cover the possible gap prior to such determination. Article 5(2) states: 'The Secretariat shall indicate the language of acts precedent to that determination.'

Many other arbitral institutions are also taking a similar approach in practice without an explicit provision like those of Article 40(2) of the NAI Rules, or Article 5 of the Milano Rules. The difference is that under the NAI and Milano rules, the institution may **require** a party to adopt a language set by the institution. Without an entitlement, the guidance given by the institution can only be

[43] There are several translations of the Croatian Act. The translation relied upon is the one published in the 2001 *Croatian Arbitration Yearbook*, 145.

[44] Published in the *Official Gazette of Serbia* No. 46/2006.

informal. In other words, in the absence of specific powers such as those given to the Administrator or to the Secretariat in the NAI and Milano Rules, the arbitral institution may give advice, but cannot validate a language of communication in the absence of a choice made by the parties, and prior to a position taken by the arbitrators. Thus, a party will address the institution in a language it considers likely to become the language of the proceedings. The institution will accept this language, or advise the party to submit its claim in another language. The choice remains with the party. After the arbitral tribunal opts for a language, this will either confirm the option taken by the party (under the guidance of the institution), or it will oblige the party to translate its submissions into the language set by the arbitrators.

In sum, the problem of the initial language is a fairly common one. A gap often emerges before the arbitrators would determine the language of arbitration. Some institutional rules have provided a solution. They either establish a criterion which will lead to a language, or designate a named language designed to fill the gap. Powers given to the administration of the arbitral institution might also solve the problem. It is important to mention, however, that quite often the problem of the initial language remains unsolved. The conclusion is simple and inevitable. Since *ad hoc* arbitration, and many institutional rules, do not provide for a reliable solution, the best strategy is that of the avoidance of the problem. The problem of initial language is avoided if the parties insert into their arbitration agreement a provision on the language of the arbitral proceedings.

C.4. **Default language, or 'official language' of the arbitral institution**

A language named in the rules of the institution may have more functions. As was just stated, one of the possible remedies to the problem of the initial language is the identification of a language of the institution, which will serve as a language of the proceedings until the regular mechanism (party agreement or determination by the arbitrators) yields a proper language of the arbitral proceedings. This is for example the solution of the Budapest Rules, and this is one of the alternative solutions under Croatian law, under Serbian law, and under the Chamber of Commerce of Bosnia and Herzegovina Rules. An identified language may, however, serve a more ambitious purpose as well. Instead of providing just a temporary solution until the arbitrators make a choice, it could possibly cover the full course of the proceedings, subject only to a different choice made by the parties themselves. In other words, it could eliminate any possible determination by the arbitrators. If this option is taken, the standard pattern is abandoned, and the emerging formula is the following: the language of the arbitral proceedings is the language identified in the rules, unless the parties would opt for another language. In this case, one could speak of a **default language** of the whole arbitral proceedings.

A well known example of this solution is the one adopted in Article 67(1) of the 2005 Rules of Arbitration of the China International Economic and Trade Arbitration Commission (hereinafter 'CIETAC Rules'):

> 'Article 67 Language
> 1. Where the parties have agreed on the arbitration language, their agreement shall prevail. Absent such agreement, the Chinese language shall be the official language to be used in the arbitration proceedings.'

The term 'official language' is suggestive of connotations that may not be compatible with the basic character of international commercial arbitration. It hints some State-prerogatives. An analysis of Article 67(1) shows, however, that the 'official language' is not superimposed, but subordinated to the will of the parties. Chinese is actually a default language. If the parties agree otherwise, their agreement will prevail.

A similar solution is provided by Article 7 of the 2002 Rules of the Court of Arbitration at the Czech Chamber of Commerce (hereinafter 'Prague Rules'), which state that the language of the arbitral proceedings is Czech or Slovak, unless the parties agree upon another language.[45]

According to the 2001 Belgrade Rules, the language of the arbitral proceedings is Serbian, unless the parties agree on a foreign language.[46] To cite another example, according to the 1998 Arbitration Rules of the Indian Arbitration Council, the language of the arbitral proceedings is English, unless the parties agree otherwise.[47]

The same position was taken by the 1995 Rules of the International Commercial Arbitration Court at the Russian Chamber of Commerce and Industry. According to Article 10 of these Rules, the language of the hearing will be Russian, but with the consent of the parties the arbitration court may conduct the hearing in another language.[48]

The 2005 Budapest Rules also provide for a default language in paragraph 9(3) which will apply in the absence of a choice made by the parties. This de-

---

[45] It is interesting to note that the Prague Rules have identified **two** default languages – Czech and Slovak – which is, in all likelihood due to the fact that the Prague Court of Arbitration (today a Czech institution) continues a Czechoslovak institution. This solution according to which the parties can equally use Czech or Slovak is also helped by the proximity of the two languages.

[46] Art. 37 (1) and (2).

[47] Art. 56.

[48] It is interesting to note that the Russian Rules speak of the 'language of the hearing' only.

fault language is Hungarian, but it is linked to another condition. Hungarian will be the language of the proceedings unless the parties agree otherwise, and on the condition that the foreign party is represented by a Hungarian counsel (possibly a Hungarian counsel in addition to a foreign counsel). If this is not the case, there is no default language, the language of the arbitral proceedings will be determined by the arbitrators in the absence of party agreement.

Staying with the question of the default language, let us take a look at its impact. First of all, the establishment of a default language of the institution brings about more certainty, because it takes care of the problem of the initial language. If the parties have failed to agree on the language of the arbitral proceedings, but submitted their dispute to an institution which has established a default language, there will be no uncertainty regarding the language in which procedural acts may be undertaken before the arbitral tribunal is constituted.[49] This is a clear advantage, which may avert problems in later phases as well. To cite an example, in a case decided by the District Court in Yokohama[50] concerning recognition and enforcement of a CIETAC award, the Japanese respondent opposed recognition arguing i.a. that the notice sent to the respondent was in Chinese only, without translation into Japanese. According to the respondent, this amounted to a violation of Article V (1)(b) of the New York Convention which states that recognition may be denied if the party against whom the award is invoked '[w]as not given proper notice of the appointment of the arbitrator or of the arbitration proceedings or was otherwise unable to present his case;'. Had the issue of initial language remained unsettled at the moment when the notice was sent, more serious difficulties could have arisen. If it is not settled which language should be the language of communication, it could be questionable whether a notice sent in Chinese to a Japanese respondent is in conformity with Article V(1)(b).[51] In the actual case, however, the Yokohama Court simply referred to the fact that the CIETAC Rules provide for Chinese as a default

---

[49] As far as the Hungarian Rules are concerned a *caveat* has to be added. Hungarian will not be the default language if the foreign party does not have a Hungarian counsel. This may be a reasonable and helpful limitation, but this also means that the question of the initial language may remain unresolved.

[50] Plaintiff: *Seller (P.R. China) v. Defendant*: Buyer (Japan), District Court, Yokohama, August 25, 1999, Docket: Heisei 10 (wa) – *Yearbook Commercial Arbitration*, Vol. XXVII (2002) at p. 515.

[51] Respondent could have still argued that by submitting to CIETAC arbitration the parties have implicitly accepted Chinese as a language of communication. However, once one enters the field of implicit indications, one may discover that there are more of them (like the language of the contract, the language of the arbitration agreement, the language of earlier correspondence between the parties); and the indications may conceivably contradict one another. Reliance on a default language is a much more straightforward and unequivocal argument.

language, and concluded that by submitting the dispute to CIETAC arbitration (and in absence of an agreement on a different language) that parties actually accepted Chinese as the language of arbitration. The Court concluded:

> '[t]he Court decides that the parties had agreed to arbitral proceedings conducted in the Chinese language. Accordingly, the Court could not find that there had been improper notice to the defendant as to the appointment of the arbitrator and/or procedures.'[52]

This specific way of solving the problem of the initial language (by way of designating a default language) has, however, some other implications as well. The language of the seat of the institution gets considerable priority.[53] A foreign language may still very well be chosen as the language of the arbitral proceedings – but only by the parties. Furthermore, the following problem might also emerge: Suppose in a dispute between a Dutch and a Serbian company the parties submit the case to the Belgrade Court of Arbitration, and the Dutch company appoints a Dutch arbitrator. The two other arbitrators are Serbs. Suppose further on, that neither Dutch nor Serbian is a common language of all arbitrators – but all three of them speak English, and would be willing to agree on English as the language of the arbitral proceedings. In a system of a default language (the language of the institution prevails, unless the parties agree otherwise) such a solution remains beyond the reach of the arbitrators, because only the parties can reverse the presumption established in favor of the default language. In many cases, after the legal battle has started, the parties take a confrontational attitude, which makes it difficult to agree on anything. If the arbitrators do not have a say, the maneuvering room in the search for a rational solution becomes somewhat restricted.

C.5. **Language or languages?**

The UNCITRAL Model Law (Art. 22) and Model Rules (Art. 17) state that the parties or the arbitrators shall determine the 'language or languages' of the arbitral proceedings. This formulation is quite common in legislative acts and in

---

[52] *Yearbook Commercial Arbitration,* Vol. XXVII (2002) at pp. 517-518.

[53] One may note here that the language of the seat of a given institutional tribunal often becomes the language of the proceedings anyway, even if it is not designated as a default language. The balance is tilting towards the language of the seat of the arbitral tribunal, because the contract is often written in the language of the domestic party, and the arbitrators are also often from the country of the institution. The establishment of the language of the seat as a default language goes, however, on step further, and sets a presumption.

institutional rules as well. One might add that those acts and rules which only mention in the singular the 'language of arbitration' or 'language of arbitral proceedings', need not be interpreted (short of other indication) as a denial of the option of determining more than one language as the language(s) of the arbitral proceedings.

Within the setting of a given case, there may be circumstances and reasons bespeaking reliance on more languages within the same proceedings. Whether such reasons and circumstances exist may be a contested issue before the arbitrators. To cite an example, in a case decided before the Arbitration Institute of the Stockholm Chamber of Commerce between a Swedish claimant and a Chinese respondent, the Chinese party asked the Tribunal '[t]o order that all written submissions by both parties be made in both Chinese and English on account of the fact that the respondent's executives do not have a command of English;'.[54] The Chinese respondent thus asked the Tribunal to establish Chinese (in addition to English) as a language of the arbitral proceedings in a way that all communication should be bilingual. This request was rejected. It was held:

> 'The Tribunal is of the opinion that since Counsel for the respondent is English-speaking, the fact that translations are necessary in his relationship with his clients is an element of time and cost, and essentially cost, which will be considered in the context of allocation of costs and is not a sufficient reason to impose a significant additional burden on the claimant. It would also introduce difficulties for the Tribunal, only one of whose members has a command of Chinese, and needlessly add to the expenditure of both time and money. This request by the respondent is therefore denied.'[55]

Let us note that, at the juncture where the question was raised, it would have been irrational to designate Chinese as a language of the arbitral proceedings in any fashion (parallel or alternative). Had English and Chinese **initially** been chosen as equal alternative (or parallel) languages of the arbitral proceedings, the actors of the proceedings (counsels and arbitrators) would have been appointed having on mind the requirement of speaking both languages. It is most

---

[54] Interim award of July 17, 1992 – published in *Yearbook Commercial Arbitration,* Vol. XXII (1997) 197 at p. 203.

[55] *Yearbook Commercial Arbitration*, Vol. XXII (1997) at pp. 203-204. The Swedish holding also raises the issue of costs, an issue to which we shall return in Chapter IV. Let me just mention here that the Tribunal could have taken a different position as well. Instead of considering the costs of translation for the executives of the Chinese party as costs which would be allocated depending on the success of the claim, the Tribunal could have held that costs of translation to a language which is not the established language of arbitral proceedings, are outside the purview of the tribunal.

difficult to designate an added language **after** the actors of the proceedings have already been chosen.

If more languages are chosen (by the parties, or by the arbitrators), the question of the position of these languages arises. Again, there are several options. The designation of more languages could conceivably mean that all submissions and communications have to be duplicated in each language. This is the approach adopted by some special institutions established for a bilateral purpose, like the Iran-US Claims Tribunal.[56] The same approach has also been taken in a number of International Centre for Settlement of Investment Disputes (ICSID) cases. If the parallel use of more languages is mandated, the arbitrators might also specify the sequence and timing of submissions in more languages.[57]

In the majority of cases, however, the adoption of more than one language does not mean full parallel use of these languages. It is much more common to designate more languages on the understanding that submissions, communication or evidence may be submitted in **either** of the designated languages. This also means that documents written in a language that is not one of the languages of arbitral proceedings, need not be translated into all, but only into one of the languages of arbitral proceedings. Arbitral tribunals are – with good reasons[58] – reluctant to impose a duplication of all communication.

Assuming that the languages of arbitral proceedings are set alternatively, rather than in parallel (cumulatively), the question still arises how the use of more languages within the same proceedings can be accommodated There are basically two types of accommodation: a) the languages may have equal stand-

---

[56] According to Art. 7 of the Administrative Directive No. 1 issued by the Tribunal on July 4, 1981 the statement of claim and all documents annexed thereto shall be submitted by the Claimant in both English and Farsi. The 1983 Rules of the Tribunal have adopted Art. 17 of the UNCITRAL Model Rules, but this was supplemented by an Agreement of the Agents, stating that documents filed with the Tribunal shall be submitted in both English and Farsi, unless otherwise agreed by the parties. This supplemented Art. 17 has been relied upon in a number of procedural orders instructing the parties to present submissions in both languages. (E.g., *Vera-Jo Miller Aryeh et al v. The Islamic Republic of Iran*, Award No. 581-842/843/844-1 of May 22, 1997.)

[57] In a 2004 ICSID case decided between MTD Equity (Malaysia), MTD Chile (Chile) as Claimants and the Republic of Chile as Defendant, it was agreed that the proceedings would be in English and Spanish, and the arbitrators specified that 'Documents filed in one language would be followed within five business days by a translation in the other language'. (*MTD v. Chile*, Award of May 25, 2004, paragraph 18 – International Law in Brief, prepared by the Editorial Staff of the ASIL International Legal Materials, August 13, 2004.)

[58] A duplication of all communication would, first of all, be quite costly. Furthermore, extensive translation is likely to yield dilemmas and misunderstandings – and these cannot be easily resolved if all implicated languages are of an equal standing.

ing, and b) there is one prevailing or basic language, while one or more other languages may also be relied upon under specified conditions.

a) The parties (or the arbitrators) may designate two, or even more fully equal languages of the arbitral proceedings. Such an option is explicitly provided in the ICSID Rules.[59] According to Article 22, the parties may agree on the use of one **or two** of the three official ICSID languages (English, French, and Spanish). With the permission of the Secretary General of the ICSID, they may also agree on a language that is not among the three official languages. Moreover, in the absence of party agreement, any party may use any of the three official languages. This solution is prompted by the fact that international organizations (like multilingual States) have typically more than one official language, and the equality of these languages needs to be safeguarded. As it is generally known, the International Court of Justice regularly proceeds in two languages of equal standing (French and English). Outside the framework of institutions like the ICSID it is also perfectly possible to agree on the use of more fully equal languages of the arbitral proceedings, on the understanding that submissions, arguments, or documents are validly submitted if they are submitted in either of the designated languages. Such arrangements are, however, rather rare.

b) It is more common to have a 'basic' language of the arbitral proceedings (a language on which any pleading, evidence, or communication may be submitted, the language of the minutes, and the language of the award), and to agree in addition on a limited use of other supplementary languages. For example, in a case in which the language of the arbitral proceedings is German but a part of the relevant correspondence and of the documents is in English, it appears rational to agree on the presentation of all evidence in its original version (German or English) without translation. Assuming that all arbitrators have an adequate command of both German and English, this is clearly a preferable solution. It avoids costs and delay of translation – and avoids misunderstandings stemming from possibly imperfect translations.

The function of such 'supplementary languages' is usually restricted to presentation of evidence, but it may be extended to pleadings as well. The range and limits of such language(s) is sometimes spelled out by the parties or by the arbitrators, while in some instances the limited use of another language is simply tolerated. It is clearly better to spell out and to specify what languages can be used and precisely in what function. If the use of another language (which is

[59] 2003 Rules of Procedure for Arbitration Proceedings of the International Center for the Settlement of Investment Disputes, Art. 22.

not established as either an alternative or as a compulsory added language of the arbitral proceedings) is just tolerated, this might open a gate in court proceedings for the argument that 'the arbitral procedure was not in accordance with the agreement of the parties' (Art. V(1)(d) of the New York Convention), or for the argument that the principle of equal treatment of the parties was violated.[60]

C.6. Any language?

In *ad hoc* arbitration the parties (or the arbitrators) may in principle agree on the use of **any** language. In the domain of institutional arbitration the situation is typically the same. There are exceptions – some of which will be mentioned later in this text – but in most cases institutional rules do not provide for any restriction.

Such openness may, of course, entail some risks. If the parties agree on a language which is not widely spoken, it might be difficult to find suitable arbitrators. The degree of difficulty depends on whether there are restrictions regarding the nationality of the third arbitrator. In the case of institutional arbitration the question also arises whether the institution can or cannot communicate in the language chosen by the parties. (It is, of course, a possibility for the institution to hire a competent translator, but this might cause delays, and would also add certain costs).[61]

In practice, the problem does not really emerge frequently. It simply does not happen that let us say a Polish Court of Arbitration is seized by a request to conduct arbitration in Urdu or Korean, while cases submitted to arbitration in Pakistan or Korea are unlikely to have Polish, Hungarian, Estonian or Norwegian as the designated language of arbitral proceedings. Normally, the cases submitted to a given court of arbitration either stem from a language environment which matches the specific language environment of the arbitral institution, or the chosen language is one of the 'world languages' for which the institution is prepared. This is why most institutional rules do not provide for

---

[60] A similar argument was raised before the Paris *Cour d'appel* in a case in which the party challenging the award objected that the Spanish party had sent his pleadings to the Spanish-speaking arbitrators in Spanish as well, in addition to English. (In spite of the fact that the language of arbitration was English.) The *Cour d'appel* held that there was no violation of the principle of equal treatment of the parties, since documents had been produced in English as well, and the content of the pleadings in the two languages was not different – *Revue de l'Arbitrage*, 1991, 97.

[61] The problem will be avoided if the institutional rules establish a distinct language of communication to and from the institution.

any limitations regarding the choice of the language of the proceedings. More problems might emerge, however, if the institutional rules (or the parties) provide that the third arbitrator must have a different nationality from that of the parties – and the home language of the institution is not one of the widely spoken languages. It is easy to conduct proceedings in Bulgarian in Sofia between Bulgarian and foreign partners, or in Lithuanian in Vilnius between Lithuanian and foreign parties – assuming that all arbitrators are Bulgarian or Lithuanian nationals. But it might be quite difficult to find a third arbitrator who is not a Bulgarian or Lithuanian national who could conduct arbitrations in Bulgarian or Lithuanian. Having an arbitrator who does not speak the language of proceedings is not impossible, but certainly not desirable. To cite an example, in an ICC case in which I acted as party-appointed arbitrator, the language of arbitration agreed upon by the parties was Serbian. This was agreed between an American party of Serbian origin and a Serbian party.[62] The arbitrator appointed by the Serbian party and myself, we faced a considerable difficulty in choosing a third arbitrator, since – under Article 9(5) of the ICC Rules '[t]he chairman of the Arbitral Tribunal shall be of a nationality other than those of the parties'. Thus, we had to find a Serbian speaking chairman who was not a Serbian national – not even a dual national one of whose nationalities were Serbian. A solution was eventually found and a Slovenian chairman was appointed, but the search caused a considerable delay. (Had this case emerged 15 years earlier when Serbia and Slovenia were parts of the same State, the Socialist Federal Republic of Yugoslavia, finding a solution would have been even more difficult.)

Speaking of options in adopting language, I would like to mention at this point two cases described to me by the arbitrator, a Croatian colleague of mine.[63] Both cases were between the same parties, submitted to the International Arbitration Center of the Federal Economic Chamber in Vienna. One of the parties was an Austrian businessman who spoke Croatian, the other party was a Croatian company.[64] The parties agreed in both cases to use Croatian as the language of the arbitral proceedings, and chose a Croatian arbitrator from the list of the Vienna institution as sole arbitrator. My colleague (the sole arbitrator) conducted the proceedings in Croatian, and he recorded the oral hearing himself in Croatian (by way of drafting a summary of the oral hearing). The awards were rendered in Croatian. This leads to some conclusions – and to some questions. First, one may conclude that it is possible to have even institutional arbitration in an 'un-

[62] ICC case 13798/AVH.

[63] Professor Krešimir Sajko from Zagreb.

[64] Cases SCH-4480, and SCH-4502, both decided in 1997.

expected language'; a language – although not excluded – not contemplated by the institution as a likely language of arbitral proceedings. This may be easier or more difficult, depending on some specific solutions in the given institutional rules. For example, the question arises how such a situation can be handled by institutions that provide for a scrutiny of the award by the institution (as it is provided by Art. 27 of the 1998 ICC Rules).[65] I would also like to mention that in the Vienna cases referred to above, the communication between the institution and the parties was limited – and it was in German. Thus, a distinction emerged between the language of the arbitral proceedings and the language of the communication to and from the institution.

It has to be mentioned that there are some (few) institutional rules, which do provide for restrictions regarding the choice of the language of the arbitral proceedings. We have already considered Article 22 the ICSID Rules, according to which the consent of the Secretary General is needed for the use of a language that is not one of the three official languages. The 2004 Rules of the Japan Commercial Arbitration Association have set a stricter rule: the language of the proceedings may be Japanese or English, or both. No third language is permitted.[66] The 2003 Rules of the Court of Arbitration at the Polish Chamber of Commerce (hereinafter: 'Warsaw Rules') have also opted for a limitation, but they permit a broader range of languages. Article 20 of the Warsaw Rules identifies five languages among which the parties may choose the language of arbitral proceedings. (These languages are: Polish, English, French, German and Russian.) A flexible restriction is provided by the 2005 Budapest Rules. According to Article 9(1) of these Rules:

> 'The parties may freely determine the language of the proceedings, provided the conditions for the proceedings conducted in such language may otherwise be ensured.'

---

[65] In the case of the ICC itself, the Court of Arbitration will either rely on the language expertise of one of its members, or a translation will be provided by the arbitrators or by the Secretariat. (Information provided by courtesy of Mr. Detlev Kühner, counsel of the ICC International Court of Arbitration.)

[66] Art. 11.

D. Questions Relating to the Language of Communication with the Arbitral Institution

D.1. The language of communication with the arbitral institution as a distinct category

As mentioned earlier, some institutional rules make a distinction between the language of arbitral proceedings and the language of communication with the arbitral institution. The Rules of the International Arbitration Center of the Austrian Federal Economic Chamber (hereinafter: 'Vienna Arbitral Center') are quite explicit. According to Article 4(a) of the 2001 Rules (now Art. 6 of the 2006 Rules):

> 'Correspondence by the Parties with the Board and the Secretary shall be conducted in German or English.'

Article 17 of the LCIA Rules distinguishes as a separate category the language of correspondence with the institution, speaking of 'communication to and from the Registrar'. To cite a further example, according to Article 37(4) of the Belgrade Rules:

> 'The written correspondence of the Secretariat with the foreign party that is not represented by a domestic person, and that clearly has no knowledge of the Serbian language, is conducted in English or in some other foreign language.'

Let us also mention that the lesser known set of ICSID Rules – the Rules Governing the Additional Facility for the Administration of Proceedings by the Secretariat of the ICSID – state in Article 30 that one of the official languages of the ICSID shall be used 'for all communications to and from the Secretariat', notwithstanding the language of the proceedings.[67]

The ICC Rules themselves do not distinguish a language of correspondence with the institution,[68] yet one of the most authoritative commentaries makes this distinction. Derains and Schwartz make the following point:

---

[67] 2003 Rules Governing the Additional Facility for the Administration of Proceedings by the Secretariat of the ICSID, Schedule C, Arbitration (Additional Facility) Rules. (The Additional Facility may administer certain disputes which fall outside the scope of the ICSID Convention.)

[68] Neither do the Statutes of the International Court of Arbitration of the ICC, or the Internal Rules of the International Court of Arbitration of the ICC – See *ICC Publication* No. 581, 1999.

> 'Finally it should be noted that the language chosen as the language of the arbitration does not bind the Court and its Secretariat. As already indicated, the working languages of the Court are French and English, and it is under no obligation to use any other languages. The Secretariat and its counsel are nevertheless fluent in numerous language and presently also administer in both German and Spanish in addition to using other languages, as required, from time to time.'[69]

At present, the number of institutional rules which devote separate norms to the language of correspondence with the institution is still scarce. Furthermore, these norms are quite recent,[70] and thus there has been insufficient opportunity to clarify the emerging dilemmas in practice. The proposed distinction between the language of arbitral proceedings and the language of correspondence with the institution raises a number of questions.

The first question with which I would like to deal within this introductory chapter is whether the language of communication with the arbitral institution encompasses only communication between the institution and the parties, or whether it also extends to communication between the institution and the arbitrators. The Vienna Rules speak of communication between the institution and the parties. The LCIA Rules contain a broader (and less explicit) reference. The formulation of the ICSID Rules referring to 'communications to and from the Secretariat' also support a broader understanding. As a matter of fact, it is difficult to imagine that the Vienna Rules would have made a deliberate choice to restrict the language of administrative communication to correspondence between the parties and the institution. It is rather generally understood that when the arbitrator submits his/her statement of fees and expenses, or seeks an extension of the time limit for rendering the award this will be done in the language of communication with the institution, rather than in the language of the arbitral proceedings. One could nevertheless observe that once a separate rule is devoted to the language of communication with the institution, it would be advisable to make it clear that it covers all communication of the institution, including communication with the parties, but also communication with the arbitrators.

I would also like to raise some further questions, having in mind first of all the primary facet of the language of communication with the institution – communication between the institution and the parties. One may ask first, whether a separate regulation of the language of communication with the arbitral institution is consistent with other rules and principles pertaining to the language of arbitral proceedings. The next question is whether such a separate regulation is

69 Derains-Schwartz, *A Guide to the New ICC Rules of Arbitration* (Kluwer 1998) p. 216.

70 The separate treatment of a language of administrative correspondence may have existed in practice, but this was a tolerated, rather than regulated practice.

desirable. I would also like deal with two further questions. It needs to be clarified what communication is actually encompassed by the language of correspondence with the institution. Furthermore, the question arises whether there can be more languages of correspondence in the same case.

D.2. Is separate regulation consistent with rules and principles pertaining to the language of arbitral proceedings?

As far as consistency is concerned, the relevant point of reference is the definition of the language of arbitral proceedings itself. Section B of this chapter cited definitions adopted in various arbitration acts and institutional rules. The majority of these definitions encompass an enumeration of various procedural acts – and this enumeration does not contain correspondence between the parties and the arbitral institution. The best-known formulations are those adopted by Article 22 of the Model Law,[71] and Article 17(1) of the UNCITRAL Model Rules.[72] Let me repeat that, according to the Model Law, and according to various acts which have adopted the wording of the Model Law, the language of arbitral proceedings extends to: '[a]ny written statement by a party, any hearing and any award, decision or other communication by the arbitral tribunal'. According to the Model Rules – and according to institutional rules which have followed the wording of the Model Rules – the language of the arbitral proceedings extends to 'the statement of claim, the statement of defence, and any further written statements and, if oral hearings take place, to the language or languages to be used in such hearings'. These and similar wordings designate a domain which is clearly separable from the area of correspondence between the institution and the parties – and thus, separate regulation of the language of administrative correspondence is not inconsistent with the established concept and scope of the language of arbitral proceedings.

[71] Accepted in a considerable number of national arbitration acts, e.g., in Tunisia (1993) Cyprus (1987), Russia (1993), Hungary (1994), Zimbabwe (1996), New Zealand (1996), Peru (1996), Iran (1997) Germany (1998), Croatia (2001), Spain (2003), Thailand 2002, Ukraine 2003, Chile 2004.

[72] E.g., the wording of Art. 17(1) of the Model Rules has also been adopted by a number of institutional rules, such as the 2001 PCA Rules for Arbitration of Disputes Relating to Natural Resources and/or the Environment, the 1996 PCA Optional Rules for Arbitration Involving International Organizations and States, the 1993 PCA Optional Rules for Arbitrating Disputes Between Two Parties of Which Only One Is a State and the 1996 PCA Optional Rules for Arbitration Between International Organizations and Private Parties; the 1998 CRCICA Rules, the 2004 Swiss Rules, the 2002 Inter-American Commercial Arbitration Association Rules, the 1997 SIAC Rules.

A different conclusion could possibly be inferred from other wordings, like that adopted by the ICC Rules which do **not** contain specifications, but simply refer to the 'language or languages of arbitration'. Such a broad wording may support a position taken against the separate treatment of the language of correspondence with the institution.

One may add here, however, some caveats as well. The definitions contained in legislation envisage both institutional and *ad hoc* arbitration. Since the question of communication between the parties and the institution obviously does not emerge in *ad hoc* arbitration, general definitions not specifically focused on institutional arbitration may not be sufficiently indicative. The UNCITRAL Model Rules are devoted to *ad hoc* arbitration.[73] Definitions adopted in institutional rules may provide guidance, but such definitions are often missing, or do not provide a clear-cut answer to the question as to whether the language of administrative correspondence should or should not be treated separately. The existing designations may provide a foothold for speculations, but they do not bear the mark of a deliberate choice.[74] It is an open question whether designations like those adopted by the Model Law and the Model Rules, which do not include a reference to communication with the institution, resulted from a considered decision not to cover the regulation of such communication. If there had been an intention to treat the matter of administrative communication separately, it would have been logical to treat it, indeed, separately, i.e., to set special rules covering this communication. Yet institutional rules modeled after the Model Law or the Model Rules, typically do not devote separate rules to this matter. Likewise, broad designations like the one adopted by the ICC Rules ('language or languages of arbitration') are not necessarily evidence of the intention to rule out any separate status of the language of correspondence with the institution.[75] Again, there are no indications showing that a deliberate choice was made between two options. Furthermore, the phrase 'language or languages of arbitration' may very well be interpreted either more narrowly and more broadly, encompassing or not encompassing communication between the institution and the parties.

It follows that a possible separate regulation of the language of communication between the institution and the parties may not be mandated,[76] but would

---

73 Although they represent a model for institutional rules as well.

74 With the exception of those few rules, of course, which have explicitly accorded different treatment to the language of correspondence with the institution.

75 As it was noted above, the commentary of Derains and Schwartz take the view that the 'language of arbitration' does not bind the Secretariat, which has two working languages (French and English) for its own communication – see n. 69.

76 Except in those few institutional rules which explicitly provide for such separation.

not be inconsistent with positions taken or with adopted wordings. The question still arises whether such a distinction and separate treatment is desirable.

D.3. Possible advantages and disadvantages of separation

It is quite clear that the designation of one or two languages as languages of administrative correspondence is certainly rational and convenient from the point of view of the institution. The institution would have a clear guidance in hiring policies, it would have an opportunity to be fully prepared for proper communication in a given number of languages – and it would not have to communicate in whatever language is chosen as the language of the arbitration proceedings, facing problems prompted by the emergence of unexpected languages.

Another advantage of this solution (and this time not only for the institution) is the – at least partial – resolution of the problem of initial language. This is a problem of the first steps. Within the setting of institutional arbitration, these are steps to be undertaken in communication between the parties and the institution. The designation of a language of communication with the institution helps, it solves at least a part of the problem. Under the Vienna Rules for example, the parties know in what language to address the Institution, even if they did not agree on the language of arbitral proceedings. They can do it in either English or German. The question is what chunk of the problem of the initial language is actually solved by a solution like that of Article 6 of the 2006 Vienna Rules. This depends on the question to what communication does the language of correspondence with the institution actually extend. (This question will be addressed in Section D.4 below.)

Speaking of initial language in connection with the language of correspondence with the institution, it is also important to point out significant differences between the two. They cover different areas of communication, and extend to a different time span. The initial language is the language of communication before the language of the proceedings was chosen. After a choice has been made (by the parties or by the arbitrators), the chosen language prevails. The language of correspondence with the institution is restricted to a narrow field, but is not of a temporary nature. It may resolve some problems of initial communication, **but it remains the language of communication between the parties and the institution even after the language of arbitral proceedings was determined**. In other words, even if French were chosen as the language of arbitral proceedings, the Vienna Arbitral Center would still communicate with the parties in English or in German. The language of correspondence with the institution is meant to prevail within its own field, even if the parties have chosen another language already in their arbitration agreement.[77]

Turning to possible arguments against the separation of a language of correspondence, the point can be made that it is more rational to have all communication with regard to one dispute in the same language. Furthermore, some logistical difficulties may arise for the parties if they have to communicate in one language with the institution, and in a different language (or different languages) with the arbitral tribunal. Keeping files might also be simpler if the language of arbitral proceedings were not divorced from the language of communication with the institution.

D.4. What does the language of correspondence with the institution encompass?

Two questions may be raised in connection with the scope of the language of correspondence with the institution: a) to what part of procedure can a distinct language of communication with the institution extend; and b) to what type of submissions and documents does this language extend?

a) As far as the *definition of the relevant part of procedure* is concerned, one may use as a starting point the fact that the arbitral proceedings envisage communication with the arbitral tribunal (or with the sole arbitrator). If all communication between the parties and the arbitrator(s) belong to arbitral proceedings proper, this would mean that correspondence with the institution could only cover a space outside that of communication with the arbitral tribunal. What is the range and what are the limits of this space of communication with the institution? It is obvious that seeking and sending general information and brochures are within the separate space of correspondence with the institution. Drawing the line becomes much more difficult when we are talking about communication in connection with an ongoing arbitration case. There are several conceivable ways of delimitation.

First, the narrowest understanding would be to consider that the language of administrative communication is limited to communication to and from the in-

[77] At this point some dilemmas might arise. Arbitration rules apply on the grounds of party autonomy. The parties are, in principle, free to modify the chosen institutional rules. If this were to happen, the institution could not disregard the proposed change. It could accept it, it could try to persuade the parties to change their position – and it could refuse to arbitrate. The issue might also be a matter of interpretation. If the parties simply agree e.g., that 'the language of arbitration shall be French', this may very well be interpreted as a choice not extending to the language of correspondence with the institution.

stitution until the commencement of the arbitral proceedings. This point is usually identified explicitly in institutional rules – and it is typically tied to the first step. The first step in a case under practically all rules is the request for arbitration (or notice of arbitration) submitted by the claimant to the administration of the institution. After this, the institution will send this request to the respondent.[78] According to Article 4(2) of the 1998 ICC Rules: 'The date on which the Request is received by the Secretariat shall, for all purposes, be deemed to be the date of the commencement of the arbitral proceedings.'[79] A possible inference from this rule is that only the language of the notice of arbitration (request for arbitration) can be regulated by rules pertaining to the language of administrative correspondence, since after that the arbitral proceedings begin, and thus, the language of arbitral proceedings takes effect. The date of the commencement of the arbitral proceedings is a logical procedural dividing line but it is not so logical as far as communication of the institution itself is concerned. It is not so logical to divorce the language in which the statement of claim (or request for arbitration) is submitted from the language in which the institution notifies the respondent of the receipt of the first submission of the claimant. The problem also has another angle. It has to be kept in mind that the request for arbitration normally contains a description of the dispute and a statement of the relief sought, and it is a communication intended to reach the other party as well, rather than just the arbitral institution. (This leads to the question to what types of documents does the language of administrative correspondence extend.)

Another possible option is to consider that the language of administrative correspondence covers all communication – before or after the commencement of arbitral proceedings – in which the institution acts **on its own behalf**, rather than on behalf of the arbitral tribunal. This would mean that the sending of the request for arbitration to the respondent (by the institution) also belongs to the domain of administrative correspondence (since it precedes the formation of the arbitral tribunal), and one could also place here any later communication in which the institution did not act on behalf of the tribunal. Invitations for a hearing ordered by the arbitral tribunal and sent to the parties by the secretariat of the institution would, however, have to conform to the designated language of arbitral proceedings. The dividing line between communication on behalf of the institution proper and communication on behalf of the arbitral tribunal may emerge as an issue, depending on the given rules. Under some institutional

[78] Under some rules, the claimant is supposed to send the request directly to the respondent.

[79] The date of commencement of arbitral proceedings is defined in the same or similar manner in many other rules as well. E.g., in Art. 2(a) of the AAA Rules, Art. 2(1) of the LCIA Rules, Art. 13 of the CIETAC Rules, etc.

rules the arbitrators themselves undertake all communication with the parties after the tribunal is formed; they only send to the institution a copy of their communication with the parties. Under these circumstances, there are no tensions between the language of proceedings and the language of administrative correspondence, because the institution does not communicate on behalf of the arbitrators. According to other institutional rules, the institution provides assistance to the arbitrators by taking care of their correspondence with the parties. The language of correspondence with the institution can more easily be divorced within the setting of rules which – like the Vienna Rules – do not envisage communication by the institution on behalf of the tribunal.

A third conceivable understanding is the extension of the language of administrative correspondence to all communication between the institution and the parties, including communication in which the institution is acting on behalf of the tribunal, providing administrative assistance to the tribunal. Such a perception would, however, create an intrusion into the sphere of the language of arbitral proceedings, and could result in difficult borderline disputes. Some odd results could also follow if some orders of the arbitral tribunal were transmitted by the secretariat of the institution in one language, while the tribunal itself communicates with the parties in another language. In sum, it is much easier to justify the separation of a language of correspondence with the institution, if this language is kept within boundaries outside the territory of communication to and from the arbitral tribunal.

A possible dividing line is the one drawn in the 2005 Budapest Rules. According to paragraph 8(4) of these Rules, the Secretariat will correspond with the parties in one of the three languages of administrative correspondence (Hungarian, German, or English) up to the moment when the arbitrators determine the language of arbitral proceedings. From that moment, the Secretariat should use the language determined by the arbitrators.

b) A further dilemma pertains to the *type of submissions and documents to which the language of administrative correspondence extends*. To take an example, let us follow the question within the setting of the Vienna Rules. It appears to be beyond dispute that the arbitral proceedings are not yet pending at the time when the claimant first writes to the institution.[80] Thus, the first communication from the claimant to the institution is certainly within the realm of communication with the institution. Does this mean that the **claim** sent to the Secretariat of the Vienna Arbitral Center can be (and has to be) in English or German, or are we just talking about the **cover letter** addressed to the institu-

[80] The proceedings become pending upon receipt of the statement of claim by the institution.

tion? The wording of Article 6 ('correspondence by the Parties with the Board and the Secretary...') supports the narrower interpretation.[81] Such an understanding (restricted to the cover letter) is more in line with the basic idea of distinguishing a language of correspondence with the institution proper. This also means, however, that the contribution of an established language of administrative correspondence to the resolution of the problem of initial language is quite modest.

D.5. One or more languages of correspondence with the institution in the same case?

Another emerging question is whether the concept of the language of administrative correspondence supposes the use of **one** language of correspondence with both parties within the same case. According to Article 37(4) of the Belgrade Rules (one of the few rules which explicitly distinguish the language of communication with the institution) the Secretariat will communicate in English (or in some other foreign language) **with the foreign party who is not represented by a domestic person, and does not speak Serbian.**[82] This clearly implies that the language of communication will always be Serbian with the Serbian party, while it might be English with the other party. This might cause difficulties, since all correspondence has to be accessible to both parties. Since the language of correspondence is divorced from the language of the arbitral proceedings, it follows that the language of communication between the arbitral institution and the domestic party will be Serbian, even if the language of the arbitral proceedings is English, and the language of administrative communication with the other party is also English.[83] The Vienna Rules do not mandate such a solution, yet they allow it. According to Article 6 of the Vienna Rules, the language of correspondence with the institution is German or English. The wording clearly allows English to be used towards the foreign (say, US) party and at the same time German to be used towards the Austrian party, even if the language of the arbitral proceedings were English. Communicating

[81] This understanding was confirmed during a telephone interview with Dr. Manfred Heider, counsel of the Vienna International Court of Arbitration.

[82] According to Art. 37(4): 'The written correspondence of the Secretariat with the foreign party that is not represented by a domestic person, and that clearly has no knowledge of the Serbian language, is conducted in English or in some other foreign language.'

[83] More about Art. 37 of the Belgrade Rules in Várady, *O jeziku arbitraže – Opaske i sugestije povodom člana 37 Pravilnika Spoljnotrgovinske arbitraže pri Privrednoj komori Srbije* ('On the Language of Arbitration – Observations and Suggestions in Connection with Art. 37 of the Rules of the Foreign Trade Court of Arbitration at the Serbian Chamber of Commerce') – in «*Arbitraža*» (Belgrade 2003) p. 11.

with different parties in different languages may be a forthcoming gesture. At the same time, problems may arise due to the fact that all communication will have to be accessible to both parties. If the Austrian party addresses an inquiry to the institution regarding technicalities of the oral hearing and receives an answer in German, will the US party receive copies of this communication in German?

Article 37 of the Belgrade Rules puts into focus a question in connection with the language of correspondence with the institution, pointing to a choice which has to be made either in the rules themselves, or through their interpretation.

E. Concluding Remarks

The articulation of issues pertaining to language has followed – maybe somewhat belatedly – the same line of development that has characterized the evolution of international commercial arbitration in general. We have witnessed a shift from spontaneity towards more explicit articulation. When modern international commercial arbitration emerged as an alternative to litigation, its hallmarks were speed, informality, low cost, and simplicity. These traits emerged in part as a result of intrinsic characteristics of arbitration, but also as a result of the specific structure of cases typically submitted to arbitration. Several decades ago, cases submitted to arbitration (rather than to litigation) were relatively simple, with fairly modest amounts in dispute; they were typically cases in which some common ground still existed. As, however, arbitration became the dominant method of settlement of international trade disputes, the spectrum of cases submitted to arbitration became much broader. It now includes most difficult and complicated cases as well; it includes acrimonious confrontations, and disputes about huge sums of money. The newly emerging environment prompted some transformation. Informality has ceded ground to regulation, spontaneity has found a rival in conceptualization. Informality is still on the banner of arbitration, it is still one of its actual comparative advantages, but the proportions have shifted.

During the past one or two decades, we have witnessed an unparalleled proliferation of legislative acts devoted to international commercial arbitration, and at the same time arbitration rules and party stipulations have become more detailed, and more discerning. Specific questions are being raised, they are getting articulated and elaborated, rather than being left to the actors to work them out in a 'natural', informal way. It is in this context that the issue of language is not an esoteric topic anymore; it emerges as a problem which needs articulation, and categorization. It is becoming more and more evident that the same answer cannot cover the growing variety of questions. Ramifications which were not manifested, and which were not detected (or which were considered to be a remote theoretical possibility only) are now coming into sight, and seeking conceptualization and responses.

Scholarly attention devoted to the question of language is still very scarce, but there is a growing number of specific norms devoted to this problem in legislation and institutional rules, and there are more and more issues shaped in practice. Questions are emerging with regard to basic concepts and definitions, the consequences of using the wrong language, the organization and costs of translation, the logistics in connection with the use of more languages, the consequences of mistranslation, etc. In this chapter, our aim was to contribute to a scrutiny of notions and concepts. It is submitted that the semblance of a simple notion of the 'language of arbitration' does not hold anymore. It is being replaced by dilemmas regarding the delimitation and interplay of manifestations that may, and need to be conceptualized. This leads us to categories like 'the language of arbitral proceedings' (as contrasted with the 'language of communication with the institution'), the 'initial language', the 'default language' and to further questions.

The subsequent chapters of this book will follow the stages of the arbitration process. We shall deal with issues of language and translation emerging prior to the constitution of the arbitral tribunal (Chapter II). The subsequent chapter (Chapter III) is devoted to determination of the language of arbitration and ordering translation by the arbitrators. Chapter IV is devoted to translation in arbitration proceedings after the constitution of the tribunal. Chapter V will investigate language and translation as issues emerging in post-award proceedings.

Chapter II

Language Issues and Language-Related Srategies Prior to the Constitution of the Arbitral Tribunal

A. Choice of Language by the Parties – and the Consequences of Such a Choice

A.1. Options and considerations in making the choice

Before the constitution of the arbitral tribunal, the parties may agree on the language of arbitration, and it is certainly in the interest of efficient proceedings to do so. The best suited setting for reaching an agreement is that of the drafting of the arbitration agreement. An effective arbitration agreement will normally establish a mechanism for the constitution of the tribunal and identify the applicable procedural rules. Many potential problems will be eliminated if it also settles the issue of the language of the proceedings.

It has to be said that the parties sometime agree on the language of the arbitral proceedings without giving full consideration to the consequences. This may confront one of the parties (or both of them) with some difficulties, but it will nevertheless contribute to more efficient and predictable proceedings. (The potential arbitrators will have a better picture of their task; the parties will know in what language they should draft their submissions.)

If the parties devote proper attention to the issue of the language of arbitration in their negotiations, they will be typically guided by rather obvious interests and considerations. It is, of course, in the interest of the party to be able to articulate arguments in a language which it not only understands, but in which it is capable of feeling and conveying nuances, and articulating distinctions. It is not irrelevant whether an emphasis (or lack of emphasis) is determined by a strategy of persuasion or by the limits of command of language. Having these considerations in mind, the optimal solution is the native tongue. The second best choice is a second language.

In some cases a less practical consideration is also gaining some importance. Intercultural communication and accommodation may also bring to the surface cultural rivalries. I remember a case in which I learned from the parties (from Russia and Ukraine) that the language they originally contemplated was Russian, of which both parties had a perfect command. The Ukrainian party felt, however, that negotiations about the language of arbitration were an opportunity to underline the dignity of the newly independent State which just declared Ukrainian in its constitution to be the only official language of the country[1] (instead of Russian, or Ukrainian and Russian). After one party proposed Russian and the other party proposed Ukrainian, English was eventually accepted as a compromise. Arguments motivated by pride and rivalries are, I am sure, not restricted to confrontations between Russians and Ukrainians – but they are relatively rare.

Returning to the more common – and more rational – consideration (that of actual command of language), the question may be asked whose command of language is really pertinent. A Bulgarian company would obviously prefer proceedings in Bulgarian. This may or may not be a realistic target. Suppose this cannot be achieved, and the CEO (or the owner) of the Bulgarian company has an adequate command of English, while a trusted attorney has a fitting command of French. In this setting, the Bulgarian company might argue in favor of French, since the command of language of the actual player in the proceedings is more important. The CEO (or the owner) will in all likelihood not draft submissions; he/she may or may not attend hearings. The command of language of an important witness may also amount to a consideration in shaping language-related strategies. It is unlikely that a party would give priority to the language spoken by a key witness and not to the language with which its attorney is at ease. However, if the attorney has a similar command of two languages and one of them is the native tongue of the witness, the language abilities of the witness may determine the aspirations regarding the language of arbitration.

The command of language of a potential arbitrator may also represent a consideration in negotiations. This circumstance may be kept in mind by one of the parties who is planning to appoint a given person as arbitrator. The language abilities of an arbitrator (or of arbitrators) may also represent a strategic consideration for both parties. The choice of any language will, of course, restrict the pool of potential arbitrators, but this will normally not amount to any problem. In some cases, however, the choice of some languages might yield quite considerable restrictions, which need to be heeded. As it is stated by G. Born, 'Language clauses can influence choice (and background) of arbitrators, and thus may have considerable practical importance.'[2] There may be cases in which the choice of a language combined with the requirement that the chairman must not have the same nationality as any of the parties could create serious hurdles, and

---

1 Constitution of the Ukraine of June 28, 1996, Art. 10.

2 Gary B. Born, *International Commercial Arbitration in the United States* (Kluwer 1994) p. 78.

the parties may consider combining the choice of a specific language with a waiver of the restrictions regarding the nationality of the third arbitrator.

One of the factors influencing a choice of language is, quite understandably, the bargaining position of the parties. At this point there is actually no significant difference between negotiations pertaining to language and negotiations with regard to other elements of the arbitration agreement, or of the contract. A new and distinct choice- influencing consideration will appear in those cases in which the parties are submitting their dispute to an institution which has a default language,[3] i.e., a language which will become the language of arbitral proceedings unless the parties agree otherwise. This is, for example, the solution of Article 67(1) of the 2005 CIETAC Rules, which have posited Chinese as a default language. If the default language happens to be the preferred solution of one of the parties, the negotiating position of this party will be considerably enhanced. Not only the desired agreement, but a lack of agreement will lead to victory. This does not mean, however, that the default language always winds up being the language of arbitral proceedings. Not rarely, the provision on language is the result of a more complex compromise involving other elements of the arbitration agreement or of the contract. Commenting on an earlier version of the CIETAC Rules (which contained the same solution regarding default language) J. Crook notes that the parties may agree on a language other than Chinese, but adds that 'Whether such agreement can be reached, however, will depend on the strength of the respective bargaining positions of the parties.'[4] It also has to be noted that while a provision on a default language creates a bargaining advantage for the party whose preferred language is the same as the default language, such provisions may represent a certain disincentive in choosing the arbitral institution itself. A possible compromise, for example, could be the choice of the CIETAC as the arbitral institution, balanced by the choice of a language which is more convenient to the non-Chinese party.

A.2. Choice of law and choice of language

As a rule of thumb, parties tend to choose their own language and their own law. This is actually more logical with regard to language than with regard to law. Familiarity with the language of arbitration is not only an advantage, but a prerequisite which cannot be produced on short notice, and which can only find a

---

[3] See *supra* Chapter I, Section C.4.

[4] Jonathon Crook, 'Leading Arbitration Seats in the Far East: A Comparative View', in S. Frommel and B. Rider, eds., *Conflicting Legal Cultures in Commercial Arbitration* (Kluwer 1999) 63, at p. 70.

less-than-perfect substitute in interpretation. Familiarity with a legal system is also an advantage, but at this point there are other important considerations which are (or should be) borne in mind. The law in force in the country of a party may have norms which are not in line with the interests of the party from that country. Some commercial laws are often labeled as being more 'friendly' towards the seller (or towards the buyer). If this is so, the choice of such a law should not be the strategic aim of both buyers and sellers just because this is the law of their home country. I have heard from several sources a credible (although not documented) anecdote about a seller who was proud of a strategic victory when he managed to nail down an agreement on the application of the law of his country after the dispute arose. The same seller became aware thereafter that his claim was time-barred, since the statute of limitation in the law of his own country provided for a shorter time period than that in the law of the buyer's country.

It is true that at the time when the parties agree on the applicable substantive law, it may be difficult to foresee which issues might emerge in a dispute and which norms might become relevant. Still, it remains a fact that – unlike with regard to language – familiarity need not be a critical consideration in choosing the applicable law; the choice of a party's own law may very well bring a disadvantage rather than an advantage.

Several authors have argued that there are reasons for linking the choice of language with the choice of the applicable law. In an article inspired by an actual case,[5] Breitenstein submits that English may not be the best-suited language if the applicable substantive law is Swiss law, because it is difficult to dissociate the law from the language in which it was shaped. He states that in the given case he had the impression that it was not possible to reach the core of the problems because the language of arbitration was 'ill suited'.[6] Breitenstein explains that one cannot adequately perceive within, say, the French language such typically English legal categories as 'consideration', 'implied terms', or 'misrepresentation'; likewise, categories like 'positive Forderungsverletzung' or 'Gewährleistung', or the distinction between 'Unmöglichkeit' and 'Unvermögen' need the context of the German language. The roots of legal concepts are in a given language. Unlike court proceedings, arbitration may adopt a 'lingua conveniens' which would be suited to the applicable law.[7]

---

[5] Detlev von Breitenstein, 'La language de l'arbitrage – une language arbitraire?' 13 *ASA Bulletin* (1995) pp. 18-21.

[6] [q]u'on ne pouvait aller au fond des problèmes, puisque la language d'arbitrage n'y était adaptée'. Breitenstein, op. cit. 18.

[7] Breitenstein, op. cit. 20-21.

Lazareff also points out that '[t]here are considerable disadvantages linked to the opposition [...] between the law applicable to the merits of the case and the language used'.[8] He stops short, however, of positing the linkage between the language of arbitration and the applicable law as a dominant consideration.

At this point one has to specify that the arguments in favor of such a match normally have in mind the applicable **substantive** law. As far as procedural norms are concerned, they will normally be supplied by institutional rules (or by the UNCITRAL Model Rules in case of *ad hoc* arbitration), and these rules typically have more than one equally valid language version. Also, while cultural characteristics still have an imprint on arbitration rules[9] there is more international harmony in the language of procedural rules compared with the language of substantive law.

Staying with the linkage between the language of arbitration and the applicable substantive law, a match between the language of arbitration and the applicable law would certainly bring some advantages. These cannot amount, however, to a crucial and decisive consideration. In his article, 'Practicalities of Cross-Cultural Arbitration', M. Wilkey argues that in choosing the language of arbitration: 'Neither the language of the site nor that of the applicable law is automatically to be preferred.'[10] He concludes that 'The choice to be made is one of comparative utility...'.[11] It is true that it is easier to perceive 'consideration' in an English context and it is easier to perceive 'imprévision' in a French context, but one must not forget that arbitrators facing terms outside their original context usually have the guidance of a substantial number of scholarly analyses, and can also rely on experience (particularly court experience). Furthermore, there are other considerations of significant weight which may point in a different direction. If a German and a Dutch party form a joint company in Lithuania and an arbitration case arises out of this joint venture, Lithuanian law might be unavoidable, but this still does not mean that the choice of Lithuanian as the language of arbitration is a rational choice. In choosing a language of arbitration, command of language (or ability to hire actors with the requisite command of language) remains the dominant consideration.

---

[8] Serge Lazareff, 'The Language of Institutional Arbitration', 8/1 *The ICC International Court of Arbitration Bulletin* (May 1997) 18, at p. 26.

[9] See Giuliana Garzone, 'Arbitration Rules across Legal Cultures: An Intercultural Approach', in V. Bhatia, Ch. Candlin and M. Gotti, eds., *Legal Discourse in Multilingual and Multicultural Contexts* (Peter Lang Publisher 2003) pp. 177-220.

[10] Malcolm Wilkey, 'The Practicalities of Cross-Cultural Arbitration', in S. Frommel and B. Rider, eds., *Conflicting Legal Cultures in Commercial Arbitration* (Kluwer 1999) 79, at p. 82.

[11] Wilkey, op. cit. p. 82.

A.3. Consequences of a choice made by the parties

A.3.1. *Consequences for the arbitrators (adaptation of the arbitrators to a given choice)*

In a study devoted to arbitration in (South) Korea, three Korean authors and an American author explain:

> 'In deciding whether to include one or more foreign arbitrators on a panel, a party should also consider the issue of language to be used during the arbitration. Unless the parties' arbitration agreement specifically requires the arbitrators to be fluent in a particular language, the arbitrators may or may not be fluent in the language that is used primarily during the arbitration.'[12]

As a matter of fact, specific provisions requiring language skills are quite rare in arbitration agreements. Explicit provisions requiring fluency of the arbitrator in a designated language are typically missing even in those arbitration agreements which do contain a provision on the language of the proceedings. It is quite clear, however, that the (usual) absence of explicit stipulations regarding language skills of the arbitrators does not relieve the prospective arbitrator from the duty to heed the language chosen by the parties. If the parties did choose a language of arbitration, the basic rule is simple: a person invited to act as arbitrator should not accept appointment unless he/she has an adequate command of the designated language (or of one of the designated languages). This has been made quite clear in the 1996 International Bar Association (hereinafter 'IBA') Rules of Ethics. Article 2 of these Rules identifies the considerations which should guide a prospective arbitrator. It is stated that a prospective arbitrator shall only accept appointment if he is fully satisfied that he is able to discharge his duties without bias, if he is fully satisfied that he is competent to determine the issue in dispute, and also if he 'has an adequate knowledge of the language of the arbitration.'

This means that as far as arbitrators are concerned, adaptation to the language of arbitration actually means acceptance of personal consequences of a choice made by the parties. If the person invited to arbitrate does not have an adequate command of the designated language, he/she should draw consequences and should not accept the appointment. Beyond this basic rule, adaptation might mean preparation by way of clarification and checking of technical terms which

---

[12] Byung-Chol Yoon, Jung-Keol Suh, Dai-Hyun Kim, and Grant L. Kim, 'Arbitration in Korea', in Ph. McConnaughay and Th. Ginsburg, eds., *International Commercial Arbitration in Asia* (JurisNet Publ. 2006) 201 at p. 225

are relevant in the case – but this is practically only possible after the receipt of the first submissions of the parties which will reveal the focus of the dispute and the relevant area of technical terms.

Let me repeat that arbitrators must have an adequate command of the language chosen as the language of arbitration. Acting as an arbitrator with the assistance of an interpreter is conceivable, but certainly not desirable. It also has to be noted that even where this option is not ruled out, the person invited to act as arbitrator who does not have adequate language skills should inform of this the party (and the arbitral institution).

If the key consideration and dividing line is 'adequate knowledge of language', the question arises what command of language could be qualified as adequate. Courts have been reluctant to set a standard. I would like to use as examples two French cases in which awards were challenged i.a. on the grounds of allegedly inadequate language skills of the arbitrators. In *JDA Software France and JDA Worldwide v. SA Kiabi*,[13] the arbitrators rendered on February 5, 2001 a preliminary award dealing with a number of procedural issues including that of the question of the language of arbitral proceedings. JDA Software and JDA Worldwide moved to set aside this award. One of their allegations was that the arbitrators had opted not to invite the parties to a debate prior to rendering the preliminary award because the arbitrators did not want to reveal that they did not have an adequate command of English. The parties requesting set aside further alleged that the arbitrators also refused to have a conference call with the parties 'during which their command of English could have been verified'.[14] In its decision of April 11, 2002, the Paris *Cour d'appel* rejected the request for annulment. The court did not discuss the standard of adequate command of language and did not investigate the linguistic skills of the arbitrators, but stated that the 'linguistic qualifications' ('qualifications linguistiques') should have been contested at the moment of the constitution of the arbitral tribunal.[15]

In another case decided by the Paris *Cour d'appel* (*Bargues Agro Industrie v. Young Pecan*[16]), Bargues opposed enforcement of the award. One of the arguments raised against enforcement was that the chairman of the arbitral tribunal '[d]id not have a sufficient knowledge of the French language, the language in which the arbitration was conducted'.[17] This argument against enforcement

[13] 4 *Revue de l'Arbitrage* (2003) p. 1252.

[14] 'Les sociétés JDA Software France et JDA Worldwide soulignent que, postérieurement au prononcé de la sentence, les arbitres sont d'ailleurs refusé de participer à une conference téléphoniques au cours de laquelle leurs connaissance en anglais auraient pu être verifiées comme de confirmer par écrit leurs aptitudes linguistiques' – *Revue de l'arbitrage* (2003) p. 1261.

[15] *Revue de l'arbitrage* (2003) p. 1262.

[16] *Yearbook Commercial Arbitration*, Vol. XXX (2005) 499.

[17] *Yearbook Commercial Arbitration*, Vol. XXX (2005) 504.

(along with other arguments) was rejected. Again, the court did not discuss standards and did not verify linguistic skills; it simply stated that

> 'Bargues' questioning whether the chairman of the arbitral tribunal had the linguistic skills to hear and settle the case in French – after rendition of the award, which appears to have indeed been written in the language of the arbitration, French – is not proof of violation of due process.'[18]

While on the one hand one may regret that the Cour d'appel did not face head on the difficult issue of adequate linguistic skills and did not contribute to the shaping of a dependable standard, on the other hand the attitude taken by the French court appears to be rational. Verifying arbitrators' linguistic skills would not only be cumbersome, but in all probability a controversial undertaking. Moreover, a scrutiny of the challenge regarding linguistic skills could support dilatory tactics, particularly when the objection is only raised in enforcement or setting-aside proceedings.

In scholarly writings one may find various characterizations of appropriate language skills. Lew, Mistelis and Kröll set, for example, a rather modest standard, stating that 'An arbitrator should be able to follow the proceedings without the need for translation.'[19] This standard may be met even by those arbitrators who would have difficulties in drafting an award or, say, dictating the minutes in the language of the proceedings, but who can still 'follow the proceedings without the need for translation'. The question arises whether this unassuming standard will satisfy requirements of efficient proceedings if it is not surpassed by any of the three arbitrators (or by a sole arbitrator).

A somewhat higher standard is put forward by T. Arnold. He suggests that parties should specify '...[a]s a minimum, that each arbitrator have the ability to effectively communicate in the language agreed to for the arbitration hearing so as to avoid translation associated problems and costs'.[20]

Lazareff formulates a more demanding criterion. In his opinion '...[i]t is clear that the arbitrator must have perfect knowledge of the language of the arbitration'.[21]

It has to be born in mind that with regard to language skills a consequential difference exists between litigation and arbitration. Judges are citizens of the

---

[18] *Yearbook Commercial Arbitration*, Vol. XXX (2005) 504.

[19] Julian D. Lew, Loukas A. Mistelis and Stean M. Kröll, *Comparative International Commercial Arbitration* (Kluwer 2003) p. 235.

[20] Tom Arnold, 'Checklist of Arbitration Considerations', in *Patents, Copyrights, Trademarks, and Literary Property Course Handbook Series (*Practising Law Institute 2000) 1059, at p. 1074.

[21] Lazareff, op. cit. 24.

country of the court, and hence, the official language of the court (or one of the official languages of the court) is normally their native tongue. Some exceptions may arise with regard to those judges who belong to a linguistic minority within the country, but these judges would typically also acquire law degrees in the official language (or in one of the official languages) of the country to which their court belongs, and in most cases they would have a perfect command of the language of the court (the official language, or one of the official languages of the country of their citizenship). With regard to arbitrators, this is neither normal nor typical. If a case is decided by three arbitrators (which is the most common pattern) they will typically belong to different countries, have different mother tongues, and have law degrees acquired in different languages. Such a structure of the arbitral tribunal is frequently supported by institutional rules. Quite often, the applicable procedural rules set as a principle that the third arbitrator must not have the nationality of either of the two parties. Thus, it is quite common for the three arbitrators to be citizens of three different countries, and to have three different first-languages. Having this setting in mind, it is probably unrealistic to insist on a 'perfect command' as an inescapable requirement.

Returning to the question what language skills are adequate, one has to note first that there is no formula which could readily distinguish adequate from less-than-adequate commands of language. Introducing a TOEFL score or some similar measuring procedure is not a realistic option. It is also a fact that although linguistic aptitudes may be categorized, they still have strong individual traits. The reading ability of a person may belong to one level, while the same person's ability to speak or write may belong to different levels; the command of a legal language is again a different matter. It is a fact that it is simply not possible to rule out the impact of individual judgment and of the conscience of the person invited to act as an arbitrator.

It is important to point out that the type of proceedings also has an influence on requisite language skills. It matters whether an oral hearing will be conducted or whether the arbitrators will decide on the grounds of written submissions only. (In the latter case, a somewhat lower standard may be adequate, because it is typically easier to read than to speak in a foreign language, and because the arbitrator is under no time pressure while he makes sense of what was communicated, and while he is reacting to what was communicated.) Moreover, to take another example, minutes of oral hearings may be taken in various ways. One of the possible options is that the chairman of the tribunal draws up and dictates a summary of what the parties, the witnesses and experts said (allowing the parties to propose modifications). Such a role of the chairman requires an excellent command of the language of arbitration, but this role need not be assumed in all arbitrations and by all arbitrators.

It is important to add that in typical cases a certain distinction may be drawn between the required language skills of the chairman of the tribunal and the required language skills of the co-arbitrators. If the option chosen is that of dictating the minutes, this is in most cases performed by the chairman only. If this is the case, the language skills of the two co-arbitrators need only meet the standard for the proper performance of less demanding tasks: they should be able to follow the oral hearing without an interpreter, and they should be able to ask some questions in the language of the proceedings. As far as the drafting of the award is concerned, the role of the chairman is, again, often different. If different parts of the award are drafted by different arbitrators, they all have to meet a rather high standard of writing skills in the language of arbitration. The situation is different if the chairman drafts the award and the role of the co-arbitrators is that of commenting and making suggestions. Such comments and suggestions may be effectively made even if they are drafted in less than perfect grammar – as long as the final wording of the award (and of the content agreed upon) remains the responsibility of the chairman. In practice, there are arbitrators who are not ready to accept the role of a chairman because they could not draft a proper award without outside help in the language chosen, but are ready to accept the role of a co-arbitrator in the same case, if the language chosen is a language in which they can read and speak without much difficulty. This may be a gray zone, but probably still within the standard set by the IBA Code of Ethics, which says that a prospective arbitrator should only accept appointment if he has 'an adequate knowledge of the language of arbitration'.

In sum, adaptation to the chosen language (or drawing consequences of a choice made by the parties) by the prospective arbitrator actually means an examination, or rather self-examination, with the purpose of establishing whether one's command of the chosen language is adequate for the performance of the required tasks. These tasks may vary depending on the type of proceedings (which may or may not be fully foreseeable) and on the proposed role within an arbitral tribunal. The bottom line is to be able to read and communicate effectively in the chosen language. The ability to write a proper award is also a clear requirement for a sole arbitrator, or for the chairman of the tribunal – and a highly desirable ability (but not an absolute must) for the co-arbitrators.

A.3.2. *Consequences for the parties (adaptation of the parties to a given choice)*

The choice made in the arbitration agreement is either one proposed or one accepted by a given party. Whichever is the case, strategies have to be adapted to this fact. The chosen language may simply represent a comfort, but it might also represent a task – or a combination of the two. Regarding the task, one may distinguish three components: a) the presentation of arguments has to be adjusted to the language of arbitration; b) the same applies to the submission of documents; and c) the language of arbitration must also be heeded in contemplations regarding witnesses and expert witnesses.

a) *Presentation of arguments*

If the chosen language is not the first language of the given party, a strategic decision has to be made. The options are to hire an attorney who has an adequate command of the language of the proceedings or to hire an interpreter. There are also situations in which it is not clear whether the party (or the attorney who would be his first choice) does or does not have a fitting command of the language of arbitration.

Experience has shown that interpretation is usually the less effective choice. Translation simply cannot fully mirror both the arguments and the art of advocacy. It cannot reflect every emphasis, gambit of persuasion, or undertone. Often, the arguments are not reflected clearly either. Interpreters are often people who do indeed have an excellent command of both languages, but do not have legal education and do not fully understand the subtleties and ramifications of the argument they are supposed to express. They may also use as synonyms terms which do not have the same meaning within a legal context. Furthermore, the person presenting the arguments through an interpreter remains somewhat divorced from the actual scene. Presenting arguments through an interpreter is certainly a possible and legitimate option, but it is a handicap too. Direct communication, even with a less than perfect command of the language of arbitration, may be a better option. Finding a competent attorney who has an adequate command of the language of arbitration is probably the best solution. A trusted attorney (or the party itself) who does not have a fitting command of language may cooperate with the attorney who was chosen primarily for reasons of adaptation to the language of arbitration.

As far as written submissions are concerned, translation is less risky because there are more opportunities for controlling the final product. A possible option is for the party (or for the attorney to whom the case would otherwise be confided) to draft the submissions and to submit it to a proof-reader who will control language and grammar. This is an option if the party (or the trusted attorney) has a certain command of the language of arbitration and is also able to check the substance of the final version after language and grammar are corrected.

b) *Documents*

As far as documents are concerned, translation is often not needed. The first reason for this is that the parties often choose a language of arbitration having in mind the language of the contract, of their correspondence, and of other pertinent documents. If this is not the case, or if correspondence was conducted in several languages (and there are also other relevant documents in more languages) it still makes sense to propose the presentation of all documents in their original version. This will typically be the case when the languages in question are spoken by both parties – and this is also expected from all arbitrators. In such a situation, translation would only represent a waste of time and money, and an added risk. Arrangements allowing the presentation of documents in their original language are sometimes made in the arbitration agreement proper. Such an arrangement might also be initiated later on by a party, and this might be equally convenient for both parties.

In the absence of such an arrangement, translation of pertinent documents is a one of the tasks of the party preparing its case.

c) *Witnesses, experts*

Once the language of arbitration is known and the party is in a position to choose between proposing a witness who does and one who does not speak that language, it is obviously more advantageous to propose a witness who can present his testimony directly, without the interposition of an interpreter. The same logic applies to hiring experts (assuming that the party has a say in choosing an expert).

If the witness the party would like to propose does not speak the language of the arbitral proceedings, inquiries should be made to establish whether under the applicable rules it is a task of the parties or of the arbitrators to make arrangements for interpretation. Following the rules, the party should either find an interpreter, or should signal to the arbitrators that interpretation is needed.

B. Absence of Choice Made by the Parties – and the Consequences of the Absence of Choice

Absence of choice made by the parties has no impact on the standards themselves. Irrespective whether the language of arbitration is known in advance, an arbitrator has to have an adequate command of the language of the proceedings in order to be able to fulfill his/her tasks. By the same token, the parties also have the same strategic aims, and have to consider and to meet the same standards in organizing their presentation. Thus, the standards of adequacy are the same, but in the absence of a choice of language in the arbitration agreement the question arises what is the language of which the arbitrators (and other actors in the proceedings) must have an adequate command.

B.1. Consequences for the arbitrators (adaptation of the arbitrators to an absence of choice)

If the language of arbitration is not known at the time when a prospective arbitrator is approached, he has to rely on logic and experience in trying to establish what language will likely become the language of the arbitral proceedings. This may be more or less difficult depending on the circumstances of the case. Qualified professionals may very well disagree on the question what ought to be the language of arbitration under the given circumstances. The crux of the matter is that a prospective arbitrator has to make guesses – one could say educated guesses – and he/she has some points of support.

One circumstance which may provide guidance is the nationality of the parties. It is not difficult to guess that German will most likely be the language of arbitration in a dispute between an Austrian and a German company. In a case between a French and a Belgian company, the names of the Belgian actors may provide a necessary additional information showing whether the Belgian party is French-speaking or Flemish-speaking. The nationality of the parties will not offer guidance, however, in a dispute between a Hungarian and a Polish party. A further point of support is the language of the contract and the language of correspondence between the parties. If the Hungarian and Polish party corresponded in English, and executed their contract in English, it will be fairly safe to assume that English will be the language of arbitration. It happens, however, with some frequency, that the language of correspondence changes; it also happens that the contract is executed in two languages. In such cases, this point of support may vanish.

A prospective arbitrator could also consult the party who nominates him/her, and furthermore may suggest to the party to try to reach an agreement on the language of arbitration with the other party. This approach will yield results if the party has more information regarding language than the arbitrator does, or if the party is ready to approach the other party (and if the two parties do reach an agreement on language).

Another possible option is to contact the other arbitrator (if the other arbitrator has already been nominated). This might yield information on the command of language(s) of the other arbitrator. In the absence of a choice made by the parties, the command of languages of the arbitrators is a legitimate consideration in determining the language of arbitration. Raeschke-Kessler and Berger submit that – in addition to the language of the contract – the linguistic abilities of the arbitrators themselves represent a relevant criterion.[22] This observation

[22] Hilmar Raeschke-Kessler and Klaus Peter Berger, *Recht und Praxis des Schiedsverfahrens* (Köln 1999) ('Ein maßgebliches Kriterium für die Entscheidung des Schiedsgerichts ist die Vertragsprache und die Sprachfähigkeiten der Schiedsricher selbst', pp. 162-163).

was made in the context of designating the language of arbitration by the arbitrators, rather than in the context of guessing the language of arbitration by a prospective arbitrator. Nevertheless, information on the command of language of a co-arbitrator is relevant because it sheds light on a possible solution (a language of which both arbitrators have an adequate command) – or shows that there is no solution (if the two arbitrators have no language in common).

Let me finally mention that there are several situations in which the absence of a choice made by the parties does not necessitate guesses. Such is the situation where institutional rules provide for a default language. If this is the case, the arbitrator should accept or decline nomination depending on his/her command of the default language. Likewise, the problem will not emerge if we are talking about a sole arbitrator – since in the absence of a choice made by the parties, the language of arbitration will be determined by the sole arbitrator himself (herself).

B.2. **Consequences for the parties (adaptation of the parties to an absence of choice)**

As far as the parties are concerned, the best way to deal with an absence of choice is, of course, to make a choice. If this cannot be achieved, a party – just as an arbitrator – will have to rely on logic and on the circumstances of the case. The nationality of the parties, the language of the contract, and the language of correspondence will be, if not the only, then the most prominent indicators.

Choosing between potential arbitrators, the party should include among relevant considerations whether the arbitrator has an adequate command of the language which will likely become the language of arbitration. The party may know this because he/she knows the arbitrator and he/she is familiar with the qualifications of the potential arbitrator. The party may also establish this through the C.V. of the arbitrator, or by way of an interview. If the party takes this approach, it will be much easier for the arbitrator to make a decision.

The party (particularly the claimant) will also have to face the dilemma of deciding in which language the first communication (statement of claim or request for arbitration) should be submitted. If we are dealing with institutional arbitration, the party should first establish whether the rules of the institution provide for an initial language.[23] If no solution is provided by way of an initial language, one is forced to fall back on educated guesses relying essentially on the points of support mentioned in connection with the arbitrators.

---

[23] See on the initial language Chapter I.C.3.

A diligent party will also make arrangements regarding its pleadings, considering the factors which may influence the determination of the language of arbitration – and will consider fallback arrangements if there are more likely outcomes.

C. Language Issues in Court Proceedings in Assistance of Starting Arbitration

If the parties and the arbitrators do not succeed in establishing an arbitral tribunal, a solution may be provided by an appointing authority, by the arbitral institution, or by courts. Courts will typically represent the last resort in the absence of party agreement on some other mechanism. The question I would like to raise is whether courts will consider – or maybe even verify – language skills in making the appointment. According to Article 11(5) of the UNCITRAL Model Law

> 'The court or other authority, in appointing an arbitrator, shall have due regard to any qualifications required of the arbitrator by the agreement of the parties and to such considerations as are likely to secure the appointment of an independent and impartial arbitrator… .'

This is a broadly accepted standard. Individual national legislations may add or omit some detail, but typically do not spell out requisite skills or relevant considerations in the legislative norm. The same approach has been taken in most institutional rules as well. A rare exception is the solution adopted in the OHADA Rules[24] which include provisions on the competencies of a 'common court of justice and arbitration' (*cour commune de justice et d'arbitrage*). Article 3(3) of the OHADA Rules states that in making the nomination, the court should consider the language of the parties (along with the nationality and residence of the parties, the residence of the counsels, the nature of the disputed issues, and the applicable law.)

It is clear that when the arbitration agreement specifies some required language skills, the court should look for arbitrators who do have such qualifications. The same obviously applies when the parties do not spell out that the arbitrators need to have an adequate command of, say, English, or French or Polish, but do state that the language of arbitration is English (or French or

[24] OHADA – Organization for the Harmonization of Business Law in Africa (*Organisation pour l'Harmonisation en Afrique du Droit des Affaires* – OHADA) *Règlement d'arbitrage de la cour commune de justice et de l'arbitrage de l'OHADA*, adopted on March 11, 1999.

Polish, etc.). In this latter case, the requisite language skills may not be a qualification explicitly 'required of the arbitrator by the agreement', but this is clearly implied. If the arbitration agreement contains no provisions on the language of arbitration, the appointing court will have no direct guidance, but could still heed the issue of language by trying to find persons who could proceed with competence in the language which will likely become the language of arbitration.

The question arises how far the court needs to go in ascertaining (or verifying) the linguistic skills of the arbitrators. In one of the quite rare cases in which this question was explicitly raised, the court took a cautious approach. In *Société La Belle Créole v. Société The Gemtel Partnership*,[25] after the decease of the arbitrator nominated by La Belle Créole (Mr. Carcassonne), the same company nominated a substitute arbitrator. Gemtel objected, stating that by the death of Mr. Carcassone, the arbitration agreement providing for *ad hoc* arbitration became extinguished. La Belle Créole addressed the President of the Tribunal de grande instance, arguing that under Article 1493 of the French Code of Civil Procedure, the President of the Tribunal de grande instance has competence 'if any difficulty arises in the constitution of the arbitral tribunal'. Gemtel argued that this provision only applies to the initial constitution of an arbitral tribunal. In its first decision of July 12, 1989, the President held that Article 1493 applies to any difficulty, including difficulties emerging after the initial constitution, and invited the parties to nominate their arbitrators.[26] After La Belle Créole nominated Mr. M.A., Gemtel challenged him before the President of the Tribunal de grande instance, stating i.a. that he did not have adequate knowledge of technical terms in English. This argument was later abandoned, but the President of the Tribunal de grande instance nevertheless considered it and held that

> 'it is not within the mission of the President of the Tribunal de grande instance to value the competence of an arbitrator and his linguistic aptitude to participate in an arbitral tribunal, since it belongs to the conscience of the arbitrator to accept or not to accept his mission... considering the specific traits of the dispute and the expectations of the parties.'[27]

---

[25] *Société La Belle Créole v. Société The Gemtel Partnership*, First decision of July 12, 1989, *Revue de l'arbitrage* (1990) p. 176.

[26] *Revue de l'arbitrage* (1990) p. 177.

[27] *Revue de l'arbitrage* (1990) at p. 184. The French text reads: '[I]l n'apparaît pas relever de la mission attribuée au Président du Tribunal de grande instance d'apprécier la compétence d'un arbitre et de son aptitude linguistique à participer à un tribunal arbitral alors qu'il ressortit à la conscience de l'arbitre d'accepter ou non la mission de juge qui lui est proposée, en fonction des spécificités du litige et de la prévision des parties;'.

In his supportive comments on this decision, Ph. Kahn stresses that a challenge procedure cannot submit each arbitrator to an entrance examination regarding his qualifications. The question of proper qualifications should not be assessed by a judge, but should rather be left to the conscience of the arbitrators. Kahn adds that there cannot be many arbitrators who would at the same time be 'perfect technicians, perfect jurists, perfect linguists, and who would have the wisdom of Solomon and the patience of Penelope'.[28]

The issue of the attitude of the appointing judge towards language skills of prospective arbitrators also arose in another case decided by the Tribunal de grande instance in 1991. In *Société Campenon Bernard v. Eurodisneyland SCA*,[29] the arbitration agreement provided that if the parties cannot agree on the choice of arbitrators, the arbitral tribunal should be nominated by the Tribunal de grande instance, and the arbitrators should be chosen from a list submitted by the ICC Court of Arbitration. The arbitration agreement at issue in this case is one of the quite rare ones which stipulated explicitly that the arbitrators had to have the requisite language skills. In addition to setting as a requirement that all arbitrators should have experience in international construction disputes, it also stated that all arbitrators need to have a full command of English ('une pleine maîtrise de la languge anglaise'). Before the Tribunal de grande instance, Eurodisney submitted that the list proposed by the ICC Court of Arbitration did not show the requisite qualifications, and asked to court to seek additional information. In its decision of December 12, 1991, the Tribunal de grande instance decided to seek additional information regarding the qualifications of the arbitrators.[30] After such additional information was provided by the ICC Court of Arbitration, in its second decision of December 20, 1991[31] the Tribunal de grande instance nominated three arbitrators from the list proposed by the ICC Court of Arbitration. In his comments on these decisions, Fouchard addresses the issue of language skills and states that the 'full command of English' ('pleine maîtrise de la langue anglaise') was easily verifiable since the persons on the list were well known. Fouchard added, however – referring to the Gemtel decision – that the President of the Tribunal de grande instance refuses, as a matter of principle, to control the linguistic aptitude of the arbitrators.[32]

The *dictum* of the Gemtel decision, according to which issues of competence and linguistic aptitude must be left to the conscience of the prospective arbitrator, raises an important question. What should be the attitude of the judge (or of

---

[28] *Revue de l'arbitrage* (1990) p. 194.
[29] Reported in *Revue de l'arbitrage* (1996) p. 516.
[30] *Revue de l'arbitrage* (1996) p. 517.
[31] *Revue de l'arbitrage* (1996) p. 518.
[32] *Revue de l'arbitrage* (1996) p. 523.

other appointing authority) towards the language requirement? It is certainly not realistic to expect that an appointing judge (or any appointing authority) will test and verify the language skills of a prospective arbitrator. Even legal qualifications may be difficult to assess, but here, at least, whether the arbitrator does or does not have a law degree may represent a dividing line which is easy to heed. Most arbitrators who have an excellent command of several languages cannot, however, present as evidence language degrees or tests passed. Still, the question remains whether linguistic aptitude is simply a matter to be left to the conscience of the prospective arbitrator. The *Gemtel* case was (in this respect) a rather easy one. What was specifically challenged was Mr. M.A.'s command of technical terms in English. Whether Mr. M.A. did or did not have a command of the relevant technical terms in English need not be a consequential issue. One cannot learn English between appointment and the first hearing – but one can very well learn and clarify the pertinent technical terms in the course of preparations for the case. As a matter of fact, a native speaker may also need to do this. The real question emerges when the basic command of language – rather than acquaintance with technical terms – is at issue. While one cannot expect the appointing judge to administer a language test, he/she could (and should) certainly make inquiries, and could also ask direct questions. The Eurodisneyland decision may be interpreted as a certain departure from the dictum in the Gemtel case, according to which matters of competence and language skills must be left to the conscience of the prospective arbitrator. In Eurodisneyland, the *Tribunal de grande instance* did indeed seek additional information regarding the competence and language skills of the proposed arbitrators before making the appointment.[33] Assistance to the constitution of the tribunal should certainly be understood as assistance to the constitution of a viable tribunal. Such assistance supposes choice of arbitrators who could adequately perform their job – and this also supposes choice of arbitrators who have an adequate command of the language of arbitration. Quite often, choice will be made between prospective arbitrators whose qualifications (including language skills) were already proven, and this is known to the court. The conscience of the prospective arbitrators remains a critical factor, but judges should also gather information before putting the authority of the court behind a choice – and such information should include indications about language skills required to participate in the proceedings.

---

[33] It has to be noted that in the given case, legal competence was more at issue than language skills, but the fact remains that additional information was sought with regard to the qualifications described in the arbitration agreement, and these included 'full command of English'.

Chapter III

Determining the Language of Arbitration and Ordering Translation by the Arbitrators After the Constitution of the Arbitral Tribunal

A. Determination of the Language of Arbitration by the Arbitrators

A.1. When are the arbitrators entitled to determine the language of arbitration?

It has already been pointed out in the preceding chapters that the arbitrators will determine the language of arbitration if this has not been done by the parties (and if there is no mandatory default language). This is a rather straightforward solution, accepted worldwide. Thus, the question raised in the title of this subsection has in most cases a simple and obvious answer: the arbitrators will determine the language of arbitration when this was not done by the parties. Still, there are issues and questions which are not covered by the obvious answer. In some (probably quite exceptional) cases the question emerged whether a party choice actually existed or not, and this dilemma led to the question whether the arbitrators are or are not entitled to determine the language of arbitration themselves. More frequently, the question arises as to what is actually covered by the choice made by the parties, and whether such a choice did or did not leave some maneuvering room to the arbitrators. This latter question has typically emerged with regard to the issue of translation of documents.

I can refer to two cases in which it became an issue whether the parties actually agreed on the language of arbitration, and thus, whether the fallback solution (determination by the arbitrators) was needed and justified. In an ICC case[1] referred to earlier in which I participated as arbitrator, the parties executed their contract in two languages (English and Serbian). It was stated in the contract that the English version had priority. At the same time the arbitration clause provided for Serbian as the language of arbitration. This may not have been the most rational solution, but it was certainly a possible arrange-

[1] Case No. 13798/AVH.

ment. One could guess that the motive behind this arrangement may have been some bargaining balance, rather than an endeavor to create a congruent legal environment for dispute settlement. In spite of the provision in the arbitration clause, the claimant submitted its request for arbitration in English. The respondent insisted that the language of arbitration should be Serbian. The claimant argued that English would be better fitted to communication with the Secretariat, and it would make the choice of the third arbitrator easier. The respondent simply stated that the arbitration clause provided for arbitration in Serbian, thus Serbian should be the language of arbitration. The claimant also raised a somewhat unexpected argument. It submitted that since the parties were debating the issue of language, the language of arbitration should be determined by the arbitral tribunal, because under Article 16 of the ICC Rules, 'in the absence of an agreement by the parties' the arbitral tribunal shall determine the language or languages of arbitration. This way, a somewhat unusual question arose. It became an issue whether the parties had or had not reached an agreement on the language of arbitration. The question may have been unusual, but it was not a difficult one. The arbitration clause did contain a clear stipulation opting for Serbian as the language of arbitration, and this provision cannot be overruled by an *ex post facto* contestation.

In another case decided under the UNCITRAL Model Rules, the question arose again whether the basic precondition for a determination by the arbitrators was met; namely, whether party agreement on the language of arbitration was or was not missing. In *JDA Software France v. SA Kiabi*[2] the framework agreement concluded between the parties contained an arbitration clause providing for *ad hoc* arbitration under the UNCITRAL Model Rules. This arbitration clause did not specify the language of arbitral proceedings. The framework agreement had several annexes. The arbitration clause in Annex 4 provided for English as the language of arbitration. In their preliminary award of February 5, 2001, the arbitrators decided on several procedural issues, including that of the language of arbitration. One of the parties insisted that the language of arbitration should be English, as stated in Annex 4. The *ad hoc* tribunal decided, however, that the language of arbitration should be French with regard to the framework agreement and its first three annexes, and that it should be English regarding Annex 4.[3] The arbitrators added that the parties should be free to express themselves in either French or English. This case shows that genuine dilemmas may emerge as to whether the parties did or did not agree on the language of arbitration. In *JDA Software*, difficulties in interpretation were trig-

[2] See a decision of the Paris *Cour d'appel* on a request to set aside the award in *JDA Software v. Kiabi*, in *Revue de l'arbitrage* (2003) p. 1252.

[3] *Revue de l'arbitrage* (2003) p. 1256.

gered by a lack of full consistency within a set of contractual arrangements. One can also imagine cases (and there may have been cases) in which the stipulation pertaining to language has been indirect. For example, acting as a consultant I noted an arbitration clause stating that 'the language of the contract will also control the language of arbitral proceedings'. The contract was executed in two languages. Had it come to arbitration, this provision would have necessitated interpretation by the arbitrators. Let me note, however, that interpretation of indirect – or unclear – party stipulations needs to be distinguished from absence of party agreement on language. In the first case, the arbitrators are not free to determine the language of arbitration ('failing agreement of the parties'), they are obliged instead to seek and establish the intention of the parties.

In sum, in the overwhelming majority of the cases it is clear whether the parties did or did not agree on the language of arbitration, and whether the fallback provision was or was not triggered. Situations in which a party agreement on language exists but it needs interpretation, are also quite rare.

A.2. **Considerations in choosing the language of arbitration**

Considerations on the grounds of which the arbitrators will determine the language (or languages) of arbitration are essentially the same as those which serve – in the absence of a choice made by the parties – as a basis for guesses made by the party who has to prepare for a case, or by the prospective arbitrator who has to speculate whether he/she can accept appointment.[4]

Arbitration acts and institutional rules in most cases do not give much (or any) guidance to the arbitrators in determining the language (or languages) of arbitration. Instead, they usually just reiterate the principle that in the absence of a choice made by the parties, the language of arbitration shall be determined by the arbitrators. To take one of many examples, the DIS Rules state in Article 22(1):

> 'The parties are free to agree on the language or languages to be used in the arbitral proceedings. Failing such agreement, the arbitral tribunal shall determine the language or languages to be used in the proceedings.'

A bit more guidance is given by those (very few) rules which instruct the arbitrators to consult the parties before making their determination. For example, according to Article 23 of the Stockholm Rules:

---

[4] See Chapter II.B.

'Unless the parties have agreed in the arbitration agreement on the language or languages to be used in the proceedings, the Arbitral Tribunal shall, after consultation with the parties, make such decision.'

A certain number of acts and rules offer some guidance by a broad reference to the 'circumstances of the case'.[5] Some acts and rules are somewhat more specific, referring for example to the 'place of arbitration and the language used by the parties in their legal relationship',[6] or, more often, by pointing out the language of the contract among the circumstances of the case.[7] The emphasis given to this latter indicator (the language of the contract) varies. One of the best examples of strong emphasis was the rule of Article 15(3) of the (former) 1988 ICC Rules which stated:

'The arbitrator shall determine the language or languages of the arbitration, due regard being paid to all relevant circumstances and in particular to the language of the contract.'

Practice has shown that this particular emphasis on the language of the contract may amount to a presumption, but only to a rebuttable presumption. Occasionally, the arbitrators chose a different law. In a case decided by a German court[8] between a Danish claimant and a German respondent, the respondent opposed recognition and enforcement of an ICC award. The respondent argued i.a. that the arbitrator's choice of English as the language of proceedings constituted a violation of due process, considering Article 15(3) of the 1988 ICC Rules, and given that the language of contract was German. This argument was not accepted, and recognition was granted.[9]

The present (1998) ICC Rules still single out the language of the contract, but with less emphasis. This does not amount anymore to a presumption or

[5] E.g., Art. 18 of the 1988 Nigerian Arbitration and Conciliation Decree No. 11; Art. 28 of the Spanish Arbitration Act No. 60/2003 (in force since March 26, 2004).

[6] See Art. 35 of the 2006 Serbian Arbitration Act.

[7] See e.g., Art. 13(1) of the 1990 Scottish Law Reform Act adopting the Model Law; Art. 21 of the 1994 Italian Arbitration Association Rules for International Arbitration; Art. 14 of the 2005 CEPANI Arbitration Rules; Art. 9(2) of the 2005 Budapest Rules; Art. 22 of the 1997 Rules of the Arbitration Center of Mexico (*Centro de Arbitraje de Mexico*); or Art. 14 of the AAA 2006 International Rules.

[8] *Oberlandesgericht* Köln, December 16, 1992 – Reported in *Yearbook Commercial Arbitration,* Vol. XXI (1996) p. 535.

[9] It has to be mentioned that in this case the arbitrators designated two languages of the proceedings: English and German. Respondent was allowed to file his pleadings in German, while the claimant was communicating in English. The position of the respondent was that German should be the only language of the proceedings, since this was the language of the contract.

clear priority, as was the case with the 1988 Rules. According to Article 16 of the present Rules:

> 'In the absence of an agreement by the parties, the Arbitral Tribunal shall determine the language or languages of the arbitration, due regard being given to all relevant circumstances, including the language of the contract.'

Other rules which mention the language of the agreement[10] include the 2006 AAA Rules, which have adopted a distinctive nuance (and precision) by referring to the document containing the arbitration agreement, rather than to the contract. According to Article 14:

> 'If the parties have not agreed otherwise, the language(s) of the arbitration shall be that of the documents containing the arbitration agreement, subject to the power of the tribunal to determine otherwise based upon the contentions of the parties and the circumstances of the arbitration.'

In their Commentary on the UNCITRAL Model Law, Holtzmann and Neuhaus note that there were several proposals aiming to give more strict guidance to the arbitrators, proposals which, however, failed. One was to require that all languages of the parties be used where the parties had neither come to a different agreement nor did they specifically ask the tribunal to choose the language. Another suggestion was to require that a party should always be permitted to present his/her own case in his/her own language.[11] The logic of this latter proposal apparently found an echo in the *JDA Software v. Kiabi case*[12] in which the arbitrators allowed the parties to each use his/her own language, and explained this option by the due process requirements of the European Convention of Human Rights.[13]

The option adopted by the arbitrators in the *JDA Software* case is a sensible solution, but it is hardly mandated. There are other ways to satisfy the due process standard set by Article 6 of the European Convention on Human Rights and Fundamental Freedoms as far as the language of the proceedings is concerned. Article 6 says that 'everyone is entitled to fair ...hearing'. This requirement will, indeed, be met if a party is allowed to express himself in his own

---

[10] See examples in n. 6.

[11] Howard M. Holtzmann and Joseph E. Neuhaus, *A Guide to the UNCITRAL Model Law on International Commercial Arbitration: Legislative History and Commentary* (The Hague, Kluwer 1989) at p. 629.

[12] *Revue de l'arbitrage* (2003) p. 1252.

[13] *Revue de l'arbitrage* (2003) pp. 1256, 1260.

language, but it will also be met if he can avail himself of the services of a translator.

In sum, in determining the language (or languages) of arbitration, the arbitrators have a considerable maneuvering room. They will normally take into consideration the language of the contract and/or of the arbitration agreement, the language of correspondence between the parties, as well as the nationality of the parties. Consulting the parties is normally a helpful step. The language skills of the arbitrators themselves will set the range of options within which a choice will be made.

B. Ordering Translation

B.1. **The scope of the term 'translation'**

As far as ordering translation is concerned, a preliminary question arises. This is the issue of the scope of translation within the arbitration process. It has been questioned what is the actually contemplated scope of term 'translation' in statutes and arbitration rules, to what does the obligation to translate extend, and what translation can be ordered by the arbitrators. A related and particularly sensitive question is whether the arbitrators are free to order presentation of documents in a language which is not the language of arbitration.

In addressing these questions we shall subject to scrutiny the formulations used in UNCITRAL enactments, since they have served as a model for a very considerable number of legislative acts and institutional rules. Speaking of the formulations adopted in UNCITRAL enactments, Chapter I(B) raised the question whether Article 22(1) of the Model Law and Article 17(1) of the Model Rules have purposefully (and adequately) demarcated the presumptive scope of choice of language. Article 22(1) of the Model Law states that the choice of language extends i.a. to the language of the award. In Article 17(1), the Model Rules also contain an enumeration explaining to what elements of the proceedings the established language extends, but this enumeration does not include the award. It is not really likely that either the parties or the arbitrators would opt for a language assuming that it will not apply with respect to the award. It is hardly realistic to suppose that when the parties choose a language to govern the arbitral proceedings, they do not assume that this is the language in which award will be written. Nevertheless, questions have emerged with regard to scope of the chosen language, as well as with regard to the scope of the notion of translation used in the UNCITRAL enactments, and in arbitral proceedings in general. One of the disputed issues has been the language of documentary evidence presented to the arbitrators.

B.2. The standard set by UNCITRAL enactments regarding the notion and scope of translation

As far as the scope of translation is concerned, the UNCITRAL Model Law may serve as a starting point of investigations. Article 22 of the Model Law is devoted to language. Section 2 of Article 22 contains a sentence about translation:

> 'The arbitral tribunal may order that any documentary evidence shall be accompanied by a translation into the language or languages agreed upon by the parties or determined by the arbitral tribunal.'

Like many other rules of the Model Law, the provision concerning translation has become a widely accepted standard, not only in countries which have been qualified as 'Model Law countries',[14] but in a considerable number of other countries as well. Legislators have typically adopted the same sentence (or a variation of it).[15] The question is whether the sentence in Article 22 offers guidance regarding the scope of translation. This sentence (the only one referring to translation) actually deals with one variant of translation: it speaks about translation of **documentary evidence**. This is obviously less than the whole spectrum. The need for translation might also emerge with respect to witness

---

[14] According to the UNCITRAL evidence August 2006), legislation based on the ML has been enacted in 52 jurisdictions, plus six states of the United States – UNCITRAL, Status of Conventions and Model Laws on http://www.uncitral.org.

[15] See e.g., (in alphabetical order) Art. 33 of the 1999 Law of the Republic of Belarus on International Arbitration Court; Art. 22(4) of the 1998 British Columbia International Commercial Arbitration Act; Art. 21(2) of the 2001 Croatian Arbitration Act; Art. 29(2) of the 1994 Egyptian Act Concerning Arbitration in Civil and Commercial Matters – last amended in 2000; Section 26(2) of the 1992 Finnish Arbitration Act; Section 1045(2) of the 1998 German Arbitration Act; Art. 22(2) of the 1999 Greek Arbitration Act; Art. 27(2) of the 1995 Guatemala Arbitration Act; Section 48(2) of the 1994 Hungarian Arbitration Act; Art. 22(4) of the 1996 Indian Arbitration and Conciliation Act; Art. 30(4) of the 2003 Japan Arbitration Act; Art. 28(b) of the 2001 Jordanian Act No. 31/2004; Art. 23(4) of the 1995 Kenya Arbitration Act; Art. 25 of the 1996 Lithuanian Arbitration Act; Art. 459(2) of the 1998 Madagascar Arbitration Act; Art. 51(3) of the 2000 Mauritania Code of Arbitration; Art. 1438 of the 1993 Mexican Commercial Code, Book V on Commercial Arbitration; Art. 22(2) of the 1997 New Zealand Arbitration Act; Art. 18(3) of the 1998 Nigerian Arbitration and Conciliation Decree; Art. 29(3) of the 1997 Oman Act on Arbitration in Civil and Commercial Disputes; Art. 111(2) of the 1996 Peru General Arbitration Act; Art. 22(2) of the Act of the Russian Federation on International Commercial Arbitration; Art. 25(1) of the 1998 Taiwanese Arbitration Act; Art. 28(2) of the 2002 Thailand Arbitration Act; Art. 67(2) of the 1993 Tunisia Arbitration Act; Art. 10(2) of the 2001 Turkish Act on International Arbitration; Art. 22(2) of the 2003 Ukrainian Act on International Commercial Arbitration; Art. 22(2) of the 1996 Zimbabwe Arbitration Act.

statements presented during the oral hearing. It may also happen that one of the arbitrators does not understand the language of the proceedings and he/she needs translation.[16] Furthermore, although the parties have to suit their pleadings to the language of the proceedings, they may opt to present their oral argument with the assistance of an interpreter.

The question has also been raised what the term 'translation' itself actually encompasses. In a more restrictive sense, translation encompasses written translation only, in which case translation at an oral hearing should be called 'interpretation'. In a broader meaning, the term 'translation' covers both written and oral translation. The terminological distinction between 'translation' and 'interpretation' has some foundations, but in practice the two terms are often used interchangeably; hence, reliance on this distinction would entail risks. The distinction is not supported by the UNCITRAL enactments. The Model Law does not contemplate translation (or interpretation) of statements made at oral hearing. The Model Rules contemplate these situations – and use the term 'translation' both with regard to translation of written statements or documentary evidence (Art. 17(2)) and with respect to translation of statements made at oral hearings (Art. 25(3)). Furthermore, an unbending distinction would be further inhibited by the fact that not all languages have a matching pair of terms. Therefore, unless otherwise indicated, we shall use the term 'translation' in its broader meaning, encompassing both translation of documents and translation (interpretation) offered during oral hearings.

Not all legislative acts devoted to arbitration have provisions on language and translation. Some important acts which have otherwise exerted wide influence (such as the 1925 US Federal Arbitration Act, Chapter 12 of the 1987 Swiss Private International Law Act, or Book IV of the 1981 French Code of Civil Procedure) do not contain rules on language and translation within the arbitration proceedings. Most arbitration acts which devote attention to translation within the arbitration proceedings only deal with translation of documentary evidence. (This is the case with the 28 legislative acts cited above.) Only a very few legislatures have devoted explicit attention to other variants of translation. For example, the Romanian Code of Civil Procedure speaks in Article

---

[16] This may happen in cases in which the parties agree on a language after the arbitrators have been chosen. If this language is understood by only two of the three arbitrators, we have a problem. Reliance on a translator is a possibility but not a desirable solution. There is a difference between communication via an interpreter between the arbitrators and a party (or a witness) and communication through an interpreter among the arbitrators themselves. Deliberations without a common language are not inconceivable, but certainly not advisable. Direct communication is preferable given both the sensitive nature of the communication and the aim of having a clear and direct mutual understanding.

369(4) of translation in the case that 'a party is ignorant of the language in which the proceedings are carried on'.[17] The Arbitration Legislation in Costa Rica contemplates both translation of documentary evidence and 'translation of testimonies of non Spanish-speaking witnesses'.[18] The Arbitration Act of Malta contemplates translation of 'oral statements made at a hearing'.[19]

The 1976 UNCITRAL Model Rules – as well as many other institutional rules – have devoted attention to more situations in which translation may be effected (beyond that of translation of documentary evidence). Article 17(2) of the Model Rules repeats the position taken by the Model Law (adding an explanation to the effect that documentary evidence may include documents annexed to the statement of claim or statement of defense, but also 'any supplementary documents or exhibits submitted in the course of the proceedings'). This is actually not a broadening of the scope set in the Model Law; Article 17(2) of the Model Rules is only more explicit in spelling out details regarding documentary evidence. Article 25(3) of the Model Rules, however, covers more ground than the Model Law. It states:

> 'The arbitral tribunal shall make arrangements for the translation of oral statements made at a hearing and for a record of the hearing if either is deemed necessary by the tribunal under the circumstances of the case, or if the parties have agreed thereto and have communicated such agreement to the tribunal at least 15 days before the hearing.'

A considerable number of arbitration rules have tracked the formulations adopted by the Model Rules. For example, the 2004 Swiss Rules of International Arbitration have adopted the exact wording of Articles 17(2) and 25(3) of the Model Rules. The essence of the solution adopted by the UNCITRAL Rules has also been followed e.g., by the 2000 British Columbia International Commercial Arbitration Center International Commercial Arbitration Rules (Art. 21 and 25), the 1998 CRCICA Arbitration Rules (Art. 17(2) and 25(3)), the 1998 NAI Arbitration Rules (Art. 40), the 1983 Iran-US Claims Tribunal Provisionally Adopted Arbitration Rules (Art. 17 and 25), and the various arbitration rules of the PCA.[20]

---

[17] Code of Civil Procedure, Book IV on Arbitration (as amended by Law No. 59 of July 23, 1993).

[18] See Art. 41 and 51 of the 2000 Costa Rica Act on Alternative Resolution of Disputes and Promotion of Freedom from Social Unrest.

[19] Art. 37(2) of the February 13, 1996 Malta Arbitration Act.

[20] The 2001 Rules for Arbitration of Disputes Relating to Natural Resources and/or the Environment (Art. 17 and 25), the 1996 Optional Rules for Arbitration Involving International Organizations and States (Art. 17 and 25), and the 1996 Optional Rules for Arbitration Between International Organizations and Private Parties (Art. 17 and 25).

The wording of Article 25(3) of the Model Rules (like similar wordings adopted in other rules) extends to translation of party pleadings and witness statements during an oral hearing. There is one – albeit rare – situation which is not covered by the formulations adopted in either the Model Law or in the Model Rules. This is translation for the benefit of one of the arbitrators who does not speak the language used in the proceedings. Very few institutional rules deal explicitly with this matter. One example may be found in Article 9(6) of the 2005 Budapest Rules, which reads: 'If the foreign arbitrator is not familiar with the language of the proceedings, upon request, the Secretariat of the Court of Arbitration shall provide an interpreter (translator).'

This short survey of the various designations of the scope of translation gives rise to the question whether formulations which contemplate a more narrow scope (typically, translation of documentary evidence only) actually pose some restriction on translation which may be ordered or produced? I suggest that it does not make sense to interpret Article 22(2) of the Model Law in a restrictive and exclusive way. An example will help to illustrate this point. Suppose arbitration is conducted under ICC Rules (which do not have special provisions on translation) and the *lex arbitri* is the law of say Greece (or of any other country which adopted the formulation of Article 22(2) of the Model Law). Suppose further that an important witness who is invited to testify during the oral hearing does not speak the language of the arbitration proceedings. Article 22(2) speaks only of translation of documentary evidence. Could this mean that this witness will not get a translator? Or will the witness not be invited to testify because he/she does not speak the designated language?) Obviously not. This was clearly not the intention – and could not have been the intention – of the drafters.

What is then the reason for mentioning 'translation' only in the context of translation of documentary evidence in Article 22(2) of the Model Law? Translation may indeed be needed across the board, both in situations covered by Section 1 of Article 22 (like the oral hearing), and in situations which are not covered by this same section, but are covered by Section 2 of Article 22 (documentary evidence). Witness statements given in a language other than the language of arbitration may need to be translated just as documents drafted in a language other than the language of arbitration. Why does Article 22(1) refer to 'language' while Article 22(2) refers to 'translation'?

What explains the terms chosen in Article 22(1) and in Article 22(2) respectively, is in all likelihood the fact that in practice, the **language** of documentary evidence cannot be chosen by the parties (or be determined by the arbitrators); regarding documentary evidence, options which are open to the parties (or to the arbitrators) only extend to **translation**. Documentary evidence either pre-exists, or is drafted outside the arbitral proceedings, and according to rules different from those which determine the language of the arbitral proceedings. The language of the document is shaped outside the arbitral proceedings. Thus, it makes sense to speak of 'language' to be determined, when one has in mind written statements of the parties, hearings, the award, or communication by the arbitral tribunal, but one can only speak of 'translation' having in mind documentary evidence. In other words, with regard to documentary evidence, the arbitrators cannot choose the language of the document; they can only choose whether to require translation. This is the most logical purpose behind the use of the term 'translation' only with regard to documentary evidence. As far as submissions, pleadings, and witness statements are concerned, the arbitrators do not order translation, because they may determine the language in which submissions, pleadings or statements have to be presented. One way of adjusting to this language is translation (the other way is to find advocates or witnesses who speak the language determined as the language of arbitration). In sum, there can be little doubt that Article 22(2) of the Model Law, while using the term translation only in the context of documentary evidence, does not exclude other instances of translation.

B.3. The authority (and the limits of the authority) of the arbitrators in ordering translation of documentary evidence

B.3.1. *Are the arbitrators free in opting for a language while ordering translation of documentary evidence?*

The question arises whether the arbitrators can decide to accept documentary evidence (or part of documentary evidence) in a language different from the language agreed upon between the parties to govern the arbitral proceedings? Article 22(2) of the Model Law states that the arbitrators may order that any documentary evidence shall be accompanied by a translation into the language (or languages) agreed upon by the parties, or determined by the arbitrators. This leads to the question whether Article 22(2), (and rules in force in modeled after Article 22(2)) allow a disjunction of the language of arbitration from the translation of documentary evidence.

There are two conceivable interpretations which could lead to such a result. First, one could argue that since the language of arbitration is contemplated in Article 22(1) (which says that it will be chosen by the parties or determined by the arbitrators), Article 22(2) envisages a separate choice by the parties, or determination by the arbitrators. This would mean that the arbitrators may themselves determine the language into which documents need to be translated if the parties did not specifically agree on the language in which the documents may be presented. In their well-known commentary on the Model Law, Holtzman and Neuhaus offer support to this position. They explain that Article 22(2) gives discretion to the arbitrators in areas which are typically not covered by party agreement. Article 22(1) defines the presumptive scope of a choice of language, stating that a party agreement (or determination by the arbitral tribunal) extends – 'unless otherwise specified therein' – to '[a]ny written statement by a party, any hearing and any award, decision or other communication by the arbitral tribunal'. In the words of Holtzman and Neuhaus:

> 'Thus, "unless otherwise specified therein", the agreement applies to written statements by a party, to hearings, and to communications by the arbitral tribunal. The agreement presumably will not apply to documentary evidence, which, under the terms of paragraph 2, is left to the discretion of the tribunal. In the light of the suggestion in paragraph 1 that parties may stipulate the scope of the agreement, paragraph 2 should probably be read as nonmandatory. That is, if the parties specifically agree that documentary evidence should—or should not—be translated, the arbitrators should presumably be deemed to lack discretion on the point.'[21]

In this interpretation, the language of the hearing (including witness testimony given at a hearing) is normally covered by party agreement pertaining to language, but such agreement presumably does not cover the question whether documentary evidence may be presented in the original language or has to be translated. This is left to the discretion of the arbitrators. In other words, with reliance on the wording of Article 22, and in line with the arguments of Holtzman and Neuhaus, one could possibly take the following position: Article 22(1) spells out to what elements of the procedure the choice of a language extends. Documentary evidence is not among these elements. Thus, one may assume that if the parties do not explicitly say that their choice extends to documentary evidence, the arbitrators are free to make a decision on the language of documentary evidence. This argument may hold water if the *lex arbitri* is the law of a Model Law country. But even then, this is likely to take the parties by surprise. Parties almost never spell out to what elements of procedure the choice of language should extend. If they agree that the language of the proceedings is, say, English, they are in all likelihood assuming that they have at least created a presumption that everything has to be in English, unless otherwise stipulated. In the opinion of Karrer:

> 'Once a language has been selected as the language of the arbitration, it is only fair to require any evidence supplied in the language other than that language to be translated or interpreted into the language of arbitration.'[22]

---

21 See Holtzmann, Neuhaus, op. cit. pp. 628-629.

22 P. Karrer, 'Arbitration and Language, Look for the Purpose', 11 *Croatian Arbitration Yearbook* (2004) p. 7, at p. 12.

Thus, it is just not realistic to assume that the parties making the choices have in mind the scope defined by Article 22(1). Agreeing on a language of arbitration normally means setting a standard to which all procedural steps have to be adjusted. This applies to party pleadings, as well as to witness statements, or to documents.

Another possible interpretation yielding a possible disjunction relies on the 'may' language. Article 22(2) says that the arbitrators **may** order presentation of documents accompanied by translation into the language determined by the parties (or by the arbitrators). Does this mean that the arbitrators may opt for presentation of documents in their original language only? This could be the case, for example, if the language of the original is not the same as the language of arbitration (chosen by the parties or determined by the arbitrators) but it is understood by the parties. In such cases, it is certainly rational to make arrangements allowing presentation of documents without translation. The question is whether the arbitrators are allowed to make such an arrangement themselves. The answer is, of course, easier when the language is determined by the arbitrators rather than chosen by the parties. In this case, one can safely assume that the decision to accept documents in their original language is a part of that determination. Just as the parties can choose a language or languages, and they can therefore also choose and accept different languages with regard to different elements of the procedure, the arbitrators can do the same (in the absence of party agreement). To give an illustration, in a World Intellectual Property Organization (hereinafter 'WIPO') Domain Name Panel Decision, the parties did not agree on the language of the arbitral proceedings and submitted evidentiary material in English and Chinese. The Panel acted in expedited proceedings, without 'in-person hearings', and reached the following decision regarding language and translation issues:

> 'The language of the proceeding is English, being the language of the Domain Name Registration and Service Agreement, pursuant to paragraph 11(a) of the Rules, and also in consideration of the fact that there is no express agreement to the contrary by the parties. In addition, pursuant to paragraph 10(b) of the Rules and in consideration of the circumstances of this Administrative Proceeding, the Panel, for the purposes of ensuring that each party is given a fair opportunity to present its case, takes into account the evidential materials provided in Chinese.'[23]

---

[23] *Citizens Watch (China) Co. Ltd. v. Cheng Zhi Zang*, Administrative Panel Decision of January 1, 2002 in Case No. D2001-1305 – http://www.arbiter.wipo.int.domains/decisions/html/2001/d2001-1305.html.

Thus, if the determination of the language (or languages) of arbitration is left to the arbitrators, they can clearly make distinct arrangements regarding documentary evidence. The difficult question is whether the arbitrators can decide on translation of documents (or, more precisely, on the waiver of the duty to translate documents) when the language of the proceedings was chosen by the parties. Given the paramount importance of party autonomy in international commercial arbitration, it appears to be advisable at least to consult the parties before the arbitrators decide to accept documentary evidence not in the language chosen by the parties as the language of the arbitral proceedings.

It has to be said that if the arbitrators were to order presentation of documents in their original language (which is not the language chosen by the parties), the problem may be somewhat alleviated by the fact that parties have an opportunity to provide for a translation themselves. An order of the arbitration tribunal stating that documents produced by the claimant will not be translated into the language of the arbitral proceedings does not render the respondent helpless. In order to understand the document, it could still get a translation outside the arbitration process, and it will be able to present arguments based on that document. The situation is different when a witness statement made at the oral hearing is not translated into the language of the proceedings. In this latter case, translation outside the arbitration process will not bring a solution. A translation of the minutes recording the statement of the witness is possible, but would not really help, because it would come too late, only after a chance for cross- examination had been missed. In such a situation, the party could very well argue that it lacked the opportunity to present its case. As far as documentary evidence is concerned, even if lack of translation might not deny the opportunity to present one's case,[24] the principle of the equality of the parties might possibly be impaired by a failure to order translation of documents. Equality of the parties does not mean, of course, that parties in unequal position and with unequal talent should have an equal opportunity to win. Equality is always measured against some standards. There is no impairment of the principle of equality if the language of the proceedings is Italian, and this happens to be the native language of one of the parties, while the other party speaks less than perfect Italian. Here, the standard set is Italian, the parties have to adjust to that standard – just as they have to adjust to the seat of arbitration, which may be the home city for one party and a city on a different continent from the perspective of another party. Yet if the parties choose Italian as the language of the proceedings, the standard and the yardstick of equality is set. Equality of the parties

[24] Except in a conceivable situation where the time needed for translation would cut the time limit for the submission of a brief unreasonably short.

might possibly be impaired if translation of a document into Italian from, say, the Polish original is not ordered – and Polish is the native language of the other party.

Let me summarize that the choice of a language of arbitration is normally understood as a choice covering all procedural steps in the proceedings. Taking this assumption, it follows that the arbitrators are not entitled (without the consent of the parties) to admit documents in another language than the language of arbitration chosen by the parties.

Even assuming that Article 22(2) of the Model Law does not allow the arbitrators to order presentation of documents in a language different from that agreed upon by the parties, some dilemmas may still emerge with regard to the range of the maneuvering room of the arbitrators. Within the setting of Article 22(2) the question arises whether the arbitrators may order translation of documents into only one of the languages of the proceedings and whether they may distinguish between those documents which have to be translated and those which do not.

B.3.2. *Translation into only one of the several designated languages*

It is clear that the parties (or the arbitrators) may designate more than one language as the language of the proceedings. Suppose the designated languages of the proceedings are English and German, and a relevant document is drafted in Croatian. Does it have to be translated into both English and German? Article 22(2) says that the arbitral tribunal may order translation 'into the language or languages agreed upon by the parties or determined by the arbitral tribunal'. This wording may be interpreted in two possible ways. First, one could assume that the choice between translation into 'the language' or the 'languages' depends on the choice already made by the parties or by the arbitrators. Hence, if one language was designated, translation will have to be ordered into that language; if more languages were designated, translation will be ordered into more languages (in our example into both English and German). Another possible interpretation would allow the arbitrators to opt freely between translation into one or more languages. Under this interpretation, the arbitrators in our hypo could order translation from Croatian into either German or English only. The Holtzman-Neuhaus commentary opts for the latter interpretation using legislative history as its basis:

> 'One point raised during the Commission's deliberations was a proposal to make it clear that, in arbitrations being conducted in more than one language, the arbitral tribunal could, if it seemed appropriate, accept documentary evidence in only one of the languages of the arbitration. The concern was that the phrase "the lan-

guage or languages agreed upon" in paragraph 2 might be interpreted to require translation into all of the chosen languages, whereas it might be sufficient in some circumstances to accept various documents in only one language.[25] The Commission accepted this principle and asked the Drafting Group to decide whether it was expressed by the existing language of Article 22. The Drafting Group did not change the applicable language.'[26]

It might be open to discussion whether possible further clarifications in the text of Article 22(2) would or would not have been superfluous.[27] At any rate, it appears to be sensible to allow the arbitrators to decide whether to order translation into one or both (or all) designated languages. If the languages of the proceedings are determined by the arbitrators, special arrangements concerning translation of documents may very well be perceived as part of that determination. If languages are chosen by the parties, some dilemmas might emerge, but there is no real tension between the wording of Article 22 and the principle of party autonomy. As stated earlier, such tensions might emerge regarding the question whether one might assume that party choice of the language of the proceedings does not encompass documentary evidence (and hence, whether the arbitrators are free to accept documentary evidence drafted in a different language from that – or those – chosen by the parties). If the issue is the possible restriction of translation into one of the languages actually chosen by the parties, considerations of rationality are not opposed to party autonomy, since translation will be effected into a language which was indeed chosen by the parties. (An opposite conclusion could only be reached if party stipulation explicitly insisted on parallel use of both languages in all situations.)

---

[25] The Secretariat also noted that some documentary evidence can be voluminous and may be relevant only in part. Seventh Secretariat Note, A/CN.9/264, Art. 22, paragraph 5, p. 639 *infra* [the text of this footnote is footnote 15 in the Holtzmann – Neuhaus, Commentary at p. 630].

[26] *Compare* Fifth Draft, A/CN.9/246 (Annex), Art. 22(2), p. 636 *infra,* with Art. 22(2) in the final text. In its commentary on the Fifth Draft, the Secretariat had interpreted the draft Article as already providing this discretion. *See* Seventh Secretariat Note, A/CN.9/264, Art. 22, paragraph 5, p. 639 *infra* [the text of this footnote is footnote 17 at p. 630 of the Holtzmann-Neuhaus Commentary].

[27] A more specific wording was adopted e.g., in the Egyptian Arbitration Act (Act No. 27 of 1994 for Promulgating the Act Concerning Arbitration in Civil and Commercial Matters, last amended by Act No. 8 in 2000). According to Art. 29(2): 'The arbitral panel may order that all or part of the documentary evidence submitted in the case shall be accompanied by a translation into the language or languages used in the arbitration. In the case of multiplicity of such languages, the arbitral panel may limit the translation to some languages to the exclusion of others.'

B.3.3. *Ordering translation of some of the documents only*

Considerations of rational and cost-effective proceedings might also give rise to the question whether **all** documents relied upon need to be translated. The 1996 UNCITRAL Notes on Organizing Arbitral Proceedings (hereinafter 'UNICTRAL Notes') make the following suggestion in Section 18:

> '(a) Possible need for translation of documents, in full or in part
> 18. Some documents annexed to the statements of claim and defence or submitted later may not be in the language of the proceedings. Bearing in mind the needs of the proceedings and economy, it may be considered whether the arbitral tribunal should order that any of those documents or parts thereof should be accompanied by a translation into the language of the proceedings.'

The Rules of the Iran-US Claims Tribunal (which adopted the UNCITRAL Rules and supplemented it by its own Notes), specify what documents filed with the Tribunal shall be submitted in both English and Farsi, and then state in subsection 4 of the Note annexed to Article 17:

> 'The arbitral tribunal shall determine in each particular case what other documents, documentary exhibits and written evidence, or what parts thereof, shall be submitted in both English and Farsi.'

The Rules and the Note were further explained by the 1985 'Guidelines for the translation of documentary evidence' circulated within the Tribunal by the President of the Tribunal with the suggestion that the Chambers follow them when scheduling the filing of evidence.[28] These Guidelines point out certain categories of documents which should be filed in both English and Farsi,[29] and state

[28] A copy of these Guidelines was provided by courtesy of Ms. A.M. van Luijt from the Registry of the Tribunal.

[29] These are the following categories of documents:
a. Affidavits, depositions and other forms of written evidence prepared or submitted for the purpose of this case;
b. In addition to those documents falling within the provisions of Note 3 (a) – (d) to Art. 17, any portion of the contract or other document relied upon with respect to matters at issue in the Case should be filed in its original language together with a complete translation. If such a contract or document was signed in both English and Farsi, both versions should be submitted as signed;
c. Portions of laws, decrees, proclamations and procès-verbaux relied upon, e.g., as evidence of a taking;
d. Letters and other written communications, telexes and records of oral communications between one Party and someone other than the other Party to this Case; provided they do not fall within paragraph 2(b) below.

for some other categories of documents that they may, in the first instance, be submitted in their original language only.[30]

The chambers have implemented the Rules of the Tribunal with a fair degree of flexibility. In *Sylvania Technical Systems Inc. v. Iran*, the Tribunal accepted all documentary submissions as they were submitted, although some were presented in one language only. The arbitrators relied on their discretionary powers granted in Article 17 and concluded in their Award of June 27, 1985 that:

> '[r]equests have been made that the Tribunal disregard certain submissions because they were made in one language only, or, alternatively, that it order the submitting Party to provide translations. Pursuant to Article 17 of the Tribunal Rules, the Tribunal decides to accept all submissions which were made by the Parties in one language only.'[31]

In *Harza v. Iran*, the Tribunal considered which documents needed to be translated and held that not all documents, but only 'important documents such as laws, proclamations, contracts, and *proces verbaux*, as well as communication between a Party and third Parties and communications internal to a party' needed translation. The Tribunal also held that – 'at present' – it did not require translations of 'brochures, invoices, accounts, charts, cheques, technical reports, communications between the Parties or books and newspaper articles'.[32] Commentators note that the Tribunal 'has been quite lenient' with regard to translation of documentary evidence.[33] While this statement may be true (particularly

---

e. Internal reports, memoranda, minutes, etc. prepared by a Party for its internal use; provided they do not fall within paragraph 2(b) below.
f. Correspondence and communications that passed between the Parties in one language only and were not required to be translated at that time, where they are relied upon as creating or altering the contractual rights or obligations of the Parties or as primary evidence of a taking.

[30] According to the Guidelines, the following categories of documents may be submitted (in the first instance) in their original only:
a. Correspondence and communications that passed between the Parties in one language only and were not required to be translated at that time, provided they do not fall within paragraph 1(f) above;
b. Contemporaneous material which was not required to be translated at the time it came into existence, such as draft contracts and technical reports (except any extracts which are relied upon as a primary source of evidence); studies; brochures; invoices; financial and other accounting statements; shipping documents; charts and plans; blueprints and diagrams; tender documents; checks; newspaper articles and extracts from publications; computer printouts; technical data; and schedules or tables of figures.

[31] *Sylvania Technical Systems Inv. v. Iran,* Award No. 180-64-1, 8 *Iran-US C.T.R.* at 300.

[32] *Harza v. Iran*, Presidential Order 120-2, 1 *Iran-US C.T.R.* at 234.

[33] See J.J.van Hof, *Commentary on the UNCITRAL Arbitration Rules, The Application by the Iran-US Claims Tribunal* (Kluwer 1991) at p. 114.

when translation **from** English was at issue), there are nevertheless cases in which one of the parties sought exemption from translation with reliance on the 'Tribunal's practice', but such exemption was not granted. In *Vera-Jo Miller Aryeh et al. v. The Islamic Republic of Iran*, the issue arose whether the Claimants should file a Persian translation of a valuation report submitted as Volume IV of Claimant's Book of Exhibits. The arbitrators decided to order such translation. As was noted in the Award of May 22, 1997:

> '[t]he Claimants argued that, according to the Tribunal's practice, the expert reports were allowed to be submitted without translation. By Order of 15 January 1992, the Tribunal, referring to Article 17 of the Tribunal Rules, requested the Claimants to provide a Persian translation of Volume IV of the Claimant's Exhibit Book by 2 March 1992, and annexed thereto the Tribunal's guidelines for the translation of documentary evidence. In compliance with this order, the Claimants filed the Persian translation of Volume IV of their Exhibit Book on 19 February 1992.'[34]

In the case of the Iran-US Tribunal, the entitlement of the arbitrators to require translation of selected documents only has a clear foothold in the Rules accepted by the Parties. As far as other situations are concerned, it might be helpful to take a glance at the possible reasons behind selection. There may be several reasons for not ordering the translation of all documents. One possible reason is the consideration of **relevance.** Parties often submit with their briefs a variety of documents, some of which are highly unlikely to have an impact on the outcome of the case. In this situation, translation of all submitted documents will be a waste of time and money. Of course, the arbitrators cannot take a conclusive position on the relevance of evidence before the parties fully present their case. This might explain determinations like the one in the *Harza v. Iran* case where the Tribunal held that 'at present' some documents do not need to be translated. (Such a position might be later reversed if it appears that some documents might have relevance, or when party insistence on a document makes it necessary to take the document into consideration.) The question remains whether it is advisable for the arbitrators to pre-select documents on ground of their relevance.

A further possible reason for selection is that some documents might be **understandable** to all participants even without translation. In a fair number of cases the language skills of the participants make translation superfluous. Depending on the level of these skills the translation of some (or of all) documents

---

[34] *Vera-Jo Miller Aryeh et al. v. The Islamic Republic of Iran*, Award No. 581-842/843/844-1, of May 22, 1997, paragraph 6, 33 *Iran-US C.T.R.* at 278.

may be waived. In some instances documents of a more technical nature (such as an invoice) might be understood even with somewhat limited language skills.

In international commercial arbitration the purpose of translation is understanding, overcoming difference, rather than assertion of a distinct sovereign identity. One could argue that the designated language of the arbitration proceedings does not need to be observed and confirmed the way the official language of a court does. It often happens that both parties and all arbitrators have a sufficient command of both the language of the proceedings, and of the language of documents in question (even if some of them would be unable to write a proper brief in that language). In such situations, translation is simply unnecessary: it would only increase costs and might also entail some hazards if the translation is imperfect. (Under such circumstances the waiver of all translation might also be an option.) Still, the point remains that a departure from the language posited by the parties as the language of arbitration may exceed the powers of the arbitrators.

The question faced at this point is whether an order of the arbitrators restricting translation to certain documents only is possible (and advisable) under Article 22 of the Model Law, assuming that the language of the proceedings was chosen by the parties. I suggest that the typical reasons which justify restriction (or even elimination) of translation of documents fall short of justifying a discretionary decision of the arbitrators without consulting the parties. If the reason for waiving translation are language abilities of the participants, this would normally need to be established in consultation with all participants (arbitrators and parties). If the reason is relevance (or rather lack of relevance), the elimination of translation of some documents without party consent tends to be provisional, since decisions regarding translation are normally made before the case was presented. On balance, it has to be said that a *prima facie* screening of the documents submitted often yields uncontroversial determinations and saves considerable cost and time.

Chapter IV

Translation in International Arbitration Proceedings

A. Introduction

In her essay 'On Being Translated' Susan Sontag explains:

> 'Translation is about differentness. A way of coping with, and ameliorating, and, yes, denying difference – even if [...] it is also a way of asserting differentness.'[1]

Let me rush to say that, of course, these lines were not written with an eye to translation in international arbitration proceedings. The backdrop of Susan Sontag's essay is an experience in Sarajevo while the city was under siege in the Summer of 1993. Defying war, siege, and shelling from the mountains around the city, she and a group of Sarajevo theater enthusiasts were putting on stage Beckett's *Waiting for Godot*. The essay dwells on one of the by-products of the war, the emergence of three languages (Bosnian, Serbian, Croatian) instead of Serbo-Croatian. In order to get around in the city, Susan Sontag was using a Serbo-Croatian – English dictionary, and everybody in Sarajevo was telling her that this was fine. But a new translation of *Waiting for Godot* was being prepared in Bosnian. From this point of departure she embarks on an exploration of the ontological roots of translation and on the variants of the idea of translation.

Susan Sontag's focus is primarily on literary translation, and on ways of coping with differentness. Our topic is much more narrow and specific, yet the basic points of reference are the same. Coping with difference, denying and asserting difference, are marks which are defining the field of translation within the arbitration process as well.

Within these introductory remarks I would like to make one more observation explaining – and further narrowing – the subject-matter of this chapter. The issue of translation may come up **within** the arbitration proceedings proper, or **in connection with** arbitration proceedings. In a most considerable number of arbitration cases translation is needed while the procedure is ongoing. The parties – or their attorneys – may not have a language in common. Furthermore,

---

1 Susan Sontag, *Where the Stress Falls – Essays* (Vintage 2003) at p. 339.

witness statements or documents may need to be translated in order to be understood by both parties and by all arbitrators. The need for translation – and problems with translation – may also emerge, however, in another setting: that of court proceedings in connection with arbitration. The relevant considerations and guiding principles pertaining to the two situations (translation within the arbitration process and translation in other proceedings in connection with arbitration) need not be the same.

This chapter endeavors to deal with the first setting, focusing on translation within the arbitration proceedings. (Post-award proceedings will only be mentioned where this is necessary for a better understanding of the nature and relevance of deficiencies of translation during the arbitration proceedings proper. We shall focus specifically on post-award proceedings in Chapter V.) In the following five subchapters of this chapter we shall consider the function of translation in international arbitration proceedings, the ways in which translation is being organized and effected, the consequences of various deficiencies pertaining to translation, and we shall conclude this chapter with two specific questions (the issue of the hidden anchor language and the question of translation between closely-related languages).

B. The Function of Translation in International Arbitration Proceedings

B.1. **What purpose does translation serve?**

In the context of international dispute settlement, translation serves two basic purposes. (Here we are getting near Susan Sontag's dichotomy between denying difference, or overcoming difference on the one hand and asserting difference on the other hand.)

First, translation is used to **overcome** difference by making it understandable what was written or said in a different language that is not understood by some participants in the proceedings. This function is an essential precondition to the observance of one of the most pervasive procedural principles – that of the equality of the parties. A party who does not speak the language of the proceedings (or does not understand the language of a witness or of a document) cannot participate in a meaningful way without translation and thus, cannot be equal without translation. There is no due process without a chance of making oneself understood and without understanding the other participants.

The second purpose of translation is more in line with **assertion** of difference. Translation is sometimes needed not because a party (or a judge, or an arbitrator) would not understand the language of, say, a witness, but because the language of that witness is not the official language of the court. In this context, translation is a tribute to sovereignty, a required acknowledgment of a distinct identity. Just as parties have to adjust to the procedural norms which govern court proceedings in a given State, they also have to adjust to the official language (or one of the official languages) of the same State. A given judge may understand the arbitral award in its original language, yet translation is nevertheless a precondition to recognition and enforcement.[2] Asserting its sovereign identity, a State is also affirming its own (different) language on which the proceedings are being conducted and the files are being kept. Another rationale behind translation in court proceedings – even if it is not needed for the purpose of understanding – is the hierarchic system of courts. Even if the translation of a document were not really needed in the given court proceedings (because the judge speaks the language in which the award is rendered), translation of all files may be needed for the purpose of appellate proceedings.

If one limits considerations to translation **within** the arbitration process, the second purpose – that of 'assertion of difference' – practically loses its relevance. Arbitration tribunals cannot be identified with a State, because the official attributes of the State of the seat of the arbitral tribunal (or of any other State) do not become official features of the arbitral tribunal itself. The language of an arbitration proceeding is normally the language (or languages) established either by the parties or by the arbitrators for that given case. There is no pre-determined language with the purpose of safeguarding the distinct identity of a community. The dominant solution is that of Article 22(1) of the 1985 UNCITRAL Model Law, which states:

> '(1) The parties are free to agree on the language or languages to be used in the arbitral proceedings. Failing such agreement, the arbitral tribunal shall determine the language or languages to be used in the proceedings.'

Thus, translation is in the hands of the parties (and of the arbitrators); its purpose is the facilitation of understanding, rather than the safeguarding of the distinct identity of a State.

Having said this, I must add that a small number of institutional rules provide for translation into one or two pre-determined languages in all cases. A

---

[2] This principle is clearly set in Art. IV of the New York Convention, and it is followed in practice – but there are some exceptions. In recent years there have been some departures from this standard in court practice. Furthermore, the 1999 Swedish Arbitration Act has made the submission of a translation of the award (by the party seeking recognition) a waivable obligation (See Várady, 'Challenge of Arbitral Awards in Recognition Proceedings on Grounds of Shortcomings Pertaining to Language', in *Balancing of Interests, Liber Amicorum Peter Hay* (Frankfurt 2005) p. 435. We shall return to this question in more detail in Chapter V.)

scrutiny of these rules may yield the conclusion that one of the purposes of translation is the safeguarding of an institutional design. Proceeding in a given language and keeping files in a given language may be a part of that pattern. For example, according to Article 25 of the 2002 Rules of Procedure of the Arbitration Chamber of Paris:[3]

> 'Documents in foreign languages must be accompanied by a French translation However, if the arbitration so requires, the Chairman of the Arbitration Chamber of Paris may decide to allow documents that are drafted or translated in English.'

Another example may be found in the 2004 Rules of the Japan Commercial Arbitration Association,[4] which state that the language of arbitral proceedings can only be Japanese or English – and accordingly, translation will always be made into one of these two languages (Rule 11). Similarly, the 1998 Rules of Arbitration of the Indian Council of Arbitration (as amended in January 2005)[5] have also set English as the language of the arbitral proceedings. This is not conclusive, however, because in the context of the Indian Rules, English is posited as a default language rather than as an official language; the parties may agree on another language if they so wish. Nevertheless, it appears from the wording of the Indian Rules that documents filed in another language will always have to be translated into English. According to Rule 56:

> 'The language of the arbitration proceedings shall be English unless otherwise agreed by the parties. If any documents filed by a party are in a language other than English, the party filing such documents shall simultaneously furnish an English translation of the documents. [...]'

These examples may suggest the conclusion that before some institutions the purpose of translation is not only the understanding of an unknown text but also the affirmation of a particular language chosen by the institution on the grounds of policy considerations which are independent from the circumstances of the given case. It is important to note at the same time that the situation created by institutional rules cannot be identical with the situation created by statutory norms such as Article IV of the New York Convention. Institutional rules only apply on the grounds of party choice, and the parties are, in principle, also entitled to modify solutions set in institutional rules.

In sum, there is a certain difference between the purpose of translation within the arbitration process and the purpose of translation in court proceedings in

---

3 Available at http://www.arbitrage.org/us/Proceedings/Rules_july2004.pdf.
4 Available at http://www.jcaa.or.jp/e/arbitration-e/kisoku-e/shouji-e.html.
5 Available at http://www.ficci.com/icanet/clause1.htm#1.

connection with arbitration. In both cases the obvious primary purpose of translation is the creation of understanding in spite of the use of different languages. In arbitration-related court proceedings, the protection and endorsement of one (or more) particular language(s) may appear as an additional or different purpose, in line with the rationale of manifestation of State sovereignty. A somewhat similar purpose may be discerned in the context of some institutional rules, which also endeavor to affirm a particular language as an element of a model of institutional proceeding; yet the number of these rules is small, and their effects are not conclusive.

B.2. **The limitations of translation**

The focus of this paper is on translation with the purpose of creating understanding. It is hardly necessary to explain why understanding is needed, and why the accuracy of translation is important. But it may not be a redundant or futile exercise to say a few words about the limitations of translation. The identification of such limitations is certainly not a new discovery, and it does not deny the values of translation either. One can find an inspired description of the confines of translation in the works of Saint Jerome (Hieronymus), who has been known as the patron saint of translators.[6] Translating the Chronicle of Eusebius of Caesarea into Latin, he made the following observations:

> 'It is difficult in following lines laid down by others not sometimes to diverge from them, and it is hard to preserve in a translation the charm of expressions which in another language are most felicitous. Each particular word conveys a meaning of its own, and possibly I have no equivalent by which to render it, and I make a circuit to reach my goal, I have to go many miles to cover a short distance. To these difficulties must be added the windings of hyperbata, differences in the use of cases, divergencies of metaphor; and last of all the peculiar and if I may so call it, inbred character of the language. If I render word for word, the result will sound uncouth, and if compelled by necessity I alter anything in the order or wording, I shall seem to have departed from the function of a translator.'[7]

This characterization stemming from the fourth or fifth century has not lost its relevance, even the nuances remain pertinent. There is a difference, of course, between translating the Chronicle of Eusebius (or any literary translation) and translation of legal documents. In the latter context, it is less important 'to pre-

---

[6] Saint Jerome lived between 347 and 419 (or 420). He translated the Holy Script from Hebrew to Latin and thus created the *Vulgata*, the official version of the Holy Script for more than a millennium.

[7] Saint Jerome, 'To Pammachius on the Best Method of Translating' – Letter LVII, available on the web: http://www.newadvent.org/fathers/3001057.htm.

serve the charm of expressions which in another language are most felicitous', or to consider 'divergencies of metaphor'. At the same time, specific traps are being set by notions, connotations, and turns of phrases known only to those initiated into the legal profession (and jargon). It has been noted that legal translation is more culture-specific than many other types of translation. In his article on problems in legal translation, Weston explains: 'The most important general characteristic of any legal translation is, rather, that an unusually large proportion of the text is culture-specific.'[8]

Turning to translation in international commercial arbitration, it may be said that translations produced within the arbitration process are quite often less than perfect. As a matter of fact, there are many reasons bespeaking the avoidance of translation – if this is an option. In his article 'Arbitration and Language, Look for the Purpose', Pierre Karrer states:

> 'In international arbitration one sometimes encounters people who are truly unilingual. Their ideas about translation are often extraordinarily naïve. [...] However, even many multilingual people have also surprisingly naïve ideas about translation. The idea that there is only one correct way of translating is a fallacy.'[9]

It is certainly true that it would be unrealistic to expect a translation to possess everything the original possesses. In Old English, a word used for 'translator' was 'versionist'. Somebody who has a talent for advocacy will try persuade with logic, style, rhythm, intonation, pauses, nuances, choice of emphasis. One simply cannot expect a translator to reproduce all this; a **version** will be rendered.

Furthermore, it has been proven time and time again that it is more effective to speak directly – even if the speaker has a less than perfect command of the language of arbitration – than to present arguments indirectly through translation. (Assuming, of course, that the speaker's command of the language of arbitration is not **too** imperfect.) As stated in Chapter II, language is a quite important part of arbitration strategy, which is sometimes overlooked. The attorney who speaks the language of the arbitration proceedings has a clear advantage over a colleague who does not. This may or may not be balanced by extraordinary legal talent, or by special trust. It is conceivable, that after weighing the pros and cons, a party will opt for an excellent attorney who enjoys his confidence, even though this attorney does not speak the designated language. This is a possible choice, but it should only be made after a careful weighing of consid-

---

8 Martin Weston, 'Problems and Principles in Legal Translation', 22(4) *The Incorporated Linguist* (Autumn 1983) p. 207.

9 Karrer, op. cit. at p. 13.

erations. One must not simply assume that a good translator will be able convert from, say, English into, say, French or Polish, all the nuances, subtle refinements, gestures, and suggestive emphases. Communicating via a translator **is** a handicap. It may not be an insurmountable one, but it is a serious one enough to be considered.[10]

Let us also mention that the reason why documents are scrutinized during the arbitration process is, quite often, because they are ambiguous. Parties will often take different positions interpreting the same text. Sometimes, one of these interpretations is simply wrong – but often there is more than one plausible interpretation because the text of the document is genuinely ambiguous. How will a translation mirror such ambiguity? Will a translation offer the same chances to the possible interpretations as those offered by the original? In his book on translation, Alan Duff says: 'Questions not answered by the writer cannot be answered by the translator; what is obscure in the original is likely to be even more obscure in the translation:'[11] Let me add that this is the result when the translation is a correct one. We have a less professional (and more dangerous) situation when the translation does suggest an answer, when the translator replaces ambiguity with a meaning of his own choice, rather than leaving it to the arbitrators (or judges) to come up with the interpretation they deem to be the right one considering the whole context.

Multilingualism is in many domains a fact of life; it is certainly a fact of life in international commercial arbitration. Translation can bridge differences, but it cannot extinguish them. Differences will appear – and will have to be dealt with – even where the original drafting takes place parallel in more languages. (And more so if there is an original and a translation.) To take an example from a legal area broader than that of arbitration, let us mention that English and Chinese were both established as official languages of Hong Kong. Statutes are equally valid in both languages. Yet the authorities have been fully aware of the fact that differences cannot be ruled out. The Drafting Division of the Hong Kong Department of Justice published in May 1998 a twelve-page (plus three pages of footnotes) 'Paper Discussing Cases Where the Two Language Texts of an Enactment are Alleged to be Different'.[12] Staying with the example of Hong Kong, let me cite an introductory sentence from a Hong Kong judgment reflecting a wise caution. The judgment starts by stating that it has two versions: English and Chinese. The next sentence states:

---

[10] A possible solution is to add an attorney who has an adequate command of the chosen language, which is safer than relying on a translator only.

[11] Alan Duff, *The Third Language – Recurrent Problems of Translation into English* (Pergamon Press 1981) at p. 3.

[12] See http://www.justice.gov.hk/inprmain.htm.

> 'Both the English and the Chinese Versions are of the same legal effect and they should not be taken just as a translation of the other. Having said that, however, the rule of thumb is that reference should be made to the original language of a document in question be it cited authority, book or document.'[13]

Probably the highest standard of translation in international adjudication is that provided in proceedings before the International Court of Justice. In translations provided before the I.C.J., meaning is almost never missed (if it is missed, a rectification will typically be provided) and nuances are usually accurately reflected. But the circumstances before the I.C.J. are quite specific. The I.C.J. has a 'Linguistic Department'. In 2005, seven revisers and twelve translators were employed as 'staff revisers and interpreters'. During periods of intensive activity, additional translators and interpreters are hired. Legal qualifications are not a prerequisite, but they are valued as an asset, and every interpreter has to familiarize himself/herself with legal terminology, as well as with concepts and matters related to activities of the I.C.J.[14] Furthermore, translation is between two languages only: French and English.[15] The terms and the jargon faced by the translators are rather specific, but pretty much consistent. It is possible to build on experience – including the experience of colleagues. Let us compare this setting with that of translation in arbitral proceedings. Arbitral institutions do not have and cannot have translators as full-time employees (with regard to *ad hoc* tribunals this is obviously out of the question). The number of possible languages is, in principle, without limitations. The translators face turns of phrases, specific terms and jargon of many fields of law,[16] and often also

---

[13] To *Kan Chi and others v. Pui Man Yau and others*, High Court of the Hong Kong Special Administrative Region, Court of First Instance, Judgment of November 26, 1998 – HCMP 002084/ 1994.

[14] Information kindly supplied by Ms. L. Blairon from the Office of the Registrar of the I.C.J.

[15] When one speaks of the special high standard of I.C.J. translations, one has in mind translations which take place in each case: the simultaneous translation of arguments presented at oral hearings and the translation of written briefs submitted by the parties. This is all in French and English. Most cases do not involve witnesses. If witnesses were heard, translation from another language might be necessary, but this will not be translation provided by the regular I.C.J. staff. The translation of documents into French or English from a third language has to be arranged and certified by the parties (Art. 51(3) of the Rules of the Court). The parties are also responsible for the translation of witness statements or other evidence presented at the oral hearing in a language other than French or English; the Registrar shall make, however, arrangements for the verification of interpretation (Art. 70(2) of the Rules of the Court).

[16] Expertise in various fields of law is an important consideration in choosing arbitrators. The Questionnaire of the ICC Court of Arbitration presented to prospective arbitrators lists the following 'fields of legal expertise': Civil law, Common law, European law, International law, Islamic law. Furthermore, 19 different specializations are listed, including Competition, Con-

have to cope with the terms and the jargon of a given trade. The possibility of reliance on earlier experience of the same kind or on the experience of fellow translators is quite limited. Furthermore, translators are usually linguists without legal education.[17] Linguists typically have advantages regarding grammar, but they also have to cope with some handicaps. A non-lawyer may very well be at loss when translating an argument focusing on the issue whether the contract was void or voidable. How will 'tortious interference with the contract' be translated by a linguist? (Would he/she know that 'tort' is a delict?)

In spite of its limitations, translation is a consequential and frequent element of the process of international commercial arbitration. What is also important is that the flexibility of arbitration proceedings allows arrangements which provide filters, checks and balances. One such filter is the fact that typically at least one of the arbitrators and someone on the side of the parties has a command of the language from which translation is made into the language of arbitration. Reliance on the product of translation therefore need not be unconditional. If translation takes place during an oral hearing, errors are often noted by some of the participants, and rectification becomes possible on the spot. If one of the parties contests the accuracy of the translation, the arbitrators might be able to clarify the matter themselves. International arbitrators often speak more than one language; their command of certain languages might very well influence their selection for a particular case. Hence, it is likely that the arbitrators (or at least some of them) will have a command of the relevant language from which translation is being made. This likelihood is enhanced by the fact that the arbitrators chosen by the parties are often from the country of the respective party, which makes it likely that they will speak the language from which some of the documents in the case have been translated. Let us add that the arbitrators are free to verify on their own motion the accuracy of translations submitted to them, and they frequently do so. If they uncover any relevant discrepancies, they could (and should) inform the parties of their findings and give them a chance to react. If not all arbitrators can compare the translation with the original, one can imagine opportunities for abuse on the part of the arbitrator who speaks both languages, but this is hardly a real danger. The safeguard against abuse lies not only in the ethical standards of arbitrators, but also in the fact that this is a type of misconduct that is quite easy to discover and to prove. An alertness (and sometimes an active role) of the arbitrators and of the parties

struction and Engineering, Corporate Law, Finance and Banking, Joint Ventures Consortia and Cooperation, Sales and Purchases, etc.

[17] This is logical, since the fees of translators are considerably below attorney's fees. If somebody has a proper law degree and a good command of more languages, he/she would rather work as a lawyer.

with regard to translation will often weed out imperfections and balance inherent limitations.

C. How is Translation Organized and Effected?

This subchapter will endeavor to consider more closely how translation is actually organized and effected. We shall investigate who are (and who should be) the translators in international commercial arbitration, who is entitled to hire them and who is actually hiring them, who pays for translation, and which are the possible and favored methods of translation.

C.1. **Who are the translators?**

Arbitration acts and arbitration rules typically do not contain provisions regarding the qualifications of the translator. Among arbitration acts, a rare exception is the 1985 Saudi Arabian Arbitration Regulation, which states in Section 25 that a party or an arbitrator who does not speak Arabic '[s]hall be accompanied by an **accredited** translator, who shall sign with him the minutes of the hearing, approving the statements made' [emphasis added]. Most institutional rules are also silent on the qualifications of the translator (or of the translation) or use some quite general description. One such general description was contained in the 2001 Vienna Rules, which mentioned that the arbitrator may order an **appropriate** translation of documents not drafted in the language of the proceedings.[18] In a similar vein, the 1993 Rules of the Hong Kong International Arbitration Center refer to translation by a '**suitably qualified person**'.[19] A more specific designation can be found in the 2003 BANI Rules, with regard to translation of documents. The BANI Rules provide that at the request of the arbitrators, an '**authentic translation by a sworn translator**' shall be provided.[20] Essentially the same requirement is set in the 1991 Conciliation and Arbitration Rules of the European Development Fund and in the 1990 MIGA Arbitration Rules, both of which require **certified translation**, when documents

---

[18] Art. 14(2) of the 2001 Rules of Arbitration of the International Arbitral Center of the Austrian Federal Economic Chamber. These Rules apply to proceedings in which the claim was filed before June 30, 2006. From July 1, 2006 the new 2006 Vienna Rules apply. The new Rules have a provision in Art. 20(2) which essentially adopted the wording of Art. 14(2) of the 2001 Rules, but in the new 2006 Rules the word 'appropriate' was omitted.

[19] Art. 14(3) of the 1993 Domestic Arbitration Rules of the Hong Kong International Arbitration Center.

[20] Art. 14(2) of the 2003 Procedural Rules of the Indonesian National Board of Arbitration (BANI).

are at issue.[21] Apart from these and a very few similar exceptions (mostly pertaining to translation of documents), the choice of the translator is left to the parties or to the arbitrators. The UNCITRAL enactments also contain no specifications regarding the qualifications of the translator. The issue was raised during the drafting of the Model Law whether certification of translation was needed, but the answer was negative. Holtzman and Neuhaus explain:

> 'One final point noted in the legislative history was that there is no requirement of certification for translations submitted to the arbitral tribunal under Article 22. Although Article 35(2) contains such a requirement for submission of the award to a court for enforcement, the Commission considered that requiring certification before the arbitral tribunal might unnecessarily add to the costs of proceedings.'[22]

Provisions regarding impartiality of the translator are also typically missing. A rare provision can be found in Article 19 of the 2005 Budapest Rules, which allows the parties to challenge the translator on the same grounds as those on which they can challenge the arbitrators. Article 19 entitled: 'Challenging the Arbitrators or the Presiding Arbitrator', sets the procedure and the grounds for challenge. According to Article 19(6): 'The provisions of the present Article shall also apply, where appropriate, to experts and interpreters.'

One may conclude that (with a few exceptions) neither arbitration acts nor arbitration rules mandate the required qualifications of the translator. Let us turn now our attention from the mandated profile to the desirable one. The ideal translator is a person who has a legal education, an excellent command of the languages concerned, experience with translation, who is a certified translator, and who is independent from the parties. This ideal profile is, however, not the typical profile. As mentioned above, translators' salaries are typically insufficiently attractive to lawyers. Moreover, while a license or certification is certainly desirable, some authors have expressed doubts about the necessity of obtaining such a translator. In the opinion of Karrer:

> 'An officially licensed interpreter or translator will not necessarily provide a better interpretation or translation than somebody who is not licensed. One should not

21 See Art. 15(2) of the 1991 Procedural Rules on Conciliation and Arbitration of Contracts Financed by the European Development Fund; and Art. 29(3) of the Rules of Arbitration for Disputes under Contracts of Guarantee of the Multilateral Investment Guarantee Agency (MIGA).

22 Holtzmann and Neuhaus, op. cit., p. 630. (To these sentences of the Holtzmann-Neuhaus Commentary the following footnote is added: 'Commission Report, A/40/17, paragraph 192, p. 645 *infra*; Summary Record, A/CN.9/SR.322, paragraphs 15–17, pp. 642–43 *infra*. This presumably does not prevent the arbitral tribunal from requiring certified translations in appropriate cases, however.')

even presume that the interpretation provided by a licensed person is better than any other interpretation.'[23]

Be that as it may, the choice of a qualified translator is an important and sensitive task. In institutional arbitration the experience of the institution often serves as helpful guidance.

As far as the 'impartiality' of the translator is concerned, the question that must first be asked is whether one can really equate the grounds for challenging an arbitrator with the grounds for challenging a translator, as the Budapest Rules do.[24] The arbitrator is a decision-maker. The translator is not; yet he/she is a person whose professional (or unprofessional) work may have an impact on the case. Both the arbitrator and the translator are, in principle, supposed to be neutral. Nevertheless, some difference clearly exists. For example, it is obvious that the wife, or husband, or brother or a business associate of a party cannot be an arbitrator, and cannot be a neutral decision-maker. But is there a persuasive reason why a person should be prevented from translating the pleadings of his/her brother? Or, to take a more common example, what if the pleadings of a party are translated by an employee of that party who is a professional translator? In this case the perceived bias is perfectly in line with legitimate party interests: The interest of the party is to get across exactly what he/she said, and the interest of the translator having been hired by the party whose pleadings he/she is translating will also be to give an accurate translation.[25]

The situation is different when an expert testimony or a witness statement is being translated. In this setting, the translator may, in principle, exert an undue influence- particularly if he/she is translating from a language not known to any of the arbitrators. Under such circumstances it is justified to screen possible translators on the grounds of considerations of bias or appearance of bias – and a possible challenge makes sense.

Another important point concerns the reliability of translation. Since translation within the arbitration proceedings is less formal, it offers more room for informal methods of checking and screening. As it was already mentioned, a control is often provided by the arbitrators themselves. In many cases, the arbi-

---

[23] Karrer, op. cit. at p. 13.

[24] Some flexibility is nevertheless allowed by the Budapest Rules, which state that the general rules on challenge will apply to translators 'where appropriate'.

[25] One can imagine situations which might raise doubts. The translator might correct some mistakes of the person who is speaking for the party. The translator might also alert the speaker to some unwanted admission and postpone the translation until the speaker decides whether he/she really wants to say this. This would be clearly off-limits with regard to witness statements. As far as party presentation is concerned, the situation is not so clear, but at least questions can be raised with regard to the mixing of the role of the party speaker and party translator.

trators (or some of them) have a command of both the language of the proceedings and the language from which translation is being made. The arbitrators can therefore be the first to alert the translator to a problem. The same might be done by the parties or by one party. If a simple error is at issue, it will usually be corrected without debate. If there is more than one plausible translation (and if the difference is consequential), the choice will be left to the arbitrators, assuming that the arbitrators have a command of the relevant languages. If the translation of a legal document or legal argument is at issue, it is quite logical for the arbitrators to take a more active role. Such an approach might actually be more effective, and it might take us closer to the true meaning of the original than trust in certified translation.

Multiple translation is also an option which has to be mentioned when dealing with the question who are the translators. In an ICC case,[26] for example, the question arose whether the arbitration clause in a Russian language contract did or did not exclude recourse to the courts. Relying on one translation, the Claimant argued that the parties had agreed to settle their dispute by ICC Arbitration, while the Respondent, relying on another translation, submitted that 'ICC arbitration would be possible only in the event that ordinary courts are not competent'. The pertinent phrase in the Russian contract read:

> 's izkloutcheniem podsoudnosti obchim soudam podlejat razrecheniou Arbitrajnom soudie pri Mejdounarodnoi Torgovo-Promychlennoi Palate'.

According to one translation (the one submitted by the Respondent) this meant that:

> '...[all disputes], except those for which common tribunals are competent, have to be solved by an Arbitration Court of the ICC...'.

Another translation was, however, provided by the ICC Secretariat, which read as follows:

> '[any dispute or controversy] without recourse to common courts shall be settled by the International Court of Arbitration of the ICC...'.

The sole arbitrator gave credit to the translation provided by the ICC Secretariat, and concluded:

---

[26] *Seller (Central Europe) v. Buyer (Western Europe),* Final award in case No. 8790/2000, reported in *Yearbook Commercial Arbitration,* Vol. XXIX (2004) p. 13.

'The arbitral tribunal is of the opinion that the Russian text clearly excludes the competence of the common courts.'[27]

In the case of multiple translations, there is normally no prescribed hierarchy. The arbitrators will have to decide which translation they should trust. If one of the translations provided is supplied by the arbitral institution, the arbitrators will likely rely on that one (because the neutrality and the experience of the institution), but this is not a mandated position.

C.2. Who hires the translator?

The issue of the choice of a competent translator takes us to the question who actually hires the translator. The obvious options are the arbitrators and the parties. There is some support for both solutions, and divided competences (depending on the type of translation) might also represent an answer. At the outset, a distinction has to be made between translation for the purposes of the parties themselves, and translation which is presented to the arbitrators and will become part of the record of the proceedings. If one of the party representatives does not have an adequate command of the language of the proceedings, he/she may bring a translator to the oral hearing who will translate – just for this party representative – the statements made at the hearing. Such translation is clearly the responsibility of the party; the translator will be hired and paid by that party.

If a party representative would not only like to understand statements made on the language of the proceedings but would also like to make statements with the assistance of the translator, the translation becomes a matter of interest for all participants concerned. In this case, it is no longer obvious who will hire the translator.

As far as translation submitted to the arbitrators is concerned, the provisions of UNCITRAL Model Law and Model Rules may serve once again as a starting point. The UNCITRAL enactments are not the only model which has had an influence on the shaping of arbitration acts and institutional rules. The solutions of some national legislators were followed by later legislation in other countries, and some institutional rules (like the ICC Rules) have also been influential. As far as the language of the proceedings is concerned, however, **arbitration acts** (other than those that followed the UNCITRAL model) are mostly silent or less precise than the UNCITRAL enactments. Different **arbitration rules** contain, of course, different provisions regarding the language of the proceedings and translation, but no other influential pattern has been established except the one crafted in the UNCITRAL enactments.

---

[27] *Yearbook Commercial Arbitration*, Vol. XXIX (2004) at p. 17.

Within the Model Law, Article 22(2) – which refers to translation of documentary evidence – states that the arbitral tribunal **may order** such translation. The 'may order' language was also adopted in the legislations which tracked the solution of Article 22(2) of the Model Law.[28] The Model Rules (and many other rules which have followed the Model Rules)[29] also use the 'may order' language when referring to documentary evidence. But the Model Rules (and many other rules) use another formulation when referring to translation of oral statements. According to Article 25(3) of the Model Rules, the arbitral tribunal '**shall make arrangements**' for the translation of oral statements. The question is whether these different formulations actually yield different entitlements and limitations. The answer should be yes. Distinction does not only flow from difference between the terms 'may' and 'shall', but also from difference between 'ordering' and 'making arrangement'. In the context of Article 22(2), the addressees of the order of the arbitrators are the parties. Within the language 'the arbitral tribunal may order that any documentary evidence shall be accompanied by a translation…' the order is directed towards the party submitting documentary evidence (and who is instructed to accompany this evidence with translation into the language or languages of the proceedings). Some rules which

---

[28] See e.g., (in alphabetical order) Art. 33 of the 1999 Law of the Republic of Belarus on International Arbitration Court; Art. 22(4) of the 1998 British Columbia International Commercial Arbitration Act; Art. 21(2) of the 2001 Croatian Arbitration Act; Art. 29(2) of the 1994 Egyptian Act Concerning Arbitration in Civil and Commercial Matters –last amended in 2000; Section 26(2) of the 1992 Finnish Arbitration Act; Section 1045(2) of the 1998 German Arbitration Act; Art. 22(2) of the 1999 Greek Arbitration Act; Art. 27(2) of the 1995 Guatemala Arbitration Act; Section 48(2) of the 1994 Hungarian Arbitration Act; Art. 22(4) of the 1996 Indian Arbitration and Conciliation Act; Art. 30(4) of the 2003 Japan Arbitration Act; Art. 28(b) of the 2001 Jordanian Act No. 31/2004; Art. 23(4) of the 1995 Kenya Arbitration Act; Art. 25 of the 1996 Lithuanian Arbitration Act; Art. 459(2) of the 1998 Madagascar Arbitration Act; Art. 51(3) of the 2000 Mauritania Code of Arbitration; Art. 1438 of the 1993 Mexican Commercial Code, Book V on Commercial Arbitration; Art. 22(2) of the 1997 New Zealand Arbitration Act; Art. 18(3) of the 1998 Nigerian Arbitration and Conciliation Decree; Art. 29(3) of the 1997 Oman Act on Arbitration in Civil and Commercial Disputes; Art. 111(2) of the 1996 Peru General Arbitration Act; Art. 22(2) of the Act of the Russian Federation on International Commercial Arbitration; Art. 35 of the 2006 Serbian Arbitration Act; Art. 25(1) of the 1998 Taiwanese Arbitration Act; Art. 28(2) of the 2002 Thailand Arbitration Act; Art. 67(2) of the 1993 Tunisia Arbitration Act; Art. 10(2) of the 2001 Turkish Act on International Arbitration; Art. 22(2) of the 2003 Ukrainian Act on International Commercial Arbitration; Art. 22(2) of the 1996 Zimbabwe Arbitration Act.

[29] See e.g., Art. 15 of the 1996 Arbitration Rules of the Commercial Arbitration and Mediation Center for the Americas (CAMCA), Art. 17 of the 2000 CRCICA Rules of the, Art. 22.2 of the DIS Rules, Art. 5 of the Milano Rules, Art. 14 of 2002 Rules of the Inter-American Commercial Arbitration Commission (IACAC), Art. 17 of the1983 Provisionally Adopted Rules of the Iran-US Claims Tribunal, Art. 11 of the 2004 Rules of the Japan Commercial Arbitration Association, Art. 17 of the 2004 Swiss Rules, Art. 17 of the LCIA Rules, or Art. 40 of the 2002 WIPO Arbitration Rules.

have adopted the UNCITRAL concept have made this even more clear. According to Article 17(4) of the LCIA Rules:

> 'If any document is expressed in a language other than the language(s) of the arbitration and no translation of such document is submitted by the party relying upon the document, the Arbitral Tribunal or (if the Arbitral Tribunal has not been formed) the LCIA Court may order **that party** to submit a translation in a form to be determined by the Arbitral Tribunal or the LCIA Court, as the case may be.' [emphasis added]

In other words, translations of documents (if ordered) have to be submitted by the party who presents the document, thus the translator will be hired by the party.[30] The wording of Article 25(3) of the Model Rules suggests a different role for the arbitrators. Article 25(3) speaks of translation of 'oral statements made at the hearing' and of the 'record of the hearing', and states that the arbitral tribunal **shall make arrangements** for such translations. This formulation indicates that the arbitration tribunal shall organize the translation, thus implying (although not requiring) that the tribunal will hire the translator.

There are only a very few arbitration rules which contemplate more variants of translation, and which do not follow the distinction made in the UNCITRAL Rules. One such example can be found in the 2005 Hong Kong Rules.[31] According to Article 15 of these Rules: 'Any necessary arrangements for live or written translation or interpretation services will be made by the HKIAC upon request of the parties.' Thus, under the Hong Kong Rules arrangements will be made by the arbitral institution pertaining to both written translation (translation of documents) and oral interpretation – upon request of the parties.

The question arises whether it is rational and advisable to leave the organization of translation of documents to the parties, while having the arbitrators make the arrangements for translation in connection with the oral hearing. There are indeed reasons which support such a distinction. The parties prepare their first briefs (the claim and the answer to the claim, or the request for arbitration and the answer to the request) before any contact with the arbitrators. They may submit documents, and it would be rational to submit translations along with these documents if the documents have not been drafted in the language which is already established as the language of the arbitral proceedings (or that which

[30] One may note that the LCIA Rules add another detail which is missing in the Model Law and the Model Rules (although not excluded by either of the two UNCITRAL enactments), stating that the arbitrators may determine the form of translation to be submitted by the parties.

[31] Procedures for the Administration of International Arbitration of the Hong Kong International Arbitration Centre (HKIAC) – in force since March 31, 2005.

is likely to become the language of the proceedings). Arbitrators shall only intervene if the parties have not done so, and then they may order the submission of translations. It is also important to mention that Article 22(2) of the Model Law, Article 25(3) of the Model Rules, and many other provisions molded according to the UNCITRAL model, apparently do not contemplate any and all documentary evidence but only consider documentary evidence submitted by the parties. According to Article 25(3) of the Model Rules, the arbitral tribunal may order the translation of 'any documents annexed to the statement of claim or statement of defense, and any supplementary documents or exhibits submitted in the course of proceedings'. This does not extend to those rather rare instances in which documents are not submitted by the parties, but requested the arbitral tribunal itself, *ex officio* (typically from an authority, or from a third party).

Having in mind the overwhelming majority of cases (those in which documents are submitted by the parties), one may ask whether the fact that translation is left to the parties opens the gate for potential abuses. It is certainly conceivable that a party might submit a distorted or biased translation, but there are circumstances impeding such attempts, and there are also mechanisms to rectify possible distortions. A circumstance which impedes the submission of documents tainted by (mis)translation is the fact that documents typically submitted in international commercial arbitration are jointly drafted by the parties or at least known to both parties. Hence, it is most unlikely that an alteration of the meaning of a document would remain unnoticed. Furthermore, since originals will also be submitted, both the other party and the arbitrators have the opportunity to check and to raise issues. In typical cases, the other party and/or at least some of the arbitrators have a command of the language of the original. If this is not the case and the document is consequential, parallel translations may be commissioned for the purpose of verification. As mentioned above, the safeguard of accuracy in international commercial arbitration is not only the authority of the source, but also the checks and balances offered by the arbitration process.

As far as translation of statements made at the oral hearing is concerned, the prevailing solution suggests that this should be arranged by the arbitrators rather than by the parties. This may be the prevailing solution, but it is certainly not the only possible one, nor is it the only one relied upon in practice. One could say that translation arranged by the arbitrators is more in line with the general nature of the arbitration proceedings, which is closer to the Continental European model of civil litigation, and thus more arbitrator-driven than party-driven. Parties may, of course, shape different solutions and compromises, and sometimes they do so, but it is generally understood that the prevailing model of proceedings is more of an inquisitorial rather than of an adversarial nature. Arbitral proceedings are organized and steered by the arbitrators. Witnesses and expert witnesses are invited by the arbitrators (although, in most cases they are proposed by the parties). According to Article 25(6) of the UNCITRAL Model Rules, 'The arbitral tribunal shall determine the admissibility, relevance, materiality and weight of the evidence offered.'

Translation at oral hearings might imply translation of witness statements, expert testimonies, party pleadings, or translation for an arbitrator who does not speak the language of the proceedings; the record of the oral hearing (the minutes) may also need to be translated. The 'shall make arrangements' language of Article 25(3) of the Model Rules is rather flexible, and it certainly allows different arrangements for different facets of translation. The acceptance of a translator hired by a party is one such permissible arrangement. The new 2005 CIETAC Rules go one step further, providing for translation commissioned by the institution, but also allowing (on an equal footing, it seems) the parties to bring their own interpreter. According to Article 67(2):

> 'At an oral hearing, if a party or its representative(s) or witness requires language interpretation, the Secretariat of the CIETAC or its Sub-Commission may provide an interpreter, or the party may bring its own interpreter.'

The acceptance of a translator hired by a party appears to be particularly justifiable when the translation at issue concerns the pleadings of that party. As far as witness statements are concerned, the appointment of a translator hired by the arbitral tribunal appears to be the better solution, although other arrangements are not unknown in practice. If a party were to hire the translator for witness statements or expert testimony, the arbitrators should not approve of the arrangement without the consent of the other party. If translation is needed for an arbitrator who does not speak the language of the proceedings, party-hired translators would be inappropriate.

C.3. Who pays for the translation?

The UNCITRAL Model Law and the Model Rules do not contain specific provisions on the costs of translation, and few institutional rules have devoted explicit provisions to this issue. Therefore conclusions must be drawn on the grounds of broad-spectrum provisions and general principles. It is probably safe to assume, for example, that the 'shall make arrangements' language of Article 25(3) of the Model Rules extends to arrangements made in connection with costs as well.

Somewhat more specific instructions may be found in the UNCITRAL Notes (which, of course, only offer advice).[32] Section 20 of the Notes offers some assistance by outlining several options:

> 'In taking decisions about translation or interpretation, it is advisable to decide whether any or all of the costs are to be paid directly by a party or whether they will be paid out of the deposits and apportioned between the parties along with other arbitration costs.'

In general, there are two basic principles that mold the allocation of costs of translation. First, once a language is determined, the standard is set and the parties have to adapt to this standard and bear the costs of such adaptation, which might imply costs of translation. Second, costs are generally allocated in proportion to success (or lack of success) in the proceedings. The application of these two principles supposes coordination and mutual adjustments.

Approaching the question of distribution of costs, a distinction also has to be made between paying for translation during the arbitration process, when translation is being made (advancing the costs), and final allocation of costs. The specific purpose of translation might also be relevant.

C.3.1. *Advancing the costs*

Where the translator is hired by a party, it is quite logical for that party to advance the costs of translation, i.e., to pay the translator. If documents submitted by a party have to be accompanied by translation, the costs should be borne (or at least advanced) by the party submitting the documents. The same goes for the costs of an interpreter hired by a party to translate its oral pleadings into the language of the arbitration proceedings. As far as translation of witness statements and expert testimony is concerned, the arbitrators should decide who pays (or advances) the costs; the same applies in other cases where the translator is hired by the arbitral tribunal. This is spelled out in some rules, but it is also a broadly accepted practice where no specific rules exist.

One of those (few) rules which have devoted explicit attention to this problem are the 2006 Vienna Rules. According to Article 35(1):

> 'If the sole arbitrator (the arbitral tribunal) considers certain actions entailing costs, such as the appointment of experts, **interpreters or translators,** making

[32] The UNCITRAL Notes define their purpose with the following words: 'The purpose of the Notes is to assist arbitration practitioners by listing and briefly describing questions on which appropriately timed decisions on organizing arbitral proceedings may be useful.'

> verbatim records of the proceedings, a visual inspection [Lokalaugenschein], or relocation of the proceedings, to be necessary, he(it) must make arrangements to cover the expected costs and inform the Secretary General thereof.' [emphasis added]

A similar rule can be found in Article 11 of the 2004 Arbitration Rules of the Japan Commercial Arbitration Association. It states that the arbitral tribunal shall determine the language or languages of the arbitral proceedings, and 'The arbitral tribunal shall, in so determining, take into consideration whether interpreting or translating will be required and how the cost thereof should be allocated.'

These rules – although mentioning costs of translation explicitly – do not really give specific guidance, except for making it clear that it is for the arbitrators to make the appropriate arrangements. The formulations are broad enough to be extended to the final allocation of the costs as well (again, without much guidance). Essentially the same position was taken in the 2005 CEPANI Rules[33] which state in Article 14(2) that 'The Arbitral Tribunal shall have full authority to decide which of the parties shall bear the translation costs, if any, and to what extent.' The 2000 Commercial Arbitration Rules of the Korean Commercial Arbitration Board[34] are a bit more specific, stating in Article 30 that the party requesting interpretation or translation '[s]hall deposit an advance payment to the Secretariat of the expenses involved…'.

A somewhat atypical position has been adopted by the 2001 Belgrade Rules. Article 37(1) of these Rules states that the default language of the arbitral proceedings is Serbian, while according to Article 37(2) and 37(3):

> '(2) The parties may agree that the proceedings be conducted in some other (foreign) language, provided that they pay all the additional costs (translation of documents, evidence and hearings).
> (3) If the members of the Arbitral tribunal or the sole arbitrator are foreign citizens appointed by the parties, the party that appointed the arbitrator shall bear the costs of translation of the documents, evidence, the hearing and the in camera deliberations of the Arbitral tribunal.'

Article 37(2) qualifies costs of translation caused by the choice of a different language than the default language (Serbian) as 'additional costs'. This qualification should probably be understood as a reference to costs which are not

33 CEPANI – Belgian Center for the Study and Practice of National and International Arbitration.

34 As amended by the (South) Korean Supreme Court on April 17, 2000.

covered by the arbitration fees and therefore have to be added by the parties. As a matter of fact, this is how costs of translation are generally perceived. It has to be mentioned, however, that such costs could also emerge if the language of the proceedings is Serbian, but translation is needed by the foreign party. This option is not contemplated explicitly by Article 37, but from its context it would follow that such costs must be advanced by the party in need of the translation (rather than by both parties). It is unclear whether this approach is extended to the final allocation of such costs.

Article 37(3) represents a rare provision dealing explicitly with costs of translation caused by the arbitrator's lack of command of the language of the proceedings. The problem is viewed under the angle of a foreign arbitrator not speaking Serbian, which is probably the most common form of appearance of this problem. It might, however, be more suitable to perceive the issue in more neutral terms, contemplating all situations in which one arbitrator does not speak the language of the proceedings.[35] The solution which has been adopted may be questioned. Considering the principle that the arbitrators (including the party appointed arbitrators) are neutral, it might be a better approach to treat the costs of translation for the benefit of an arbitrator as common costs rather than as costs of the party who appointed the arbitrator.

A solution similar to that adopted by the Serbian Rules has been espoused by the 2002 Rules of Arbitration of the Court of Arbitration at the Bulgarian Chamber of Commerce (hereinafter 'BCCI'). The Bulgarian Rules have also posited the default language (Bulgarian) as the point of reference, and as the dividing criterion of costs. The Bulgarian Rules are more explicit than the Belgrade Rules regarding the final allocation of costs. Article 23 of the Bulgarian Rules stipulates that the arbitral tribunal '[s]hall appoint an interpreter for the party having no command of Bulgarian. The fee of the interpreter shall be for the account of that party, irrespective of the outcome of the case'. Thus – unless the parties have agreed on another language – costs of translation into and from Bulgarian will not only have to be advanced but also finally be borne by the party in need of such translation.

Let us add that, although rarely, the parties sometimes themselves stipulate specific arrangements regarding the costs of translation. To cite an example, in a case referred to earlier (*JDA Software v. Kiabi*),[36] the parties reached an agreement regarding costs of translation and this was recorded in the terms of reference. It is interesting to note that the agreement was reached while the language

[35] See in more detail on Art. 37, Várady, *O jeziku arbitraže* ('On the Language of Arbitration'), in *Arbitraža* (Beograd 2003) at pp. 11-27.

[36] *Revue de l'arbitrage* (2003) p. 1252.

of arbitration was still an open issue. The parties agreed that witnesses would be allowed to testify in their own language, on the understanding that the party who called the witness would organize simultaneous translation of the witness statement into the language established as the language of arbitration. It was added in Article 9(2) of the terms of reference that the costs of translation would be born by the party concerned[37] (i.e., by the party who proposed the witness). It appears from the formulation of this stipulation that the principle set does not only apply to advancing of costs of translation, but will also determine final allocation.

In arbitral practice, the issue of costs of translation is not always raised in advance. When it is, in the absence of party stipulation the arbitrators settle this issue by a procedural order. Payment is either requested from both parties, or it is requested from the party who is proposing the procedural step which incurs costs of translation. I would like to mention as examples procedural orders issued in two ICC cases. In case No. 5926, the procedural order of the arbitrators of September 26, 1988, included the following provision:

> '5. Appearance of the witnesses and translation into English, if needed, will have to be arranged, at its cost, by the party producing such witnesses.'[38]

In a 1992 procedural order,[39] ICC arbitrators provided that translation for the benefit of the counsel for the respondent will be advanced by the claimant. It was stated in point 4 of the Order:

> 'Counsel for defendant may be present and may put questions. In that case simultaneous translation is to be provided into English, provisionally at the expense of the plaintiff.'[40]

At first sight it may appear that the two procedural orders are relying on different principles, but only at first sight. In the second case, the witness, who was supposed to testify at his home, was proposed by the claimant (plaintiff). The language of arbitration was English, but witness was expected to testify in Italian. Thus, although translation was for the benefit of the counsel of the respondent (defendant), departure from the language of arbitration took place on the

---

[37] 'Le frais relatifs à cette traduction seront à la charge de la partie concernée', *Revue de l'arbitrage* (2003) at p. 1261.

[38] ICC No. 5926, *Collection of Procedural Decisions in ICC Arbitration 1993-1996*, 2nd edn. (Kluwer – ICC Publishing 1998) at p. 105.

[39] Order No. 7170, 1993, *Collection of Procedural Decisions in ICC Arbitration 1993-1996*, 2nd edn. (Kluwer – ICC Publishing 1998) at p. 55.

[40] Ibidem at p. 56.

initiative of the claimant (plaintiff), and translation was a consequence of this departure. The position taken in both cases is the same: the party who proposes a procedural step which implies translation has to advance the costs of such translation. This rule was adopted in many cases, but there is also a fair number of cases in which costs of translation are advanced by both parties.

Some conclusions may be inferred from (or in connection with) the rules and practices referred to above. It appears to be generally accepted that – as this has been made explicit in the Vienna Rules – the costs of translation are treated the same way as other additional costs, such as costs of expertise or the costs of on-site inspection. These costs are normally not part of those covered by arbitration fees, which only cover the administrative costs and the remuneration of the arbitrators. Some of these costs will be normally advanced by a party (like the costs of translation of documentary evidence attached to a brief presented by the party, and possibly the costs of interpretation of party pleadings). With regard to witnesses and experts, the question arises whether the arbitrators should invite one party (the one proposing a witness or an expert) or both parties to submit a share of the costs of translation. Both solutions have found support in practice. One may submit that in line with the more inquisitorial nature of arbitration (unless otherwise stipulated), witnesses and experts are more linked to the arbitral tribunal than to one of the parties. Relying on this principle, it seems to be more appropriate to invite both parties to each deposit one half of the costs. If one party should fail to do so, it is always possible to resort to a fallback solution and invite the more interested party to advance the full amount. The argument can be made that this is a more logical solution, but other solutions (as in the two ICC cases mentioned above) have also gained acceptance in practice. The rather broad formulation of the Model Law, which is widely adopted, allows more options, since it simply states that arrangements shall be made by the arbitral tribunal.

C.3.2. *Final allocation of costs*

The next question is how the costs of translation should be finally allocated in the award. Allocation is normally guided by success and by the rationality of the costs. Arbitration rules tend to be flexible on this point, allowing the arbitrators considerable maneuvering room. There is no pre-established formula, but one can point out some considerations (and dilemmas) that influence the distribution of costs of translation. A recurring question is whether costs of translation advanced by a party should or should not be considered as part of the overall costs which shall be allocated depending on the success (or lack of success) of the claim. One of the circumstances influencing the answer is whether the costs are rational and justified.

If witness statements or expert testimonies are at issue and if the translator is hired by the arbitrators, it is unlikely that the arbitrators would question the rationality of the translation (i.e., the actual need for translation). In such a case, the costs of translation will normally be distributed between the parties in the same proportion as other costs (including arbitrator's fees); this proportion is dependent on the outcome of the case. With regard to translation of party pleadings, other considerations are also gaining relevance. As mentioned earlier, the language of the proceedings (chosen by the parties or determined by the arbitrators) is the standard, and all participants have to adjust to that standard. If arbitration takes place, say, in Prague, and if the language of the proceedings is Czech, the parties are supposed to present their case in Czech. An Austrian attorney who does not speak Czech may choose to plead with the assistance of a translator. (Another option would be, of course, to hire a Czech attorney.) Now suppose the Austrian party opts for a translator, and then either hires one himself/herself, or asks the arbitral institution to arrange for translation. Is this a justifiable cost? According to Section 7 of the 2002 Prague Rules, the default language of the oral hearing shall be Czech (or Slovak), but the hearings shall be translated into another language upon request of a party. One possible line of argument would be that by accepting the jurisdiction of the Prague Court of Arbitration (and without agreeing on a different language), the Austrian party accepted proceedings in Czech, and that therefore – although it is entitled to translation – it cannot justify and claim such costs of translation. This is the solution which follows for example, from the explicit provision adopted by Article 23 of the 2002 Bulgarian Rules discussed earlier in this subchapter.

Different arguments may, however, also be raised. For instance, one may question whether it is true that if the language of the proceedings is Czech, the Austrian party can only choose between hiring a Czech attorney, or hiring a translator on the understanding that the Austrian party will bear the costs of the translator regardless of the outcome of the case. One could also argue that the choice of an attorney should not be restricted, not even indirectly, and the party should be able to choose the person in whom it has the greatest confidence; if such a choice necessitates translation, this is not an unreasonable luxury. Following this logic, the party which prevails would be entitled to a compensation of the costs of translation of its own pleadings.

The arbitrators will have to opt between these (conflicting) considerations, taking into account the circumstances of the given case. In one of the few known arbitration cases which have addressed this issue, the Arbitration Institute of the Stockholm Chamber of Commerce hinted at an interesting (and questionable) proposition. This case was already discussed in Chapter I,[41] but from a different

[41] Chapter I.C.5.

angle. In this case, unlike in the Czech-Austrian hypo considered above, all party attorneys had a command of the language of the arbitral proceedings (which was English), but the executive officers of the Respondent did not. In this dispute between a Swedish claimant and a Chinese respondent, the Chinese party asked the Tribunal to order that all written submissions by both parties be made in both Chinese and English.[42] This request was rejected. It was held:

> 'The Tribunal is of the opinion that since Counsel for the respondent is English-speaking, the fact that translations are necessary in his relationship with his clients is an element of time and cost, and essentially cost, which will be considered in the context of allocation of costs and is not a sufficient reason to impose a significant additional burden on the claimant. It would also introduce difficulties for the Tribunal, only one of whose members has a command of Chinese, and needlessly add to the expenditure of both time and money. This request by the respondent is therefore denied.'[43]

What is pertinent here for our purposes – and what is somewhat perplexing – is the statement that the costs for such translation 'will be considered in the context of allocation of costs'. This hints at the possibility of adding these costs to the overall costs of the proceedings which will be distributed depending on the success of the claim. A final position in this respect was not taken, because the final award on the merits went in favor of the Swedish claimant and costs were awarded to the claimant.[44] It was never raised as an issue which costs of the Chinese party were justified costs, because no costs were awarded to the Chinese party. It is an open issue how the costs of translation would have been allocated had the Chinese party prevailed. The primary context of the position taken by the Stockholm tribunal is that of ordering or not ordering translation of the submissions; the wording pertaining to costs may be suggestive, but it is not conclusive. One may submit, however, that translation designed for understanding on the home ground of one of the parties rather than on the playing field of arbitration proper should be an option for the party, and the costs should stay with that party irrespective the outcome of the arbitration case.

As far as costs of translation of documentary evidence are concerned, the 'adjustment to the standard' principle has less relevance than with regard to translation of pleadings. As far as pleadings are concerned, the party has a choice. It can choose an advocate who speaks the language of the proceedings – and

[42] Interim award of July 17, 1992 – published in *Yearbook Commercial Arbitration*, Vol. XXII (1997) 197, at p. 203.

[43] *Yearbook Commercial Arbitration*, Vol. XXII (1997) at pp. 203-204.

[44] Final award of July 13, 1993, *Yearbook Commercial Arbitration*, Vol. XXII (1997) 204 – the decision on costs is on p. 210.

there are many reasons supporting such a choice – or it can opt for an advocate who does not speak the language of the proceedings, and who will communicate with the assistance of a translator. As far as documents are concerned, however, they normally predate the arbitration proceedings, and they are not crafted with the possible language of future arbitration proceedings in mind. Hence, the cost of such translation is, at least in principle, an unavoidable and rational cost which is normally advanced by the party and which should be allocated at the end of the proceedings in line with the outcome of the case.

The question of the rationality of the translation of some specific pieces of evidence may nevertheless be raised. If translation was extended to documents which did not and could not have had any impact on the outcome of the case, the question may be raised whether this was a rational expenditure. This takes us back to the issue of whether it is advisable for the arbitrators to pick and choose pieces of documentary evidence when they order translation. At this point, I would only like to mention that an ex-post assessment of the relevance of the translated documents for the purpose of allocation of costs remains a possibility.

Costs of translation for an arbitrator only deserve special consideration. There are basically three options. First, one may take the position that this is an obvious cost of the proceedings, and not an avoidable cost of one of the parties. Following this logic, the costs of translation for the benefit of the arbitrator who does not speak the language of the proceedings should be allocated in proportions dictated by the outcome of the case. The Serbian Rules discussed above adopt a second option, and state that such costs will be borne by the party who appointed the arbitrator who does not speak the language of the proceedings. It is not clearly spelled out in the Serbian rules whether this solution extends to the final allocation of costs as well. This solution cannot apply, however, where the arbitrator who does not speak the language of the proceedings is not a party appointed arbitrator. It has to be added that although the Belgrade Rules have devoted special attention to this option, the relevance of this option is very modest. According to information received from the Secretariat of the Belgrade Court of Arbitration, in the period of 1995–2005 there were only seven cases in which translation was provided for the party-appointed arbitrator, while during the last five years (2000–2005) there were three such cases.[45] Another possible option is to deduct these costs from the fees of the arbitrator. This latter option appears to be more justified in cases in which the language of the proceedings was established before the appointment of the arbitrators. In such cases, the

---

45 Information provided by Ms. Čukavac, Secretary of the Court of Arbitration at the Serbian Chamber of Commerce and Industry.

arbitrator had an option not to accept the appointment because of his/her lack of fluency of the language set as the language of the proceedings – and this is a reasonable option from the point of view of professional ethics.[46] If, for some reason, the arbitrator nevertheless accepted to act in a case in which his/her language abilities did not match the procedural standard which was preset – and thus translation was needed in order to balance his/her shortcomings – it would make sense to deduct the costs of such translation from the fees of the arbitrator. This is the solution which has been adopted in the practice of the Court of Arbitration at the Russian Chamber of Commerce and Industry.[47] Situations have also emerged where the language was not predetermined (and it was not readily foreseeable either) and after the arbitral tribunal is constituted it becomes evident that the arbitrators do not have a common language. If in such a case a language is chosen which is not spoken by one of the arbitrators, this arbitrator could still resign, but this may cause undue delays, and translation might be the lesser evil. In this setting the parties could have avoided the extra costs of translation by providing for the language of the proceedings in their arbitration agreement, and therefore more arguments can be advanced in favor of adding the costs of such translation to the costs of the procedure allocated between the parties.

C.4. **Methods of translation**

When identifying methods of translation in international commercial arbitration, a distinction must first be made between translation of documents and translation of oral statements. As far as translation of documents or written statements is concerned, there are no discernible methodological differences from the point of view of ordering and organizing translation. The only difference of a similar nature is that between certified translation and translation without certification, which issue was addressed earlier. Thus, speaking of various methods of translation we shall focus primarily on translation of oral statements.

C.4.1. *Simultaneous and consecutive translation*

With regard to translation of oral pleadings and testimonies several methods may be distinguished. The basic options are simultaneous and consecutive trans-

---

[46] The Code of Ethics of the International Bar Association state in Section 2.2: 'A prospective arbitrator shall accept an appointment only if he is fully satisfied that he is competent to determine the issues in dispute, and has an adequate knowledge of the language of the arbitration.'

[47] Information provided by Mr. Kaj Hobér partner at Mannheimer Swartling.

lation. Both have some merits and limitations. Simultaneous translation is less time consuming. Some practitioners argue that simultaneous translation is fairer because it offers no advantage to the party who has a command of both the original language and of the language to which translation is being made. (With consecutive translation, the party who understands both languages will get the content earlier, and will therefore have more time to prepare a rebuttal or a question. This party will also get the message twice.) This is, indeed, a certain advantage, but hardly an unfair one which would amount to a violation of due process if tolerated. There are also arguments in favor of consecutive translation. Most importantly, it will give much more opportunity to both the arbitrators and to the parties to check the accuracy of the translation and to alert the translator to problems. With simultaneous translation, the arbitrators who have a command of both languages have to choose between listening to the original testimony and listening to the translation via earphones. Thus they will not be in a position to compare and to intervene. Furthermore, the consecutive translator is working under less pressure, which also contributes to the quality of the translation. Redfern and Hunter qualify simultaneous translation as a method which is 'invariably unsatisfactory'. In their opinion, 'However skilled the interpreters, simultaneous interpretation – by its very nature, cannot be sufficiently accurate for the purpose of recording the testimony of a witness in a transcript form.'[48]

C.4.2. *Translation by the arbitrators themselves*

In some instances translation is provided by the arbitrators themselves or by one of them. To cite an example, in a case argued before the Budapest Court of Arbitration,[49] the Claimant was from Serbia and Montenegro, the Respondent was from Hungary, and the language of the proceedings chosen by the parties was English. There were several oral hearings and several rounds of exchange of submissions, all in English. Before one of the oral hearings each party proposed one witness, and this was accepted by the arbitral tribunal. Neither of the two witnesses spoke English. The witness proposed by the Serbian party spoke Serbian; the witness of the Hungarian respondent spoke Serbian and Hungarian, and he chose to speak Hungarian. It was anticipated that the witness' testimonies would be short (and, indeed, they were). Finding a translator (or more, likely, two translators) and making the appropriate arrangements would have

---

48 Redfern and Hunter, *Law and Practice of International Commercial Arbitration*, 4rd edn., Student Version (London 2004) at p. 263.

49 Case No. Vb/03501.

taken time. The rationality of the arrangement would also have been questionable, since one would have had to invite two translators for about thirty or forty-five minutes of translation each. Under these circumstances a shortcut was desirable. For reasons of the economy of the proceedings, no translator was hired for this rather short segment of the oral hearing. Instead, the chairman of the tribunal translated both witness' statements into English and dictated the translation to the minutes, allowing the parties to intervene if they wish. The arrangement which was proposed by the arbitral tribunal was accepted by the parties and recorded in the minutes. Regarding the questioning of the witness proposed by the Claimant it was stated:

> 'Before proceeding with the questioning of Mr. A. the Arbitral Tribunal has decided in agreement with the parties that the Chairman of the Tribunal will conduct the investigation in Serbian language and will dictate the answers of Mr. A. in English. Since representatives of both Parties have a command of Serbian they will be allowed to intervene if in their opinion the translation would need to be modified.'[50]

Such arrangements may be practical, but only in a limited number of situations. They only come into question when the arbitrators – or some of them – have an adequate command of the languages concerned. Furthermore, in the given case, translation of the witnesses' statements by the chairman of the tribunal was further justified by the circumstance that the testimonies were only a short episode in the proceedings and therefore this added role could not hinder the arbitrator in carrying out his primary task.

In another case decided by the Budapest Court of Arbitration, the following procedural order was rendered during the hearing of May 12, 2005:

> 'The Arbitral Tribunal orders that:
> 1. the language of the proceedings in accordance with the arbitration agreement of the parties is English language, but the language of the oral hearings will be in Hungarian, the minutes of these hearings will be taken in English.
> 2. all submissions of the Parties have to be in English.
> 3. all exhibits have to be submitted in English language as well. This order also relates to exhibits annexed to earlier submissions of the Parties.'[51]

In this case all participants (including party representatives, all three arbitrators and the recording secretary as well) were more at ease with Hungarian. Having

---

[50] Case No. Vb/03501, from the Minutes of the oral hearing of June 23, 2005.

[51] Minutes of the oral hearing May 12, 2005, Case No. Vb/04362.

this in mind, an agreement was reached that party representatives would plead in Hungarian. The minutes – in line with one of the options established in comparative practice – contained a summary of the statements dictated by the chairman. This time, it was agreed that the chairman would dictate this summary in English rather than in the language in which the parties spoke. Since all participants had a command of English, they were able to follow the making of the summary, and they were also in a position to make suggestions. This case is somewhat different from the previous one. Here – just as in some like cases – the purpose of translation was not the standard purpose. Translation was not arranged in order to bridge a language gap between the participants. All participants spoke English, although some of them were not at ease with English. Moreover, both the nationality and the first language of all participants was Hungarian so they could have easily agreed on Hungarian as the language of the proceedings. The following background may explain the solution adopted in the Procedural Order of May 12, 2005. In Hungary, like in many new EU-member countries, (and like in many other countries) privatization brought to the scene owners from many countries. It is not a rarity that the owner of a Hungarian (or Polish, Estonian, Czech, etc.) company does not speak the language of the home country of the company. For this reason, managers try, wherever possible, to keep records (or parallel records) in a language understood by the owners. It is in this context that some arbitration agreements provide for English (or sometimes German) as the language of the arbitral proceedings, although the first language of both parties is the same, and is not English (or German). In such a situation it appears to be a sensible solution to have the record in English, but to allow the parties to plead in a language with which they are more at ease. Summarizing the minutes by way of translation takes an extra effort by the third arbitrator, but it appears to be better fitted to this specific purpose than the hiring of an interpreter. This is another variant of 'translation by the arbitrators themselves', a different manifestation of translation from the one in the previous case where translation (by the arbitrator) served the conventional purpose of making some participants understand what they would not understand without translation. In the case in which both parties spoke in Hungarian but the third arbitrator summarized their pleadings in English, the actual function of translation was not to provide understanding between the participants, but to leave a record in a language which is understood by interested persons who are not direct participants of the arbitration proceedings.

In connection with translation made by the arbitrators themselves, it has to be mentioned that it may not be prudent to make such arrangements without the explicit consent of the parties. It is true that the entitlement of the arbitrators to make arrangements for translation is usually formulated in quite broad terms, not excluding the possibility of confiding this function to themselves. At the same time, however, it is clear that such arrangements are out of the ordinary, and they endow the arbitrators with functions different from those normally contemplated by the parties. Under these circumstances it appears to be sensible to seek specific party consent for an arrangement under which an arbitrator would assume the role of the translator.

D. Deficiencies Pertaining to Translation and Their Consequences

D.1. The problem

Shortcomings in connection with translation often come with consequences. Such deficiencies may have an impact on the conduct of the proceedings, they may influence the outcome of the proceedings, and they may impair the regularity of the proceedings. One may distinguish three types of deficiencies in connection with translation during the arbitration proceedings. First, there may be no translation; second, the translation may be erroneous; and third, translation may be offered where this was not foreseen in stipulations and arrangements pertaining to language. As far as specific consequences are concerned, these may be manifested both in the arbitration proceedings proper, and in the post-arbitration proceedings. If a document is not translated into the language of the arbitral proceedings, the arbitrators may decide not to consider it, and this may influence their decision either on jurisdiction or on the merits. Shortcomings regarding translation may also affect the validity of the award in post-award proceedings. A deficiency pertaining to translation may lead to the setting aside of the award or refusal of recognition. (With these issues we shall deal in more detail in Chapter V.) Speaking of consequences, the question also arises whether the arbitral institution or the arbitrators may also have to bear some consequences if shortcomings are due to lack of action or to improper action of the arbitrators or of the arbitral institution. In this chapter we shall focus primarily on shortcomings and their consequences within the arbitration proceedings proper.

D.2. Lack of translation

Lack of translation might affect the conduct or outcome of the arbitration case. Documents submitted without translation may not be taken into consideration. Lack of translation might also amount to a violation of due process. If a party does not speak the language of the proceedings, or does not speak the language in which a witness makes his/her statement and no translation is provided, one could say that the party was denied the opportunity to present his/her case. Absence of translation may also represent a violation of the procedure agreed upon between the parties.

D.2.1. *Variants of lack of translation*

The consequences of lack of translation depend, of course, on the circumstances of the case. There are several variants of lack of translation. The problem is more consequential when a party statement or a witness statement is made in a language other than the established language of the arbitral proceedings, and the arbitral tribunal fails to arrange for translation. This could amount to a clear denial of due process. Such cases, however, are quite unlikely to occur. It is difficult to imagine a situation where the arbitrators would not provide for translation into English if the stipulated language of the proceedings is English and a witness speaks Estonian. But what if the stipulated language is English, one of the parties and a witness speak English, but this is not understood by the Estonian party, and the arbitrators do not provide for translation? Do we still have a violation of due process due to lack of translation? At this point, a further distinction needs to be made between two possible situations: a) the arbitrators do not make arrangements for translation, but do not prevent the party (in our hypo the Estonian party) from bringing its own interpreter, and b) the arbitrators do not arrange for translation and do not allow the party to bring its own interpreter. Article 25(3) of the Model Rules (and many other institutional rules which have followed the UNCITRAL lead) are quite flexible regarding arrangements for translation. Article 25(3) simply says that arrangements for translation shall be made if this is 'deemed necessary by the tribunal under the circumstances of the case'. It would be logical to assume that arrangements have to be made for the translation of a **witness statement or of an expert opinion** from a language other than the language of the arbitral proceedings **into** the language of the arbitral proceedings – unless all participants have an adequate command of the language used which is not the language of the arbitral proceedings. As far as translation of **party pleadings into** the language of the arbitral proceedings is concerned, such translation also has to be arranged, but this may be the responsibility of the party.

The question arises whether one should also assume that translation needs to be provided **from** the language of the arbitral proceedings when this language is not understood by one of the participants. In this situation, a failure of the arbitral tribunal to hire a translator would probably not amount to a denial of the right to present one's case as long as the party is not prevented from making its own arrangements for translation. In other words, a party should be entitled to use translation from its language into the language of the proceedings. A somewhat different position was taken by Redfern and Hunter, who endorse the principle that it should be

> '[r]egarded as the fundamental right of a party or a witness to speak at a hearing in his mother tongue if he so wishes'.

They do, however, add a qualification in a footnote:

> 'It is not unreasonable, however, for an arbitral tribunal to require that a party who wishes to engage lawyers to present his case to be required to retain representatives who are able to perform their functions in the working language of the arbitration.'[52]

This caveat, advanced with some caution, might restrict the freedom of the party to choose an advocate on the grounds of confidence. If a party has to present its case in a country where it has no previous experience with lawyers, this party may be reluctant to hire an attorney on the grounds of language abilities (which might in practice restrict the choice to local lawyers). If the language of the arbitral proceedings is, say, Slovenian, then it is clear that the parties have to adjust their strategies to that fact, but it should remain their choice whether to hire a Slovenian speaking attorney, or to hire a translator who will assist an attorney who does not speak Slovenian. Eliminating one of the two options might amount to a restriction impeding the party in the presentation of its case, and this may arguably represent a ground for setting aside or refusal or recognition of the award. This perception is also endorsed by the legislative history of the UNCITRAL Model Law. In the course of drafting, it was suggested that it be explicitly stated that a party should always be permitted to present its own case in its own language. (There were alternative suggestions regarding the costs of such translation.) The Commission observed that it was not necessary to stipulate that a party could provide for translation from and to its own language since there was no intention of preventing a party from doing so.[53] One may submit that requirements of procedural fairness include the right of a party to rely on translation both into and from the language designated as the language of the arbitral proceedings.

As far as **documentary evidence** is concerned, the discretionary powers of the arbitrators are again, quite broad. This is relevant regarding both consequences within the arbitration proceedings proper and consequences in post-award proceedings. If the parties do not provide for translation of certain documents, the arbitrators may decide not to consider such documents. A fail-

---

[52] Redfern and Hunter, *Law and Practice of International Commercial Arbitration*, 3rd edn. (London 1999) at p. 233.

[53] Holtzman-Neuhaus, op. cit. 630.

ure of the arbitrators themselves to provide for translation may influence the outcome of setting aside or recognition proceedings. In this latter context, it is important to note that the failure of the arbitrators to arrange for translation will not necessarily result in a denial of an opportunity to present one's case. Even if the arbitrators erred in not ordering translation, a diligent party can remedy this by making his own arrangements for translation.[54] If a new document were presented by a party during the oral hearing, the other party could always seek time to study the document and to react to it, irrespective of the language of the document. Thus, lack of order of the arbitrators providing for translation of documents need not amount to a ground for setting aside or refusal of recognition.

Three questions of a general nature may be raised in connection with lack of translation. The first question pertains to the specific procedural **setting** in which the lack of translation may be manifested (and may yield consequences). Second, the question also arises whether the **relevance** of the statement or document which was not translated matters. The third question is whether a party may be deemed to have **waived** its right to rely on lack of translation if it failed to protest during the arbitral proceedings.

D.2.2. *Consequences of lack of translation*

There are two basic settings in which lack of translation might emerge as an issue: a) First, it might emerge as a problem within the arbitration proceedings proper and might thereby influence the conduct of the proceedings and/or the award; b) Second, it might be raised as an issue in post-award proceedings, and might have an effect on the decision of the court. In the first setting the consequences of lack of translation are determined by the arbitrators, while in the second setting the consequences are determined by the court. In this section we shall focus on consequences of lack of translation in arbitration proceedings proper.

In an interesting case submitted to the Iran-US Claims Tribunal, the Tribunal's jurisdiction depended on the nationality of the Claimant, Ms. Juliette Allen. This is an issue which has appeared with some frequency before the Tribunal, given that the jurisdiction of the Tribunal is limited to '[c]laims of nationals of the United States against Iran and claims of nationals of Iran against the United

[54] A different conclusion might be reached in the following (probably rare) situation: Claimant submits a large amount of documents which are not drafted in the language of the proceedings. The arbitral tribunal does not order that these should be accompanied by a translation. Respondent has a short time limit for the submission of the answer to the claim, and has no time both to provide for translation, and to draft the answer considering the translated documents.

States'.[55] Given this limitation, the nationality of legal persons and the impact of dual nationality have emerged as threshold questions in a considerable number of cases. In *Juliette Allen v. The Government of the Islamic Republic of Iran*,[56] the Claimant contended that she was born in Tehran to Iranian parents, and that following her marriage to a US national in 1969, she was naturalized as a US citizen in 1973. The Respondent contested the Claimant's (Ms. Allen's) ability to have access the Tribunal on the grounds of her US nationality. In response, the Claimant submitted as evidence her US passport, a certificate of naturalization, and some other documents, but without translation. The Tribunal requested translation, but translation was either not submitted or was incomplete. On November 30, 1990, the Tribunal ordered the Claimant to submit by 28 December 1990 'full English and Persian translations of her submissions filed 6 August and 11 September 1990'. The Tribunal further emphasized that, considering the procedural status of the case, no extension of the time limit would be considered. After none of the required translations were filed, on March 5, 1991 the Tribunal issued an Order in which it informed the Parties that it would consider application of Article 28(3) of the Tribunal Rules[57] if the Claimant, without showing sufficient cause, failed to submit by 28 March 1991 the said translations. The Tribunal again added that it would not consider any extension of the time limit set by the Order. By a further Order of 14 May 1991, the Tribunal noted that the Claimant had not filed the translations within the extended time limit set by its Order of 5 March 1991, and had not provided any explanation for her failure to do so. Thereupon, the Tribunal announced its intention, pursuant to Article 28(3) of the Tribunal Rules, 'to proceed with its deliberations on the issue of jurisdiction in this Case on the basis of the evidence properly filed in both Persian and English as of 28 March 1991'. Acting in this manner, the tribunal refused jurisdiction. As it was explained in paragraphs 15 and 16 of the Award of December 11, 1992:

> '15. The Tribunal notes that the Claimant has not filed the translations required pursuant to Article 17 of the Tribunal Rules of, inter alia, her American passport and certificate of naturalization despite the Tribunal's repeated Orders for her to

[55] Art. II of the January 19, 1981 Declaration of the Government of the Democratic and Popular Republic of Algeria, Concerning the Settlement of Claims by the Government of the United States and the Government of the Islamic Republic of Iran. (often referred to as Claims Settlement Declaration or 'CSD')

[56] Iran-US C.T.R., Case No. 930, Chamber Three, Award No. 541-930-3 of December 11, 1992, 28 *Iran-US C.T.R.* at 382.

[57] According to Art. 28(3): 'If one of the parties, duly invited to produce documentary evidence, fails to do so within the established period of time, without showing sufficient cause for such failure, the arbitral tribunal may make the award on evidence before it.'

do so. Thus, there is no properly filed evidence indicating that she possesses United States nationality.
16. Consequently, the Tribunal does not reach the question of the Claimant's dominant and effective nationality. It is compelled to reject her claim for failure to comply with the jurisdictional requirement set out in Article II, paragraph 1, of the Claims Settlement Declaration, which establishes the Tribunal's purpose in relevant part as 'deciding claims of nationals of the United States against Iran and claims of nationals of Iran against the United States... .'[58]

This is a clear case in which lack of translation determined the outcome of the arbitration proceedings proper. The arbitrators relied on Article 28(3) of their Rules (which contains a provision identical to that of Article 28/3 of the UNCITRAL Model Rules, and to corresponding provisions of many other institutional rules). Article 28(3) says that if a party is duly invited to produce documentary evidence and fails to do so without due cause, the arbitrators may make an award without such evidence. The arbitrators gave a somewhat extended interpretation of this rule, applying it to a situation where the evidence was presented but without the required translation.

The question can be raised whether the position taken by the arbitrator is in accordance with the Kompetenz-Kompetenz principle that establishes the right (and duty) of the arbitrators to decide on their own competence. This may mean a right and duty to establish the relevant facts even if the parties are not fully cooperating. In this case, competence depended (at least in part) on the passport and the certificate of naturalization of Ms. Allen.[59] Under the circumstances of the case, it is rather safe to assume that the arbitrators understood the documents as presented (in English). One could argue that in line with the *Kompetenz-Kompetenz* principle they could have considered the submitted documents anyway since these were connected with their competence. Arguments support-

[58] *Juliette Allen v. The Government of the Islamic Republic of Iran*, Case No. 930, Chamber Three, Award No. 541-930-3, 28 *Iran-US C.T.R.* at 384.

[59] The passport and the naturalization certificate were certainly relevant, although not necessarily decisive. Even if it were demonstrated that Ms. Allen was a US citizen, the question still remained whether this was her effective and dominant citizenship since it was quite likely that she also had Iranian citizenship. In an earlier decision, the Tribunal took a position of principle regarding effective citizenship. On April 6, 1984, the Full Tribunal issued a decision in Case No. A18 (*The Islamic Republic of Iran v. The United States of America*), Decision No. DEC 32-A18-FT (6 Apr. 1984), reprinted in 5 *Iran-US C.T.R.* 251, in which it determined that 'it has jurisdiction over claims against Iran by dual Iran-United States nationals when the dominant and effective nationality of the claimant during the relevant period from the date the claim arose until 19 January 1981 was that of the United States'. Id. at p. 25, reprinted in 5 *Iran-US C.T.R.* at 265. Thus, even if the documents showed that Ms. Allen was a US citizen, it still remained to be determined whether this was her 'dominant and effective nationality' at the relevant time.

ing the Tribunal's decision can, however, also be made. Acceptance of the documents without translation could have violated the right of the Iranian party to present its case. At this point one has to note that the duty to provide translation was clearly a duty of the Claimant, but it is also true that the Iranian Respondent could have arranged for translation. Is the failure to do something it was not obliged to do (but could have done), an impediment to argue that it was 'unable to present its case'? In the *Juliette Allen* case, the Iranian party was, of course, **expecting** translation to be provided by the Claimant in accordance with the procedural orders. Had the arbitrators opted to rely on the original anyway, without a warning given to the Respondent, the Iranian party would have had a quite strong case for arguing that it was unable to present its case. In addition, the repeated failure to submit translations was in clear violation of procedural orders by the Tribunal. Tolerating such a procedural deficiency might have represented a ground for challenging the award in post-award proceedings. One can imagine exceptional circumstances which may justify a different result, but in principle, a failure to submit requested translations might, indeed, justify the disregarding of the original.

Staying within the setting of the arbitral proceedings, mention must also be made of the influence the lack of translation has on the **conduct** of the proceedings, not necessarily affecting the award. Absence of translation may have an impact, for example, on **time limits**. Examples may again be found in the proceedings of the Iran-US Claims Tribunal.[60] In *Houston Contracting Company v. National Iranian Oil Company et al.*,[61] the Respondents requested a Farsi translation of certain evidentiary documents filed on April 4, 1986, and sought in this connection an extension of the time limit to submit their Memorials and evidence. In its Order of January 19, 1987, the Tribunal stated i.a.:

> 'The Tribunal notes that the request for translation was raised nine months after the Claimant's submission in question, and eleven days before the filing date for the Respondents to submit their Memorials and evidence. Thus, the request was made much too late to be granted.'[62]

It is rather evident that lack of translation may have an impact on time limits – it is also evident that manipulations are also possible in this connection. On one

[60] Given the bilingual foundations of this Tribunal, it is logical that issues pertaining to language and translation appear in its proceedings with some frequency.

[61] *Houston Contracting Company v. National Iranian Oil Company, National Iranian Gas Company and the Islamic Republic of Iran*, Case No. 173, Chamber Three, Order 173-3 of January 19, 1987, 14 *Iran-US C.T.R.* at 18.

[62] Order of January 19, 1987 issued in the case cited in the previous footnote.

hand, lack of translation may impair the ability of the other party to study a brief and to prepare a counter-brief within the time limit set. One may argue that a time limit for response does not start running at all if the brief is submitted without translation (or without full translation). On the other hand, lack of translation is sometimes just a pretext for various procedural maneuvers. In the *Houston Contracting Company* case, the arbitrators did not face these issues directly but instead relied on an implied waiver stemming from the lack of objection within a reasonable time. In the absence of the waiver argument (and in the absence of clear abuse), it appears to be safer to extend the deadline to a date after the submission of the required translation – and this is what has been done in many cases.

In an interesting case decided by the Budapest Court of Arbitration,[63] the issue arose what documents submitted with the statement of claim needed to be translated and whether the time limit for the submission of the statement of defense would or would not run before translations were submitted. In this case, a British and a US party were on one side, and two Hungarian parties were on the other side. They agreed on English as the language of arbitration. The parties approached arbitration in a rather combative spirit, and this was quite visible already during the first steps in the case. The Claimants (the UK and the US party) submitted with their claim almost all correspondence and documents pertaining to the contractual relationship with the Hungarian side. A considerable part of these documents, some of which were quite voluminous, was in Hungarian. The Hungarian parties protested, objecting that the documents were not presented with a translation into English, the language of the arbitral proceedings agreed upon by the parties. The Hungarian parties also argued that the time limit for the submission of a statement of defense should not start running until the translations were submitted. The Claimants criticized this objection, stating in their letter of July 31, 2001 that 'Your clients are, of course, very familiar with all the exhibits, including those in Hungarian.'[64] The Claimants added: 'In the interests of avoiding unnecessary costs and paper generation, please would you indicate precisely which parts of which exhibits you consider translation essential.'[65] In a further letter of August 2, 2001, the Claimants pointed out once again that all exhibits are well known to both parties, that 'the exhibits about which your clients complain are in the Hungarian language – the native language of your clients, not ours;' and added that full translation would imply 'some 1400 pages' and would cost US$ 23,000 plus tax.[66] In their letters of

---

63 Case No. Vb/01089 (unpublished)

64 Files of the case Vb/01089.

65 Files of the Case Vb/01089.

66 Letter of the Claimants of August 2, 2001, in the file of Case Vb/01089.

August 10, 2001 and August 15, 2001, the Respondents reiterated that in their opinion '[t]he failure to provide translations of the exhibits to your client's Statement of Claim constituted a defect in the Statement of Claim, which prevents time running'. The Respondents also added that they did not require translation of documents which were not relevant, but they left it to the Claimants to decide which exhibits to the statement of claim were relevant.[67] Since difficulties arose with regards to the appointment of the chairman of the Tribunal, the two party-appointed arbitrators wrote a joint memorandum to the parties stating:

> 'It is strongly desirable that all parties **only place** before the Arbitral Tribunal documents, or parts of documents, which **directly bear** upon the issues that have to be decided in this arbitration. In consequence each party will only be under a duty to have translations prepared of these documents or parts of documents.'[68]

After the Tribunal was fully constituted, it extended new time limits but without explicitly mentioning lack of translation as a ground for the extension. The Tribunal returned to the issue of translation in its Procedural Order of September 23, 2002; it invited both parties to submit 'copies of all documents that they intend to rely upon in this arbitration', and added that: 'All relevant documents in a language other than English must be accompanied by an English translation.'[69]

There are two issues which deserve attention in connection with this altercation. The first – that of the selection of relevant documents – is not a difficult one. A party submitting documents cannot expect signals from anybody else regarding what is relevant (and then translate what is deemed to be relevant). It is the responsibility of the filing party (of the Claimant in our case) to screen documents for relevance – and then to submit those documents it considers relevant in the light of the claims and the arguments it makes. In principle, screening of documents **by the arbitrators** on grounds of relevance cannot be ruled out under all circumstances, but it either needs to be made with much caution or should be avoided. As far as documents introduced during the first exchange of briefs are concerned, here a screening by the arbitral tribunal is typically out of the question because under most institutional rules this first exchange of briefs **precedes** the constitution of the arbitral tribunal. In the given case it is also clear that the relevant documents had to be translated into En-

---

[67] Letters of the Respondents of August, 10 and August 15, 2001, in the files of Case Vb/01089.

[68] Section 6 of the Memorandum of Party Nominated Arbitrators of August 15, 2001 – in the files of Case Vb/01089.

[69] Procedural Order of September 23, 2002 – in the files of Case Vb/01089.

glish. Translation is not for the benefit of the parties only. Relevant documents had to be translated into English because, although both parties had Hungarian speaking attorneys in addition to English speaking ones, two of the arbitrators (one from Spain, one from the UK) did not speak Hungarian.

The second issue raised in the Hungarian case is more complex. This is the issue whether the submission of documents by the UK and the US party without translation into Hungarian did or did not '**prevent time running**' regarding the submission of the statement of defense. If the language of the arbitral proceedings is English (as was the case) and parts of the documentary evidence are submitted in Hungarian, one may very well argue that the statement of claim had a procedural imperfection. At the same time, lack of translation into English from Hungarian did not impair the ability of the Hungarian party to understand the written submissions and to respond to them. Thus, while it is clear that the Claimant had to eventually translate into English all documents on which it intended to rely (because all arbitrators had to read them), it is much less clear whether the Respondent had a justifiable cause to delay response. This issue was not addressed directly to the arbitrators. If one starts from the assumption that the purpose of translation within the arbitration proceedings is to help **understanding,** one may argue that under the circumstances of the case no such assistance was needed for the preparation of the statement of defense.

D.2.3. *Waiver*

Waiver may serve as an argument against linking consequences to lack of translation both in arbitral proceedings and in post-award proceedings. Waiver may be considered by the arbitrators themselves. This was the case in the Houston Contracting Company case decided by the Iran-US Claims Tribunal.[70] In this case, a request of the Iranian party for translation into Farsi (Persian) was submitted to the arbitrators nine months after the untranslated documents were submitted. The request was denied as having been raised too late. The arbitral tribunal also denied the request for an extension of the time limit for the submission of Respondent's Memorial on the grounds that documents attached to Claimant's submission were not translated into Persian. The parties may waive their rights by inaction, and this may be taken into consideration by the arbitrators.

The issue of waiver may come to the fore both during and after the arbitration proceedings. Let me return to a previous hypo in which the arbitrators wrongly assume that both parties understood the language of the witness and

---

[70] See n. 61.

did not arrange for a translation of the statements of the witness into the language of the arbitral proceedings. In this situation, the party who does not understand the language of the witness surely has an opportunity to protest, to alert the arbitrators, and to seek translation. The failure to do so will amount to waiver under the Model Law. According to Article 4 entitled **Waiver of right to object:**

> 'A party who knows that any provision of this Law from which the parties may derogate or any requirement under the arbitration agreement has not been complied with and yet proceeds with the arbitration without stating his objection to such non-compliance without undue delay or, if a time-limit is provided therefore, within such period of time, shall be deemed to have waived his right to object.'

A number of institutional rules also contain provisions stating that a party who does not use the opportunity to protest against a perceived procedural deficiency, will be deemed to have waived its right to object on that ground.[71] The same conclusion might follow from the principle of bona fide proceedings. If a party has an opportunity to object for lack of translation, and if the party is in a position to seek translation but fails to do so, this may indeed be construed as a waiver both in arbitration proceedings and in post-award court proceedings.

D.3. Mistranslation

D.3.1. *Variants of mistranslation*

Translations are sometimes less than perfect. These imperfections are, however, typically quite benign and do not have an impact on the outcome of the case. If translation puts consequential matters at issue, a scrutiny is possible within the arbitration process, and will in all likelihood take place. The first screening device that might eliminate mistranslations is the arbitrators themselves. The parties also serve as a screen as they typically check the translation and raise issues. Nevertheless, albeit rarely, consequential mistranslations do appear, may have consequences within the arbitration proceedings, and may serve as a basis for challenging the award.

There are several variants of possible mistranslation. One possible criterion for classification is the subject-matter of translation. Mistranslation may arise in connection with the translation of a party pleading, of a witness statement, of

---

[71] See e.g., Art. 33 of the 1998 ICC Rules, Art. 8 of the 2005 CIETAC Rules, Art. 32 of the 1998 LCIA Rules, Art. 25 of the 2006 AAA International Arbitration Rules, or Art. 58 of the 2002 WIPO Arbitration Rules.

a document, or possibly of statutes or institutional rules. Where statutes or institutional rules are concerned, an authoritative interpretation (or interpretation established in practice) may exist which can serve as guidance in identifying mistranslation. There is usually no such guidance at hand when the issue is that of the correct translation of a witness statement, of a document, or of party pleadings.

Another important criterion for classification is whether the participants were aware of the translation problem, and whether the problem was discussed and debated. We have one manifestation of the problem when the parties and the arbitrators are aware that a document (or a statutory provision or a witness statement) may be translated in more than one way, when alternative translations are competing, and when the arbitrators must then opt for one of the alternatives after having considered a confrontation of arguments. In this context, what we have has the characteristics of a decision on merit. If one of the parties still insists that mistranslation took place, he/she will have difficulties couching the argument in terms of a procedural omission. (And will be therefore in a difficult position in endeavoring to challenge the award because both the New York Convention and statutory rules on setting aside have practically restricted challenges to objections pertaining to procedure.)

We have a different scenario when all participants simply rely on a translation (possibly a certified translation), when all arguments start from the assumption that the translation gives an adequate picture of the original, only to discover after the award was rendered that a mistranslation took place. Within this variant the procedural line of argument has a better chance of success. (One can argue for example that because the arbitrators picked a less than competent translator, the party was unable to present its case.)

Another distinction can be made on the grounds of responsibility for hiring the translator. Mistranslation may be the result of the work of a translator hired by one of the parties or of a translator hired by the arbitrators. The strength of some possible challenges may be influenced by this distinction. For example, the 'unable to present his case' line of reasoning will certainly be weaker if the translator was hired by the party who makes this argument.

D.3.2. *Consequences of mistranslation*

There is a difference between the contexts in which lack of translation and mistranslation emerge as a concern. When lack of translation is at issue, this fact itself is usually common ground; it is known that there was no translation, and the consequences depend on whether translation was required. When mistranslation is in the focus, it is rarely common ground that there was any mistranslation at all; instead, it is often debated whether the translation was or was not correct.

There are also differences regarding the procedural setting in which arguments may be raised and consequences may follow. The two basic settings are a) that of the arbitration proceedings proper, and b) that of post-award proceedings. In this chapter we shall deal with the consequences of mistranslation within the arbitration proceedings.

We have seen that lack of translation may disqualify some arguments or documentary evidence, and that it may also have an impact on the time limits extended by the arbitrators. The question arises whether similar consequences may be determined by the arbitrators if mistranslation is at issue. In *Juliette Allen v. The Government of the Islamic Republic of Iran*, the Iran-US Claims Tribunal decided to disregard evidence submitted by the Claimant because it was not accompanied by the requested translation.[72] Suppose the party submitting documentary evidence (which has to be accompanied by a translation) submits a translation but an incorrect one. Can this document be disregarded by the arbitrators? Probably not. Lack of translation may be established without scrutiny and discussion of a document. Mistranslation, in contrast, can only be established as a result of some scrutiny and discussion. Thus, by the time a mistranslation becomes evident, an *ab ovo* exclusion of the document is simply no longer possible.

When speaking of the impact of lack of translation on the conduct of arbitration proceedings, the example of extension of time limits was also mentioned.[73] If translation is not submitted by one party, the other party may – in principle – seek an extension of the time limit for the preparation of an answer to the submission which included untranslated documents. At this point, there is no consequential difference between lack of translation and mistranslation, except with regard to the ascertainment of the shortcoming. The fact that no translation was submitted is obvious, and the arbitrators may – depending on the circumstances – consider this fact while allocating time limits. Mistranslation is not an obvious fact, but it is conceivable that the arbitrators would notice a mistranslation, order a substitute translation – and set time limits starting from the submission of the new translation.

Speaking of mistranslation within the setting of the arbitration proceedings, I would like to mention an interesting example linked to the threshold of the proceedings. The problem arose during the constitution of the arbitral tribunal, and it was prompted by imperfect translation of a sentence in the rules of the

72 See *supra* footnote 58.

73 See the *Juliette Allen* case, the *Houston Contracting Company* case, and Case Vb/01089 decided by the Court of Arbitration at the Hungarian Chamber of Commerce – all discussed *supra* in subchapter D.2.2.

arbitral institution. In a Hungarian case referred to earlier,[74] the parties agreed specifically to settle their disputes under the Budapest Rules in force on the date of their contract. At the time when the contract was concluded the 1995 Rules prevailed, rather than the 2000 Rules which were applicable at the time when the dispute arose. A problem emerged at the point where the two party-appointed arbitrators had to choose a third arbitrator. Under the English version of the 1995 Rules, it appeared that the two arbitrators were restricted in their choice: they had to elect an arbitrator among persons on the roll (list) established by the Budapest Court of Arbitration. The Hungarian original of the 1995 Rules, however, showed no such restriction and neither did the German version of the 1995 Rules. The 2000 Rules did not contain such a restriction in any version. (As a matter of fact, the mistranslation was already eliminated in the 1997 edition of the English version of the Rules.) It was rather clear that the 1995 Rules were tainted by a mistranslation. The question was which version should guide (and possibly restrict) the party-appointed arbitrators in choosing the third arbitrator. The language of the contract was English, the parties chose English as the language of the arbitration proceedings, and they stated explicitly that the Rules in force on the date of their contract would apply – all of which favored the 1995 English version. Against this, a counter-argument could have been raised: the original of the Budapest Rules is obviously the version in the Hungarian language. While this latter argument is not without merits, it is probably the weaker one. Institutional rules do not have an official version the way legislative acts have, and they become binding on grounds of party agreement.[75] It is true that

---

[74] Case No. Vb/01089.

[75] Institutional rules are quite often drafted and published in several languages, but they rarely devote attention to questions prompted by the parallel existence of more versions. One of the exceptions are the 2004 Rules of Procedure of the Danish Institute of Arbitration, which have Danish, English, French and German versions. According to in Section 54: 'In cases where the working language used in the proceedings is Danish, German or French, the Danish, German or French version, respectively, of these Rules of Procedure shall apply. In all other cases, the English version of these Rules of Procedure shall apply.' Thus, the basis of the solution is party autonomy. The version which applies is the one which the parties contemplated; it is assumed that if the language of arbitration is not one of the languages in which the Rules are published, the parties probably contemplated the English version. This solution leads to the conclusion that possible mistranslations probably cannot be remedied. The version which has a likely basis in party autonomy will apply. The 1983 Rules of Conciliation, Arbitration and Expertise of the Euro–Arab Chambers of Commerce are a most rare (if not the only) example of rules which have established a mechanism for choosing between conflicting versions. The Rules have been drawn up in three equally authentic languages: French, Arabic, and English. The mechanism is provided by Art. 30(2) which states: 'In the event of any dispute regarding the interpretation of the different texts of the Rules, the Higher Arbitration Board to which the matter is referred either by the arbitrator(s) or the parties shall have absolute power to resolve it.'

parties typically do not really study institutional rules before adopting them, but reliance on this circumstance might lead in a dangerous direction. It was difficult merely to disregard the 1995 English version of the Rules (including its unwanted restriction regarding the choice of the third arbitrator). The two party-appointed arbitrators opted to present this issue to the parties; they outlined reasons which gave priority to the Hungarian version of the 1995 Rules, but they then also linked further steps to a position to be taken by the parties. In their 'Memorandum of Party Nominated Arbitrators' of August 15, 2001, the arbitrators stated:

> 'Consequently, subject to any submissions by the parties which we invite them to make (if they wish to do so) within the next 14 days and which persuade us to take a contrary view, its is our intention to follow the Hungarian version of the Rules as prevailing on [...] and, in doing so, hold that the Arbitral Tribunal (in its entirety) can be properly constituted with arbitrators who either are or are not on the Roll but who otherwise meet the requirements of Article 4 of the Rules.'[76]

Positive responses from the parties (which were indeed given) could be construed as an amendment of the original procedural arrangement of the parties. It would have been dangerous to embark on a search for the third arbitrator with reliance on the Hungarian version without the (at least tacit) consent of the parties. In the given setting the tribunal concluded that the overcoming of mistranslation needed the support of both parties.

D.4. **Translation uncalled for**

Translation beyond what was arranged for by the parties or by the arbitrators may also represent a ground for contestation. In a case between *Honeywell Bull (France) and Computacion Bull (Venezuela)*, an ICC arbitral award was rendered in favor of the Venezuelan party. Honeywell Bull brought an action to set aside before the Paris Court of Appeal.[77] One of the grounds stated was that – 'contrary to the rules of procedure adopted by the parties which made English the language of arbitration' – the Venezuelan party sent copies of his pleadings in Spanish to the two Spanish-speaking arbitrators. What happened was that in addition to the submissions in English sent to all participants, the Venezuelan party sent an extra Spanish version of its submission to the two arbitrators whose first language was Spanish. The party challenging the award asserted that this

---

76 File of the Case No. Vb/01089.

77 *Compagnie Honeywell Bull S.A. c/ Computacion Bull de Venezuela*, Cour d'appel de Paris (1re Ch. suppl.) Decision of June 21, 1990, Reported in *Revue de l'arbitrage* (1991) 96.

was improper communication because it 'provided to one of the parties preferential access to certain members of the tribunal'.[78] The court rejected this challenge, stating that it was not alleged that the content of the pleadings submitted in Spanish was different from the content of the same pleadings submitted in English and that the 'incident' was resolved by a decision of the arbitral tribunal of June 21, 1988 to strike from the record the Spanish language submissions. The Court of Appeal also took note of the fact that the briefs in question had been duly produced in English, and it concluded that 'the equality of the parties had been strictly safeguarded'.[79]

This case received mixed reviews from commentators. One position was taken by Lazareff, who noted:

> 'This decision can be criticized since, whatever one might say about it, such procedure infringes the equality between the parties and, in fact, authorizes arbitrators not to work in the language of the proceedings and to create an imbalance within the Arbitral Tribunal.'[80]

An opposite opinion was expressed by Delvolvé in his comments published in the *Revue de l'arbitrage.*[81] Delvolvé submits that equality of the parties has to be scrupulously observed, but this must not mean a geometric rigor of parallels (*la rigeur géométrique des parallèles*). He adds that even though it is not appropriate, and might even be disloyal to submit to the two Spanish speaking arbitrators briefs in Spanish when English was the language of the proceedings, there was no great damage since the Spanish version of the briefs was not considered during the deliberations and since their content was not different from that of the proper English submissions.[82]

Translation uncalled-for is very rarely posited as a ground for challenge – and it is a difficult one to succeed with. To begin with, it is not easy to find an appropriate setting. Unsolicited translation can hardly result in the inability of a party to present his case. A violation of the procedure agreed upon by the parties, or a violation of the principle of equal treatment of the parties, are more plausible contexts – and these are the settings in which the arguments of Honeywell Bull were presented. Did we have a procedure which was not in accordance with the agreement of the parties? The parties agreed on English as the language of the proceedings, all briefs were submitted in English, but some

---

78 *Revue de l'arbitrage* (1991) at p. 99.

79 *Revue de l'arbitrage* (1991) 100.

80 S. Lazareff, 'The Language of Institutional Arbitration', the 18 *ICC International Court of Arbitration Bulletin* (May 1997) 18, at p. 25.

81 *Revue de l'arbitrage* (1991) 103-109.

82 *Revue de l'arbitrage* (1991) 104.

briefs were also submitted in Spanish. The Spanish briefs were later stricken from the record. One could say that the striking from the records was a symbolic remedy – but so was the wrong. As far as equality of the parties is concerned, in the given context the argument does not work directly, because it was actually the arbitrators who were not treated equally. It took some ingenuity to mold the facts in terms of inequality of the parties themselves, and a plausible formula was found in the contention that the Spanish version of the briefs 'provided to one of the parties preferential access to certain members of the tribunal'. The essence of this argument is probably not in the fact that the Spanish speaking arbitrators had access to a Spanish version of the brief submitted. If the arbitrator does not speak the language of the arbitral proceedings, it is certainly legitimate (and necessary) to provide such arbitrators with translation. Should such translation amount to a reason to set aside if the arbitrator does speak the language of the proceedings, and the translation is thus not a matter of necessity but only a matter of convenience or courtesy? The arbitrators may have obtained a kind of benefit beyond what was bargained for. Should this matter?

There is one more angle from which this case may be viewed. The motive behind the submission of the briefs in Spanish was in all probability not to communicate something to which the other party and the non Spanish-speaking arbitrator had no access. The likely purpose was a more indirect one. The Venezuelan party may have been fishing for some pro-Hispanic sympathy or bias. While this is improper, it is not really consequential. All arbitrators received the same information. The receipt of an unsolicited translation of the same brief in one's mother tongue could hardly corrupt an arbitrator with normal ethical standards. It seems that this added angle would not yield a different result as far as the claim for setting aside is concerned.

Speaking of translation uncalled-for, I would like to mention an *ad hoc* case in which I acted as the third arbitrator. The language of arbitration was English, but during the oral hearing one of the parties was trying to add emphasis to his arguments by repeating certain key phrases in my native tongue (which is not a language understood world-wide). The party said 'but the actual intent of the parties' then he raised his voice and repeated (still in English), '**the actual intent of the parties**' – and then he said again '***the actual intent of the parties***', this time in the language of the third arbitrator (not with a perfect accent, but understandably). The gambit (a pitch for some added sympathy) was rather transparent – but pretty harmless too. Under the circumstances, a reminder was probably a sufficient measure.

The *Honeywell Bull* case shows that translation uncalled-for is a variant of shortcomings pertaining to translation which may also appear as a purported ground for challenge. The chances for finding shelter for such a challenge under the provisions of the New York Convention (or under the provisions of municipal legislation) are rather modest – which is in line with the actual weight of the problem. Assuming that translation uncalled-for does not yield a different content,[83] it does not normally undermine the integrity of arbitral proceedings.

D.5. **Consequences regarding the arbitrators and the arbitral institution**

The 1989 International Arbitration Rules of the Zürich Chamber of Commerce and the 1995 Arbitration Rules of the Basel Chamber of Commerce contained[84] an interesting rule pertaining to the allocation of risks in cases of 'erroneous translation' or 'faulty translation'. According to Article 22 of the Zürich Rules:

> 'The Arbitral Tribunal determines the language or languages that must be used in written communications and in hearings. It provides for the necessary translations and, where required, interpreters and decides on the distribution of the costs and the risk of erroneous translation.
> As a rule, the procedure with the parties is conducted in the language of the arbitration agreement, and the parties may arrange at their own expense and at their own risk for their own translators and interpreters.'

Essentially the same wording is adopted in Article 20 of the Basel Rules. The relevance of these provisions today is limited, since it is restricted to cases in which the notice of arbitration was filed before the 2004 Swiss Rules came into force. They represent, nevertheless, and interesting starting point for discussion.

---

83 If it were different, one would have mistranslation as an added problem.

84 Past tense is used because the rules of six chambers of commerce (those of the Zürich International Chamber of Commerce and the Basel Chamber of Commerce including) have been replaced by one set of rules, the 2004 Swiss Rules of International Arbitration. In the Introduction of the Swiss Rules it is stated:
'(a) In the past, six Chambers of Commerce and Industry in Switzerland had their own different rules of arbitration for the resolution of international commercial disputes.
(b) In order to promote institutional arbitration in Switzerland and to harmonise the existing rules of arbitration, the Chambers of Commerce and Industry of Basel, Bern, Geneva, Ticino, Vaud and Zürich (hereinafter collectively "the Chambers") have adopted the present uniform rules, the Swiss Rules of International Arbitration (hereinafter the "Rules"), which replace the Chambers' former rules of international arbitration.
These Rules are based on the UNCITRAL Arbitration Rules… .'
The Basel Rules might still have relevance, but – unless otherwise agreed upon – for ongoing proceedings only. According to Art. 1(3) of the Swiss Rules: 'These Rules shall come into force on January 1st, 2004 and, unless the parties have agreed otherwise, shall apply to all arbitral proceedings in which the Notice of Arbitration is submitted on or after that date.'

Responsibility for improper translation may emerge in several contexts. Mistranslation may conceivably be a reason for setting aside or refusal of recognition of an award (which topic shall be dealt with in the next chapter). At this point I would like only to comment on the proposition that the institution may decide on the distribution of the risk of erroneous translation. There are two problems with this proposition.

First, if the issue of erroneous translation is raised before courts, the distribution of risks will be beyond the reach of the arbitral tribunal.

The second problem takes us to a broader question, that of the possible liability of the arbitrators and of the arbitral institution. If the risks of mistranslations are distributed by the arbitral tribunal, the arbitrators or the arbitral institution may avoid their own responsibility for choosing a less than competent translator. This is the same position as the one taken in more general and quite uncompromising terms in the 1998 ICC Rules, which state in Article 34 that 'Neither the arbitrators, nor the Court and its members, nor the ICC and its employees, nor the ICC National Committees shall be liable to any person for any act or omission in connection with the arbitration.' This position has been followed in some institutional rules, but it has also been questioned in scholarly writings. It remains to be seen whether this rule will be upheld by the courts. In one of the rare cases in which the institution itself was sued before a court, the issue of Article 34 was raised, but the decision rendered was not based on this Article. In *Cubic Defense Systems Inc. v. ICC*,[85] CUBIC sued the ICC, alleging that the ICC had failed to honor the *contrat d'organisation d'arbitrage* (the contract between the parties and the arbitral institution). One of the alternative arguments raised by CUBIC was that the *contrat d'organisation d'arbitrage* was void due to the precarious position of the obligations of the arbitral institution in the light of Article 34 of the ICC Rules. CUBIC pointed out that

> '[t]he complex system to which it had adhered did not impose any real obligation on the other contracting party, namely the ICC, such that the Contract lacked any purpose. In consequence, the obligation to which it had consented is not based on any cause;' it further added that '[t]he obligations which would appear to bind the ICA under the Arbitration Rules are not legally binding on it such that the ICA

[85] Court of Appeal of Paris, First Chamber, Section A, Judgment of September 15, 1998, corrected by a 'Judgment on Rectification of Material Errors Discovered by the Court' of October 7, 1998 *Revue de l'arbitrage* (1999) 103; English translation in 1998 Mealey's 'International Arbitration Report', Document #05–990426–109. The decision of the Paris Court of Appeal reproduced above was confirmed by the French *Cour de cassation* on February 20, 2001, *Revue de l'arbitrage* (2001) 229.

escapes all control whatsoever as regards the implementation of its duties. The services promised in reality remain at the discretion of the ICC. Thus the person having an obligation has only contracted an obligation lacking any purpose, contrary to the provisions of Article 1126 of the Civil Code; or, which comes to the same thing, an obligation subject to a condition that the party bound is entirely free to implement or not, which is void under the provisions of Article 1174 of the said Code.'[86]

Reflecting upon these arguments, the Paris Court of Appeals stated:

'Any party to an agreement, even if it be an association responsible for organizing an arbitration, is liable if it fails to meet its contractual obligations. In the present case, no clause providing for exemption from liability is relied upon by the ICC. For the exemption clause which appears in its new Rules, drawn up after the making of the agreement here considered, supposing that clause to be valid is not applicable to this case.'

Thus, the problem was not addressed directly, because the ICC did not actually rely on Article 34 – because Article 34 of the 1998 Rules was adopted after the conclusion of the given *contrat d'organisation d'arbitrage.* Still the position taken in the dictum is quite clear. Any party is liable if it fails to meet its contractual obligations, and an arbitral institution responsible for organizing arbitration is no exception.

The issue of the weight of provisions which limit (or exclude) the liability of the arbitrators and of the arbitral institution was faced more directly in a 1999 decision of the Supreme Court of Austria.[87] In this case, the focus was on the liability of the **arbitrator** rather than of the arbitral institution. An Austrian arbitral institution had rendered an award between two German companies ordering the Respondent to pay about 25 million Austrian shillings (ATS). The Respondent (in the arbitration case) then sued Dr. S., the Chairman of the Arbitral tribunal, requesting about 4 million ATS for damages covering the costs of the arbitration proceedings and the costs of the proceedings in which the arbitral award was challenged. The basis of the claim was the allegation that Dr. S.

---

[86] Mealey's provides here a translator's note: 'According to Art. 1126 of the French Civil Code, "Every Contract has as its purpose a thing that a party binds himself to give or that party binds himself to do or not to do." Art. 1174 of the Code states: "Every obligation is void where it is contracted subject to the condition that the party bound is free to implement it or not".'

[87] *H. GmbH v. Hans-Otto S*, Decision No. 1 Ob 253/97 of April 28, 1998, published in *Entscheidungen des Österreichischer Obersten Gerichtshofes in Zivil – (und Justizverwaltungs)-sachen*, (SZ) 71/76 pp. 446-455; English text in *Yearbook Commercial Arbitration*, Vol. XXVI (2001) pp. 221-229; French text and comments by C. Liebscher in *Revue de l'arbitrage* (1999) 392-400.

had worked under the influence and the control of the other party, and had failed to make appropriate disclosure. In his defense, the Dr. S. invoked Article 17 of the Rules of the arbitral institution, which stated that the arbitrators

> '[c]annot be financially liable for their activity in the context of arbitral settlement of disputes'. The court of first instance denied the claim for damages, and this was confirmed by the Vienna Court of Appeal. The Supreme Court, however, reversed these decisions and returned the case to the first instance with instructions. After an interesting conflict of laws analysis, the Supreme Court found that German law was applicable because the law applicable to the arbitration proceedings also applies to the agreement with the arbitrators. Applying German law, the Supreme Court then made a distinction between faults of the arbitrators in connection with the making of the award and faults in connection with activities 'which do not pertain to the decisional process.'

With regard to faults in connection with the making of the award, the arbitrators may enjoy the 'judge privilege' (*Richterprivileg*),[88] if not on the basis of German law (Art. 839/2 of the BGB – the German Civil Code), then on the basis of their contractual position. This privilege, the Court held, does not extend, however, to acts of the arbitrator which do not pertain to the making of the award. Focusing on Article 17 of the Rules of the arbitral institution, the Supreme Court held that under German law a party may object to unfair standard clauses not only when these were formulated by the other party, but also when these solely serve the interests of the other party. The Supreme Court added:

> 'Even the exemption from liability for ordinary negligence vis-à-vis a merchant is invalid if it concerns an essential contractual obligation of the party supplying the standard conditions in the sense of Sect. 9(2) second sentence of the ABGB [German Act on General Conditions]... There is no doubt that the arbitrator's obligation towards the parties in the arbitration, to be objective and to treat them equally, is an essential obligation arising out of the parties' agreement with the arbitrators... .'[89]

Although the Supreme Court did not render a decision on the merits, it clearly took a position holding that an institutional rule excluding all liability of the arbitrators cannot be conclusive.

What these two cases give is some guidance, but no direct answer to the question whether deficiencies pertaining to translation during the arbitration

---

[88] The 'judge privilege' means restriction of the liability of the judge to cases of intentional misapplication of the law.

[89] *Yearbook Commercial Arbitration*, Vol. XXVI (2001) at p. 228.

proceedings may result in liability of the arbitrator or of the arbitral institution. Assuming that Article 34 of the ICC Rules and similar rules are no perfect shield and cannot fully exclude the liability of the institution on ground of the *contrat d'organisation d'arbitrage* (or the liability of the arbitrators on ground of the *receptum arbitri*), the question arises what liability would come into question in connection with mistranslation which is the fault of the translator hired by the arbitrators or the arbitral institution, or what liability might emerge as a consequence of lack of translation.[90] Usually the parties would advance the costs of translation. Suppose the arbitrators order translation of a document, hire a translator, and pay this translator from the funds advanced by the parties. If the translation turns out to be substandard and a new translation must be ordered, should this be paid for again by the parties, or should the costs be shouldered by the arbitrators who made an ill-advised initial choice? Or let us raise a more consequential question: if the award is set aside, or if recognition is denied because of a deficiency pertaining to translation, can the arbitrators be held liable? (Could they, for example be sued for the costs of the proceedings?)

There are not many cases in which arbitrators have been sued for damages – and there are even fewer cases in which such damages have been granted. My research has not revealed any case in which the arbitrators have been sued on the grounds of some shortcoming pertaining to translation. The French and the Austrian case suggest that all liability cannot be effectively excluded. At the same time, it might paralyze any mechanism of dispute settlement if the decision-makers could be held personally liable for any decision which other decision-makers consider to be a wrong one. A standard reflecting a reasonable compromise is needed, but there is no such standard in international enactments. The solution has been left to the norms of the applicable municipal law, which – as demonstrated by the Austrian case – need not be the *lex fori*. A standard which may conceivably serve as a model is that adopted in Section 29(1) of the 1996 Arbitration Act for England, Northern Ireland and Wales (hereinafter 'English Arbitration Act'), which states:

> 'An arbitrator is not liable for anything done or omitted in the discharge or purported discharge of his functions as arbitrator unless the act or omission is shown to have been in bad faith.'

Envisaging possible situations in which liability of the arbitrator (or of the arbitral institution) may hinge on a deficiency pertaining to translation, it should be pointed out that the type of deficiency has, of course, an influence on the pos-

---

[90] Theoretically, liability for translation un-called for might also emerge, but the practical relevance of this problem is negligible.

sible consequences. If mistranslation is at issue, one should note the fact that – as stated earlier – cases in which a mistranslation is not noticed during the arbitral proceedings are rare. If this nevertheless happens, all parties might bear some responsibility. If the (in)correctness of the translation was noticed and discussed, and the arbitrators then accept one of the confronted positions in their award, they should be covered by the *Richterprivileg*.

If the translation prepared by a translator commissioned by the arbitrators turns out to be defective and a new translation is commissioned during the proceedings, the consequences are not grave. In this particular case, however, the solution adopted in the former Basel and Zürich rules (according to which the arbitral tribunal will decide on the distribution of the costs and risks of erroneous translation) does not appear to be best suited. In this situation the financing of the substitute translation by the arbitrators themselves (or by the arbitral institution) emerges as a sensible option. This option could be adopted by the arbitrators themselves, but courts should also be free to reach such decisions after considering all relevant circumstances (including whether the translator chosen was a person who otherwise had a fair reputation).

If lack of translation is in the focus, the liability of the arbitrators could, in principle, be more obvious, because lack of translation is more obvious than mistranslation. But it is difficult to envision a real-life case in which arbitrators might be held liable, particularly if one adopts the standard that only acting in bad faith could trigger liability. It is just not likely that the arbitrators would deny translation in a situation in which a party really needs it and claims it. Such a situation might conceivably emerge if we are dealing with translation between closely-related languages – the issue addressed in the concluding subchapter – but here the question arises whether lack of translation is indeed consequential.

E. The Issue of the Hidden Anchor Language (When the Original Is Actually a Translation)

In the domain of international transactions, contracts are often drafted in a language which is not the native language of any of the parties to the contract. A Danish principal and a Greek agent may very well choose English as the language of their agency agreement. A Croatian seller and a Polish buyer may execute a sales agreement in German. An Austrian seller has a standard contract in German, but translates it into English in order to offer it to a Moscow customer who prefers to deal in English (if not in Russian). In such situations, the original signed by the parties is actually a translation, and the language from which such translation was made remains hidden. Drafting contracts in a third language may imply translation in a literal sense. The lawyer of the Croatian seller prepares a draft in Croatian and sends it to the client company, this company gives it to its own translator or hires an outside translator to prepare the German version. The parties will discuss the German text until they reach a final (German) version. This final version becomes the original of the contract. The Croatian draft which represented the starting point never reaches the other party and does not become a part of the documents of the transaction. The primary version is even more hidden if the Croatian lawyer, relying on his/her command of German, prepares an initial draft in German (and possibly checks grammar with a linguist). In this case, there is no Croatian original on paper, but Croatian is still the actual starting point – one may call it the **anchor language**. If the anchor point during the drafting of the German-language contract is Croatian, the lawyer will try to find German equivalents for Croatian terms and phrases he/she is familiar with.[91] When there is no actual draft prepared in the first language of the lawyer who does the drafting, one cannot speak of translation in a literal sense, but the product is very much akin to that of a translation.

The original may also remain hidden when the language of the contract is not a third language, it is the language of one of the parties, but the draft is prepared by the other party. For example, the contract is concluded between a US and a Finnish party, and the Finnish party is the one who submits the first version. (In such situations, it also matters how much negotiation will actually take place and how much effort will be invested by the native speaker party in scrutinizing the language of the contract.) The question arises whether the anchor version of a contract (or of a phrase in a contract) may gain relevance before the arbitrators (or before a court).

To bring the issue closer, I would like to mention a case in which one of the parties contemplated arbitration, and I was asked to give an opinion about the arbitration clause. This was a 1997 contract concluded between a UK and a Hungarian party. In a legal sense, English was clearly the original. Section 1.3 of the Contract entitled 'Language of contract, number of copies', stated: 'This contract was produced in 2 (two) original copies in English.' The Hungarian party investigated the option to submit a claim to the Foreign Trade Court of Arbitration at the Hungarian Chamber of Commerce and Industry. The basis of jurisdiction would have been Section 9 of the Contract under the heading 'Arbitration', which contained the following somewhat baffling text: 'Legal disputes shall be settled by the chosen court accepted by the Hungarian Chamber of

---

[91] This will be the case unless the person who is drafting a contract on a third language has a near perfect command of that third language, and is well acquainted with legal practice on that third language.

Commerce.' The question arose whether this was a valid arbitration clause. Let me add that the Hungarian term for arbitration is *választottbíróság* – which literally translated means 'chosen court'. In all probability, the contract was drafted in Hungarian, and was translated by a non-lawyer, who came up with the grammatically correct – but rather misleading – translation: 'chosen court'. Let me also mention that the heading of Section 1.3 of the Contract read 'Governing right in contract'. This can again be better understood with reliance on the anchor language. In Hungarian the same term, *jog*, is used for both the words 'right' and 'law'.[92] What was meant was the 'governing law'. Under the heading 'Governing right in contract' Section 1.2 read: 'As for the contract, its interpretation as well as for the legal relations between Parties the law in the Hungarian Republic is the guiding principle.' (The anchor term for 'guiding principle' was probably the Hungarian word *irányadó* which means 'applicable' in a legal context but which may also be translated as 'guiding' or 'giving direction'.)

The question arose whether this was a pathological clause beyond repair or just an imperfect clause which nevertheless represented an arbitration agreement in writing which provided for the jurisdiction of the Budapest Court of Arbitration. '[C]hosen court accepted by the Hungarian Chamber of Commerce' does not make much sense. The heading of Section 9 ('Arbitration') might have provided helpful guidance, but the Contract limited the reliability of such guidance by adopting a rather unusual provision in Section 1.4 entitled 'Section headings'. The provision read: 'Section headings do not restrict, amend or touch the sense of the contract.' It thus became an important issue whether the anchor language could be taken into consideration, which would reveal that 'chosen court' was actually an unfortunate literal translation of 'választottbíróság', i.e., arbitration. Once 'chosen court' is replaced by 'arbitration', the arbitration clause becomes rather unequivocal.[93] In this case, the question remained open, because the dispute was settled before it would have reached the arbitrators.

In another quite similar case – again between a Hungarian and a UK party – the arbitration clause in the 'Mutual Agreement' read: 'In case of controversial matters the parties determine the selected court, which operates next to the Chamber of Commerce in Budapest.' Again, the parties did not get the name of the

[92] Just like the term *droit* in French, or the term *Recht* in German.

[93] The name of the institution is less than fully adequate, but the incompleteness is not misleading. The full name is: 'Hungarian Chamber of Commerce and Industry' rather than 'Hungarian Chamber of Commerce', but such imperfections are normally tolerated. There is only one institutional arbitration in Hungary dealing with international disputes, and this is the Court of Arbitration at the Hungarian Chamber of Commerce and Industry. The 'accepted by' language is also the result of an imperfect translation, but it does not undermine a basic understanding.

institution exactly right, which is a fairly common problem.[94] What is more important for our present purposes is that we have again a literal translation of the Hungarian term *választottbíróság* – this time as 'selected court' (instead of 'chosen court'). This case reached the Budapest Court of Arbitration. An oral hearing was held, but the UK respondent failed to appear (although it was duly notified). The absence of the UK party made it more difficult to clarify the intentions of the parties. As stated in the English language Award, Claimant offered the following explanation:

> '[t]he designation "selected court which operates next to the Chamber of Commerce in Budapest" is a literal translation. The Hungarian term "választottbíróság" means arbitration, but its literal translation is "selected court". Furthermore, "Chamber of Commerce in Budapest" can only mean the Hungarian Chamber of Commerce and Industry, since in Hungary no other chamber of commerce has a court of arbitration.'[95]

The arbitrators raised the question whether a valid arbitration agreement existed, and stated:

> 'Scrutinizing the wording of the "Mutual Agreement" the arbitrators were faced with another example of clauses falling into the category labeled "clauses pathologiques" by Eisemann. This leads to the difficult question of the limits of the power of the arbitrators in seeking the "true intent" of the parties beyond (or even in spite of) what the parties actually wrote. It is the opinion of the arbitrators, that the arbitration agreement must possess in itself a minimum level of coherence in order to serve as a foothold for a search after the true intentions of the parties.'[96]

Referring specifically to the 'selected court' language, the arbitrators stated further on:

> 'The wording of the arbitration clause does not make much sense otherwise but on the assumption that this is a translation of a Hungarian draft – which translation actually conveyed the words, more so than the meaning.'

---

[94] See on arbitration clauses which contain an imperfect designation of the institution, Várady, Arbitration Despite of the Parties?, in *Law and Reality* (in Honour of C.C.A. Voskuil) (M. Nijhoff Publ. 1992) pp. 351-376.

[95] Award of May 21, 2002 in Case No. Vb/01181 – unpublished.

[96] Award of May 21, 2002, No. Vb/01181 – at p. 4 (unpublished).

Eventually, the arbitrators found that they had no jurisdiction, but for reasons other than the imperfect reference to the arbitral institution.[97] It appears from the wording of the award that the 'selected court' language may not in itself have justified refusal of jurisdiction.

In real life international commercial contracts, it happens with some frequency that a mistranslation becomes part of the original. In many cases this will not yield true misunderstandings which might influence the outcome of the dispute, but in some cases, genuine dilemmas emerge. Observance of the hidden anchor language may indeed help the arbitrators to understand the true intentions of the parties.[98] But the issue is not a simple one. In the cases mentioned above, the intentions of the party whose language is the hidden language were quite evident. If the Hungarian term for arbitration is *választottbíróság*, i.e., 'chosen court' or 'selected court' in literal translation, then it is crystal clear what the Hungarian party had in mind. Had the other party to the agreement been a Croatian party, the situation would have been quite unequivocal. The Croatian term for arbitration is *izbrani sud*, which also means 'selected court' in a literal translation. In such a situation, reaching after the hidden anchor language is not much more than reaching after the obvious.

But in our cases, the agreement was concluded between a Hungarian and a UK party. What were the intentions and the perception of the UK party? It is quite obvious that the English native speaker party did not devote much attention to the language of the contract in either of the two cases mentioned above. It happens – unfortunately with some frequency – that contracts are concluded without sufficient scrutiny. Normally, the party that failed to devote attention to the wording but signed the contract will be bound. Will it also be bound by an arbitration agreement which refers to a chosen (or selected) court? Let us repeat that a party is normally bound by what is written in a clause, even if he/she failed to scrutinize it (though having had the opportunity to scrutinize it). The situation is somewhat different when one has to reach towards an anchor language in order to establish the proper meaning of a contractual provision. If the literal translation offers a plausible option as it stands, the party who has no command of the anchor language may possibly insist on this option, arguing that he/she was misled (led to trust the meaning flowing from the literal transla-

97 The dispute was between two companies, while the 'Mutual Agreement' containing the arbitration clause was signed by two natural persons, without indicating the names of the legal persons they represented; furthermore, the 'Mutual Agreement' was an agency agreement, while the subject matter of the dispute arose from a sales contract.

98 It is understood that, given the formal requirements, more caution and restraint needs to be exercised when the provision at issue is not just an ordinary provision in the contract but the arbitration clause.

tion). Bona fide reliance on the literal meaning may block an examination of the anchor language. In the cases referred to above, however, it would have been difficult for the UK party to argue that it did not know that 'chosen court' meant arbitration. In the given context, this argument would not have been persuasive (particularly not when the heading of the clause reads, in English, 'arbitration'). It would also be quite difficult for the English speaking party to explain what **did** it have in mind. In the case which ended with the May 2002 award, the English party did not show up at the oral hearing, and thus could not offer any explanation. Had the party appeared, it may have confirmed that both parties meant arbitration. Explaining any other meaning would have been quite difficult. It just would not sound plausible to argue that by saying that '[t]he parties determine the selected court, which operates next to the Chamber of Commerce in Budapest', the parties actually meant to submit disputes to a court which is identified by being in the proximity of the Budapest Chamber of Commerce. Even though arbitration clauses have to be interpreted with more caution, in these Hungarian cases it is difficult to see any plausible interpretation which could have blocked resort to the anchor language.

When the anchor language is not hidden

Problems might also emerge when the anchor language is not hidden. I would like to cite here a clause from a 2004 contract submitted to me for an opinion. The contract was executed between two businessmen, both of Ukrainian origin, one of them residing in the Netherlands, the other in the Ukraine. Their contract was drafted and executed in both Russian and in English. The text was printed in two columns; the Russian text appeared on the left side, while the English text was on the right side. Both versions were signed and stamped by the parties at the bottom of the last page. Article 9 of the Contract read in Russian:

> '9. Претензии и споры.
> 9.1. Претензии и споры, относящиеся к выполнению настоящего контракта, будут решаться сторонами путем переговоров и консультаций.
> 9.2. В случае отсутствия приемлемого для сторон решения споры подлежат разрешению в судебном порядке.
> 9.3. Судебные разбирательства происходят по месту нахождения ответчика.
> 9.4. Решения суда являются окончательными и обязательными для обеих сторон.'

I am giving here a translation which was checked and verified by a Russian lawyer and S.J.D student:[99]

---

[99] Ms. Yulia Guseva, J.D. Orenburg, M.A Central European University Budapest, S.J.D. candidate.

> '9. Claims and disputes.
> 9.1. Claims and disputes related to the performance of this contract shall be settled by the parties by means of negotiations and consultations.
> 9.2. In case of absence of a solution acceptable to the parties, the disputes shall be resolved in court.
> 9.3. The court proceedings shall take place at the place of the defendant.
> 9.4. The decision of the court shall be final and binding on both parties.'

The English text in the actual contract was, however, different, and the differences in question are not merely differences in style – particularly not with regard to Section 9.2. Article 9 printed in the right column of the Contract read:

> '9. Claims and debates
> 9.1 All disputes, which may arise out or in connection with the present Contract, shall be settled by means of negotiations between the Parties.
> 9.2 If the Parties cannot come to the agreement, then such a dispute can be settled by arbitration.
> 9.3 The place of dispute settlement is of defendant location place.
> 9.4 The award of the arbitration shall be final and binding upon the Parties.'

Let me add that the parties did not agree on a controlling version of the contract; they stated instead in Article 10 of the Contract that the two versions (Russian and English) have equal value.

The problem is, of course, that according to the Russian text, if the parties cannot reach a negotiated settlement the dispute shall be resolved by courts in the country of the defendant – and at the same time the equally authentic English text of the Contract provided for arbitration. The question is whether one could treat one of the two texts as the **anchor** version in a situation when both languages are equally visible and equally authentic. The problem is in essence the same as in the case of the hidden anchor language. The authentic text (in our case one of the authentic texts) is actually a translation, and reliance on the anchor might reveal the content which the parties had in mind at the time of the making of the contract. In this case the circumstances indicate that English was not the first language of the parties, and one can rather safely assume that the stipulations were originally not shaped in English but in Russian. This follows from the background of the parties, and the same conclusion is supported by a linguistic comparison of the two texts. (In this case, we are talking about a very simple linguistic comparison, which is within the abilities even of a non-linguist and even of a non-native-speaker.) For example the sentence stating that 'The place of dispute settlement is of defendant location domicile', certainly does not look like the original but rather like a not-too-successful translation. Identifying one of the two languages as an anchor language may again be a way out of the impasse – and may indicate with a rather high probability which version reflects the actual intent of the parties, i.e., whether the parties actually contemplated arbitration or litigation.

In his book on translation into English, Alan McConnell Duff introduces a chapter on meaning and ambiguity with a phrase of Orwell: 'What is above all needed is to let the meaning choose the word, and not the other way around.'[100] Taking 'chosen court' and similar products at their face value, leads us to an Orwellian result: words are choosing meaning. Therefore, in cases in which the translation conveys the words rather than the meaning, dependence on the anchor language appears to more sensible than letting the literally-translated word determine the meaning. Reliance on the anchor language may be compared with reliance on legislative history. Legislative history, just like reliance on the anchor language, take us back to the environment in which the rules were crafted, and there it may be more easy to re-discover the intended meaning. Following this approach, we need not remain baffled, for example, with a provision excluding *dommages par conséquence* in a French contract when it is known that there is a hidden English anchor which in all likelihood referred to 'consequential damages'. Behind 'one-time orders' in an English contract one may discover *einstweilige Verfügungen*, meaning provisional measures in German. Reaching after the hidden anchor language mandates caution, but it is a rational device of contract interpretation when contracts are being shaped in a multilingual environment.

F. The Issue of Closely Related Languages – Reflections on a Bulgarian Case

F.1. An introductory observation

Translation is normally needed to bridge the gap between the language skills of a party (or of an arbitrator) and the language actually used in the arbitration proceedings. If a participant in the proceedings has a command of, say, German and English, and the language of arbitration (or the language of a document) is Japanese, one needs translation. This is the simple assumption on which discussions on translation are based. We have seen that this assumption leads to a number of intricate issues, including those connected with the ways of organizing and effecting translation, or those connected with deficiencies pertaining to

[100] Alan McConnell Duff, *Into English – Writing and Translating into English as a Second Language* (Ljubljana 2000) Chapter VII: 'Meaning and Ambiguity', p. 133.

translation. Bridging the gap between the language abilities of a participant and the language used in the proceedings makes sense if the gap exists. Speaking of shortcomings of translation and of consequences of lack of translation or mistranslation also makes sense if there was a need for translation.

But in some cases, the basic assumption is tainted by controversies. It is not always obvious that one needs translation if the language of arbitration is not his/her native language, and he/she never studied the language of arbitration as a second language either. If one speaks German and English, and the language of arbitration is Japanese, than yes, one obviously needs translation. But what if one speaks Norwegian and the language of arbitration is Swedish? Or one speaks Serbian and the language of arbitration is Croatian? There are distinct but closely-related languages, and the question arises whether translation is actually needed (and makes sense) between such languages, and whether lack of translation amounts to a deficiency in such a situation. I would like to approach this problem through a Bulgarian case which has not received much publicity outside Bulgaria and Macedonia, yet which offers a most interesting insight into the problem of closely-related languages.

Let me also mention in this introductory note that this subchapter also serves as an introduction to the next chapter, since we shall have to consider positions taken in post-award proceedings as well in order to be able to demonstrate the problem.

F.2. **The facts of the Bulgarian case**

In a quite interesting – and controversial – Bulgarian case, lack of translation between Macedonian and Bulgarian represented the cause for refusal of enforcement, and for setting aside. In *Continental Export-Import (Macedonia) v. Pharmachim (Bulgaria)*,[101] arbitration took place in Sofia, under the Rules of the Court of Arbitration at the Bulgarian Chamber of Commerce and Industry. Both parties appointed an arbitrator (the Claimant appointed Professor Strezovski from Macedonia, the Respondent appointed Mr. Laskov from Bulgaria), and thereafter the party-appointed arbitrators chose Professor Tadjer (from Bulgaria) to act as chairman of the arbitral tribunal. The first hearing was held on July 10, 1990. Minutes were taken in Bulgarian by a stenographer. These minutes show

[101] The case was not published. The author expresses thanks to Professor Arsen Janevski from the University of Skoplje Faculty of Law and to Ms. Vera Atanasovska an attorney from Bitola, Macedonia, for sending copies of the Bulgarian court decisions. Translations which appear in the text were made by the author with the help of Bulgarian graduate students Ms. Bogdana Georgieva from Emory University Atlanta, and Mr. Mihail Danov from the Central European University, Budapest.

that Chairman Tadjer stated in his first sentence after opening the hearing the following: 'Since the representative of the Claimant is a Yugoslav citizen who does not understand Bulgarian well enough, the arbitral tribunal appoints Ms. Dessislava Slavova as interpreter from Bulgarian into Serbo-Croatian and vice versa.' After the first hearing four more oral hearings were held, but the services of the interpreter were no longer used.

At this point a few sentences are needed to explain the background of the case. In 1990, the Socialist Federal Republic of Yugoslavia (the 'SFRY') still existed. One of the six constituent republics of the SFRY was Macedonia. There were several official languages in the SFRY, including Serbo-Croatian and Macedonian. Serbo-Croatian was by far the most widely spoken language.[102] What makes this case even more complex is that after the award was rendered but before the start of post-award proceedings, on November 17, 1991 Macedonia became an independent State under the name 'Former Yugoslav Republic of Macedonia'. In the Former Yugoslav Republic of Macedonia, Serbo-Croatian is no longer an official language. Nevertheless, it was safe to assume that both the Macedonian arbitrator (Prof. Strezovski) and the attorney for the Claimant (Mr. Shopov) had an adequate command of Serbo-Croatian.[103] It is equally safe to assume that the first language of the Macedonian participants was Macedonian. It is common ground that Bulgarian and Macedonian are very similar. One of the (many) issues in ethnic disputes on the Balkans is whether Macedonian is actually a separate language, or whether it is just Bulgarian with a regional touch. Today, Macedonian is recognized as a distinct language (or, at least, this is officially not contested in Bulgaria), but the fact remains that Macedonians and Bulgarians can communicate with each other without real difficulty.

Returning to the case, let me just say that after several hearings and exchange of briefs, a unanimous award was rendered on June 17, 1991. By this Award, the Bulgarian Respondent was obliged to pay to the Claimant US$ 500,013.50 with costs and interest, while other claims and counterclaims were denied. Language and translation – or rather the lack of translation – emerged as issues during post-award court proceedings. The fact that closely-related languages were at issue gave an added spin to the arguments presented. During post-award proceedings, the sequence of facts pertaining to translation was

---

[102] After the dissolution of the SFRY, the Serbo-Croatian language was also dissolved. Today it is called Serbian in Serbia and Montenegro, Croatian in Croatia, and Bosnian in Bosnia and Herzegovina. There is an initiative to name 'Montenegrin' the language used in Montenegro. There are differences, but these do not impede mutual understanding.

[103] As a matter of fact, the author participated with Professor Strezovski in several arbitration cases conducted in Serbo-Croatian in Belgrade.

shaped into two narratives: one wrought in the enforcement proceedings, and the other adopted by the Bulgarian courts following a motion to set aside.

F.3. The perception which emerged in enforcement proceedings

The Macedonian Claimant sought execution of the award by a leave of enforcement under Article 49 of the 1988 Bulgarian Law on International Commercial Arbitration (hereinafter 'LICA').[104] The Respondent opposed enforcement alleging that the arbitration tribunal lacked jurisdiction and pointing out that translation was not provided for during the arbitration proceedings. We shall concentrate on the objection pertaining to lack of translation (the objection regarding jurisdiction was rejected). The Bulgarian party (Pharmachim) explained that translation was provided during the first hearing, but was not provided during four subsequent hearings. What the Bulgarian party had to explain was how this alleged shortcoming amounted to a ground for denying recognition. According to Pharmachim, this represented a violation of Article 47(1)(5) of the 1988 Bulgarian Arbitration Act (LICA).[105] Article 47(1)(5) states:

> '[The award may be set aside...if...] the composition of the arbitral tribunal or the arbitral procedure was not in accordance with the agreement of the parties unless this agreement is in conflict with a mandatory provision of this law, or failing such agreement, was not in accordance with the provisions of this law.'[106]

---

[104] The 1988 Bulgarian Law on International Commercial Arbitration (Published in the *State Gazette* No. 60 of August 5, 1988) is one of the very first arbitration acts modeled after the UNCITRAL Model Law, although it did not strictly follow the Model Law regarding recognition and enforcement. At the time of enforcement proceedings (1992) Art. 49 of the LICA described the claim for enforcement, while Art. 50 stated the reasons for which enforcement may be denied. Both provisions were abrogated by the amendments of November 1993 (*State Gazette* No. 93 of November 2, 1993). Under the present version of the LICA, awards made in Bulgaria enjoy res judicata effect without any recognition proceedings before State courts.

[105] Art. 47 actually deals with setting aside rather than recognition and enforcement, but Art. 50(1/1) which deals with recognition, states the recognition may also be denied on the grounds of Art. 47.

[106] This provision follows the wording of Art. V(1)(d) of the New York Convention and that of Art. 34 of the Model Law. The only difference is the explicit stipulation with respect to a possible conflict between the rules of procedure established by the parties and the *lex arbitri*. Today, this provision does not apply anymore with regard to domestic awards. One has to point out that Art. 47 of the Bulgarian act actually deals with setting aside. This is not the exact setting of the first post-arbitration proceeding which was a proceeding for confirmation (enforcement) of the award. Of course, it is quite common in comparative law to seek setting aside in proceedings for confirmation, opposing the move for confirmation. In this case, however, after the proceedings for confirmation (enforcement), separate proceedings for setting aside took place. An explanation may be in the fact that the 1988 version of the LICA provided for a scrutiny of domestic awards in enforcement proceedings as well. I shall leave these procedural questions aside, because they do not have an impact on the issues of language and translation.

In this context, lack of translation can possibly be posited either as a violation of party agreement on the arbitral procedure, or as a violation of the provisions 'of this law', i.e., the LICA.

In its decision of September 21, 1992, the City Court of Sofia upheld the objection pertaining to lack of translation and stated:

> 'It is evident from the protocol of the arbitration session of 10.07.1990 that the arbitral tribunal appointed an interpreter for translation from Bulgarian into Serbo-Croatian and vice versa. Even though in this protocol the appointment was motivated by the fact that the representative of the claimant did not understand Bulgarian well enough, the assistance of the interpreter was in the interest of all participants of the lawsuit in view of normal communication during the presentation of positions and consideration of evidence. It is evident from the protocols that no interpreter participated at subsequent hearings up until the conclusion of the proceedings. The absence of an interpreter when an arbitrator, an expert and some witnesses were foreign citizens and spoke a language different from Bulgarian which was explicitly specified as the language of the arbitration proceedings, is to be viewed as a serious violation of the arbitration procedure, on ground of which the respondent objected, and on this ground the claim for a leave of enforcement of the Award of 17 June 1991 is denied.'

This statement exposes the following perception of facts and shortcomings pertaining to the language of the proceedings. The language of the arbitral proceedings was 'explicitly specified'. This language was Bulgarian. Accordingly, translation should have taken place to and from Bulgarian. Since there was no such translation, Article 47(1)(5) was violated, which speaks of 'arbitral procedure not in accordance with…'.

The question arises how Article 47(1)(5) exactly became relevant. Do we have here arbitral procedure not in accordance with the LICA, or arbitral procedure not in accordance with party stipulation? Article 47(1)(5) allows set-aside if the arbitral procedure was not in accordance with the agreement of the parties, or failing such agreement, was not in accordance with the provisions of the LICA.[107] The court says that Bulgarian was 'explicitly specified' as the language of arbitration, but this was not followed by the arbitrators. Having this in mind, it would be difficult to argue that the procedure was not in accordance with the LICA, because there is no provision in the LICA which would 'explicitly specify' Bulgarian as the language of the arbitral proceedings. Such determination may have resulted from the order of the arbitrators at the first hearing,

---

[107] Let me repeat that we are now talking about enforcement rather than set aside proceedings, but according to Art. 50 of the LICA, Art. 47 was also applicable in recognition proceedings.

or from the Rules of the Court of Arbitration at the Bulgarian Chamber of Commerce (hereinafter 'BCCI' or Bulgarian Rules) which posited Bulgarian as a default language.[108] The position taken in the decision of the Sofia City Court is more compatible with the assumption that it was the agreement of the parties that the arbitrators departed from. One may argue that the agreement of the parties yielded (indirectly) the establishment of Bulgarian as the language of the proceedings. (Because the parties gave power to the arbitrators to make decisions, and/or because the institutional rules chosen by the parties – and providing for Bulgarian as a default language – may be perceived as a part of party agreement.)

The question still remains how the explicit (or if not explicit, then indirectly made) party agreement was infringed. There was no translation from Bulgarian to Serbo-Croatian (except during the first hearing). Can this represent a violation of Article 47(1)(5)? Hardly so. If Bulgarian was spoken, the assumed party agreement pertaining to language was properly observed. The only question which could have been raised was whether the right of the Macedonian party to present its case was thereby impaired. This would not belong, however, under Article 47(1)(5), and such issue could only be raised by the party whose rights were supposedly infringed.[109] In other words, it was for to the Macedonian party to assess whether it could follow proceedings in Bulgarian, and to insist on translation had it concluded that it needed such assistance in presenting its case. The Macedonian party never raised such an issue. Under these circumstances, absence of translation **from** Bulgarian could not have represented a ground for denying enforcement. Was there a lack of translation **to** Bulgarian? This would make the allegation concerning the violation of Article 47(1)(5) more plausible, and this is, indeed, what is hinted at in the decision of the Sofia City Court, which found that '[a]n arbitrator, an expert and some witnesses were foreign citizens and spoke a language different from Bulgarian'. What language did they speak? Was it Serbo-Croatian? The court says it was 'a language different from Bulgarian'. Summarizing the arguments of the Bulgarian party, the court uses another designation but fails again to name the language. It mentions that the Bulgarian party objected that the representative of the Claim-

[108] According to Art. 16 of the 1989 version of the BCCI Rules that was applicable at the time of the dispute: 'The hearings of the case shall be made [sic] in Bulgarian. By agreement with the parties an arbitral hearing could also be made [sic] in another language.'

[109] This point was made by A. Janevski in his comments on this case ('Language of Arbitration as a Ground for Non-Enforcement and Setting Aside: Tracing a Bulgarian Case', 5 *Croatian Arbitration Yearbook* (1998) 101. Janevski states that the Respondent '[c]alled upon the violation that jeopardized the position of the claimant, but not his own rights, since the proceedings were conducted in Bulgarian', at p. 108.

ant, one of the members of the arbitration tribunal, one of the experts and two witnesses were citizens of the former[110] Yugoslavia, and 'spoke in their native language'. This 'language different from Bulgarian' or 'native language' was in all likelihood Macedonian. Whether the designation 'Macedonian language' was purposefully avoided is difficult to say. The Balkans are full of conflicts and sensitivities relating to identity.[111] (And not only the Balkans.) There has been (or, at least, there was) a Bulgarian–Macedonian debate regarding the issue whether Macedonian is actually a separate language, and it is conceivable that the Bulgarian courts wanted to avoid the identification of Macedonian as a distinct language. Indeed, none of the several court decisions in this case refer to Macedonian language. This may be a matter of style, but other explanations are also conceivable.

Let me repeat that although it is not spelled out explicitly what language the Macedonian actors did speak, there can be hardly any doubt that this was Macedonian. All participants 'from the former Yugoslavia' were participants from Macedonia and had Macedonian names. What is even more indicative, the assumption that they spoke Macedonian may very well explain why there was no translation, and why the Bulgarian party failed to object **during** the arbitration proceedings. If Bulgarian and Macedonian are not identical, they are certainly very close. Assuming that the Bulgarians were speaking Bulgarian, and the Macedonians were speaking Macedonian, one could understand why was translation not requested by any party after the first hearing. Had the Macedonian participants spoken Serbo-Croatian, it is difficult to imagine that the Bulgarian party would not have objected during four full hearings after the first one. It is also most difficult to imagine that the arbitrators (two of whom were Bulgarian) would have failed to notice that some participants were speaking a language which was not understood by the Bulgarian party (probably not understood by themselves either), and that they would have failed to order translation had they noted that this was needed.

---

[110] By the time of the enforcement proceedings the SFRY ceased to exist.

[111] An excellent contemporary analysis of conflicting identities and conflicting legends regarding identities was given by Ms. Adela Peeva, a Bulgarian author, in her documentary movie 'Whose is this song' which won in 2003 and 2004 a number of European awards. The main storyline of Adela Peeva's, 'Whose is this song' is the following. The author listens to a song in a group of people having different nationalities, and everybody believes that the song belongs to his/her culture. After this, the author travels to Istanbul, to the Greek island of Lesbos, to Albania, to Bosnia, to Macedonia, to Serbia, and finally to her home country, Bulgaria. The song is known everywhere, among villagers, among musicians, and among experts. The music is the same and everybody likes it. Every person is convinced that the song belongs to the tradition of his/her ethnic group, that it is undoubtedly a traditional Turkish, (Greek Albanian, Bosniac, Serbian, Bulgarian) song and that the others are just trying to snatch it. No one has doubts.

Taking the – I believe quite safe – assumption that the Macedonian participants spoke Macedonian and no translation was provided into Bulgarian, the question arises whether this might amount to a reason for denying recognition. This is the juncture where translation (or lack of translation) between closely-related languages becomes a specific issue.

The Bulgarian party chose to rely on Article 47(1)(5) of the LICA. Reliance on this argument could be further explained in the following terms. The arbitrators ordered translation from Bulgarian to Serbo-Croatian and *vice versa*, such translation was only effected during the first of the five hearings, and this leads to the argument that 'the arbitral procedure was not in accordance with the agreement of the parties'. This argument is supported by the understanding referred to above, that the term 'agreement of the parties' may be interpreted in an extended way to encompass provisions of the institutional rules chosen by the parties, and to encompass the procedural orders issued by the arbitrators (who also derive their authority from party agreement). We have here, however, a big stumbling block – and this is the issue of waiver, or lack of objection. The Bulgarian party did not object on the grounds of lack of translation during four hearings; it only raised this issue in the enforcement proceedings (after an award was rendered in favor of the Macedonian party). This amounts to waiver.[112] The LICA takes a very clear position with regard to waiver. According to Article 5:

> 'A party which knows that any provision of this Law from which the parties may derogate or that any requirement under the arbitration agreement has not been complied with and yet proceeds with the arbitration without stating its objection, cannot rely on the non-compliance.'

Thus, Article 5 of the LICA clearly states that a party cannot rely on non-compliance with party agreement if this party was aware of the non-compliance, yet proceeded without objection. Under the circumstances of the case it appears that Article 5 should have been conclusive. Reliance on waiver is particularly justified in a situation where the irregularity against which no objection was raised did not actually yield a meaningful disadvantage. Lack of translation between closely related (and mutually understandable) languages is an obvious example of such a situation.

---

[112] A point also made by Janevski, op. cit. at p. 109.

F.4. The perception which emerged in setting aside proceedings

After enforcement was denied, the Bulgarian party attempted to confirm victory, and moved to set aside the award. Like its opposition to enforcement, its motion to set aside was also based on Article 47(1)(5) of the LICA, but with a different emphasis. While in enforcement proceedings the emphasis was on 'proceedings not in accordance with the agreement of the parties', this time it was stressed that the arbitral procedure was not in accordance with the *lex arbitri* (the LICA). In its December 12, 1992 motion for annulment, the Bulgarian party alleged that an infringement of Articles 22 and 26 of the LICA has taken place.[113]

In its motion of December 12, 1992, Pharmachim (the Bulgarian party) articulated the well-known facts the following way: On the first oral hearing, translation was ordered and effected from Bulgarian to Serbo–Croatian and *vice versa*, but this arrangement was not heeded during four later hearings, and this failure 'seriously encumbered and delayed the proceedings'. Pharmachim argued further that one of the arbitrators and other participants on the Claimant's side were Yugoslav citizens, and that they acted without a translation. A new detail was added to this argument. The Bulgarian party explained that statements made by the Macedonian actors were 'rendered for the protocol in Bulgarian, by the Chairman of the Arbitral Tribunal' (Professor Tadjer). In the opinion of the Bulgarian party the principle of equality of the parties set in Article 22 of the LICA was violated. The argument was also made that Article 26 of the LICA was violated, because the arbitrators did not determine the language of the proceedings (for the oral hearings after the first one.)

This line of argument was accepted by the Sofia City Court on July 22, 1994,[114] and it was confirmed by the Supreme Court of Bulgaria on February 20, 1995.[115] The Sofia City Court held that since the parties did not agree on the language of the proceedings

> '[i]t was the duty of the arbitral tribunal by virtue of Article 26 of the LICA to determine the language. This was not done, moreover, the hearing of July 10, 1990 was assisted by an interpreter, but the subsequent hearings were conducted without such assistance. Thus the parties were not granted equal opportunities for

---

[113] Art. 22 sets the principle that the parties have to be treated with equality, while Art. 26 states that failing party agreement, the arbitral tribunal shall determine the language of the proceedings.

[114] Decision No. 168 of the Sofia City Court of July 22, 1994.

[115] Supreme Court of Bulgaria, Third Civil Law Chamber, Decision No. 141 of February 20, 1995.

> participation in the proceedings and for the defense of their rights, and thereby the law applicable to the arbitration procedure was violated. A ground for setting aside exists under Art. 47 para. 1 point 5 of the LICA, and for this reason the award in of the Court of Arbitration at the Bulgarian Chamber of Commerce and Industry in Arbitration Case No. 223/89 has to be set aside.'

The Macedonian party appealed, but the Supreme Court of Bulgaria confirmed the annulment. In its decision of February 20, 1995 the Supreme Court stated that in the absence of party agreement, the language of the arbitral proceedings should have been determined by the arbitrators, but this was not done. The Supreme Court stated further that:

> 'The majority of the hearings were held without the assistance of an interpreter, written evidence was not accompanied by a Bulgarian translation, the parties were not granted equal opportunities for participation in the proceedings and for defense of their rights. The provision of Article 22 of the LICA was violated. Having this in mind, the decision of the Sofia City Court to set aside [the award] on the grounds of Article 47 para.1 point 5 of the LICA is well-founded and lawful.'

The facts relied upon in the setting aside proceedings are not in contradiction with those that were pointed out in the enforcement proceedings, but there are some new details, and the specifics are linked into a somewhat different narrative. It remains common ground that there was translation (between Bulgarian and Serbo-Croatian) during the first oral hearing, and there was no translation at subsequent hearings. The deficiency which (allegedly) flows from these facts was, however, perceived from a different perspective. During the enforcement proceedings, it was assumed by the Sofia City Court that Bulgarian was indeed set as the language of the arbitral proceedings, yet this was not observed during four oral hearings, and hence the Bulgarian court concluded that Article 47(1)(5) was violated (apparently on the grounds that **the proceeding was not in accordance with the agreement of the parties**). During the setting aside proceedings, the failure to provide for translation during four hearings was seen from a different angle. The Sofia City Court stated that under Article 26 of the LICA, the arbitrators were obliged to determine the language of the arbitral proceedings in the absence of party agreement, but they had failed to do so (meaning presumably that they had failed to do so with regard to four oral hearings). Such non-observance of Article 26 also led to a violation of Article 22 (equal treatment of the parties and full opportunity for each party 'to defend its rights'). Since Articles 22 and 26 of the LICA were violated, **the procedure was not in accordance with the LICA** and thus the condition for annulment under Article 47(1)(5) was met. Within this new narrative, the conclusion is the same, but the basis for the conclusion is different. Article 47(1(5) may be either invoked when the arbitral procedure was not in accordance with the agreement of the parties, or when it was not in accordance with the provisions of the LICA. In the enforcement proceedings it was assumed that the proceeding was not in accordance with the agreement of the parties. In the set aside proceedings a different perception was adopted, and it was stated that the arbitration proceeding was not in accordance with the *lex arbitri* (Art. 22 and 26 of the LICA).

Two basic questions may be raised in connection with the narrative which came to the fore during the set aside proceedings. a) First, whether Article 26 of the LICA was, indeed, infringed (whether the arbitral tribunal failed to determine the language of the proceedings) and b) Second, whether the principle of equal treatment of the parties (set in Article 22 of the LICA) was violated. I would like to address now these two questions:

a) Whether there was a failure to determine the language of the arbitral proceedings in the given case is questionable at best. At the first hearing, the Chairman of the Tribunal ordered translation between Bulgarian and Serbo-Croatian '[S]ince the representative of the Claimant is a Yugoslav citizen who does not understand Bulgarian well enough…'. This wording reveals quite clearly the assumption that Bulgarian was the language of the proceedings and translation was thus ordered because the representative of the Claimant did not speak the language of the proceedings 'well enough'. This assumption is substantiated by Article 16 of the Bulgarian Rules, which provides for Bulgarian as the language of the arbitral proceedings unless the parties agree otherwise. The existence of Article 16 actually contradicts the argument that Article 26 of the LICA was violated. Article 26 of the LICA says that the arbitrators will determine the language of the proceedings if the parties have failed to do so. This provision is simply not applicable whenever arbitration is conducted under BCCI Rules, since these Rules state that Bulgarian will be the language of the proceedings unless the parties agree otherwise. Since the Rules chosen by the parties are considered to be a part of party agreement, and since these Rules provide for a solution, the hypothesis of Article 26 of the LICA (no solution provided by the parties) will simply never materialize if the parties accept arbitration under the BCCI Rules. In other words, considering that Article 16 of the BCCI Rules was applicable, the arbitrators had no duty to make a determination regarding language; the arbitrators did not even have a right to do so, since this had already been done by Article 16 of the Rules. The arbitrators only had a duty to observe the designation made by Article 16. Having this in mind, the finding that the arbitrators failed to determine the language of the proceedings is quite unpersuasive.

But even if one were to accept as an assumption that the arbitrators failed to specify the language of arbitration, the question would arise whether the absence of an explicit determination may in itself trigger annulment or refusal of recognition without investigating what language **was** actually used and whether the language actually used did or did not cause impairment. Sometimes the question of the language of arbitration is simply not raised as an issue by either the parties or by the arbitrators, because there is no debate, and because it is fairly obvious what should be the language of the proceedings. In a number of cases the language of the proceedings is not chosen by the parties, and the record does not show any determination by the arbitrators either – but some language is, of course, used. This may be less than fully scrupulous, but it is hardly a sufficient ground for challenge. After an arbitral proceeding has ended and an award has been rendered, procedural challenges pertaining to language must be based on the language which was actually used, rather than on a failure of an explicit determination.

b) Was there a violation of Article 22 of the LICA (which spells out the principle of equality of the parties and stresses that each party should have a 'full opportunity to defend its rights')? In its motion to set aside, the Bulgarian party submitted and explained that the Macedonian participants were speaking without the assistance of a translator. If the arguments of a party (or of a witness) are not translated to the language of the other party, this may amount to a violation of due process. The question is whether this is still the case when the languages at issue are closely related. At this point, another circumstance is also relevant. The Bulgarian party pointed out as an argument – and this was not contradicted – that the Macedonian participants were speaking their native language, and their statements and pleadings were rendered in Bulgarian by the third arbitrator (Professor Tadjer) who was dictating the minutes. Is this a confirmation of a violation of some procedural rights, or is this an indication which leads towards an opposite conclusion? There are various forms of minutes in international commercial arbitration.[116] Dictating a summary by the chairman of the tribunal (or by the sole arbitrator) is one of the possible options. It seems that during the Bulgarian arbitration proceedings the method of taking the minutes changed. The first oral hearing was recorded by a stenographer. This hearing (during which translation between Bulgarian and Serbo-Croatian was provided) was a very short introductory hearing, which lasted only 30 minutes. During later hearings, the minutes were dictated by Chairman Tadjer who summarized the statements which were made. It is difficult to perceive any other reason behind

[116] See Várady-Barcelo-Von Mehren, *International Commercial Arbitration – A Transnational Perspective*, 3rd edn. (Thomson & West 2006) pp. 490-495 (including a discussion concerning the taking of minutes in a hypothetical case from: Peter Sanders, ed., *ICCA Comparative Arbitration Practice and Public Policy in Arbitration* (1987) 137-140)).

this change but the circumstance that following the first oral hearing the participants came to the conclusion that no translation was really necessary. Furthermore, awards are normally made on the grounds of the record – and the record was in Bulgarian. The minutes were dictated by the chairman of the tribunal. Thus, while the Macedonian party and the Macedonian witness spoke Macedonian, what was recorded was in Bulgarian. The minutes recorded all party pleadings, witness statements, and expert testimonies. Thus, the Bulgarian party had heard what was dictated (in Bulgarian), and had access to all the testimonies and the arguments which may have influenced the outcome of the case. Accordingly, Pharmachim clearly had an opportunity to raise questions on the grounds of what it heard and what became a part of the record. It was never alleged that the arbitrators had relied on something that had been said but was not recorded in the minutes. It appears that the circumstance pointed out in the setting aside proceedings (that the minutes were dictated in Bulgarian) actually weakens the argument and weakens the challenge on the grounds of equality of the parties and the right to defense. Let us add that here again, waiver (lack of objection) appears to be another strong argument against the position of the Bulgarian party.

F.5. **General guidance from the Bulgarian case?**

A question of a more general nature arises pertaining to the need for translation between closely-related languages, and regarding the consequences of absence of translation between closely-related languages. The question is whether lack of translation between closely-related languages should or should not have an effect on the regularity of the proceedings (and on the validity of the award). It obviously matters how close is close – and this is often controversial. The Bulgarian case may not have yielded consistent and persuasive guiding principles, but it demonstrated the complexity of the issue.

The Bulgarian case also raises the question whether some ethnic rivalries with a long history may find an added arena in international commercial arbitration. One would hope that such patterns of rivalry will not mark the province of international commercial arbitration. (This hope was not really bolstered by the Bulgarian case but it was not seriously undermined by it either.) Let me stress that within the arbitration proceedings proper, the Bulgarian and Macedonian arbitrators established a working arrangement which was not tainted by ethnic debate. The tension did not become an explicit issue in either arbitration or post-arbitration proceedings, although some formulations – and the avoidance of the designation 'Macedonian language' – may be suggestive of an awareness of the controversy. Arguments and judgments may have also been influenced by other considerations. One could say that the Bulgarian decisions may bear the stamp of ethnic rivalry, but this is not the factor which determined their main characteristics (and shortcomings).

It is important to add that it is very likely that the hesitations, shifts, and wavering in the search of a fitting provision of the LICA can be explained by the fact that closely-related languages were at issue. If lack of translation has manifest adverse effects, the conceptualization and categorization of these effects is relatively easy. If these effects are questionable and inchoate, it is much more difficult (if possible at all) to fit them under specific procedural shelters designed to offer protection against distinct instances of procedural unfairness.

As far as the outcome of the Bulgarian case is concerned, the positions taken can hardly serve as general guidance. It is difficult to see how the proceedings before the Bulgarian court of arbitration could have possibly violated either the party agreement or Bulgarian law. First of all, in all likelihood, there were no real difficulties in understanding. This conclusion is supported not only by the fact that the two languages are very similar, but also by the fact that there was no protest or initiative to introduce translation during any of the four hearings. Second, even if there was some difficulty in communication, this was remedied by the act of dictating and recording the minutes in Bulgarian. And finally, lack of objection amounted to a clear waiver.

F.6. The advantages and the predicament of closely-related languages

Speaking of the treatment of closely-related languages in general terms, the question arises whether we have here a chance for a helpful shortcut, or whether we are just embarking on further complications. As stated in the introductory note to this subchapter, it is not irrelevant whether translation was not provided between English and Japanese, or whether we are facing a situation in which translation was not provided between Swedish and Norwegian. Can one in both cases speak of a violation of the principle of equality, or denial of opportunity to present one's case? Could a Norwegian party seek annulment of the award because there was no translation from Swedish into Norwegian?

Arbitrators should probably not attempt to resolve linguistic issues which have remained unresolved among linguists and politicians. Whether translation is needed or is not needed between Macedonian and Bulgarian, Swedish and Norwegian, Czech and Slovak, Serbian and Croatian, Dutch and Flemish, and between other closely related (or arguably identical) languages, is not for arbitrators to decide. But arbitrators can heed the fact that some languages are closely related and that people speaking such closely-related languages may very well understand each other. This circumstance also places an added burden on the party that challenges the award on ground of lack of translation, and this makes counter-arguments based on waiver more powerful. The waiver argument makes sense even in a context where the party's ability to present its case is actually impaired. The argument is obviously even stronger where the impairment is at best questionable. If a party accepts to proceed without translation between Macedonian and Bulgarian, his rights to present his case have probably not been impaired at all. If closely-related languages are in question, there is every reason to insist on timely, clear and explicit objection because of a lack of translation – and there is every reason to dismiss the challenge in the absence of such objection.

What if such an objection is indeed made? One can imagine a situation where a party insisted on translation even though he/she understood the language spoken by the other party. It is also possible that someone might insist on translation just in order to demonstrate the distinctness of a language. This may be politically motivated; it may even be close to abuse, but it would be difficult not to tolerate it. The question is whether arbitrators can decide whether translation between two languages is or is not needed. Courts have, indeed, made such decisions. The International Criminal Tribunal for the former Yugoslavia (hereinafter: 'ICTY') took a position regarding the relevance of differences between Bosnian, Croatian and Serbian. Here, of course, the situation is different. The ICTY is an international criminal court before which the same judges have to treat a large number of cases involving the same languages. Since the issue of possible differences between Serbian, Croatian and Bosnian may very well emerge in each case, it would have been difficult to proceed in a principled way without taking a general position. There is no translation before the ICTY between these languages, but there is, of course, translation between Bosnian, Croatian or Serbian and the working languages of the ICTY (English and French[117]). The ICTY accepted separate names (Serbian, Croatian, Bosnian) but also accepted as a fact that these languages can be used interchangeably. An abbreviation was adopted, the 'S/B/C' language (sometimes with a different sequence of the abbreviating letters, thus S/C/B, C/S/B, or B/S/C). The bottom line is that a Croat, a Serb, or a Bosniac is entitled to translation into and from English or French, and will receive a C, B, or S translation depending on the availability of the translator; he or she will not be entitled, however, to translation between Serbian, Croatian and Bosnian. What is also important is that, while translating to and from the working languages of the ICTY, the sequence of S, C, or B interpreters is dictated by working hours and availability. Thus, it happens with some frequency that the statement of a witness from Serbia is interpreted by an interpreter from Bosnia or Croatia (or *vice versa*). It is (rightly)

---

[117] According to Art. 33 of its Statute, the ICTY has two working languages, English and French. In practice, the dominant language is English.

assumed that the differences between Bosnian, Croatian and Serbian do not amount to an obstacle in mutual understanding.

In *Prosecutor v. Vojislav Šešelj*, the Trial Chamber II rendered a specific Order on Translation of Documents.[118] The Order was prompted i.a. by the request of Mr. Šešelj to be provided with translation into just Serbian, rather than Bosnian or Croatian or Serbian (B/C/S). The Trial Chamber relied on Article 21 of the Statute of the ICTY which guarantees to the accused information 'in a language which he understands'. In the concluding sentence of the Order of March 6, 2003 it is stated that the Trial Chamber

> '**FURTHER ORDERS** the Registry to provide the Accused with translations of any future motions filed by the Prosecution (without attachments) in B/C/S... thereby guaranteeing the right of the Accused to be heard in a language he understands.'[119]

To take different example, the Supreme Court of Bronx County, New York took a position whether Krio was a separate language and whether translation to and from Krio was required to prevent deprivation of the defendant's right to a fair trial. In *The People of the State of New York v. G. Smith*,[120] the court undertook an investigation and established that

> 'In sociolinguistic terms, Krio is a derivative of Creole English and had its source in native contact with speakers in English. Historically, it became a makeshift from of speech called Pidgin. Eventually it evolved into a distinct language of its own.'[121]

---

[118] *Prosecutor v. Vojislav Šešelj*, Case No. IT-03-67-PT, Order on Translation of Documents of March 6, 2003.

[119] During the trial, on March 25, 2003, Judge Schomburg responded to Mr. Šešelj by giving the following explanation: 'Dr. Šešelj, we are here in a tribunal where we use the—all three variants of the same common Serbo-Croatian language, and everybody is treated equally… . So you have to accept and you have to show some tolerance. Language is a tool bringing persons, bringing people together, and to make us understand each other, but we can't expect that everybody speaks the same variant or, even worse, the same dialect. In this Tribunal, for example, we have English as one of the official languages. Sometimes also for us it is difficult to understand a person speaking Irish English, French English, German English [meaning English spoken by a Frenchman or by a German person] American English, but we have to live with this in the spirit of tolerance and trying to understand each other… . And to be honest, we don't care about this from where a person comes, be it Zagreb, Novi Sad, Belgrade, or wherever. The main point is that it's translated into a language you understand, and there should be not the slightest problem with this.' ICTY, Transcript of the Šešelj trial of March 25, 2003, available at http://www.un.org.icty/transe67/030325IA.htm, at pp. 76-77.

[120] 195 Misc.2d 434, 759 N.Y.S-2d 315, decision of April 4, 2003.

[121] 759 N.Y.S.2d 315, at 316.

After the analysis, the New York court came to the following conclusion: 'The court finds that Krio, although related to English, is a separate and distinct language that cannot be readily understood without an interpreter.'[122] Thus, courts sometimes take a position with regard to distinctness of languages, and the need for translation between closely-related languages.

Such a position may, in principle, be taken by the legislator as well, but this is quite exceptional. One (and possibly the only) exception is paragraph 24 of the new Norwegian Arbitration Act[123] which states that 'Swedish and Danish may also be used if the language of arbitration is Norwegian'. This settles the issue, at least in cases in which the seat of arbitration is in Norway, and thus Norwegian law is the *lex arbitri*. The 1999 Swedish Arbitration Act and the 2005 Danish Arbitration Act do not contain corresponding provisions.

The question arises whether arbitrators could or should undertake investigations regarding the proximity of languages, and whether they should reach decisions on such matters without legislative or judicial guidance. First of all, doubts might exist as to whether such questions are arbitrable. It is true, of course, that the question of the status of a language will not appear as an issue pertaining to the merits of the claim submitted to the arbitrators, but it is an open question whether limitations imposed by the requirement of arbitrability do or do not extend to preliminary questions as well. Given these doubts, arbitrators are better advised not to decide how closely related some languages are and whether translation is needed between such languages. Thus, if one of the parties insists on translation, it might be more prudent to arrange for translation (or to allow translation) between closely-related languages even when the arbitrators tend to think that translation is probably not really needed. Arranging for unnecessary translation may be an error, but it is certainly a much less consequential error than a failure to order translation when one party does not fully understand the language of a pleading or of a witness statement. But again, in the absence of insistence or objection, lack of translation cannot amount to a ground for challenging the award – particularly not when the languages concerned are closely-related languages.

---

122 759 N.Y.S.2d 315, at 317.

123 In force since January 1, 2005.

Chapter V

Language and Translation in Post-Award Court Proceedings

A. Introduction

In this chapter we shall focus on arbitration related court proceedings in which the award is challenged and scrutinized. Court control over the language of arbitral proceedings remains a possibility after the arbitration process has ripened into an award which is submitted for recognition and enforcement, or challenged in setting aside proceedings. One of the hallmarks of contemporary treatment of arbitral awards is a resolute restriction of possible avenues of challenge. The global trend is to provide two opportunities for control of the award. First, the party dissatisfied with the award may seek set aside (annulment) before a court which considers the award to be domestic (normally a court of the country where the award was rendered). The second option is to oppose recognition and enforcement of the award before a court which considers it to be a foreign award (normally a court outside the country in which the award was rendered).

There is a recurring question which has left a mark on challenges on the grounds of language-related deficiencies. The question has repeatedly arisen whether a proven error pertaining to language justifies in itself setting aside or refusal of recognition, or whether the party challenging the award also has to demonstrate that such an error had a consequential impact. As far as the language of the documents[1] submitted for post-award scrutiny is concerned, the question has emerged whether the 'right language' can only be the language prescribed following a strict reading of Article IV of the New York Convention (or of similar provisions in municipal law). In other words, the question has arisen whether, for example, recognition should always be refused in the absence of translation, or if translation and certification do not strictly comply with the requirements of Article IV, or whether one should, in balance, also consider whether such imperfections do or do not yield a serious danger of distortions or misunderstandings under the circumstances of the case. Likewise, in the context of Article V of the New York Convention (or of like munici-

[1] The documents at issue are typically the award and the arbitration agreement.

pal norms), the question has arisen whether a proven shortcoming (e.g., lack of translation, or mistranslation) is a sufficient basis for challenge, or whether the award can only be set aside (or refused recognition) if it is proven that this shortcoming actually undermined the fairness of the proceedings in the given case. This chapter will endeavor to follow these issues in various settings in which language and translation emerge as issues in post-award proceedings.

A.1. The standard of an understandable award fit to be considered in court proceedings

In a 1958 UK case[2] the question arose whether the award – considering its style of articulation – was capable or incapable of being enforced as a judgment. Giving the leading judgment in this case, Lord Evershed stated:

> '[y]ou cannot enforce a document which merely says by way of declaration (in effect) that certain contracts with three numbers should be set against certain other contracts with three other numbers, and that Dafnis Thomaides & Co. (UK), ought to pay differences between them.'[3]

Dilemmas similar to those which arose in the UK case due to a professional shortcoming, may also arise due to differences in culture and language. Arbitration awards need to be understandable, and need to have some logical consistency in order to be confirmed or recognized and declared enforceable by a court. Cultural differences may have an impact on this standard. It is also possible that as a result of imprecise translation – or as a result of a strictly literal translation – it becomes questionable whether the award is fit to be recognized as an enforceable title.

Having said this, let me also mention that cases in which the formal appropriateness of the award for recognition is questioned for reasons of language and culture are quite rare. This is to a considerable extent due to the fact that standardization and globalization in the realm of international commercial arbitration has not been limited to a harmonization of statutes and arbitration rules. This harmonization of statutes and rules, along with a steadily growing transnational exchange of experience, have also yielded a certain standardization of patterns of expression.

---

[2] *Margulies Brothers Ltd. v. Dafnis Thomaides & Co. (UK) Ltd.*, Court of Appeal, (1958) 1 *Lloyd's Rep.* 205

[3] Ibidem at 207.

To mention an exception, I shall refer again to a UK case,[4] which is one of the truly rare cases in which differences in language and culture cast into question the appropriateness of the award for recognition and enforcement. After a Chinese (CIETAC) award was rendered, leave to enforce the award was rendered in the UK. The defendant sought to set aside this order arguing, i.a., that the language used in the Chinese award was not a language '[w]hich the English courts would recognize as language requiring one party to deliver up goods to another'. In its decision of January 19, 2001, the High Court of Justice, Queen's Bench Division Commercial Court cites the relevant (and contested) part of the 'dispositif' of the award in its English translation. I would like to reproduce this part:

> 'The NVLG-10 Liquid Bagging Machine and spare parts purchased by the plaintiff from the defendant shall be returned. The defendant shall return to the plaintiff 85% of the money for goods which has been paid through negotiation with the use of the letter of credit, totaling US $ 131,750. The defendant shall pay the plaintiff the interest calculated at 7% of the annual interest rate for the above-mentioned money for goods from the day of negotiation from the bank to the date of actually returning the money to the plaintiff. The plaintiff does not need to pay US $ 7.750, the remaining sum for the NVLG-10 Liquid Bagging Machine which has not been paid, because the equipment is to be returned.'[5]

The defendant objected that from the language of the award it does not follow clearly

> 'who is to deliver the machine or to whom, nor does it [the Chinese award] use language which the English courts would recognize as language requiring one party to deliver up goods to another'.[6]

The English court **did** recognize the award. It stated that it remained unpersuaded that there are such uncertainties about the drafting of the paragraph at issue as would make it incapable of enforcement as a judgment. It was said that the court should not be 'astute to find difficulties of construction' of foreign awards. In the statement of reasons the court stressed:

> 'This award, of course, was made in China, and made in the Chinese language. The document from which all those in court have worked is a certified translation.

[4] *Tongyuan (USA) International Trading Group (China) v. Uni-Clan Ltd.*, High Court of Justice, Queen's Bench Division Commercial Court, decision of January 19, 2001, 2001 WL 98036 (QBD – Comm.Ct.)

[5] Ibidem at p. 3 of the WL printout.

[6] Ibidem.

> But even when a foreign award is made in the English language, it must be rare that it will use terms precisely mirroring those which an English court would use for the purpose of drafting a judgment. The question, in my judgment, is whether the award as it stands (in this case the award in translation) is sufficiently certain to be capable of enforcement as it stands.'[7]

This English case may not have been a really difficult one, but it is important for demonstrating and drawing attention to the need to approach foreign awards with a sense of cultural tolerance – which at the same time does not exclude proper procedural scrutiny. The translation into English of a Chinese arbitral award will not, and need not, yield an English style judgment. Globalization in international commercial arbitration does not only mean the shaping of standardized rules and patterns of arbitral proceedings, it also means a growing global readiness to discern essential components of say, an award, behind different linguistic instruments of expression and behind different styles of articulation.

A.2. Two settings in which language and translation emerge as an issue in post-award court proceedings

Before courts, the issue of language arises under an angle different from that obtaining in arbitration proceedings. Courts have an official language (or official languages), and proceedings will be conducted in the official language (or in one of the official languages) of the court. It is not within the power of the parties or of the arbitrators to determine the language of post-award court proceedings. Thus, in many cases the language of arbitral proceedings and the language of the award will not be the same as the language of subsequent court proceedings. The question arises, how the two proceedings may be synchronized language-wise. Should the arbitral award challenged before a court (or submitted to the court for recognition) be submitted in its original, or in a translation, or in both. The question may also arise whether the whole award needs to be translated, whether the arbitration agreement needs to be translated, whether translation needs to be certified, or how the court will treat shortcomings in translation.

There is also another setting in which language issues emerge in post-award court proceedings. The limited control defined by Article V of the New York Convention may include a scrutiny of the appropriateness of choices and decisions pertaining to language during the arbitral proceedings. The question may arise whether lack of translation, mistranslation, or translation uncalled-for, may

---

7 Ibidem pp. 3-4 of the WL printout.

be qualified as a procedural deficiency which amounts to a ground for denial of recognition and enforcement. The same questions may emerge in **setting aside proceedings** as well. With regard to setting aside we do not have the same world-wide uniformity of possible grounds for challenge as that provided by the New York Convention with regard to recognition and enforcement of foreign awards. Yet court control over the language of arbitration in setting aside proceedings follows the same patterns and gives rise essentially to the same problems as those emerging during court control in recognition and enforcement proceedings. One of the characteristics of modern arbitration law is the convergence (if not identity) of the standards of scrutiny in setting aside and in recognition proceedings respectively. The difference is that with regard to recognition and enforcement, the grounds on which an arbitral award may be challenged are set clearly in Article V of the New York Convention, which is accepted today (August 2006) in 137 countries around the world.[8] There is no world-wide convention covering setting aside, but there is a strong movement towards convergence and harmonization. The grounds which justify setting aside are becoming identical or very similar on a global scale, and these grounds are modeled on those which are set in the New York Convention. According to the 1985 UNCITRAL Model Law, the grounds on which an arbitral award may be challenged – either in set aside or in recognition proceedings – are the same. This is clearly the dominant trend. Accordingly, conclusions which may be drawn regarding control over the language of arbitration in recognition and enforcement proceedings are typically pertinent in setting aside (annulment) proceedings as well. This is the main reason why we are treating the two post-award court proceedings (recognition and enforcement on the one hand, and setting aside on the other hand) in the same chapter. Some occasional differences have arisen, but essentially the same conclusions apply, and the same inferences may be drawn from both proceedings regarding language and translation. We shall concentrate primarily on recognition and enforcement, since the standard was set by the New York Convention, and since most pertinent positions (and controversies) both in practice and in scholarly writings have been shaped on the basis of the New York Convention. Specific features of setting aside proceedings will be pointed out where appropriate.

Following this introduction, this chapter contains two subchapters ('B' and 'C') reflecting the two basic settings in which issues pertaining to language and translation arise in post-award court proceedings. Subchapter 'B' will deal with the rules and considerations pertaining to the formal requirements in the pre-

[8] See the UNCITRAL website at http://www.uncitral.org/pdf/english/texts/arbitration/NY-conv/XXII_1_e.pdf.

sentation of the results of arbitration proceedings to the court, i.e., with translation and authentication of the documents submitted. Section 'C' will focus on court control of procedural irregularities (or alleged procedural irregularities) in recognition or setting aside proceedings, when the shortcoming which is raised as an issue pertains to language and translation within the arbitration proceedings.

B. Translation and Certification of the Documents of the Arbitration Proceedings

B.1. The standard set in Article IV of the New York Convention, and some questions

Article IV of the New York Convention makes it clear that the party seeking recognition and enforcement of a foreign award has to submit to the court both the award and the arbitration agreement on the grounds of which the arbitrators assumed jurisdiction. The focus is on the basis of the arbitration process (the arbitration agreement), and on its result (the award); and a language standard is set with the endeavor to make it sure that the arbitration agreement and the award are presented without distortions and can be properly understood by the recognizing court.

The document which needs to be submitted is the original (of the award and of the arbitration agreement) or a duly certified copy thereof. As far as the award is concerned, the original needs to be authenticated. The award and the arbitration agreement may, of course, be written in different languages, and it is quite possible that only one or none of these languages is an official language of the court before which recognition is sought. Section 2 of Article IV is designed to handle these issues. According to Article IV(2):

> 'If the said award or agreement is not made in an official language of the country in which the award is relied upon, the party applying for recognition and enforcement of the award shall produce a translation of these documents into such language. The translation shall be certified by an official or sworn translator or by a diplomatic or consular agent.'

This is, of course, quite logical. Arbitrators do not represent a State; they are not officials who are supposed to proceed in the official language of the sovereign State which they are serving. Arbitrators will instead follow a language chosen by the parties, or (in the absence of a choice made by the parties) they may determine a language which in their opinion is best suited for the given dispute.

On the other hand, courts are authorities of a sovereign State, and they have an official language; thus, documents presented to the court should, in principle, be suited to this official language. The same logic applies when we are dealing with setting aside proceedings. Again, we have court proceedings which are conducted in the official language (or in one of the official languages) of the given court. Some differences between recognition and setting aside proceedings may emerge, however, with regard to the need for certification, the form of certification, and possibly with regard to the range of documents which need to be submitted. The Model Law, while adopting the solution of Article IV of the New York Convention regarding recognition and enforcement,[9] does not set any standard regarding translation of the documents for the purposes of court proceedings prompted by a motion to set aside the award. This is left to municipal codes of civil procedure and other pertinent norms. The basic rule is usually the same as that of Article IV of the New York Convention, but variations may emerge regarding details.[10]

Several questions have arisen in the course of the application and interpretation of Article IV(2). In a number of cases, the scope of Article IV emerged as an issue. The question was also asked whether the 'shall produce a translation' language of Article IV(2) does or does not leave any maneuvering room, for example for a judge who has a good command of the language of the award (and of the arbitration agreement), and does not need a translation. A further related question is whether the circumstance that the content of the award is undisputed has an impact or not. The nature and scope of certification have also emerged as an issue. The question has been further asked whether the whole award (and every page of it) needs to be certified; and whether the person effecting the certification must have a command of the languages at issue. Another important question is that of the consequences of non-observance of Article

[9] Without specifying what is understood by certified translation. The Model Law simply speaks of the duty to supply a 'duly certified translation' (Art. 35(2)), while the New York Convention specifies that 'The translation shall be certified by an official or sworn translator or by a diplomatic or consular agent.' One may add that the provisions of the Model Law on recognition and enforcement have a most limited practical relevance given the world-wide adoption of the New York Convention.

[10] To cite just one example, the Peruvian Arbitration Act No. 26572 (in force since January 6, 1996) states in Art. 126 that the documents submitted in setting aside proceedings (primarily the award) need to be translated into Spanish – if they are not drafted in Spanish. Art. 96 of the same Act specifies that translation of the document has to be made '[b]y a diplomatic agent or Peruvian consul or someone serving in such stead, at the place of its issue, or by an official translator'. Certification of such translation is not posed as a requirement (but the persons entitled to translate are essentially the same as those who are entitled to certify the translation under Art. IV(2) of the New York Convention).

IV(2); should this result in a final judgment rejecting recognition and enforcement, or should resubmission with conforming documents be allowed. In a number of cases it has been raised as an issue whether the requirements of Article IV may be superseded by other statutory provisions or treaty provisions. Finally, the question has arisen what the consequences of a mistranslation are. We shall deal with these questions in the following pages of this subchapter.

B.2. The scope of the standard set for translation of documents

Let me repeat that the standard is set in Article IV of the New York Convention, and this standard is an expression of principles which apply in the domain of setting aside proceedings as well.

Questions have emerged regarding the range of the principle set in Article IV of the New York Convention. In this connection, I would like to refer first to a setting aside case decided by the Swiss Federal Tribunal.[11] In this case the party seeking annulment requested the production of the complete case file to be ordered from the arbitral tribunal, and 'as far as necessary' the translation of all records which were not drafted in one of the Swiss official languages. The arbitral tribunal did produce the case file, but the Federal Tribunal decided that a translation of the file was not necessary, 'since the complaints made by the Plaintiff can be adjudicated without such translation'. Thus, translation of the whole arbitration file was not excluded as an option, but it was not considered to be necessary under the circumstances of the case. The question arises whether a difference exists in this regard between recognition and enforcement on one hand, and setting aside proceedings on the other hand. A related question is that of the scope and range of Article IV regarding recognition and enforcement proceedings proper.

Article IV of the New York Convention is quite specific regarding the range of documents which need to be submitted (and translated). It mentions two items: the award and the arbitration agreement. Does this mean that submission and translation of other parts of the file may not be requested? This hypothesis is not persuasive. Article IV of the New York Convention does not set limits to the gathering of evidence. The courts are normally free to request or accept evidence, including pieces of the file of the arbitration case. If it is contested, for example, whether an objection against a procedural deficiency was or was not raised, party submissions (or a record of the oral hearing) may very well be relied upon as evidence. At the same time, the maneuvering room of the court is

[11] *A. Ltd. v. Republic of Turkey*, Federal Tribunal, First Civil Chamber, Judgment of October 18, 2004, reported in 23 *ASA Bulletin* (2005) pp. 164-174.

greater outside the limits of the wording of Article IV. Article IV of the New York Convention sets as a formal precondition to recognition and enforcement the presentation of a certified translation of the award and of the arbitration agreement (unless they were made in an official language of the court). As we shall see below, it is questionable whether a court is entitled at all to proceed without such translation. In a setting aside case (unless the procedural norms of the forum would repeat the requirements of Article IV of the New York Convention), the court may decide freely whether to require translation of the required documents (including the award and the arbitration agreement), and if so, whether to require certification. The same applies to recognition and enforcement cases with regard to documents other than the award or the arbitration agreement. Even if one were to accept the position that Article IV envisages the presentation of certified translation as a formal precondition (rather than just as a vehicle which has to ensure better understanding), this position could only extend to those documents which are specified in Article IV: the award and the arbitration agreement. In other words, if other elements of the arbitration file are at issue (other than the award or the arbitration agreement), they are beyond the scope of Article IV, and the court is free to rely on other norms and principles in deciding whether it will or will not accept the original of the document without certified translation into the official language of the court.

Staying with the issue of the scope of Article IV, I would like to mention that the question arose as to what the duty to present a translation of the arbitration agreement actually extends to. In a case decided by the Court of First Instance (*Bezirksgericht*) of Zurich in 2003,[12] the party requesting recognition and enforcement of an Italian award submitted a translation of the arbitration clause contained in a license agreement. (The award was in Italian, but the original of the license agreement containing the arbitration clause was in English.) The party opposing recognition and enforcement objected, arguing that a translation of the arbitration clause only does not meet the conditions of Article IV(2) of the New York Convention because the overall meaning of a contractual provision can only be determined on the basis of the complete text of the contract. Thus, the question arose to what document – or what part of what document – Article IV actually refers. The Zurich court held that an explanation is contained in Article II of the New York Convention, which provides for a definition of the terms used in Article IV. Article IV actually refers to Article II, regarding the 'original agreement' to be supplied.[13] According to Article II, the term 'agree-

[12] *Italian party v. Swiss company*, *Yearbook Commercial Arbitration,* Vol. XXIX (2004) 819-833. The decision of the *Bezirksgericht* Zurich of February 14, 2003 was confirmed by a decision of the *Obergericht* (Court of Appeal) of Zurich on July 17, 2003.

[13] According to Art. IV(1)(b) the party seeking recognition has to supply 'The original agreement referred to in Art. II or a duly certified copy thereof.'

ment in writing' shall include an arbitral clause in a contract, or an arbitration agreement. Having cited this provision, the Zurich court concluded that Article IV(2) of the New York Convention only requires the translation of the relevant arbitration clause, and not of the entire contract which contains the arbitration clause.

Another question relating to the exact documents which have to be submitted was raised in a case decided by the Spanish Supreme Court in 1985.[14] Here, recognition of an award rendered in London was sought in Spain. Acting under the authority given by the former Spanish norms, the office of the Attorney General requested that certain formal defects in the documents presented by the claimant be cured. One of these alleged defects was the absence of authentication of photocopies of some documents which were relied upon during the arbitration proceedings. The Spanish Supreme Court held that the duty of authentication of these photocopies is not mandated by Article IV of the New York Convention, which only requires the presentation of the award and of the arbitration agreement in a duly authenticated (or certified) form.[15]

The position taken in these cases is helpful in clarifying an important point. Article IV of the New York Convention sets as a requirement that the party seeking recognition has to provide the original (or a duly certified copy) of the award and of the arbitration agreement, and also has to provide a certified translation of these two documents if they were not made in the official language (or in one of the official languages) of the court. Both the original and a translation have to be submitted; the translation cannot replace the original.[16] These are formal requirements, and it is at best questionable whether the court deciding on recognition and enforcement may waive some of these requirements. But these requirements are restricted precisely to those documents which are specifically mentioned in Article IV: the award and the arbitration agreement.

As far as other documents are concerned, in deciding about the need for translation and/or certification, the court is not bound by the prerequisites set in Article IV.

---

[14] *Pastrederiet m/v Jytte Dania v. Más S.A. Yearbook Commercial Arbitration,* Vol. XIV (1989) 704; also published in 2 *Revista de la corte española de arbitraje* (1985) pp. 223-224.

[15] The Spanish Supreme Court also stated that an evaluation of the documents at issue was already made by the arbitrator, who is competent to make both a formal and a substantial evaluation of these documents. This evaluation cannot be revised to affect the merits of the case.

[16] This was explicitly confirmed in some court cases. For example, in *Inter Maritime Management S.A. v. Russin & Vecchi*, the Swiss Federal Tribunal (Supreme Court) took an explicit position according to which, under Art. IV the translation must accompany the original or the duly certified copy of the arbitration agreement, it does not take its place. (10 *International Arbitration Report* (1995) pp. D-1-D-13, decision of January 9, 1995.)

Let me mention that the issue of the scope of Article IV has also arisen in a quite different context. In another Swiss case,[17] the party opposing recognition made a rather imaginative attempt to restrict the application of Article IV in order to make room for the application of another multilateral treaty which posed more stringent requirements regarding translation. The applicant sought recognition of a Luxemburg award rendered in French. No translation was submitted, given that French is one of the official languages in Switzerland, and Article IV of the New York Convention requires translation into one of the official languages of the country in which the award is relied upon. The party opposing recognition submitted, however, that it should have received the award (in the recognition proceedings) in German, in the light of the reservation made by Switzerland to the 1965 Hague Convention on Service Abroad of Judicial and Extrajudicial Documents in Civil or Commercial Matters (hereinafter 'Hague Convention'). According to this reservation, if the party which is being served refuses to accept, service should take place in either German, or French, or Italian, depending on which part of Switzerland service is effected in. In this case, service took place in a German-speaking part of Switzerland, and this circumstance served as a basis for the argument that the Swiss party was not properly served (since he received the award in French). The Basel court established first that a basic precondition for the application of the Swiss reservation to the Hague Convention was not met because the Swiss respondent did not refuse acceptance. What is more important for our considerations, the Basel court also investigated the question of the scope of Article IV in conjunction with the Hague Convention. The party opposing recognition argued that the Hague Convention, rather than the New York Convention applies regarding documents submitted to a **party**. This supposes a most narrow interpretation of Article IV, assuming that it only speaks of submission of documents (and of translation) to the court, rather than to the other party. This narrow perception of the scope of Article IV would lead to a distinction which would be most unhelpful – and which has no support in the wording of Article IV, which simply speaks of the duty of the applicant to supply documents and translation of documents, without specifying the addressee. The obvious addressees are the court and the other party. The (somewhat twisted) argument of the party opposing recognition also opened the question of the relationship between the two conventions. The Basel court held that the New York Convention applies. Since the New York Convention only requires translation if the award was not made in one of the official languages of the country in which recognition is sought – and

---

[17] Basel-Stadt, *Appelationsgericht*, decision of November 5, 2003, Reported in 24 *ASA Bulletin* (2006) 125.

since French is one of the official languages of Switzerland – the objection of the respondent was rejected.

One of the relevant inferences from this case is that Article IV does not use as a basis of comparison the language which is dominant within a region (the region where recognition is sought), but it only considers official languages on the level of the State. If the award is rendered in one of the official languages of the State of recognition, translation is not needed, irrespective whether the language of the award is the language of communication in the region where the court is situated.

B.3. Can a foreign-language award (or arbitration agreement) be considered in post-award proceedings without translation?

I would like to turn now to the question of the nature of the requirement set in Article IV regarding the two documents which are specifically mentioned: the arbitration agreement and the award. One may submit that translation of the award and of the arbitration agreement is posited in Article IV(2) as a mandatory requirement. The wording of Article IV is quite firm. It states that in order to obtain recognition and enforcement, the applicant **shall** supply duly authenticated originals (or duly certified copies) of the award and of the arbitration agreement, and that the applicant **shall** produce a certified translation of these documents if they were not made in an official language of the country where the award is relied upon. This is one of the rare points where the New York Convention is more stringent than its predecessor the 1927 Geneva Convention on the Execution of Foreign Arbitral Awards.[18] The Geneva Convention only provides that translation of the requisite documents 'may be demanded', which wording allows a greater room for maneuver.[19]

One may submit that the wording of Article IV(2) of the New York Convention leads to the conclusion that the possible fact that the judge has an adequate command of the language of the award is not contemplated as a circumstance which would relieve the moving party of the duty of submitting a proper translation. In a case which invited some negative comments (and which was mentioned briefly in Chapter I), the Commercial Court of Tashkent City (Uzbekistan) refused to enforce an English award which was presented to it accompanied by a Russian translation.[20] The truth of the matter is that Russian was the official

[18] The 1927 Geneva Convention is still in force, but its importance has been very much reduced due to the success of the New York Convention.

[19] Art. IV(2) of the 1927 Geneva Convention on the Execution of Foreign Arbitral Awards.

[20] Award of the Grain and Feed Trade Association (GAFTA), London, between Romak S.A. Geneva and FTC Uzdon Tashkent, reported in 16-10(2) *Mealey's International Arbitration Reports* (2001).

language in Uzbekistan **earlier**, when Uzbekistan belonged to the Soviet Union, but after the dissolution of the USSR, Uzbekistan became a new sovereign State, and adopted Uzbek as its official language. It is practically certain that the Russian translation was perfectly understandable to the judges of the Tashkent City Commercial Court. It is possible that the judges who gained their earlier experience in Russian were actually more at ease with Russian. Yet even if the outcome may not have been rational, the rules of the New York Convention were not infringed. Article IV(2) clearly entitled the Uzbek judges to insist on an Uzbek translation.

It has to be mentioned that some departures from a strict interpretation of Article IV(2) have nevertheless emerged. Three types of departures may be pointed out: a) some legislators have expanded the number of languages for which no translation is needed; b) some authors (and courts) have taken the position that the court may, if it so wishes, consider the award and the arbitration agreement without translation; and c) the requirement of translation has occasionally been waived on the grounds of the more-favorable-right provision of the New York Convention.

B.3.1. *Extension of the range of languages from which no translation is needed*

In a few countries some added flexibility has been provided through an extension of the list of languages from which no translation is needed. What follows from Article IV(2) of the Convention is that translation is needed if the award and/or the arbitration agreement were not made in an official language of the country where recognition is sought. Some legislators have waived the duty of translation regarding some **other** languages as well, which are not official languages of the country of recognition. For example, according to Israeli legislation, translation is not needed if the award was made in Hebrew, Arabic, French or English – not all of which are official languages in Israel.[21] In the same vein, the Ukrainian Arbitration Act provides that translation is not necessary if the award is in Ukrainian or in Russian, although Russian is no longer an official language of the Ukraine.[22] Furthermore, the Ukrainian Act has provided that if translation is needed, it may be made into either Ukrainian or Russian.

---

[21] Regulations for the Execution of the New York Convention (Foreign Arbitration) 5738 – 1978, Art. 3.

[22] Art. 35(2) of the February 24, 1994 Act on Commercial Arbitration. (It is important to mention, that according to Art. 10 of the Ukrainian Constitution, 'The state language of the Ukraine is the Ukrainian language'.)

B.3.2. *Can the court waive the duty to produce translation?*

While it is clear that under the New York Convention courts do not have to consider an award which was not translated into the official language of the court, the question still arises whether the judges are entitled to do so, if they so wish.

Some scholarly writings have taken the position that the obligation set in Article IV(2) is waivable. Notably, this position was taken by Van den Berg in his well known commentary on the New York Convention. In the opinion of Van den Berg, '[a] party seeking enforcement of an award need not produce translation when he applies for enforcement if the court is deemed to know the language of the award'. Van den Berg adds that the party can only be required to supply a translation if the court or the other party with a justified interest requests it.[23] In other words, the duty to supply translation into an official language of the court is not absolute. No translation needs to be presented if neither the court nor the other party insists on it.

Some court cases have demonstrated a further step of departure from the strict reading of Article IV. While in the opinion of Van den Berg no translation is needed if neither the court nor the other party insists on it, some judgments show that absence of translation was tolerated even though the other party did insist on it.[24] To take an example, in a case decided by a Norwegian court in Vardǿ[25] the party seeking recognition and enforcement did not submit a Norwegian translation of the ICC award rendered in English. The Norwegian party who opposed recognition relied on this omission and asked the court to reject the claim for recognition. The Norwegian court opted to follow a different logic. It held that recognition is possible on grounds of the English text of the award, and even pointed out some advantages of reliance on the original award. It was stated in the Norwegian decision that:

> '[the court] does not deem that the New York Convention sets an absolute requirement for a translation. The original language of the award is English, and if the court has sufficient command of this language to understand the relevant wording with regard to the award's conclusions, the cost of translation seems unreasonably

---

[23] A. Van den Berg, *The New York Arbitration Convention of 1958*, (Kluwer) 1981 Edition (reprint of 1994) at p. 259.

[24] The position of Van den Berg has a nuance here, he speaks of party requests based on 'justified interest'. This nuance was not identified as an issue in the cases to which we shall refer on the following pages.

[25] *Pulsarr Industrial Research B.V. (Netherlands) v. Nils H. Nilsen A.S. (Norway)*, Judgment of July 10, 2002 – reported in *Yearbook Commercial Arbitration,* Vol. XXVIII (2003) 821.

high compared to what a translation may achieve. A translation from English into Norwegian may also fail to provide a correct transcription of the contents of the award as it may cause inconsistencies between the original text and the translated version of the award. Hence, the request for enforcement dated 4 December 2001 complies with the formal requirements of the New York Convention... .'[26]

In a similar vein, a Dutch court held that the arbitration agreement does not have to be submitted in a Dutch translation as long as the agreement is written 'in an understandable language' (understandable to the court). Following this logic, the Zutphen Court of First Instance (Arrondissementsrechtbank) recognized a Chinese (CIETAC) award against a Dutch party, in spite of the fact that the arbitration agreement was not submitted in a Dutch translation.[27] Even more explicit is another Dutch court, the District Court of Amsterdam, in deciding on the recognition and enforcement of an arbitral award rendered between Southern Pacific Properties (Middle East) Ltd. and the Arab Republic of Egypt.[28] In its 1984 decision the District Court of Amsterdam stated:

'Petitioner has submitted duly certified copies of the arbitral award and the arbitration agreement. The aforementioned award and agreement are drawn up in the English language which language we master sufficiently to have taken full cognizance of the contents of these documents. We therefore consider that the provisions of Article IV para. 2, of the applicable Convention on the Recognition and Enforcement of Foreign Arbitral Awards, done at New York, June 10, 1958 [...] are complied with.'[29]

In this interpretation the requirements of Article IV(2) may be met either by supplying proper translation, or by the circumstance that the language of the award and of the arbitration agreement is 'sufficiently mastered' by the judges (and these judges accept the documents without translation).

Deciding on recognition and enforcement of a Ukrainian award, the Court of Appeal (*Oberlandesgericht*) of Schleswig (Germany)[30] raised the issue of the nature of the obligations flowing from Article IV. The exact issue which emerged was that of certification (rather than of translation proper), but the conclusions

---

[26] *Yearbook Commercial Arbitration*, Vol. XXVIII (2003) at p. 824.

[27] *China Packing Design Corporation v. SCA Recycling Reukema Trading B.V.*, decision of the Arrondissementsrechtbank in Zutphen of November 11, 1998 – Reported in *Yearbook Commercial Arbitration*, Vol. XXIV (1999) 724.

[28] District Court of Amsterdam, decision of July 12, 1984, reported in 24 *International Legal Materials* (1985) 1040.

[29] Ibidem.

[30] *Oberlandesgericht* Schleswig, Judgment No. 16 Sch 01/03 of July 15, 2003, reported in *Yearbook Commercial Arbitration*, Vol. XXX (2005) 524-527.

reached by the court purport to cover the whole range of Article IV. The court asked whether Article IV actually sets conditions for the admissibility of a claim for recognition and enforcement, and answered in the negative. The court made first a clear determination establishing that the conditions set by Article IV were not met:

> 'Admittedly, the documents submitted by the claimant do not satisfy the formal requirements of Art. IV [of the] Convention. The claimant supplied namely only uncertified originals, with translations carrying only a certification stamp by a Ukrainian notary public on their last page.'

In spite of this finding, the Schleswig court found that it might proceed. After the sentences quoted above, the court continued and held:

> 'This suffices in the present case, however, because Art. IV [of the] Convention does not set conditions for the admissibility of the enforcement proceedings, and the authenticity of the arbitral award is undisputed. Requiring strict compliance with the formal requirements for recognition in Art. IV [of the] Convention in the present case would be unnecessarily formalistic and, consequently, it would create a difficulty not appropriate to the situation.'[31]

These examples suggest that while the obligations of the party seeking recognition are firm, and while a party cannot require exemption from its duty to supply documents as this is prescribed in Article IV, the court need not be bound by this obligation. In other words, a position has been gaining ground according to which the court may accept the relevant documents without translation, if it finds that translation is not necessary under the circumstances of the case.

B.3.3. *The impact of the more-favorable-right provision*

The position taken in the decision of the Schleswig court had an additional point of support. In addition to the quite bold interpretation of the nature of Article IV, the Schleswig court also relied on the more-favorable-right provision of Article VII of the New York Convention. Since the essential aim of the New York Convention is to **facilitate** recognition and enforcement, its drafters made it clear that the norms of the Convention do not prevent the application of more favorable rules (more favorable from the point of view of the party seeking recognition). To make this idea explicit, Article VII states that the Convention shall not deprive '[a]ny interested party of any right he may have to avail

[31] *Yearbook Commercial Arbitration*, Vol. XXX (2005) at p. 526.

himself of an arbitral award in the manner and to the extent allowed by the law or the treaties of the country where such award is sought to be relied upon'.

Thus, if treaties or municipal procedural norms of the forum State contain more favorable provisions (more favorable for the party seeking recognition) these provisions may supersede the norms of the New York Convention. The Schleswig court relied on Section 1064 of the 1998 German Arbitration Act (Book X of the German Code of Civil Procedure devoted to arbitration). According to Section 1064:

> 'At the time of application for a declaration of enforceability of an arbitral award the award or a certified copy of the award shall be supplied. The certification may also be made by counsel authorized to represent the party in the judicial proceedings.'

It follows that – unlike Article IV of the New York Convention – the German Arbitration Act does not mandate translation, and does not require the submission of the arbitration agreement. (The presentation of a translation and the presentation of the arbitration agreement in its original and/or in translation may be required as evidence in the course of proceedings, but the submission of these documents does not represent a formal precondition to admissibility of the application for recognition and enforcement.) The Schleswig court found that the (more lenient) requirements of Section 1064 were met.[32]

German courts have been quite consistent in softening the strictness of Article IV with reliance on Section 1064 (or on bilateral treaties), and in accordance with the more-favorable-right principle. To cite another example, in its decision of September 23, 2004, the Higher Court of Appeal of Bavaria (*Bayerisches Oberstes Landgericht*) proceeded to consider a request for enforcement, and enforced a Syrian award, in spite of the fact that the party seeking enforcement did not submit the arbitration agreement and its translation. The court held: 'According to the more-favorable-right principle of Article VII(1) of [of the] Convention, the translation and submission of the arbitration agreement is not a requirement for admissibility... .'[33]

The duty to submit translations and to submit the arbitration agreement was also waived in a number of other German decisions, with reliance on the more-favorable-right provision.[34]

---

32 *Yearbook Commercial Arbitration*, Vol. XXX (2005) 527.

33 *K. Trading Comp. (Syria) v. Bayerische Motoren Werke A.G. (Germany)*, *Bayerisches Oberstes Landesgericht*, decision No. 4Z Sch 005-4 of September 23, 2004 – reported in *Yearbook Commercial Arbitration*, Vol. XXX (2005) 568 at p. 571.

34 See e.g., *Trading company (Israel) v. Buyer (Germany),* the decision of the Cologne Court of Appeal (*Oberlandesgericht Köln*) No. 9 Sch 01-03 of April 23, 2004 (*Yearbook Commercial*

In addition to the German act, some other legislative acts have also espoused solutions which are more flexible than the position adopted by Article IV of the New York Convention. For example, the 1999 Swedish Arbitration Act[35] makes the duty to supply a translation of the award into Swedish a waivable obligation. According to Article 56: '**Unless the Court of Appeal decides otherwise**, a certified translation into the Swedish language of the entire award must also be submitted'. [emphasis added] Essentially the same solution was adopted in the 1992 Finnish Arbitration Act.[36]

A waiver of some requirements of Article IV with reliance on the more-favorable-right provision is on firm ground, clearly in line with the New York Convention. This option is, of course, only available if the procedural norms of the forum – or applicable treaties other than the New York Convention – provide for more flexible solutions regarding presentation and translation of required documents.

The more difficult question is whether Article IV may itself be interpreted in a more flexible way. The wording of Article IV does not offer much foothold for flexibility. Article IV states that in order 'To obtain recognition and enforcement...' the applicant 'shall, at the time of application, supply...'. This is, indeed, phrased as a formal precondition to obtaining recognition. At the same time, there are many practical reasons favoring a more flexible interpretation. The reason for requiring the submission of both the award and of the arbitration agreement in both the original and in a certified translation, is to make sure that the arbitrators proceeded on the grounds of consent of the parties, and that the content of the award is exactly that which was submitted for recognition. In 1958, when a new and liberal transnational system of recognition of foreign arbitral awards was presented for acceptance, and when dangers were perceived more by way of anticipation than by way of experience, it was logical to put more emphasis on safeguards, and to set more stringent formal requirements. Today, more than a half century later, recognition of foreign arbitral awards has become common practice world-wide, and this practice has shown the actual dimensions of the problem. In this situation, there is less need to abide by stan-

Arbitration, Vol. XXX (2005) 557, and SchiedsVZ 2005, 163); Claimant: *Lawyer (Austria) v. Defendant*: Client (Germany), decision of the Higher Court of Appeal of Bavaria (*Bayerisches Oberstes Landesgericht*) No. 4 Z Sch 09/04 of July 5, 2004 (*Yearbook Commercial Arbitration*, Vol. XXX (2005) 563); *Company X (Russian Federation) v. Company Y (Germany)*, decision of the Court of Appeal of Bavaria (*Bayern Oberlandesgericht*) No. 4 Z Sch H5/00 of August 11, 2000 (*Yearbook Commercial Arbitration*, Vol. XXVII (2002) 451.

[35] Arbitration Act of March 4, 1999 (SFS 1999:116).

[36] Art. 54 of the Finnish Arbitration Act No. 967/1992, in force since December 1, 1992.

dards set a half century ago against potential dangers. Flexibility has become more justified; it is more practical and more logical simply to ask the question whether the safeguard of translation is needed under the circumstances of the given case. The fact that unnecessary translation may actually create (rather than dispel) uncertainties, and may yield needless costs, is also a relevant consideration.

As far as the translation of the arbitration agreement is concerned, it is difficult to imagine any real danger or impairment of justified interests as a consequence of not submitting a translation of the arbitration agreement if the party opposing recognition (or the party requesting setting aside) does not deny the existence of a valid arbitration agreement, and does not challenge jurisdiction. Accordingly, a flexible interpretation of Article IV, allowing the court to insist or not to insist on the submission of a certified translation of the arbitration agreement, may yield more efficient proceedings and does not jeopardize procedural guarantees. Should the decision of the court be conditioned by lack of insistence of the party opposing recognition? Probably not. The original of the arbitration agreement is the arbitration agreement which was signed by both parties. It is difficult to imagine a legitimate interest of the parties who signed the original to insist on the submission of a translation. It is much easier to presume dilatory tactics behind such a move.

As far as the most important document (the award) is concerned, most of the arguments outlined above remain pertinent. The original of the award is the award yielded by the arbitration proceedings agreed upon by the parties, this is the award which is addressed to the parties – and this is the same award which the parties validly received from the arbitrators (or from the arbitral institution). Again, it is difficult to discern a legitimate party need for translation if the court itself does not need translation. One may conclude that once one accepts a more flexible interpretation of Article IV regarding the need to supply translation, the decision whether translation will or will not be required should belong to the court deciding upon the request for recognition.

B.4. The issue of certification

Assuming that the court does have maneuvering room in ordering or not ordering translation (of the award and of the arbitration agreement), the use of this maneuvering room will be restricted to those still rare cases in which the court is confident that it can rely on documents drafted in a foreign language. Thus, in a typical case, translation of the award and of the arbitration agreement will be requested – and will be provided. This leads us to the next requirement set regarding the presentation of translation. Article IV(2) of the New York Convention and like rules in municipal statutes request **certification** of the translation. At this point, several questions have arisen. It has been asked what exactly needs to be certified and by whom? The purpose of certification has also been raised as an issue. A further question is whether the duty to supply certification is waivable, in other words, whether the court may opt not to seek certification under justified circumstances (first of all, when the accuracy of the translation is not disputed).

B.4.1. *Persons qualified to issue certification, and the purpose of certification*

According to Article IV(2) of the New York Convention, translation can be certified by either an official or sworn translator, or by a diplomatic or consular agent.[37]

The options set in Article IV(2) are rather straightforward, but they have nevertheless given rise to some debate in practice. In a French case,[38] for example, the party opposing recognition stated that translation of the award could only be effected by a person on the list of French judicial experts (interpreters). This argument was not accepted. The French court cited Article IV(2) of the New York Convention stating that translation may be certified by 'an official or sworn translator, or by a diplomatic or consular agent', and this wording does not restrict the circle of potential translators to those who are listed as an expert in France.[39] Similarly, in an Italian case, the Messina Court of Appeals (*Corte di Appello*) held that Article IV(2) constitutes a derogation from Article 123 of the Italian Code of Civil Procedure which provides that translation should be made by an official translator appointed by the judge.[40] The court accepted the certified translation (from German to Italian) submitted by the Austrian applicant, which translation met the conditions of Article IV(2), but did not meet the conditions of the Italian Code of Civil Procedure. Let me mention that a stricter

---

[37] One may assume that the 'diplomatic or consular agent' contemplated by Art. IV(2) is normally a diplomatic or consular agent of the country were recognition is requested, positioned in the country of origin of the award. The wording of Art. IV allows, however, the acceptance of translations certified by other diplomatic or consular agents as well.

[38] *S.A.R.L. Synergie v. Société SC Connect SA*, decision of the Paris *Cour d'appel* of March 18, 2004 – reported in *Revue de l'arbitrage* (2004) pp. 454-455.

[39] One may note that a clear distinction was not made here between providing translation and providing certification of translation. The issue raised was not restricted to certification, but the Paris *Cour d'appel* cited the provision of the New York Convention which enumerates persons who are qualified to certify a translation.

[40] *S.a.S. Wieland K.G. (Austria) v. Società Industriale Meridionale (S.I.M.) (Italy)*, *Corte de Appello di Messina*, decision of May 19, 1976 – *Yearbook Commercial Arbitration*, Vol. V (1980) 266.

standard was also set by The Uniform Arbitration Act of the Organization for the Harmonization of Business Law in Africa (*Organisation pour l'Harmonisation en Afrique du Droit des Affaires* – OHADA). Article 31 of this Uniform Act states that if the arbitration agreement and the award are not drafted in French, the party seeking recognition should submit a translation certified by a translator who is on the list of experts in the country concerned.[41] One may assume that this requirement would also cede ground to Article IV(2) of the New York Convention in cases in which the New York Convention applies.

The choice of the persons qualified to issue certification is certainly linked with the purpose of certification. The question arises whether certification means verification of the authenticity of the document from which translation was made, whether it possibly implies a verification of the identity of the translator and the authenticity of his/her signature, or whether we are talking about verification of the accuracy of the translation. In the latter case, the person effecting certification has to have a fitting command of the languages concerned. An answer to the question regarding the purpose of certification is needed in order to establish who can provide adequate certification.

A position on this issue was taken in a South Korean case[42] in which recognition and enforcement of a Swiss award was requested in South Korea. The Seoul Court of Appeals granted leave of enforcement, and on appeal, the case reached the Supreme Court of South Korea. One of the issues raised was that of the nature of certification. The Korean Supreme Court held:

> 'The requirement [that] the translation of the arbitral award be certified by an official or sworn translator or by a diplomatic or consular agent under Art. IV(2) of the New York Convention does not go so far as to require that such translation be done personally by any of [the] said persons. This requirement is met if anyone of them duly certifies that the translation is the translation of the arbitral awards concerned, even though the text of the arbitral awards is not translated personally by anyone of said persons. Thus, an affixation of the signature of a diplomatic or con-

---

[41] Organisation pour l'Harmonisation en Afrique du Droit des Affaires (OHADA). Acte uniforme relatif au droit de l'arbitrage (Entré en vigueur depuis le 11 juin 1999)
« Art. 31
L'existence de la sentence arbitrale est établie par la production de l'original accompagné de la convention d'arbitrage ou des copies de ces documents réunissant les conditions requises pour leur authenticité.
Si ces pièces ne sont pas rédigées en langue française, la partie devra en produire une traduction certifiée par un traducteur inscrit sur la liste des experts établie par les juridictions compétentes. »

[42] *Adviso N.V. (Neth. Ant) v. Korea Overseas Construction Corp. (South Korea)*, decision of the Supreme Court of Korea No. 93Da53054 of February 14, 1995, reported in *Yearbook Commercial Arbitration*, Vol. XXI (1996) 612-616.

> sular agent is not necessarily required; nor does the meaning of the term "certified" encompass the certification of the accuracy of the translations.'[43]

The first point made by the Korean decision – that certification does not have to be made by the same person who does the translation – is quite common ground. The second point made is that certification does not imply a control of the accuracy of the translation. This is not common ground.

A different position was taken in a Swiss case decided in 1998. Unlike the Korean Court, the Swiss court (in Zug) found that the purpose of certification was the verification of the accuracy of the translation. The court of first instance denied enforcement, finding that the applicant had failed to provide a duly certified translation of the Russian award into German. This was confirmed by the Court of Appeal (*Obergericht*) in Zug.[44] In this case, the Russian award was translated into German by an employee of a Moscow notary public. Certification was issued by the notary public. The Swiss court considered the notary public to be an 'official', thus belonging to the persons entitled to execute certification under Article IV(2). The question arose what the notary public actually certified. The court established that the text of the certification actually confirmed that translation was effected on the basis of a true copy of the original award. This would have met the standard adopted by the Korean court. The Swiss court held, however, that what was needed was a certification of the **correctness of translation** rather than a certification of the authenticity of the copy of the award on the grounds of which the translation was made. Since the notary public did not certify the correctness of the translation, the application for recognition was dismissed holding that the conditions set in Article IV(2) were not met.

The wording of Article IV(2) appears to give somewhat more support to the Swiss interpretation. Article IV(2) speaks of certification of the translation. ('The translation shall be certified...'.) Although this is not fully explicit, one could reasonably argue that by 'certifying the translation', the person executing certification actually needs to certify whether the translation is accurate, rather than whether the right document was translated. One may also note that the first sentence of Article IV(2) speaking of translation, does not set any requirement regarding the person of the translator. It is merely stated that the party seeking recognition shall produce translation. Requirements and qualifications are specified, however, regarding **certification** of translation in the second sentence of Article IV(2).[45] The reference to 'an official or sworn translator' is certainly a

---

[43] *Yearbook Commercial Arbitration*, Vol. XXI (1996) 614.

[44] *Obergericht* Zug, decision of 27.II. 1998, – reported in 18 *ASA Bulletin* (2000) 363.

[45] In practice, the function of the translator and the function of the person who issues the certificate need not be divorced. For example, a sworn translator may, of course, not only certify but also perform the translation.

reference to qualifications which lead to the assumption that we are talking about certification of the accuracy of translation, rather than just about certification that the translation submitted is indeed a translation of the award concerned (or that the signature affixed is that of the actual translator). Further references in the second sentence of Article IV(2) to 'a diplomatic or consular agent' are less unequivocal, and may allow other conclusions as well.[46]

It appears to be closer to both the wording and to the context of Article IV(2) to assume that certification of the translation actually implies a verification of the content of the translation. Accordingly, translation could only be certified by a person who has a command of both the source language and of the target language. Let us add that this does not mean that all translations have to be checked by two persons (the translator and the certifier). If the translator is a person qualified under Article IV(2) to issue certification, this person may certify his/her own translation. If, however, the translator does not possess the qualifications described in Article IV(2), his/her translation will have to be certified 'by an official or sworn translator or by a diplomatic or consular agent'. This latter situation is the one in which the question emerged regarding the purpose of certification. As we stated, there are more arguments favoring the position that certification of the translation implies a verification of its accuracy.

B.4.2. *What type of documents and what parts of the document need to be certified?*

In a case decided by the Ontario Court of Justice[47] the recognition of a Japanese award was requested in Canada. The applicant submitted a Japanese and an English text of the award. The question arose as to whether the Japanese text needed certification under Article IV(2) of the New York Convention. Had the award been issued by the arbitrators both in Japanese and in English, both texts would have been deemed to be the original, and accordingly, there would have been no need to certify the English text as a translation. The applicant did indeed submit that the award was issued in both Japanese and English. This was, however, contradicted by a Japanese solicitor of the applicant corporation, who mentioned in his affidavit that 'We have translated into English, for your refer-

---

[46] It is certainly desirable for a diplomatic or consular agent, let us say in Romania, to speak Romanian, and to be able to translate a Romanian award into the language of the country he/she is representing. Yet, the assumption that a diplomatic or consular agent will speak the requisite languages is not so obvious as it is with regard to a sworn translator.

[47] *Kanto Yakin Kogyo Kabushiki-Kaisha v. Can-Eng Manufacturing Limited*, Ontario Court of Justice, Judgment of January 30, 1992, 4 B.L.R. (2d) 108, 40 C.P.R. (3d) 451.

ence, the Text of the Award as follows.' An original needs to be duly authenticated under Article IV(1), but does not need to be certified as a translation under Article IV(2). The Ontario court concluded that the English text was not an original but a translation, and hence it needed to be certified as a translation. Thereupon, the applicant submitted an additional affidavit by a sworn translator certifying that the English text was a true and correct translation of the award made by the Japan Commercial Arbitration Association. This episode shows that not only the language, but the character of a document also matters. If the arbitrators themselves issue an award in a second language, there will be no need to certify that the award drafted in the second language is a true and correct rendition of the award in the first language; in fact, both versions are equal originals.

The question has also arisen whether the whole award or only some parts of it (or none of it) needs to submitted in a certified translation. The question of partial certification became an issue in a case decided by the Geneva Court of Appeal (*Cour de Justice*) on April 15, 1999. The award submitted for recognition was an award of CIETAC. The original of the award was in Chinese. It was submitted together with a translation into French. The first and last pages of the translation were certified by an official of the Swiss Embassy in Beijing. These pages contained data concerning the parties, the decisional part (*dispositif*), the names of the arbitrators and a clause stating that the award was final. The party opposing recognition objected that the whole translation was not certified. Rejecting the objection of the party opposing recognition, the Geneva court held that this objection was 'purely formal', given that the correctness of the translation was not contested. In the words of the court: 'The Court concludes that this objection is again a purely formal one, given that the Appellant does not contest in any way the conformity of the translation with the original.'[48]

This is an illustrative example showing that the absence of disagreement regarding the accuracy of the translation may (and probably should) guide the court towards a flexible position – particularly when we are not facing a total absence of certification, but rather a certification which may be less than comprehensive.

B.4.3. *Is it relevant whether the content of the award (or the accuracy of the translation) is disputed?*

There are several reasons behind the requirement that the party seeking recognition should produce a certified translation of the award and of the arbitration

---

[48] '[l]a Court constate que ce reproche est à nouveau purement formel, l'appelante ne contestant aucunement la conformité de la traduction avec le text original.' *R. SA v. A. Ltd, Cour de Justice*, Genève, arrêt du 15 avril 1999, 18 *ASA Bulletin* (2000) p 786, at p. 792.

agreement. The first and most simple reason is that the court which considers these documents needs to have a reliable version in the language it understands. A further reason pertains to the equities of the parties. A translation may be imprecise, it may even be biased; it could impose more (or less) burden on one of the parties than what would follow from the original award. Hence, it is important to make the translation as reliable as possible, and this may be done through certification (particularly if we assume that certification implies a control of the accuracy of the translation). It has to be added that adequate certification does not establish conclusive truth. It is, in principle, possible to contest and investigate a certified translation as well.

But what if the submitted translation is not contested between the parties? Would insistence on certification make any practical sense under these circumstances? We have seen earlier that the language skills of the judges represent a consideration which may lead to an exemption from the duty to submit translation. At this point we shall lend attention to another circumstance which has also been interpreted as a reason for relaxation of formal requirements, at least regarding certification. Several courts have opted not to seek certification of the translation, irrespective of language skills, on the basis of the fact that the content of the translated document was not contested.

In its decision of August 17, 2000,[49] the German Supreme Court (*Bundesgerichtshof*) took a position regarding the nature of Article IV(1) of the New York Convention. It held that the rule which requires the submission of 'a duly authenticated original award or a duly certified copy thereof' is actually a provision concerning evidence. It becomes relevant when authenticity is disputed. In the given case between a German investor and the Republic of Poland, Poland opposed recognition and enforcement of a Swiss award in Germany, alleging, i.a., that the German party did not submit duly certified documents. The Supreme Court held that it was not necessary to discuss whether the award was or was not duly certified, since its authenticity was not disputed. The Court stated that Article IV of the New York Convention should be interpreted as a mere rule on evidence (*blosse Beweismittelregelung)* and it would be an empty formality (*leere Förmelei*) to request certification when the content of the submitted award was not contested.[50]

[49] *Bundesgerictshof* (BGH), Beschluss vom 17 August 2000, III ZB 43/99 – website: www.bundesgerichtshof.de.

[50] 'Hier hat die Antragsgegnerin nicht im Zweifel gezogen, dass der von der Antragsstellerin vorgelegten Abschrift des Schiedsspruchs eine damit übereinstimmende authentische Urschrift zugrunde liegt. Es wäre eine leere Förmelei, von der Antragstellerin dennoch zu Verlangen, dass sie die – unstreitige – Existenz und Authentizität des abschriftlich mitgeteilten Schiedsspruchs zuusätzlich mittels der in Art. 4 Abs.1 lit.a UNÜ gennanten Urkunden nachweisst.' BGH, Beschluss vom 17 August 2000 – on p. 5 of the text on the website quoted in the previous footnote.

The same logic was followed in a 2001 decision of the German Supreme Court.[51] In a case in which the German party opposed the recognition of an award of the London Maritime Arbitrators Association (hereinafter 'LMAA'), the Bundesgericht stated i.a. that a possible shortcoming in legalization (certification) would be without consequences, since the existence and the authenticity of the award were not disputed.[52]

The two German decisions actually deal with Article IV(1), but their logic also extends to Article IV(2). If no certification of the original of the award were needed in case the authenticity and the content of the award were not disputed, the same should apply to lack of certification of a translation of the award if the content and the authenticity of the award (the accuracy of the translation) is not disputed. Following the logic of the German courts, insistence on a certified translation (instead of a simple translation) when the accuracy of the translation is not disputed could also be qualified as an empty formalism (*leere Förmelei*).

A flexible interpretation of Article IV will be compatible even with the letter of the Convention when an additional foothold is given under Article VII, i.e., when more favorable rules of the *lex fori* can apply.

When Article VII does not come into play,[53] the arguments of the German Supreme Court are still relevant. One also has to bear in mind, however, that the courts have some *ex-officio* duties as well under the New York Convention. The court will consider *ex-officio* issues of arbitrability and public policy, even if these issues were not raised by the party opposing recognition. Thus, the court needs to have a translation it can trust. In a case referred to earlier, a Swiss court (*Obergericht Zug*), describing the ratio legis behind Article IV(2), stated that the reason and the aim of this provision is to provide a firm ground to the judge who has no command of the language of the original, and who has the duty to investigate not only the objections raised by the debtor, but also the grounds described in Article V(2) of the New York Convention which have to be observed *ex officio*.[54]

---

[51] BGH, Urteil, 1 Februar 2001 III ZR 332/99 – website: www.bundesgerichtshof.de; also reported in 19 *ASA Bulletin* (2001) 325-334.

[52] According to Section II.2. of the statement of reasons (*Entscheidungsgründe*) of the February 1, 2001 Judgment: 'Möglicherweise bestehende Legalisationsmängel des Schiedsspruchs wären unschädlich. Denn die Existenz und die Authentizität des abschriftlich mitgeteilten Schiedsspruchs sind unstreitig…' (pp. 6-7 of the text on the *Bundesgerichtshof* website).

[53] Art. VII does not come into play when a more permissive regulation is not provided by either the local procedural rules or by applicable international agreements.

[54] 'Sinn und Zweck dieser Bestimmung ist es, dem der Sprache der Urschrift nicht mächtigen Anerkennungs- und Vollstreckungsrichter eine sichere Grundlage in die Hand zu geben, um neben den vom Schuldner eingewendeten auch über von Amtes wegen zu beachtenden Verweisungs-

One may note that while the point is well taken, the practical relevance of the caution expressed by the Zug court is limited. Article V(2) of the New York Convention refers to arbitrability and to public policy. Arbitrability rarely represents a ground on which awards are questioned. Furthermore, although this is not inconceivable, it is difficult to imagine a real-life case in which the translation of the 'dispositif' of the award is not contested (it is not contested which claims are awarded and which are denied), yet some mistranslation would nevertheless hide the problem with arbitrability. In other words, it is difficult to imagine a mistranslation which would not be misleading with respect the outcome of the dispute, but would nevertheless be misleading regarding the subject matter of the dispute (would be misleading regarding the question whether the subject matter of the dispute was capable of settlement by arbitration.) As far as public policy is concerned, while it is true that the court may deny recognition on this ground *proprio motu*, in the overwhelming majority of cases the party opposing recognition will also object where an arguable violation of public policy exists. Thus, while it is true that safeguards for the accuracy of the translation do not only serve to shield the party opposing recognition, the practical relevance of this fact is quite limited. If mistranslation yields a result which might violate public policy, it is highly unlikely that this issue would not be raised by the aggrieved party. In cases in which the party opposing recognition does not contest the accuracy of the translation, it is just not realistic to assume that a mistranslation would exist which would amount to violation of public policy.

One may also submit that certification is not an absolute guarantee either, and in most cases, the absence of contestation by any of the parties will probably contribute more to the trustworthiness of the translation than a certification would. Taking into consideration the absence of challenge regarding the content of the award is particularly justified in cases where there is some certification, but it is disputed whether it meets all requirements of Article IV(2).

B.5. Mistranslation in the text of the award

A translated award which is the subject matter of post-award court proceedings may contain some mistranslations. Not every mistranslation is pertinent. Comparing adequacy of literary and legal translation, Cachard states that the concept of an erroneous translation within the domain of law is narrower: 'For lawyers, a faulty translation is an erroneous translation that so deforms the text

---

gründe gemäss Art. V Abs 2 NYU befinden zu können…', *Obergericht Zug*, decision of 27.II. 1998, – reported in 18 *ASA Bulletin* (2000) 363.

of origin that it injures those who trust the translation. Mistranslation leads a judge to decide a case differently.'[55]

Mistranslation has to be relevant regarding the outcome. A mistranslation in the 'dispositif' of the award is an obvious example, although even within the 'dispositif', not every mistranslation matters. If the debtors name and address is correctly rendered in the French translation of the Italian original, but the translators translates Signor Luigi Coppi as 'Seigneur Luigi Coppi', instead of Monsieur Luigi Coppi,[56] this would not alter the decision.

If mistranslation in the award is raised as an issue, the court may order different translations in order to come to a conclusion– irrespective whether the translation was or was not certified. It even happens that the applicant itself raises the issue of (mis)translation. In a Hong Kong case,[57] a Chinese (CIETAC) award was presented for recognition, and the translation submitted showed some errors. The errors were obviously relevant. Using Cachard's standard, they would have 'led the judge to decide the case differently'. One of the two errors mentioned in the Hong Kong judgment pertained to the interest rate. The original award provided for 0.75% per month, while the translation (obviously by way of a clerical error) showed 7.5% per month. This was noted by the applicant itself, and the court ordered a court translation to clarify the imprecisions and mistakes. The party opposing recognition advanced mistranslation as one of the reasons for which recognition should be denied. The court held, however, that this was not a ground for refusing to enforce the award 'because it was clearly a translation error and is being corrected on the application of the plaintiffs'.

The question also arose whether the party opposing recognition may waive his/her right to object on the grounds of mistranslation. For example, if the defendant does not object before the court of first instance which grants recognition, can the defendant rely on mistranslation during appellate proceedings? This is the situation which arose in a dispute between a sister domiciled in Iran, and a brother with residence in the United States (in Oregon). Their dispute was submitted to arbitration in Iran, and an award was rendered (in Farsi) requiring the brother to pay US$ 220,000 to the sister. The sister sought confirmation of the award, filing both the arbitration agreement and the award in their original and with translations in Washington County Circuit Court. The brother was properly served, but did not participate in the proceedings. The award was con-

---

[55] O. Cachard, 'Translating the French Civil Code: Politics, Linguistics and Legislation', 21 *Connecticut Journal of International Law* (2005) 41, at p. 56.

[56] 'Seigneur' comes close to 'Lord' or 'God'.

[57] *Zhejiang Province Garment Import and Export Company (China) v. Siemssen & Co. (Hong Kong)*, Supreme Court of Hong Kong, decision of June 2, 1992, published in *HK Law Digest* (1992) F8.

firmed by a judgment on November 23, 2001, and several writs of garnishment were issued. On December 13, 2001, the brother moved for set aside. One of the reasons for set aside was the alleged incorrectness of the translation of the award. The defendant pointed out that the translation used the phrase 'arbitration judgment' or 'arbitral award', while the correct translation should have been 'arbitration opinion'. The defendant alleged that the difference between these terms is consequential under Iranian law. The award was set aside, and the applicant (the sister) appealed. Dealing with the issue of the alleged mistranslation, the Court of Appeals of Oregon[58] held that even if the translation was incorrect, and even if it was fraudulently filed, the fraud would have been 'intrinsic fraud', rather than 'extrinsic fraud', and intrinsic fraud is not sufficient to set aside a judgment. The Court of Appeals relied on an earlier judgment in which the relevant distinction between intrinsic and extrinsic fraud was drawn, and it was held that: 'Intrinsic fraud will not provide a basis for relief from a judgment, because the litigant had the opportunity to refute the presentations.'[59] Following this logic, the Oregon Court of Appeals found that 'Defendant could have corrected the perceived error by filing an exception before judgment [on confirming the award] was rendered.'[60] The decision on set aside was reversed and remanded with instructions to reinstate the judgment.

In a case which has similar traits (but also some distinctive features), the Supreme Court of Austria reached a different conclusion.[61] The case concerns a Swiss award rendered in English. Recognition was requested in Austria, and the submission of the applicant met all conditions of Article IV of the New York Convention. The applicant submitted, in addition to the original, a certified translation of the award and of the arbitration agreement. The translation was made and certified by a sworn translator. Still, in spite of the fact that all formal conditions were met, the translation contained an obvious and consequential mistake. A whole section of the 'dispositif' (Section 6, dealing with costs) was simply missing in the translation. What makes this case even more unusual, is that this was not noticed by the parties, and it was not detected by the court of first instance either. Recognition was granted to the text which did not contain Section 6 of the original award. The question arose whether the error in translation could and should be remedied in subsequent proceedings. The position taken by the Oregon Court would suggest a negative answer. The Austrian courts

---

58 *Marzieh Geranghadr v. Abdolreza Entagh*, decision of July 30, 2003, 189 Ore.App. 567; 2003 Ore.App.Lexis 1333.

59 *Wimber v. Timpe*, 109 Ore.App.139, 146 (1991).

60 189 Ore.App. 567, 572.

61 *S*** (United States) v. A***, H***, Andre H*** and Stefan S****, OGH decision No. 30b347/99x of June 20, 2000 – available on website http://www.ris.bka.gv.at/jus/.

took a different position. After recognition was granted by the court of first instance (*Erstgericht* – in the given case the *Bezirksgericht* Schwechat), the appellate court (*Rekursgericht* – in the given case the *Landesgericht* Korneuburg) set the decision of the *Bezirkgericht* Schwechat aside, and remanded, ordering supplementary proceedings (*Verfahrensergänzung*). Upon revision, the decision of the Korneuburg appellate court was confirmed by the Supreme Court of Austria.

The Korneuburg appellate court raised the issue whether an appellate court may consider problems with regard to translation when these were not raised before the court of first instance. The court came to the conclusion that in principle, it is not possible to raise issues of mistranslation in appellate proceedings, but it added that the situation is different when the translation is so erroneous that a whole part of the holding is missing. In this situation, the court of first instance had to establish *ex officio* that a section was missing, and had to instruct the applicant to submit a corrected translation.

This reasoning leads to the conclusion that while the omission of the party to raise the question of mistranslation may extinguish the right to appeal on this ground, this right will not cease if an omission of the court (or of the court as well) is at issue. Before addressing this quite intricate issue, a preliminary question has to be answered, namely whether the court has a right and duty to raise the issue of the correctness of the translation *ex officio*, if some inadequacy comes to its attention. The Austrian Supreme Court addressed this question and held that there is no rule in either the New York Convention, or in the applicable Austrian norms, or in the relevant 1962 Austrian–Swiss treaty that would oblige the court to remain satisfied with an incomplete translation. The Supreme Court concluded that incompleteness has to be investigated *ex officio*, at least when this is recognizable from the structuring of the document even without a command of the language of the original. This was indeed the case, since it was evident even to a person without requisite language skills that Section 6 of the original award was lost in translation.

A comparison of the Oregon and the Austrian decisions leads to a number of important questions. The first – and probably the easiest – question is whether the court before which the award is relied upon is entitled at all to raise the issue of (mis)translation. The Austrian Supreme Court states that there is nothing in the New York Convention that would oblige the court to remain satisfied with an imperfect translation. This is true, but neither is there anything in the New York Convention which would oblige the court to investigate *ex officio* the correctness of the translation. Deducting permission from lack of prohibition is probably the only way to come to the conclusion reached by the Supreme Court. General procedural principles yield the same conclusion, and this is a sensible solution. If the court notes that a section of the holding is missing in the translation submitted, it would be contrary to fair and efficient proceedings to remain silent and to enforce the result of mistranslation. Likewise, if the court were to observe that the translation obliges the respondent to pay 7,5% of monthly interest – instead of 0.75% as actually awarded – not raising this as an issue[62] would be clearly contrary to good faith.

The difficult question is what consequences should follow if the parties do not object, and the court does not notice that the translation is defective. The failure to use a procedural right will normally lead to the loss of this right. This principle was emphasized by the Oregon court, and it was also followed by the Korneuburg court (and approved by the Supreme Court of Austria). In the Austrian case it was added, however, that even if the party fails to object during first instance proceedings, it may nevertheless raise the objection in appellate proceedings in situations where the court was also obliged to raise the objection and failed to do so. An element of this construct is the view that the court is obliged to raise the issue of mistranslation *ex officio* if the mistranslation is obvious (recognizable even without requisite language skills). In other words, an exception was created, and it was restricted to cases in which the deficiency is obvious (and hence the court had a duty to notice it *ex officio*).

Some dilemmas arise in connection with this exception. First of all, in order to consider this exception one needs some definition – or at least some standard which would guide the court in identifying those errors which are recognizable even without a command of the foreign language ('auch ohne Fremdsprachkentnisse erkennbar sind'). This was not difficult in the given Austrian case, because one can qualify without hesitation the omission of a part of the 'dispositif' as an obvious error. It is much more difficult, however, to translate 'obviousness' into a more general standard. (Let me add that we are talking about the obviousness of deficiencies which, nevertheless, remain unnoticed.)

In the Austrian case a corrective exception was recognized in order to give priority to substance over formalities. But if this is the aim, the question is whether the means were well chosen. If the deficiency in translation is so obvious that even a judge without command of the language of the original should have noticed it, this means that the neglect of the party who did not object is even greater. The argument could also be made that the party (who also failed to object) may deserve more protection when the deficiency is perhaps less obvious but more consequential.

Let me conclude first that when translation is submitted, what is actually recognized is the text of the award in the official language of the court (the text of the translation). This means that errors in translation may indeed become

[62] Raising it as an issue means in practice to alert the parties, and possibly to order a new translation.

consequential. Furthermore, it is easy to accept the proposition that if the court notices an obvious (or not obvious) error in translation, it has a right and a duty to react. It is also an established principle that if a party fails to notice a clearly detectable error in translation in recognition proceedings before the court of first instance, he/she will not be allowed to challenge the award in appellate proceedings on the grounds of this error. Should there be exceptions to this latter rule? The exception designed by the Austrian court is less than persuasive as a general standard. It has to be added that the dimensions of the problem are probably modest. It would really take a high level of negligence (at least from the party whose rights are impaired) not to notice that what the translated award grants is substantially different from what the original award ordered.

Let me finally note on the margins of the Austrian case and of the Hong Kong case discussed in this subsection that errors in translation need not stem from linguistic imperfection. A less than diligent and less than conscientious translation is an added opportunity for technical omissions and clerical errors as well.

B.6. On the consequences of a failure to submit fitting documents at the time of the application

If an award orders the Respondent to pay US$ 1 million, but the court determines that the Respondent did not have an opportunity to present his case during the arbitral proceedings, recognition will be denied, and there will be no recovery on ground of the award. But what if the only problem with the award is the fact that among the documents submitted, there is a translation of the award, but it is not properly certified? Should this represent a ground for denial of recognition (and of recovery), or should the court just invite the Claimant to furnish the missing certification (and possibly pay added costs)? Here we are not talking about the option for the court to waive the duty to submit translation (or certification). We are talking about cases in which the court did not exempt the party from submitting the documents required under Article IV. The question is what consequences should follow if the party nevertheless fails to submit the required documents.

In a 1981 Italian case, the Supreme Court of Italy refused recognition of a Romanian award on the grounds that the Romanian party seeking recognition did not submit the required duly authenticated documents or duly certified copies thereof. The Supreme Court stressed that according to Article IV of the Convention the requested documents (the award and the arbitration agreement) need to be submitted '**at the time of the application**'.[63] This logic could clearly

[63] Reported in 21 *Rassegna dell'Arbitrato* (1981) 134.

apply to the documents contemplated in Article IV(2) as well. Other courts have taken a more flexible position. In an earlier (1965) decision, the Supreme Court of Austria held that the failure of the party seeking recognition to submit the arbitration agreement (in addition to the award) does not justify denial of enforcement, because this defect can be cured.[64] The same logic was followed in a 2000 decision of the High Court of Hong Kong (Special Administrative Region). The Hong Kong court held that the lack of submission of original documents or translations at the time of the application could be remedied by subsequent submission.[65]

The Austrian and Hong Kong approach appear to be justified. In most cases a failure to provide fitting documents can be easily remedied. If a translation is submitted without proper certification, such certification could be procured after the court established that the documents do not meet all requirements of Article IV(2). One could also argue, that – unlike Article V – Article IV of the New York Convention does not mention any sanctions. Article V makes it clear that recognition may be **refused** if a defect of the award is demonstrated. Article IV merely mentions that the submission of the appropriate documents identified in subsections 1 and 2 are prerequisites for obtaining recognition. Thus, recognition cannot be granted until fitting documents have been produced, and the party that is in delay with the submission of proper documents and certificates may be liable for the costs incurred due to the delay caused – but this does not mean that the claim for recognition has to be refused on its merits.

In a 1995 decision the Supreme Court of Italy clarified its position, and established a compromise.[66] In this case the arbitral award was rendered in Budapest in favor of a Hungarian party. The Hungarian party sought recognition in Italy, without supplying all documents prescribed by Article IV. The Rome Court of Appeal held that the request for recognition was inadmissible, but added that this was not a decision on the merits of the request, and that a new request could still be submitted. The Italian defendant appealed against this holding, arguing that the proper consequence of failure to submit the necessary documents can only be a denial of the merits of the request (i.e., denial of recognition), rather than declaring the request inadmissible, but allowing resubmission. This gave the Supreme Court an opportunity to define the exact

64 *Oberster Gerichtshof*, November 17, 1965 – reported in 9 *Zeitschrift für Rechtsvergleichung* (1968) 123.

65 *Medson Co. Ltd. v. Viktor (Far East) Ltd.*, High Court of the Hong Kong Special Administrative Region, Court of First Instance, April 8, 2000 – reported in *Yearbook Commercial Arbitration*, Vol. XXVIII (2003) 270-271.

66 *Campomarzio Impianti srl. (Italy) v. Lampart Vegyipari Gépgyár (Hungary)*, Corte di Cassazione, September 20, 1995 – reported in *Yearbook Commercial Arbitration*, Vol. XXIV (1999) 698-702.

consequences of a failure to comply with Article IV. The Supreme Court reviewed various earlier Italian decisions pertaining to this issue, and confirmed the judgment of the Rome Court of Appeal. The Supreme Court held that:

> '[t]he obligation in Art. IV is a prerequisite for commencing the proceedings or, more precisely, a prerequisite for rendering a decision on the merits. Hence, the decision which finds that there is such defect does not prevent a subsequent request to enforce the same award.'[67]

This is certainly a rational position, in line with the purpose and spirit of the New York Convention, and not contradicting its wording either. Recognition can only be conclusively denied for the reasons enumerated in Article V. A failure to comply with the requirements of Article IV may result in dismissal allowing resubmission of the application. An even more simple and more practical solution is, instead of dismissal, to allow resubmission of the documents within the same proceedings.

C. Language and Translation in the Context of Control of Procedural Irregularities in Post-Award Proceedings

C.1. The issue of language in the context of control of procedural irregularities in post-award proceedings – General remarks

The preceding subchapter of this chapter has dealt with issues pertaining to the language and translation of documents submitted in post-award proceedings, investigating the possible shortcomings of these documents, and the consequences of such shortcomings. These are issues relating to documents (most importantly, the award) which are submitted in post-arbitration proceedings. I would like to turn now to the second angle under which language and translation may become relevant in post-arbitration proceedings. The focus of this subchapter is on post-award scrutiny of language and translation used within the arbitration proceedings. The question arises whether (and if so, in what way) irregularities regarding language and translation could become grounds for setting aside the award, or for denying recognition.

The main focus of this subchapter is again on the New York Convention, since it sets a truly global standard. I would like to repeat that the grounds on which setting aside is permitted in various national laws are becoming increasingly harmonized with those established in the New York Convention. The Model

[67] *Yearbook Commercial Arbitration*, Vol. XXIV (1999) at p. 702.

Law has played a pivotal role in this synchronization. Let me also repeat, however, that differences do exist, and we shall devote attention to some distinct features in municipal norms which have become relevant with regard to language and translation.

Under the New York Convention, possible grounds for denying recognition on the basis of some deficiency in the arbitration proceedings are restricted to those enumerated in Article V. Article V also controls the adequacy and fairness of the use of language(s) during the arbitral proceedings. In the course of court practice on a comparative scale, dilemmas have emerged regarding possible interpretations of the procedural requirements pertaining to language.

Not all of the grounds for refusal of recognition enumerated in Article V have become (or could have become) relevant with regard to deficiencies in the arbitration proceedings pertaining to language and translation. Finding a fitting shelter for language-related shortcomings (or alleged shortcomings) may not be easy – and we have seen this following the meanderings of the Bulgarian case discussed in the preceding chapter.[68] There are basically three settings in which the language used (or not used) during the arbitral proceedings may become a cause for denial of recognition and enforcement under the New York Convention. The first is offered by subsection 1(b) of Article V, which states that recognition may be denied if the party against whom the award is invoked '[w]as not given proper notice of the appointment of the arbitrator or of the arbitration proceedings or was otherwise unable to present his case'. The second possible setting is offered by subsection 1(d) of Article V, which provides that recognition may be refused if '[t]he arbitral procedure was not in accordance with the agreement of the parties, or, failing such agreement, was not in accordance with the law of the country where the arbitration took place;'. A third setting is also imaginable. One may possibly argue that some impropriety concerning language amounts to a violation of public policy within the meaning of Article V(2)(b) of the New York Convention. It is difficult, however, to find such cases, and it is even more difficult to find cases in which a language related argument could not have been couched in terms of Article V(1)(b) or Article V(1)(d), but only in terms of V(2)(b). For this reason, our main focus will be on Articles V(1)(b) and V(1)(d). It also has to be mentioned that it is quite possible – even likely – that the same language-related deficiency would fit under more than one provision of Article V.

As far as setting aside proceedings are concerned, the grounds defined in Article V(1)(b) and V(1)(d) are adopted in most national statutes covering setting aside. Quite often, the wording is exactly the same, or essentially the same.

---

[68] Chapter IV.F.

Some acts contain, however, distinct grounds for setting aside the award, and some of these grounds have become relevant in the context of issues pertaining to language. An important example is paragraph 10 of the 1925 United States Federal Arbitration Act (hereinafter 'US Arbitration Act') which sets **misconduct** of the arbitrators (including 'any other misbehavior by which the rights of any party have been prejudiced') as one of the grounds for vacating the award. The 1950 UK Arbitration Act also contained such a ground for setting aside.

On the following pages we shall examine setting aside and refusal of recognition and enforcement on the grounds of deficiencies pertaining to language. We shall focus on the two basic types of deficiencies: **use of wrong language (lack of translation)**, and **mistranslation**. We shall investigate what consequences are linked to these deficiencies, and in what settings these consequences are allocated.

C.2. **Use of wrong language (lack of translation)**

Use of wrong language (or lack of translation) may become relevant in post-award court proceedings in several settings. We have already identified these settings above as possible shelters under which language-related objections may be fitted in general. Article V(1)(b) of the New York Convention – or a corresponding provision in national statutes expressing the same concept of due process – is one of these shelters. The other option is Article V(1)(d) – or like provisions in national statutes – which sanction arbitral proceedings not in accordance with the agreement of the party (or not in accordance with the *lex arbitri*). We shall also investigate consequences of 'misconduct of the arbitrator' as a possible setting.

C.2.1. *Due process ('The party against who the award is invoked was not given proper notice [...] or was otherwise unable to present his case')*

Formulating a standard of due process, the New York Convention relies on the 'ability to present one's case' as a criterion. Article V(1)(b) sets one specific example (proper notice), and adds that recognition may also be denied if a party 'was otherwise unable to present his case'. We shall start with the issue of notice:

Proper notice

The propriety of notice may possibly turn on the language of the notice. This leads to the question what is (or should be) the language of notice. The basic rule is different from that in court proceedings. The language of arbitral proceedings normally covers notice as well. This rule, however, does not always provide the answer. The language of the arbitral proceedings is typically established by the parties or, in the absence of party agreement, by the arbitrators. Quite often, the parties do not contemplate the issue of language in their arbitration agreement. This leads to the issue of initial language, a question we have dealt with earlier.[69] One also has to mention that the prevailing rule (the language of the notice is the language of the arbitral proceedings) is sometimes replaced by another norm. The rules of some arbitral institutions make a distinction between the language of the arbitral proceedings and the language of communication between the institution and the parties. According to the 2006 Vienna Rules, for example, the language of communication between the institution and the parties is English or German, notwithstanding what language was established as the language of the arbitral proceedings proper.[70] Accordingly, if notices were sent by the Vienna Center, rather than by the arbitrators themselves, they should be in either English or German, even if the language of the arbitral proceedings was for example French, or Hungarian.

If the language of the notice is not in accordance with the language of the arbitral proceedings determined by the parties, or with the language determined by the arbitration rules chosen by the parties, the party opposing recognition may possibly rely on both Article V(1)(b) and Article V(1)(d). At this point it is important to note that Article V(1)(b) actually sets a standard of due process, and within the context of this provision, lack of proper notice is just one way in which a party may be impeded in presenting his/her case. I would like to demonstrate the relevance of Article V(1)(b) through several court cases from various countries.

In a case decided by the Basel Court of Appeal in Switzerland,[71] the Swiss party opposed enforcement of a Romanian award, stating that the first invitation to participate in the arbitration proceedings was in Romanian. He added that he did receive a notice in a 'comprehensible language' later on, but this was 'only 4–5 days before the start of the proceedings'. The question arose as to whether this represented 'proper notice' within the meaning of Article V(1)(b). The Basel Court scrutinized Article V, stated that it enumerates the grounds for possible refusal of recognition, and came to the conclusion that 'The fact that an invitation to arbitration proceedings was drafted in the language of the seat of the arbitration – a language that one of the parties did not understand – is not

[69] See Chapter I.C.3; See also Várady, 'The Language Issue in International Commercial Arbitration – Notions and Questions', *Prawo Priwatne Czasu Przemian (Festchrift Soltysinski)* (Poznan 2005) 923-954, at pp. 934-937.

[70] See Art. 6 of the 2006 Vienna Rules.

[71] *Apellant: N.Z. (nationality not indicated) v. Apellee: I. (Romania)*, reported in *Yearbook Commercial Arbitration*, Vol. XVII (1992) p. 581.

part of that enumeration.'[72] With regard to this conclusion, the point can be made that the fact that the language of the notice is not an explicit part of the enumeration in Article V need not be critical. Article V uses the term 'proper notice', and this may very well be interpreted as a standard which implies the use of the proper language as well. Still, the outcome reached in the Basel decision is a logical one. Even if the Romanian rules did not provide for a default language in the absence of party agreement, in other words, even if the problem of 'initial language' had not been solved, the burden on the Swiss party was not an unreasonable one, nor an unexpected one. The Swiss party might not have spoken Romanian, but finding a translator in Basel would not have been an excessive burden, particularly not for a party that had agreed to arbitrate in Bucharest. One could argue that the party receiving the notice might not even know that it comes from a court of arbitration. But this line of argument is not particularly persuasive in this case, because the Romanian name of the Court of Arbitration at the Romanian Chamber of Commerce is not very different from the French designation (it may alert the English-speaking reader as well), and it is difficult to miss the message from the letterhead. But even supposing that '**Curtea de Arbitraj International**' did not remind a French-speaking reader[73] of *Cour d'Arbitrage International*, or did not ring a bell for someone who speaks English, a party in good faith cannot just ignore a letter from Bucharest after having submitted to Bucharest arbitration, and while expecting notice from the Bucharest International Court of Arbitration.[74]

Another example of cases in which the issue of language emerged in the context of Article V(1)(b) is a 1999 decision of the District Court of Yokohama (already referred to in paragraph I.C.4)[75] In this case a Japanese respondent opposed recognition of a Chinese award relying on Article V(1)(b), stating that the notice was sent to the respondent in Chinese without a translation into Japanese. The case was not a difficult one. The Japanese court took note of the fact that according to the CIETAC Rules, the language of arbitration was Chinese, unless the parties agreed otherwise. In the given case, the parties clearly agreed on the application of the CIETAC Rules, and they did not choose another language as the language of arbitral proceedings. Thus, the language which followed from the fact that the parties opted for CIETAC Rules was Chinese – and this was the language of the notice. Recognition was granted.

---

72 *Yearbook Commercial Arbitration*, Vol. XVII (1992) at p. 583.

73 French is one of the official languages in Switzerland.

74 It is a different question whether the Bucharest court of arbitration acted in this case fully in line with its interest to promote this court of arbitration as an international forum.

75 Plaintiff: *Seller (P.R. China) v. Defendant: Buyer (Japan)*, District Court of Yokohama, August 25, 1999 (Docket: Heisei 10/wa/3851) – reported in *Yearbook Commercial Arbitration*, Vol. XXVII (2002) p. 515-518.

One might ask what would have been the outcome, had the CIETAC sent the notice in English (the contract was written in Chinese and English). A notice in English would have been in contravention of the rules governing arbitration, because according to the CIETAC Rules the default language is Chinese. Nevertheless, in my opinion a notice in English would not have represented a violation of Article V(1)(b). Unlike Article IV(2) which – at least in principle – requires formal compliance with a given language (the language of the country in which the award is relied upon), Article V(1)(b) does not set such a specific standard. It speaks of 'proper notice'. If Article V(1)(b) is invoked, notice in a language other than the language of arbitration need not amount to a violation per se. It remains important whether the ('wrong') language of the notice did or did not impede the party in presenting its case. Considering the circumstances of the case, it is quite possible that notices in more than one language may represent 'proper notice'. The circumstances of the case may be relevant, but normally, notice in one of the languages of the contract could be considered as proper notice. The Article V(1)(b) ground for refusal of recognition is generally perceived as standard of due process. This means that an irregularity will only infringe Article V(1)(b) if it amounts to a violation of due process. One also has to bear in mind that the message contained in a notice is usually quite simple. The due process standard will normally be met if the language of the notice is either the language the party bargained for (or tacitly accepted), or a language which the party can understand without much difficulty. One cannot speak of violation of due process and of inability to present one's case if, for example, the language of the notice is the official language of the country of the recipient (which is not the language of arbitration), or the native tongue of the recipient (which in the given case is neither the language of arbitration nor the official language of the country of the recipient). The use of a language which is closely related to either the language of arbitration or to the language of the recipient (e.g., Serbian instead of Croatian, Spanish instead of Catalan, Czech instead of Slovak, Swedish instead of Norwegian), would in all likelihood not amount to a violation of Article V(1)(b) either.

I would like now to refer to another case in which the language of notice was at issue, but the pertinent provisions relied upon were not those of Article V of the New York Convention, since this was a setting aside case decided under US law. In *Pacific Reliance Inc. v. Transmoreproduct*, a Russian party (Transmoreproduct) sought setting aside of an arbitral award before US courts (courts of the State of Washington) on the grounds of improper notice.[76] The arbitration clause in the contract stated that

[76] See *Pacific Reliance Inc. v. Transmoreprodukt (Russia)*, the decision of the Superior Court of Kin County, 128 Wn.App.1007, and the Decision of the Court of Appeals of Washington, Division One, June 13, 2005, 2005 Wash. App. LEXIS 1367.

> 'All disputes are subject to binding arbitration in King County, subject to the King County Mandatory Arbitration Rules and Washington Law. The parties agree to accept service of process by registered mail at their respective home offices.'

The contract also stated that it shall be executed in English and Russian, and the 'English version shall control if translations are inconsistent'. An arbitral award was rendered without participation of the Russian party. In its claim for setting aside Transmoreproduct argued that notice was inadequate, because it received it without translation into Russian. The Superior Court of King County denied the motion to vacate the award, and on appeal, the case reached the Court of Appeals of Washington. The Russian party contended that language disparities between the Russian and English language versions of the contracts make it ambiguous whether registered mail was adequate service. This argument was easily dismissed since the contract expressly provided that 'the English version will control if translations are inconsistent'. The argument was also raised that notice was not in accordance with the relevant Hague Convention and with the Russian Code of Civil Procedure, since documents were not translated into Russian. The Court of Appeals held that 'There is no requirement under the contract or under Washington law that a translation be provided.'[77] This case shows that there are still misunderstandings stemming from the failure to make a distinction between the language of notice in court cases and in arbitration cases respectively. In a court case, the provisions of the Russian Code of Civil Procedure or of the 1965 Hague Convention could indeed be relevant. Arbitration is, however, a product of the parties, and the language of communication is also set by the parties (or by the arbitrators). It appears that in the given case the parties did not agree on the language of arbitration, and hence the issue of initial language was not explicitly solved. Given, however, that one of the languages of the contract (the controlling language) was English and that the parties opted for English language arbitration rules (King County Mandatory Arbitration Rules), a notice in English could hardly be perceived as unexpected, and as a violation of due process. There is one point which may have been raised by the Russian party and which, according to the text of the decision, was not specifically raised. The US party (Pacific Reliance) in addition to sending (admittedly proper) notices to arbitrate, also moved to obtain a court order to arbitrate. It is not clear what was the exact role of this court order, since a notice to arbitrate on the grounds of an uncontested arbitration clause was quite sufficient to set into motion the arbitration proceedings. Had the order to compel arbitration been perceived as the triggering element, and had the challenge been focused on this

---

[77] 2005 Wash.App. LEXIS 1367 *8.

court order, the argument could have been made that the notice to appear before this **court** (and possibly the *ex parte* court order) had to be communicated to the Russian party in accordance with the norms of the 1965 Hague Convention, rather than under the rules pertaining to arbitration proceedings proper.

Otherwise unable to present one's case

The 'otherwise unable to present his case' part of ground V(1)(b) – or other articulations of the standard of dues process – may also come into play when the 'wrong' language is used, or when translation is not provided. Lack of translation which actually yields lack of understanding may indeed impede a party in presenting its case. If a witness had no opportunity to make a statement – or if this statement was not properly understood – because he/she had no adequate command of the language of the arbitral proceedings and no translation was provided, this may amount to a violation of due process. The argument against recognition will be strengthened if, under the applicable rules, the duty to provide for translation was a duty of the arbitral tribunal (rather than of the party who challenges the award).

At this point I would like to refer to a French setting aside case in which the standard of due process was not scrutinized on the grounds of Article V(1)(b), but on the grounds of Article 1502(4) of the French Code of Civil Procedure, which contains a formulation which is different, but follows the same principles. In the dispute between *Société Comecim* and *Société Theobroma*, and arbitral award was challenged before the Paris *Cour d'appel.*[78] One of the grounds of the challenge was violation of due process (*principe de contradiction* in the formulation of Article 1502(4) of the French Code of Civil Procedure).[79] Comecim objected that the arbitral tribunal accepted a written submission of Theobroma drafted in English, in spite of the fact that the language of arbitration was French, and in disregard of a request of Comecim to provide French translation. The Paris Court of Appeals found that under the given circumstances of the case, due process was not violated by accepting an English submission without translation. Consideration was given to the fact that most of the correspondence between the parties was in English, and the use of English was customary between them. It was also mentioned in the decision that the parties did not even translate into French (from English) documents submitted to the Court of Appeals in setting aside proceedings, which also dem-

[78] *Société Comecim v. Société Theobroma, Cour d'appel de Paris*, decision of June 27, 2002, *Revue de l'arbitrage* (2002) 793-795, and (in more detail) *Revue de l'arbitrage* (2003) 427-434.

[79] According to Art. 1502(4) of the French New Code of Civil Procedure one of the grounds on which recognition may be challenged is 'lorsque le principe de la contradiction n'a pas été respecté;'.

onstrated their familiarity with English. The Court of Appeals concluded that under the circumstances the absence of translation did not cause any impairment,[80] and rejected the request for setting aside. This confirms the position that in post-award proceedings a challenge based on alleged violation of due process due to lack of translation can only be sustained if this lack of translation actually impeded a party in presenting his/her case. The Paris court also noted that the applicable arbitration rules (Arbitration rules of the French association of cacao trade) state in their Article 37 that the language of arbitration is French and that the arbitrators may refuse to accept (*peut déclarer non receivable*) documents in another language. It was held that following this provisions the arbitrators may, but are not obliged to, reject documents in another language than French.

C.2.2. *'Arbitral procedure not in accordance with the agreement of the parties, or [...] not in accordance with the law of the country where the arbitration took place'*

Article V(1)(d) provides that recognition may be refused if the arbitral procedure was not in conformity with the agreement of the parties;[81] regarding issues not covered by party agreement, recognition may also be refused if the arbitral proceeding was not in conformity with the *lex arbitri*. These provisions may again give rise to language related issues. One should point out that the failure to provide for translation is more consequential if translation **into** the language of the arbitral proceedings is missing. This may be a direct violation of the procedural arrangement pertaining to language.

One may argue that the context of Article V(1)(d) is suggestive of strict compliance. Arbitrators derive their authority from the parties. Faced with unreasonable stipulations (including unreasonable stipulations pertaining to language), the arbitrators may try to persuade the parties to modify some terms of their agreement on procedure, they may refuse to arbitrate, but they cannot ignore party stipulations (including those concerning the language of the proceedings), because the will of the parties is the source of their authority. In *the Comecim v. Theobroma* case discussed in connection with notice and due process, while it was rather obvious that due process (or the principle of adversary proceedings) was not violated by the acceptance of a brief drafted in English, the question

[80] 'il s'en déduit que l'absence de traduction du mémoire de la société Theobroma n'a causé aucun grief à l'auteur de recours en annulation', *Revue de l'arbitrage* (2002) 794.

[81] One may submit that arbitral proceedings not in conformity with the institutional rules chosen by the parties could also be deemed as arbitral proceedings not in conformity with party agreement.

also had to be answered whether the use of English was compatible with the agreement of the parties regarding the arbitral procedure. In order to dispose of this objection the court had to establish that the acceptance of a submission in English actually did not violate the wording of the relevant provision of the arbitration rules (which were applicable on the basis of party agreement).

One also has to point out that while the wording of Article V(1)(d) is indeed suggestive of strict compliance, other interpretations have also gained ground in comparative practice both within and outside the realm of language issues. I would like to cite just a few well-known cases interpreting Article V(1)(d) which do not deal with language issues. In *Compagnie des Bauxites de Guinée v. Hammermills*,[82] the US District Court of the District of Columbia stated that under Article V(1)(d) recognition should only be denied if the violation at issue 'worked substantial prejudice to the complaining party'.[83] Another of those cases in which a flexible attitude was explicitly taken is the China Nanhai Oil Joint Service Corporation, *Shenzen Branch v. Gee Tai Holdings*.[84] In this case, Judge Kaplan from the Supreme Court of Hong Kong specifically raised the question whether the recognizing court should exercise discretion when facing the objection that the arbitration procedure was not in accordance with the agreement of the parties. Judge Kaplan took a strong position in favor of discretion, adding that 'This conclusion is, in my judgment, quite consistent with the pro enforcement bias of the Convention and the pro enforcement attitude of most enforcing courts around the world.'[85]

Arguments have also been advanced in favor of a more flexible interpretation of Article V(1)(d) having language issues specifically in mind. Fouchard, Gaillard and Goldman state that:

> 'Where there is a failure to comply with the provision as to the language of proceedings agreed by the parties, or determined by the arbitrators failing agreement of the parties, an action to set aside or refuse enforcement of the award may be entertained but will generally prevail only where the principles of due process and equal treatment of the parties are considered to have been violated.'[86]

This is certainly a sensible suggestion, even if it does not clearly follow from the language of Article V. It is reasonable to assume that not any departure from

---

[82] Memorandum Opinion of May 29, 1992, 1992 WL 122712 (D.D.C.)

[83] 1992 WL 122712 (D.D.C.) *5.

[84] Supreme Court of Hong Kong, High Court, 1994, 20 *Yearbook Commercial Arbitration* (1995) 671; Várady-Barcelo-Von Mehren, op. cit. 842.

[85] Várady-Barcelo-Von Mehren, op. cit. 844-845.

[86] Ph. Fouchard, E. Gaillard and B. Goldman, *On International Commercial Arbitration* (Kluwer 1999) at p. 679.

the language set by the parties (or set by other mechanism) amounts to a reason for refusing recognition, irrespective whether it has an actual impact on the fairness of the proceedings. It is also important to mention at this point that a corrective factor balancing strict application of Article V(1)(d) can often be found in the concept of waiver (to be discussed later under C.2.5).

With respect to Article V(1)(d), another interesting question might be raised in the context of language and lack of translation. It is commonly accepted that under most statutes and institutional rules, the language of the arbitral proceedings is either chosen by the parties or determined by the arbitral tribunal. The question arises whether it matters that Article V(1)(d) only refers to procedure not in accordance with the agreement of the parties or with the *lex arbitri*, without mentioning procedure not in accordance with determinations made by the arbitrators. Can this mean that if no translation is provided into the language of the proceedings as determined by the arbitral tribunal, the chances for challenge are more limited? Probably not. First, such a distinction does not make much practical sense and does not appear to be a fair one either, because it establishes an unexpected difference and hierarchy between the different methods of determining the language of the arbitral proceedings. Such a hierarchy is not contemplated either in the relevant provisions of arbitration acts or in the arbitration rules dealing directly with the issue of establishing the language of the proceedings. Furthermore, one can argue that a determination made by the arbitrators is also derived from party agreement or from the *lex arbitri* since the arbitrators are making such a determination either on the grounds of the applicable arbitration rules (which are chosen by the parties and may be treated as a part of party agreement) or on the grounds of the applicable *lex arbitri*.

Speaking of Article V(1)(d) of the New York Convention I would like to refer to a case which does not exactly belong to, but which is akin to cases in which the use of a wrong language or lack of translation became an issue. In a 1998 case decided by the *Oberlandesgericht* Dresden[87] the issue was not that of inadequate language, but of allegedly inadequate language skills. The dispute was originally submitted to the Commercial Arbitration Court of the Chamber of Commerce and Industry of the Russian Federation (hereinafter 'ICAC'). According to the Rules of the ICAC, the President of the Russian Chamber of Commerce and Industry acts as appointing authority if a party fails to nominate his/her arbitrator. The respondent did not nominate its arbitrator, and stated in a letter to the ICAC that the President of the Russian Chamber of Commerce and

[87] *Oberlandesgericht* Dresden, Decision No. 11 Sch.04/98 of October 20, 1998, *Yearbook Commercial Arbitration*, Vol. XXIX (2004) 673.

Industry might appoint an arbitrator (what follows from the Rules anyway), adding that the arbitrator should be able to speak German. The President initially appointed an arbitrator who spoke German, but this had to be changed, and he finally appointed an arbitrator who did not speak German. An award was rendered obliging the respondent to pay DM 610,969.94. Claimant sought recognition before the Dresden Court of Appeal (*Oberlandesgericht*). The respondent opposed recognition, and one of the reasons advanced was that the arbitrator appointed by the President of the Russian Chamber of Commerce and Industry did not speak German. It was alleged that for this reason the arbitral tribunal was not properly constituted ('the composition of the arbitral authority...was not in accordance with the agreement of the parties...'), which is one of the reasons for denying enforcement under Article V(1)(d). Unlike in other cases in which the use of wrong language (or lack of translation) was qualified as 'procedure not in accordance with the agreement of the parties' (or with the *lex arbitri*), here the focus is on the **composition of the tribunal**, rather than on the procedure – and the substance of the objection concerns language skills.

The Dresden court rejected this argument (as well as other arguments raised by the respondent), and enforced the award. It held that the arbitral tribunal was duly formed. The respondent (defendant in the court proceedings) did have an opportunity to appoint an arbitrator according to his wishes. The Dresden court stated: 'The defendant did not make use of this right. Thereafter, the President of the Moscow Chamber of Commerce and Industry had complete discretion in the choice of the arbitrator.'[88] The Court added that the President was not obliged to comply with the wishes of the respondent and, moreover, the respondent failed to challenge the arbitrator upon appointment within the time limit set by the ICAC Rules.

Language skills of the arbitrators can rarely represent a basis for challenge in the context of Article V(1)(d). For one reason, this is because language skills are most rarely specified by the parties as a requisite qualification. Another reason is that, if such a stipulation were made, it would in all likelihood be observed. In other words, there have been practically no cases in which (lack of) language skills could have represented the basis of the argument that the composition of the arbitral authority was not in accordance with the agreement of the parties. As a matter of fact, this case is no exception. A **party agreement** on linguistic skills of the arbitrator is lacking in this case as well. What we have is only the wish of one party. Had there been a party agreement to the effect that one or more arbitrators have to speak German, and had that party agreement

[88] Ibidem at p. 675.

been disregarded, we would have a different matter. In that case, one could indeed have made the argument that the composition of the arbitral tribunal was not in accordance with the agreement of the parties.

Another interesting question may be raised in connection with the Dresden case. As it appears from the facts of the case, the language of the proceedings was not German. The German party wanted a German speaking arbitrator for other reasons. Suppose the language of arbitration **had** been German. In this case it would have been certainly ill-advised to appoint an arbitrator who did not speak the language of the proceedings. Would this amount to a violation of Article V(1)(d)? Probably still not, assuming that translation was provided for the arbitrator who did not speak the language of the proceedings. If the language of the arbitral proceedings is German, the appointment of an arbitrator who does not speak German is certainly a bad choice, but not necessarily a violation of party agreement or of the *lex arbitri*, as long as translation is provided, and thus, a bridge is created between the language skills of a participant and the language of the arbitral proceedings. If translation were not provided, we would have another case in which the award could be challenged on the grounds of lack of translation.

C.2.3. *Misconduct of the arbitrator*

In *Rotheray & Sons Ltd. v. Carlo Bedarida & Co.*, a 1961 UK case[89] decided under the 1950 Arbitration Act, a motion for set aside was based on a quite rare language-related deficiency. In this case an English and an Italian company agreed to arbitrate under the Bradford Chamber of Commerce Arbitration Rules. The case was submitted to two arbitrators appointed by the Bradford Chamber of Commerce. One of the key issues in the dispute was whether a contract had been concluded. There was no oral hearing, the arbitrators decided on the basis of written evidence, and on July 7, 1960 they rendered an award in favor of the Italian party. The English party moved for set aside advancing two interrelated grounds:

> '(1) that it constituted misconduct for an arbitrator to proceed to his award on the basis of documentary evidence in a language which he did not understand, even if the documents were verbally translated to him by his co-arbitrator; and (2) it constituted misconduct for an arbitrator, in those circumstances, to state in his award that he had "carefully considered" the evidence.'[90]

---

[89] *E. Rotheray & Soons Ltd. v. Carlo Bedarida & Co.*, Queens Bench Division, decision of February 22, 1961 – 1 *Lloyd's Rep.* (1961) 220.

[90] 1 *Lloyd's Rep.* 220, at 221.

It was not contested between the parties that a part of the documents submitted to the arbitrators was in Italian, without translation. It was also commonly known that one of the arbitrators (Mr. Todd) did not speak Italian; Mr. Todd confirmed in an affidavit that he did not read Italian. The content of the documents was translated to Mr. Todd orally by his co-arbitrator (Mr. Whittingham). The court first reached the conclusion that since Mr. Todd had no knowledge of the Italian language, and since the only assistance he had was oral translation made to him by his co-arbitrator who was not proved to be a skilled translator, '[t]here has at least been a technical irregularity amounting to misconduct in these proceedings'.[91]

The more difficult question was whether this 'at least technical irregularity' justifies the setting aside of the award. The court held that it did. In his judgment Justice McNair pointed out that as the arbitral tribunal had to decide whether a contract was or was not concluded by way of correspondence,

> '[i]t is vital that those who have to determine the question should have a clear appreciation of the meaning and effect of each individual letter or cable in the chain preceding the alleged contract date, and, indeed, even subsequent to the alleged contract date, and it is very unsafe indeed to rely, in reaching a decision on that kind of point, on a rough and ready haphazard knowledge of the foreign language in which some of the documents have been prepared.'[92]

Justice McNair concluded that the irregularity which resulted in Mr. Todd's not being fully informed as to the meaning of the Italian documents '[w]as an irregularity which may have caused a substantial miscarriage of justice…'.[93]

'Misconduct' is a quite fitting characterization of the irregularity which emerged in this case. Arbitrator Todd did not do what he was supposed to do. In reaching a conclusion as to whether the correspondence between the parties did or did not yield a contract, a conscientious arbitrator has to scrutinize the language of letters and cables himself. He is professionally required to form his own opinion, based on his own assessment of the terms and phrases in the relevant letters and cables. This is only possible on the grounds of one's own direct scrutiny of the documents by way of reading them in the original, or with the help of a written translation. A 'shortcut' by reliance on oral translation of the co-arbitrator is short of what an arbitrator is obliged to do, and therefore it may be qualified as misconduct. It may happen (and probably does happen) that

---

91 1 *Lloyd's Rep.* 220, at 224.
92 1 *Lloyd's Rep.* 220, at 224.
93 1 *Lloyd's Rep.* 220, at 225.

some arbitrators do take shortcuts even in full command of the language of the documents – simply by not reading, or not reading carefully enough all documents. There may be no substantial difference between this misconduct and the misconduct in the *Rotheray v. Bedarida* case – except that when an arbitrator does not speak the language in which documents are submitted (and there is no translation either), it is more obvious and more easily demonstrable that misconduct took place.

The question arises what would be the outcome of a *Rotheray v. Bedarida* situation today, without 'misconduct' as a specifically mentioned ground for setting aside, or refusal for recognition in the present UK Arbitration Act.[94] Is there a ground in the New York Convention, or in the Model Law, or in the 1996 UK Arbitration Act,[95] which would permit challenge on the basis of the same fact pattern? One conceivable shelter is due process, or inability to present one's case. The difficulty with this option is that it normally assumes that a **party** was thwarted in presenting its case. If, for example, the party was not given an opportunity to respond to the allegations of the other party, his ability to present his case was indeed impaired. Can this situation be equated with that in which the party was given an opportunity to respond, but one of the arbitrators actually did not read his submission? One could possibly argue that one's case is not presented until the arguments actually reach the attention of the arbitrator. But in our case, the documents and arguments of the party challenging the award (Rotheray) were presented in English, and clearly did reach the attention of both arbitrators. The documents of the Italian party (the party opposing challenge) were those which were not properly scrutinized by one of the arbitrators. Can a party argue that it did not have an opportunity to present its case, when the documents presented by **the other party** are those which were not fully read? Furthermore, in the given case it was not alleged that the Italian language correspondence would have caused difficulties to the English party in reacting to those documents. (This was not alleged, and this would have been difficult to allege, since this was correspondence between the parties themselves; in other words, this was the English party's own correspondence.) It is clearly more easy (and more logical) to phrase the problem in terms of a wrongdoing (misconduct) of the arbitrator rather than in terms of inability of a party to present its case.

Do we have here proceedings which were not in accordance with the agreement of the parties, or not in accordance with the *lex arbitri*? There is no indica-

---

94 'Misconduct' of the arbitrator is rarely identified as a distinct ground for challenge in contemporary arbitration acts. An exception is paragraph 10(3) of the US Federal Arbitration Act.

95 Applicable in England, Northern Ireland and Wales – but not in Scotland.

tion that the parties would have agreed on the language of the proceedings (or on the language of the documents). Submission of documents in Italian does not appear to be a violation of party agreement. Do we have proceedings in violation of the *lex arbitri*? Again a difficult proposition, since most arbitration statutes do not provide for a fallback language.

There is one norm, however, which was obviously violated. This is the rule that the arbitrators have to read what was submitted to them. This rule is so obvious that it is rarely spelled out in statutes or in arbitration rules, but it may be covered by some general principles. If the same case were to emerge today in England, Section 33(b) of the 1996 UK Arbitration Act could possibly provide a more specific point of reliance.[96] It states that the arbitral tribunal shall 'adopt procedures suitable to the circumstances of the particular case, [...] so as to provide fair means for the resolution of matters falling to be determined'. Such adaptation of the procedure to the circumstances of the case normally implies ordering translation in order to enable an arbitrator to undertake a proper scrutiny of the documents, since this is a necessary precondition to a fair and competent resolution of the dispute.

C.2.4. *Relevance of lack of translation (relevance of the document or of the presentation which was not properly translated)*

Some procedural decisions regarding translation are motivated by considerations of relevance. A procedural imperfection has to have some weight in order to justify setting aside or refusal of recognition. There are imperfections which are obviously inconsequential. If a translator omits the introductory phrase of a witness who first says that he wishes good morning to all participants, this can hardly be a ground for setting aside or for refusal of recognition. Some deficiencies of translation may be identified as irrelevant without any scrutiny of the merits, and should be disregarded.

The issue of relevance also emerges with regard to documentary evidence. Translation of some documentary evidence may not be ordered because the arbitrators believe that it cannot have an impact. The question arises whether in post-arbitration proceedings the court should or should not take into account the pertinence of a missing translation. One could argue that taking into consideration the relevance of an untranslated statement is in line with a pro-arbitration stance. If the arbitrators fail to provide, for example, for the translation of a witness statement into the language of the proceedings (wrongly assuming that

[96] According to Section 68, a failure of the tribunal to comply with Section 33 represents a possible ground for setting aside.

all parties understand the language of the witness) and it turns out that this statement had no actual relevance and did not influence the outcome of the case, there are no reasons to sustain the challenge of the award because the procedural error had no impact on the merits of the case. The problem with this approach is, however, that it implies some scrutiny of the case on its merits, while one of the main achievements of the New York Convention is the avoidance of such scrutiny. The New York Convention has set a model which restricts the possible grounds for refusal of recognition to those enumerated in Article V, and these grounds are strictly limited to procedural deficiencies with the sole exception of the public policy ground. The same approach has been adopted in the Model Law with respect to setting aside. The fact that a post-award scrutiny does not enter into the merits of the case (with the only exception of public policy issues) is an important feature of the contemporary system of international commercial arbitration. An investigation with the purpose of establishing whether lack of translation had an impact on the outcome might render some inconsequential omissions irrelevant, but it might also undermine an important mainstay of contemporary arbitration. A possible compromise could be an investigation not whether the untranslated document did have, but whether it could have had *prima facie* an impact on the outcome of the case. This is essentially the approach followed in the *Rotheray v. Bedarida case*[97] in which the court established that the failure to translate part of the correspondence between the parties represented ' an irregularity which may have caused a substantial miscarriage of justice', given that the exact question before the arbitrators was whether the correspondence did yield a contract. Although the case was decided within the setting of the 1950 English (UK) Arbitration Act, the logic of the analysis pertaining to relevance is clearly in line with the new 1996 Act. Section 68 of the 1996 Act allows setting aside only if an irregularity – like those enumerated in Article V of the New York Convention – took place, **and** if such irregularity has caused or will cause substantive injustice to the applicant. The New York Convention and arbitration acts based on the Model Law do not contain this additional qualification, yet a *prima facie* scrutiny investigating whether the missing translation could have had an impact at all may save some awards where the missing translation was obviously irrelevant. Such a *prima facie* scrutiny does not amount to a noteworthy impairment of the principle that (apart from public policy) a post-award scrutiny does not imply a reinvestigation of the merits.

It has to be added that it is of some importance whether the challenge refers to lack of translation in the context of the 'procedure not in accordance with the

[97] Discussed above in subchapter C.2.3.

agreement of the parties' argument, or whether the party relies instead on public policy, or inability to present one's case. Public policy can only be triggered by adverse consequences of a particular intensity, and these cannot possibly be assessed without taking into consideration the relevance of the missing translation. The 'unable to present his case' ground for challenge is also closely intertwined with the weight and relevance of the circumstance which allegedly prevented a party from presenting his/her case. As far as 'procedure not in accordance with the agreement of the parties' (or with the *lex arbitri*) is concerned, the wording of Article V)1)(d) is suggestive of a stricter approach; but as was mentioned earlier,[98] court practice has permitted room for considerations of relevance within this setting as well.

C.2.5. *The issue of waiver*

Waiver is another instrument introducing flexibility to the treatment of language-related deficiencies in post-award proceedings. Waiver may, in principle, become relevant both regarding use of wrong language (lack of translation) and regarding mistranslation; its practical relevance is, however, much higher with regard to lack of translation. This is the reason why we shall address this question in somewhat more detail in this subchapter.

The concept of waiver has found an explicit formulation in Article 4 of the Model Law, which states:

> 'A party who knows that any provision of this Law from which the parties may derogate or any requirement under the arbitration agreement has not been complied with and yet proceeds with the arbitration without stating his objection to such non-compliance without undue delay or, if a time-limit is provided therefore, within such period of time, shall be deemed to have waived his right to object.'

This concept has been tracked by many national legislators.[99] One may add that waiver (or estoppel) may represent a point of reliance as a general principle as well, even without foothold in specific and explicit legislative provisions. Speak-

---

[98] Subchapter C.2.2.

[99] To mention a few examples among recent enactments, the rule adopted in Art. 4 of the Model Law was tracked, e.g., in Art. 4 of the 1993 Act on International Commercial Act of the Russian Federation; Section 6 of the 1994 Hungarian Act No. LXXI on Arbitration; Section 1027 of the 1998 German Arbitration Act (Book X of the Code of Civil Procedure); Art. 5 of the 2001 Croatian Arbitration Act; paragraph 1(4) of the 2005 Norwegian Arbitration Act; Art. 579 of the 2006 Austrian Arbitration Act (Section IV of the Code of civil Procedure); or Art. 43 of the 2006 Serbian Arbitration Act.

ing of the principle of waiver in their Commentary on the Model Law, Holtzmann and Neuhaus stress: 'In fact, it might well have been implicit in the Model Law even if it were not stated explicitly.'[100]

Waiver is a particularly important point of reliance when the objection is couched in terms of Article V(1)(d) of the New York Convention (or of like provisions in national legislative acts). As mentioned earlier, Article V(1)(d) is suggestive of a stricter reading and makes it more difficult (although not impossible) to introduce relevance as a corrective factor. Under these circumstances, the importance of another corrective factor (of waiver) increases.

Speaking of waiver in the context of the rule of Article V)1)(d) – and in connection with lack of translation – let me say first that it is quite difficult to find cases in which an arrangement on the applicable language was made[101] which was then bluntly disregarded in favor of another language. There are, however, cases in which the arrangement pertaining to language is not followed strictly, and the question arises whether the result is just a flexible interpretation of the arrangement, or a departure from it.[102] It happens for example with some frequency, that the correspondence between the parties is conducted in two languages, only one of which is later chosen as the language of the arbitral proceedings. Both the parties and the arbitrators may very well have a command of both languages. In such a situation, it is advisable to put on record an agreement to the effect that written evidence may be presented in either of the two languages. But what if the issue is not raised, and the arbitrators simply **tolerate** submission of documents in two languages (only one of which has been chosen as the language of the arbitral proceedings)? Would this amount to a reason to refuse recognition under Article V(1)(d)? There are indeed cases in which, in addition to the language which is chosen to be the language of the arbitral proceedings, another language is also used to a limited extent. It is more difficult, however, to find cases in which this took place in defiance of an explicit objection raised during the arbitral proceedings. What usually happens is that the issue is simply not raised, because all participants have a satisfactory command of both languages, and they do not perceive the use of another language as a problem. To cite one example from my personal experience following this pat-

---

[100] H. Holtzmann and J. Neuhaus, op. cit. 196.

[101] By way of party stipulation, determination by the arbitrators, or by way of designation of a default language.

[102] This problem could be reduced – or even eliminated – by more specific arrangements regarding language, which arrangements would not only designate a language of the arbitral proceedings, but would also identify situations in which limited use of another language is permitted. (E.g., submission of documents in a language which is not the language of the arbitral proceedings, but which is understood by the arbitrators.)

tern, in an unpublished case argued before the Budapest Court of Arbitration between a Hungarian and a UK party, the parties chose Hungarian as the language of arbitral procedure. The contract which represented the starting point of the dispute was in English. Both parties chose Hungarian counsels. Counsel for one of the parties, who had an excellent command of English, cited some provisions from the English original of the contract, and from these provisions he derived certain arguments which he presented in English. Counsel for the other party followed the English presentation without difficulty, and responded in Hungarian. All three arbitrators understood both Hungarian and English. Nobody reacted to the fact that the contract was not translated, and that for a few minutes oral arguments were presented in a language which was not the stipulated language of the arbitral proceedings. It is not really likely that following a similar situation one party would oppose recognition on ground of violation of the rule set in Article V(1)(d). If in hindsight such an argument were nevertheless to be raised, **waiver** might be the argument against refusal of recognition.

Another possible explanation leading to the same result would be **acceptance by conduct.** The two – waiver and acceptance by conduct – are closely intertwined. If a party accepts the fact that a document is presented in another language than that chosen as the language of arbitration, and enters into the discussion of such document, this may be qualified as waiver, but one may also assume that the agreement pertaining to language was tacitly modified (at least to a limited extent). Staying with the construct of acceptance by conduct, the question might arise whether conduct may produce effective agreements pertaining to arbitration. It is well known that the arbitration agreement has to be in writing. One may argue, however, that the rigor of Article II of the New York Convention which defines the writing requirement, only extends to the arbitration agreement stricto sensu, i.e., to '[a]n agreement in writing under which the parties undertake to submit to arbitration all or any differences which have arisen or which may arise between them…' – as defined by Article II of the New York Convention. Following this line of argument, other party stipulations may be established in a less formal way, including conduct. The parties who did not object to the use of a language other than the one set as the language of the arbitral proceedings may be deemed to have modified their stipulation. Having said this, let me add that although acceptance by conduct is a plausible argument, waiver is a much more common point of reliance with a clear anchor in Article 4 of the Model Law and in many other legislative acts and arbitration rules.

Let me summarize that although an outright disregard of the arrangement regarding the language of the proceedings is more a theoretical than a practical possibility, less than strict adherence to the existing arrangement is not uncommon. At the same time, a limited use of languages other than the language of the arbitral proceedings is quite unlikely to cause actual impairment. For this reason, waiver – when there is a waiver – is a helpful corrective factor.

C.3. **Mistranslation**

In post-award proceedings, shortcomings pertaining to translation may lead to consequences within the setting of Article V(1)(b) or Article V(1)(d) of the New York Convention, or under like provisions in national arbitration acts dealing with setting aside. Arguments concentrating on shortcomings of the translation may possibly find shelter under the principle of equality of the parties as well. Since this principle is not recognized under the New York Convention as a distinct ground for refusal of recognition, a challenge based on infringement of equality may be couched in terms of inability to present one's case, or of a violation of public policy. Under exceptional circumstances, public policy may also be brought into play without focusing on equality: for example, one could ask whether an award based on an obvious misunderstanding could be qualified as being contrary to public policy.

As far as Article V(1)(d) is concerned, it may very well offer the appropriate setting in cases of lack of translation, but it would be most difficult to stretch it to **mistranslation.** If there is no translation into the language chosen to be the language of the arbitral proceedings, one may very well argue that 'the arbitral procedure was not in accordance with the agreement of the parties'. It is difficult to make the same argument when the basic procedural arrangement is heeded, i.e., when there is translation into the language of the arbitral proceedings, but it is imperfect.

C.3.1. *Mistranslation which remains unnoticed during the arbitral proceedings*

Article V(1)(b) of the New York Convention and the principle of equality of the parties[103] offer probably the best chances as a shelter in case of mistranslation. If a document was mistranslated and this was not known to one of the parties, one could argue that this party was unable to present his case, because he was

[103] The 'otherwise unable to present his case' language of Art. V(1)(b) may be perceived as a more specific expression of the principle of equality of the parties. It is not easy to imagine cases in which an argument pertaining to translation could be couched in terms of an alleged violation of the principle of equality of the parties but could not be couched in terms of an alleged violation of the right of the party to present his case.

unaware of the misperception created by someone else (the translator), was unable to correct the miscommunication created, and was unable to rely upon the true content of the document.

In one case I remember, the language of arbitration was Serbo-Croatian, but part of the relevant correspondence between the parties was in English. The parties submitted Serbo-Croatian translations of this correspondence. In one rather important letter, the Claimant acknowledged that the contract was 'duly executed' (meaning that it was properly concluded). This was, however, translated into Serbo-Croatian as 'uredno izvršen' which actually means 'duly enforced' or 'duly performed'. This could have happened with translation into other languages as well (particularly on the assumption that the translator has no legal background) given the fact that the term 'execution' may have several meanings and the choice may be a difficult one to make for someone who does not understand the legal context. In the given case, it was not contested that the contract was properly concluded, the issue was whether it was actually performed. The error was noted by all participants (sooner by some, later by others), and it was corrected.

As a matter of fact, this is the typical epilogue. In a case decided by the Paris Court of Appeal[104] one of the reasons for which annulment was sought was a shortcoming (*défaillance*) in the translation of witness testimonies. The Paris Court of Appeal refused to grant annulment on this ground, noting that the arbitral tribunal, having received observations from the parties, had made appropriate corrections in the transcript.[105]

Languages which become relevant during the arbitral proceedings are normally languages which have been used or encountered during the shaping of the contractual relationship as well. Moreover, in most cases at least some of the arbitrators are familiar with the language from which translation is effected, and diligent parties do not forget to check translation. This is why unnoticed mistranslation which thereby impairs the right of a party to present his case is a rather unlikely variant of the problem of mistranslation.

At this point I would like to mention a case which came close to this 'unlikely variant'. In *Conlux USA Corporation v. Dixie-Narco Inc. and Maytag Corporation*,[106] Conlux submitted to the US District Court N.D. Ohio a motion to set aside an award of a sole arbitrator. The language of all participants (including the arbitrator) was English, but one of the relevant documents emerging

[104] *Compagnie Honeywell Bull S.A. c/ Computacion Bull de Venezuela*, *Cour d'appel de Paris* (1re Ch. suppl.), decision of June 21, 1990, Reported in *Revue de l'arbitrage* (1991) 96.

[105] *Revue de l'arbitrage* (1991) at p. 104.

[106] United States District Court, N.D. Ohio, Eastern Division, decision of January 25, 1996, 929 F. Supp. 269.

during the proceedings was a Japanese patent which had to be translated into English. Patentee (Conlux) brought an action against competitor Dixie-Narco alleging infringement of its patent. The arbitrator found that infringement did take place, but he also found that Conlux was guilty of inequitable conduct in failing to disclose prior art Japanese patent during the application process. The arbitrator concluded in his award that such inequitable conduct precluded recovery by Conlux. Conlux moved to vacate the award on four grounds, two of which relied on mistranslation. Plaintiff alleged that the Japanese patent submitted as evidence was mistranslated and this led to the conclusion that Conlux failed to disclose prior art at the time when it applied for a US patent. In order to couch this alleged mistranslation in terms which would allow setting aside under the 1925 US Arbitration Act, Conlux argued that a 'mistake of fact' took place, and the argument was also made that Conlux was not given an opportunity to respond.

With regard to the 'mistake of fact' construct, it has to be mentioned that para. 10 of the US Arbitration Act, which sets the possible grounds on which the award may be vacated, does not specifically include 'mistake of fact' as a ground. Case law has, however, identified and added some patterns which have been accepted as a ground within para. 10. The best known of these patterns shaped by case law is the 'manifest disregard of law'.[107] In Conlux, the Ohio District Court relied on para. 10(a)(4) of the US Arbitration Act (allowing set aside 'where the arbitrators exceeded their powers') but qualified the actual deficiency as a 'mistake of fact'. The Court stated:

> 'While this Court is not to revisit the arbitrator's factual determinations, where the record before the arbitrator demonstrates an unambiguous and undisputed mistake of fact and the record demonstrates strong reliance on that mistake by the arbitrator in making his award, it can fairly be said that the arbitrator "exceeded [his] powers, or so imperfectly executed them" that vacation may be proper.'[108]

Coming to this conclusion the District Court relied on the National Post Office case,[109] and cited the 1st Circuit in *Electronics Corp. of America v. International Union of Elec. Radio and Machine Workers*[110] stating that

---

[107] See e.g., *Wilko v. Swan*, 346 U.S. 427, 436-7 (1953); *Saxis Steamship Co. v. Multifacs International Traders Inc.*, 375 F.2d 577, 582 (2d Cir. 1967); *Amicizia Societa Navigazione v. Chilean Nitrate and Iodine Sales Corp.*, 274 F.2d 805, 808 (2d Cir.1960); *First Options of Chicago v. Kaplan*, 514 U.S. 938, 115 S.Ct. 1920, 1923 (1995)

[108] 929 F. Supp. 269, 273.

[109] *National Post Office Mailhandlers, Watchmen, Messengers and Group Leaders Division v. United States Postal Service*, judgment of January 3, 1985, 751 F.2d 834 at 843.

[110] *Electronics Corp. of America v. International Elec., Radio and Machine Workers*, AFL-CIO Local 272, 494 F.2d 1255 (1st Cir. 1974).

> '[w]hen the "fact" underlying an arbitrator's decision is concededly a non-fact and where the parties cannot fairly be charged with the misapprehension, the award cannot stand'.[111]

What is interesting in the *Conlux v. Dixie-Narco* case is that the court considered mistranslation as a possible mistake of fact, and that in this way, reliance on mistranslation may be interpreted as falling under the 'exceeded their powers, or so imperfectly executed them' standard which allows setting aside. The District Court held that mistranslation may in principle amount to such a mistake of fact, but it was not persuaded that the actual circumstances of the given case provided a ground for vacating the award. It found that the alleged mistranslation was not the sole basis for the arbitrator's finding, and added that Conlux could not claim relief from an error 'for which it can fairly be charged'. Conlux did not only fail to object to the translation submitted by Dixie-Narco, but its own translation also contained the alleged error. It was only after the award was rendered that Conlux came to the conclusion that a mistranslation had occurred in the text of the Japanese patent.

It has to be noted that the rather extensive interpretation of the 'exceeded their powers' ground is balanced by some important qualifications. The mistake has to be obvious and unambiguous, it has to be relevant (or even more strongly, it has to be the basis of the award), and the party seeking set aside must not have contributed to the error. The question arises whether the construct which was reached by interpretation of para. 10 of the US Arbitration Act could possibly find relevance within the context of the New York Convention (or of the Model Law). The 'exceeded their powers' concept was, indeed, accepted by both the New York Convention, and by the Model Law, but the formulations and the context do not allow interpretation in the direction traced by the US decisions referred to above. The 'exceeded their powers' formulation is quite close to the 'decisions of matters beyond the scope of the submission to arbitration' language of Article V(1)(c) of the New York Convention. Yet the formulation of the US Act is clearly broader, since it also contains the 'or so imperfectly executed them' added standard. Furthermore, the wording of the New York Convention and of the Model Law make it clear and explicit that 'exceeding of powers' is measured against the terms of submission to arbitration (the arbitration agreement). The focus of Article V(1)(c) is specific. An imperfect decision (including a decision based on mistranslation) cannot be challenged on the grounds of Article V(1)(c), as long as the decision stays within the scope of the arbitration agreement. This restriction of focus is not present (or, at least, not explicit) in the US Arbitration Act.

---

[111] Ibidem at 1257.

The Conlux court also considered another procedural articulation of the alleged mistranslation of the Japanese patent. Conlux submitted that it was deprived of an opportunity to respond, since it was disallowed from presenting evidence regarding mistranslation, and that thereby para. 10(a)(3) of the US Arbitration Act was violated.[112] This is a line of argument which could have been made under Article V(1)(b) of the New York Convention as well. A denial of an opportunity to bring to the attention of the arbitrators that there is a problem with the translation originally submitted may possibly be qualified as an example of those situations where the party is 'otherwise unable to present his case'. In the given case this line of argument failed too, for the simple reason that the motion came too late. As was noted by the District Court: 'It was only after the arbitrator made his final decision that Conlux reviewed the translations more carefully and discovered the alleged error.'[113] During the arbitral proceedings the mistranslation (or alleged mistranslation) remained unnoticed – and this is the reason why this case is discussed in this subchapter, rather than in the following one dealing with conflicting translations which have already emerged within the arbitration proceedings. Conlux actually asked for a rehearing before the arbitrator, after the award was rendered. This is not compatible with the basic principles of arbitral proceedings. As the District Court stated: 'Otherwise, arbitration awards could never be final.'[114]

A more difficult case would have arisen had the mistranslation been noted during the arbitral proceedings, and had the arbitrator refused to consider an alternative translation before rendering the award. In this hypo – under either the US Arbitration Act, or under the New York Convention, or under the Model Law – the question would have arisen at what point in the procedure the alternative translation was submitted. In other words, what procedural steps were permitted, and what steps were taken, before the arbitrator refused to consider new evidence. If before such refusal the party did have adequate opportunity to scrutinize translations and to submit an alternative translation (but failed to do so, because he only discovered mistranslation at a late moment), there is no violation of the right of the party to present his case. The protection guaranteed to the party who was 'unable to present his case' will only make sense if we take as a standard the assumption of a **diligent** party, rather than a party who did not present his case because he did not study the file with due diligence and in due time.

---

[112] According to Art. 10(a)(3) the award may be vacated if the arbitrators are guilty of misconduct '[i]n refusing to hear evidence pertinent and material to the controversy;'.

[113] 929 F. Supp. 269, at. 272.

[114] Ibidem p. 274.

C.3.2. *Translation contested during the arbitral proceedings*

Translation sometimes becomes a contested issue during the arbitral proceedings. The parties may submit different interpretations of the meaning of the original, the arbitrators opt for one of the translations offered, yet this may still be perceived by one of the parties as mistranslation. This pattern emerged in a number of cases decided by the Iran-US Claims Tribunal. In *Sylvania Technical Systems v. The Government of the Islamic Republic of Iran,*[115] the Respondent contested jurisdiction on several grounds. One of the arguments of the Respondent was that the contract actually excluded arbitration by providing for the jurisdiction of Iranian courts. It was not debated that the contract concluded between the parties contained a clause which had placed at least some of the possible disputes under the jurisdiction of Iranian courts. In its English version this clause read:

> 'Settlement of Differences
> All differences and disputes which may arise between the two parties resulting from interpretation of the Articles of the Contract or the execution of the works which can not be settled in a friendly way, must be settled in accordance with the rules and laws of Iran via referring to the competent Iranian Courts.'[116]

The Contract was written and signed in both English and Farsi, and it was common ground that the Farsi text was the governing version. The main translation problem arose in connection with the expression 'execution of the works' which was interpreted in a rather restrictive manner, excluding the present dispute (thus allowing it to be submitted to arbitration rather than to Iranian courts). The Farsi term used in place of 'work' was 'kar'. The Respondent argued that the term 'kar' had a broader meaning, encompassing the subject matter of the present dispute, and thus placing it under the exclusive jurisdiction of Iranian courts. After an exchange of arguments the tribunal came to the following conclusion:

> 'The fact that the word "kar" has so many different and broad meanings in Farsi does not mean, however, that all these meanings have been agreed between the Parties. The Contract was written and signed in both Farsi and English. Although it provides that the Farsi text is to govern in the event of inconsistency between the two versions, the many different meanings of the Farsi word "kar" lead to an ambiguity in the Farsi text. It is appropriate to refer to the English text to clarify

---

[115] Award No. 180-64-1 of June 27, 1985, 8 *Iran-US C.T.R.* at 298.
[116] Award No. 180-64-1 of June 27, 1985, 8 *Iran-US C.T.R.* at 306.

> this ambiguity. The best evidence of which of the Farsi meanings was intended by the Parties is the one found in the English version, namely "work".'[117]

The same problem emerged in a number of cases dealing with the same contractual provision which appeared in the 'IBEX Project'. The Sylvania decision was followed, but it gave rise to a number of dissenting opinions. In *Watkins-Johnson v. The Islamic Republic of Iran*,[118] arbitrator Assadolah Noori states the following in his rather vigorous dissent:

> 'The record in Sylvania shows that Iran correctly drew the attention of Chamber One to the extensive meaning of the phrase "anjam-e karha," and to the broad and unambiguous meanings of the word "kar". On page 12 (of the English version) of Award No. 180-64-1 (reprinted in 8 *Iran-US C.T.R.* 298, 306-7), the majority concedes that "in its Interlocutory Award No. ITL 6-159-FT the Full Tribunal did not refer explicitly to the interpretation of the Farsi word 'kar' and its impact on the scope of the Tribunal's jurisdiction."
> Unfortunately, however, instead of limiting the extent of the prejudice caused by the Full Tribunal's unjust judicial error by rendering an equitable and rational decision, and solely for the purpose of retaining jurisdiction over the claims relating to the IBEX Project – at whatever cost, and by whatever means necessary – the majority in Sylvania has suddenly become an expert in the Persian language even though totally unacquainted with that language and its literature. The majority there states, on the strength of the strange and astonishing pretext that the many different meanings of the Persian word "kar" lead to an ambiguity in the Persian text, that it is thus necessary to refer to the English text – i.e., a text which was invalid against the Persian text wherever there was a conflict between the two versions. This is absolutely unbelievable. Stating that the many different meanings (or, more correctly, the broad meanings) of the Persian word 'kar' lead to an ambiguity in the Persian text, is just the same as if the majority were to say that water burns, instead of quenching thirst, and that fire quenches instead of burning.'[119]

And he continues:

> 'The fact is that the broad meanings of the Persian word "kar" not only do not lead to the slightest ambiguity, but actually eliminate any possible ambiguity, and cause the Contract to cover every conceivable dispute arising out of the Parties' reciprocal obligations and works, and "questions of fact" in general. Even if, in arguendo, the several different meanings of "kar" did lead to an ambiguity –

[117] Award No. 180-64-1 of June 27, 1985, 8 *Iran-US C.T.R.* at 306.

[118] Watkins-Johnson company, *Watkins-Johnson Ltd. v. Islamic Republic of Iran*, Bank Saderat Iran, Award No. 429-370-1 of July 27, 1989, 22 *Iran-US C.T.R.* at 218.

[119] Idem at 294.

> which is not the case – the majority cannot arbitrarily refer to the English text on this pretext and, by its erroneous understanding (even of the English text), forcibly make itself the arbiter of the fate of the IBEX cases.'[120]

I shall not try, of course, to take a position regarding the true interpretation of the word 'kar'. The question I would like to raise is whether such debates may or may not continue in the setting of post-award proceedings, and if they may, on what provision the moving party could possibly rely. As mentioned earlier, it is difficult to qualify the problem of conflicting translations in terms of a procedure 'not in accordance with the agreement of the parties' (or not in accordance with the *lex arbitri*). In the given situation, the procedure itself is not in violation of the standards of conduct set by the parties or by the *lex arbitri*. Proceedings are conducted in the language agreed upon, translation is provided and considered, the parties have an opportunity to state their positions. Instead, a dilemma emerges which is very similar to other dilemmas appearing with regard to contract interpretation. The outcome is the acceptance of one of the possible interpretations after a confrontation of arguments regarding the 'right interpretation'. It would be difficult to find support in the New York Convention (or under most national laws) for a reopening of this argument, since the New York Convention precludes the reopening of the debate pertaining to the merits (unless violation of public policy were at issue). The search for the true meaning of the contract in a multilingual context is just one variation of contract interpretation.

There is one circumstance, however, which may cast doubt on this conclusion in the specific context of the *Sylvania* case. In this case (just as in the *Watkins-Johnson* case), contract interpretation, including the debate on conflicting translations, yielded a decision on **jurisdiction.** It is generally accepted that when jurisdiction is at issue in either recognition or annulment proceedings, courts may exercise a less deferential review. The exact limits of such a review vary – and this question is beyond the scope of our considerations. I would only like to illustrate the problem by citing a decision of the Swiss Federal Tribunal, and considering the position taken by the Swiss Federal Tribunal under the angle of the issue of mistranslation. In *Vekoma v. Maran*,[121] the Swiss court set aside an ICC award on the grounds of lack of jurisdiction, by adopting a different qualification of facts from the one accepted by the arbitrators. The

---

120 Idem at 295.

121 Transport en Handelsmaatschappij *'Vekoma' B.V. v. Maran Coal Corp*, Decision of the Swiss Federal Tribunal of August 17, 1995 – German and French text in 14(4) *ASA Bulletin* (1996) 673; English excerpts in Várady-Barcelo-Von Mehren, *International Commercial Arbitration*, 3rd edn. (Thomson & West 2006) 758-761.

Swiss court spelled out that a *de novo* review was justifiable with regard to jurisdiction, but added some qualifications. It was stated:

> 'A decision pertaining to jurisdiction in international commercial arbitration may be reinvestigated freely by the Bundesgericht (BG) from a legal point of view, while with respect to facts review is only possible within the limits of substantiated objections which claim that factual findings result from non-observance of procedural guarantees set by law (i.e. those set in Article 190/2/d and 182/3 of the Private International Law Act), or that they are incompatible with procedural ordre public.'[122]

Thus, when jurisdiction is at issue, legal conclusions may be reinvestigated *de novo*. What happened in the Swiss case was that the Supreme Court found that the seller's silence in response to a fax of the buyer communicated to the buyer something different from what the ICC Tribunal had found that it communicated. Buyer set a time-limit for a response. Seller did not respond within the time-limit. Unlike the arbitrators, the Swiss Court characterized this silence as a rejection of the offer. The content of the fax and the lack of response were not contested. This led the Swiss Supreme Court to conclude that legal conclusions are at issue (rather than facts), and that it is hence justified to embark on a *de novo* investigation.

The question emerging from our perspective is what are facts and what are legal conclusions in the context of (mis)translation – assuming the Swiss position were to guide the court. The Iran-US Tribunal opted for a given meaning of the term 'kar', considering both the Farsi and the English text. Is this the establishment of a fact, or rather a legal conclusion? If the ascertainment that the correct meaning of the term 'kar' is 'work' were a question of fact, this finding would escape a *de novo* review even if jurisdiction were at issue. One may argue, however, that what may be qualified as a fact is just the finding which document is the binding contract and what is the content of this contract. Following this line of argument, it is a fact that the binding contract in Farsi uses the term 'kar', but the interpretation of what this term actually means is closer to the category of a legal conclusion – and thus subject to a *de novo* review by courts. The latter perception appears to be closer to the standard distinction between facts and conclusions. Which document is the contract and what is the content of the contract are facts; what is the meaning of the text of the contract is a legal conclusion. Translation establishes the meaning.

---

122 Várady-Barcelo and Von Mehren, op. cit. 760-761.

This suggests that a *de novo* review of findings pertaining to **jurisdiction** is a possible setting in which arguments concerning mistranslation may be raised in post-award proceedings.

C.3.3. *Relevance and waiver*

The issues of waiver and relevance are pertinent with regard to mistranslation as well, but their significance is not the same as that with respect to lack of translation. Some further differences also emerge depending on whether mistranslation remained unnoticed during the arbitral proceedings, or whether conflicting translations were discussed.

As stated earlier, the question of mistranslation is not likely to arise in the context of Article V(1)(d) of the New York Convention. Hence, the issues of relevance and waiver are also unlikely to arise with the context of the rule of Article V(1)(d). It would be quite difficult, for example, to qualify mistranslation as 'procedure not in accordance with the agreement of the parties' (which may be a plausible qualification with regard to lack of translation). A more fitting shelter may be found if mistranslation is qualified in terms of the violation of the right of a party to present his case or violation of public policy.

Let me also mention that when conflicting translations are at issue, waiver does not emerge as a possible argument, since the problem does not pass unheeded during the arbitration process (and there is no failure to object, since the issue was debated).

Relevance

Turning to the more likely setting, where the question is whether someone was able to present his/her case, or whether public policy was violated, it is difficult not to consider relevance when mistranslation is at issue. It has been submitted earlier that one of the possible drawbacks of considering relevance is that it implies some consideration of the merits of the case. At the same time, when public policy or the ability to present one's case are concerned, the weight of the circumstance at issue is a necessary part of the analysis. A violation of public policy implies a particular intensity which reaches the foundations of domestic legal order, and the inability to present one's case can only be assessed considering of the actual impact of the alleged impediments. One may conclude that within the settings in which mistranslation is likely to emerge as a basis for challenge (inability to present one's case or public policy), the relevance of the allegedly mistranslated text should be taken into consideration. The logic of this proposition has been corroborated in the *Conlux* case.

The distinction between mistranslation which remained unnoticed on the one hand, and translation contested during the arbitral proceedings on the other hand, does not lead to different analyses when we are talking about the relevance of the mistranslated text. The same considerations which apply with regard to mistranslation which remained unnoticed also apply with regard to conflicting translations. The weight and pertinence of the error in translation (if it can be raised at all) leads to the same analysis notwithstanding whether the purported error was or was not discussed during the arbitration proceedings.

Waiver

Considering the wording of Article 4 of the Model Law, waiver is not likely to appear as a relevant argument when mistranslation is at issue. Article 4 of the Model Law qualifies as 'waiver' situations in which 'A party **knows** that any provision of this Law [...]or any requirement under the arbitration agreement has not been complied with and yet proceeds...' [emphasis added]. It is difficult to imagine situations where a party **knew** that the translation submitted was a mistranslation, but failed to contest it or raise it as an issue. One could possibly imagine the following situation: A party is aware of a mistranslation because he knows both languages, but he wrongly believes that the error works in his favor. In this example (which is not very likely to become a real-life case) waiver could, indeed, emerge as an argument against the party who with hindsight decides to challenge the award, after it has become evident that the mistranslation *worked against him, rather than in his favor.*

Waiver becomes more pertinent, however, as an argument, if we do not restrict this concept to situations in which a party was aware of a mistranslation (and failed to object), but extend the notion of waiver to situations in which the party could have (and should have) been aware of the mistranslation. One could submit that this option is within the logic of Article 4. Actual knowledge (awareness) is a subjective factor, often difficult to demonstrate otherwise than by circumstances showing that the party could and should have been aware of the problem. Thus, in practice, it would be most difficult to implement the purpose of the 'knows' standard without stretching it towards a 'had to know' or 'was supposed to know' criterion. In their Commentary on the Model Law Holtzmann and Neuhaus state: 'Presumably, the existence of knowledge, like any other fact, would not have to be proved directly in all cases. Rather, knowledge may often be proved by proof of circumstances from which such knowledge may be inferred.'[123]

Speaking of waiver in this somewhat more extended sense, the question also arises whether it matters who was in charge of organizing translation. If the translator was retained by the party that suffered from the mistranslation (and

---

[123] H. Holtzmann and J. Neuhaus, op. cit. 199.

that challenges the award on ground of mistranslation), a situation arises which may be likened to waiver. It becomes questionable whether, for example, this party could still be deemed as being unable to present its case given that the translation was within its responsibilities.

Let me finally mention that it is justified to consider relevance and waiver in conjunction – particularly if we extend the concept of waiver to those situations in which the party did not know but was supposed to know that a mistranslation existed. The purpose of both instruments (consideration of relevance and waiver) is to limit setting aside (or refusal of recognition) to those cases in which language-related deficiencies did actually yield consequential harm to a party without his fault. This is easier to establish if the two instruments are not strictly divorced. In considering whether a party did or did not lose his right to object against mistranslation (because he failed to notice a mistranslation although he could have and should have noticed it, or because he hired the translator himself), it would make sense to take into consideration the relevance or gravity of the mistranslation. At this juncture different policy arguments may be advanced. One may argue that it is pro-arbitration to deny the challenge, if the party challenging the award could have noticed or prevented the mistranslation during the arbitration proceedings. At the same time, the argument can be made that if the mistranslation yields a real turnaround of the outcome of the case, and this is established, principles of justice bespeak a correction of the error, even if a really diligent party could have and should have noticed the error earlier. The circumstances of the case might offer guidance in choosing between these juxtaposed considerations.

Annex I

International Conventions and UNCITRAL Enactments – Provisions Pertaining to Language and Translation

Table of Contents

A. International Conventions

1. United Nations Convention on the Recognition and Enforcement of Foreign Arbitral Awards, New York, 1958
(June 10, 1958)

Article IV
2. If the said award or agreement is not made in an official language of the country in which the award is relied upon, the party applying for recognition and enforcement of the award shall produce a translation of these documents into such language. The translation shall be certified by an official or sworn translator or by a diplomatic or consular agent.

2. MERCOSUR Agreement on International Commercial Arbitration, Buenos Aires, 1998
(July 23, 1998)

Art. 13 – Place and language
2. Failing an explicit determination by the parties, the language shall be that of the seat of the arbitral tribunal.

3. Arab Convention on Commercial Arbitration, Amman, 1987

Article 23
1. The language of the proceedings, pleadings and the award is Arabic.
2. The arbitral tribunal may decide to hear parties, witnesses and experts who do not speak Arabic by resorting to a translator after having him take an oath.
3. The arbitral tribunal may authorize that pleadings and evidence as well as all submissions be made in languages other than Arabic provided that they be translated into Arabic.

4. Convention on the execution of the foreign arbitral awards, Geneva, 1927
(September 26, 1927)

Article 4
[...]
A translation of the award and of the other documents mentioned in this Article into the official language of the country where the award is sought to be relied upon may be demanded. Such translation must be certified correct by a diplomatic or consular agent of the country to which the party who seeks to rely upon the award belongs or by a sworn translator of the country where the award is sought to be relied upon.

5. Organisation pour l'Harmonisation en Afrique du Droit des Affaires (OHADA), Acte uniforme relatif au droit de l'arbitrage, 1999[1]

(Entré en vigueur depuis le 11 juin 1999)

Article 31
La reconnaissance et l'exequatur de la sentence arbitrale supposent que la partie qui s'en prévaut établisse l'existence de la sentence arbitrale.
L'existence de la sentence arbitrale est établie par la production de l'original accompagné de la convention d'arbitrage ou des copies de ces documents réunissant les conditions requises pour leur authenticité.
Si ces pièces ne sont pas rédigées en langue française, la partie devra en produire une traduction certifiée par un traducteur inscrit sur la liste des experts établie par les juridictions compétentes.

B. UNCITRAL Enactments

6. UNCITRAL Model Law on International Commercial Arbitration, 1985

(United Nations document A/40/17, Annex I. As adopted by the United Nations Commission on International Trade Law on 21 June 1985)

Article 22. Language
(1) The parties are free to agree on the language or languages to be used in the arbitral proceedings. Failing such agreement, the arbitral tribunal shall determine the language or languages to be used in the proceedings. This agreement or determination, unless otherwise specified therein, shall apply to any written statement by a party, any hearing and any award, decision or other communication by the arbitral tribunal.
(2) The arbitral tribunal may order that any documentary evidence shall be accompanied by a translation into the language or languages agreed upon by the parties or determined by the arbitral tribunal.

Article 35. Recognition and enforcement
(2) The party relying on an award or applying for its enforcement shall supply the duly authenticated original award or a duly certified copy thereof, and the original arbitration agreement referred to in article 7 or a duly certified copy thereof. If the award or agreement is not made in an official language of this State, the party shall supply a duly certified translation thereof into such language.

7. UNCITRAL Rules of Arbitration, 1976

Model Arbitration Clause
Any dispute, controversy or claim arising out of or relating to this contract, or the breach, termination or invalidity thereof, shall be settled by arbitration in accordance with the UNCITRAL Arbitration Rules as at present in force.

---

[1] In spite of the designation 'uniform act', the OHADA enactment actually contains norms which are directly binding. According to Article 10 of the 1993 OHADA Treaty: 'Uniform Acts are directly applicable and overriding in the Contracting States notwithstanding any conflict they may give rise to in respect of previous or subsequent enactments of municipal laws.'

Note - Parties may wish to consider adding:
(d) The language(s) to be used in the arbitral proceedings shall be ...

Language
Article 17
1. Subject to an agreement by the parties, the arbitral tribunal shall, promptly after its appointment, determine the language or languages to be used in the proceedings. This determination shall apply to the statement of claim, the statement of defence, and any further written statements and, if oral hearings take place, to the language or languages to be used in such hearings.
2. The arbitral tribunal may order that any documents annexed to the statement of claim or statement of defence, and any supplementary documents or exhibits submitted in the course of the proceedings, delivered in their original language, shall be accompanied by a translation into the language or languages agreed upon by the parties or determined by the arbitral tribunal.

Evidence and hearings (Articles 24 and 25)
Article 25
2. If witnesses are to be heard, at least fifteen days before the hearing each party shall communicate to the arbitral tribunal and to the other party the names and addresses of the witnesses he intends to present, the subject upon and the languages in which such witnesses will give their testimony.
3. The arbitral tribunal shall make arrangements for the translation of oral statements made at a hearing and for a record of the hearing if either is deemed necessary by the tribunal under the circumstances of the case, or if the parties have agreed thereto and have communicated such agreement to the tribunal at least fifteen days before the hearing.

8. UNCITRAL Notes on Organizing Arbitral Proceedings, 1996

2. Language of proceedings
17. Many rules and laws on arbitral procedure empower the arbitral tribunal to determine the language or languages to be used in the proceedings, if the parties have not reached an agreement thereon.

(a) Possible need for translation of documents, in full or in part
18. Some documents annexed to the statements of claim and defence or submitted later may not be in the language of the proceedings. Bearing in mind the needs of the proceedings and economy, it may be considered whether the arbitral tribunal should order that any of those documents or parts thereof should be accompanied by a translation into the language of the proceedings.

(b) Possible need for interpretation of oral presentations
19. If interpretation will be necessary during oral hearings, it is advisable to consider whether the interpretation will be simultaneous or consecutive and whether the arrangements should be the responsibility of a party or the arbitral tribunal. In an arbitration administered by an institution, interpretation as well as translation services are often arranged by the arbitral institution.

(c) Cost of translation and interpretation
20. In taking decisions about translation or interpretation, it is advisable to decide whether any or all of the costs are to be paid directly by a party or whether they will be paid out of the deposits and apportioned between the parties along with the other arbitration costs.

15. Witnesses

60. To the extent the applicable arbitration rules do not deal with the matter, the arbitral tribunal may wish to require that each party give advance notice to the arbitral tribunal and the other party or parties of any witness it intends to present. As to the content of the notice, the following is an example of what might be required, in addition to the names and addresses of the witnesses: ... (b) the language in which the witnesses will testify; and ...

10. Practical details concerning written submissions and evidence (e.g. method of submission, copies, numbering, references)

42. Depending on the volume and kind of documents to be handled, it might be considered whether practical arrangements on details such as the following would be helpful:...

When translations are to be submitted as paper documents, whether the translations are to be contained in the same volume as the original texts or included in separate volumes.

9. Recommendations to Assist Arbitral Institutions and Other Interested Bodies with Regard to Arbitrations Under the UNCITRAL Arbitration Rules, 1982

B. Arbitral Institution or Other Body Acting as Appointing Authority or Providing Administrative Services in Ad Hoc Arbitration under the UNCITRAL Arbitration Rules

1. Offer of Services

19. In order to assist parties, the institution may wish to set forth in its administrative procedures model arbitration clauses covering the above services. The first part of any such model clause should be identical with the model clause of the UNCITRAL Arbitration Rules:

"Any dispute, controversy or claim arising out of or relating to this contract, or the breach, termination or invalidity thereof, shall be settled by arbitration in accordance with the UNCITRAL Arbitration Rules as at present in force."

...

As suggested in the UNCITRAL Model Arbitration Clause, the following note may be added:

"Note - Parties may wish to consider adding:

(c)The language(s) to be used in the arbitral proceedings shall be ...."

3. Administrative Services

33. In describing the various services, the institution should specify those services which would not be covered by its general administrative fee and which, therefore, would be billed separately (e.g., interpretation services). The institution may also wish to indicate which of the services it can provide itself, with its own facilities, and which it might merely arrange to be rendered by others.

Annex II

National Legislation – Provisions Pertaining to Language and Translation

(Listed alphabetically by the name of the country)

Table of Contents

33. Mauritania – Loi No.2000-06 portant code de l'arbitrage, 2000
34. Mexico – Federal Mexican Commercial Code, Title IV, Book V, Commercial Arbitration, 1993
35. New Zealand – Arbitration Act, 1996
36. Nigeria – Arbitration And Conciliation Decree No. 11, 1988
37. Oman – The Law of Arbitration in Civil and Commercial Disputes, 1997
38. Paraguay – Law Nr. 1879 on Arbitration and Mediation, 2002
39. Peru – General Arbitration Law No. 26572, 1996
40. Poland – Code of Civil Procedure Part Five, Arbitration, 2005
41. Romania – Code of Civil Procedure, Book IV on Arbitration, 1993
42. Russian Federation – Law on International Commercial Arbitration, 1993
43. Saudi Arabia – Rules for the Implementation of the Arbitration Regulation, 1985
44. Scotland – Law Reform (Miscellaneous Provisions) Act, 1991
45. Serbia – Arbitration Act, 2006
46. Singapore – International Arbitration Act, 2002
47. South Africa – Recognition and Enforcement of Foreign Arbitral Awards Act No. 40, 1977
48. Spain – Law on Arbitration, 2004
49. Sri Lanka – Arbitration Act No. 11, 1995
50. Sweden – Arbitration Act, 1999
51. Switzerland – Intercantonal Arbitration Convention, 1969
52. Taiwan – Arbitration Act, 1998
53. Thailand – Arbitration Act, 2002
54. Tunisia – Arbitration Code, 1993
55. Turkey – International Arbitration Law, 2001
56. Ukraine – Law on International Commercial Arbitration, 2003
57. United Arab Emirates – Loi sur la procédure civile des Émirats arabes unis Titre III: L'arbitrage, 1992
58. United Kingdom – Arbitration Act, 1996
59. Venezuela – Ley de Arbitraje Comercial, 1998
60. Vietnam – Textes sur l'exécution des sentences arbitrales étrangères, 1995
61. Yemen – Presidential Decree No. 22 Issuing The Arbitration Act, 1992
62. Zambia – Arbitration Act, 2000
63. Zimbabwe – Arbitration Act No. 6, 1996

1. Austria – Code of Civil Procedure, Fourth Section, Arbitration Procedure, 2006

Language of Proceedings
Article 596
The parties are free to agree on the language or languages to be used in the arbitral proceedings. Failing such agreement, the arbitral tribunal shall determine the language or languages to be used in the proceedings.

2. Bermuda – International Conciliation and Arbitration Act, 1993

(In force 29 June 1993)

41. Evidence
The party seeking to enforce a Convention award must produce –
c) where the award or agreement is in a foreign language, a translation of it certified by an official or sworn translator or by a diplomatic or consular agent.

3. Bolivia – Law Nr. 1770 on Arbitration and Conciliation, 1997

Article 77 (Language)
I. The parties may freely agree on the language or languages that shall be used in arbitral proceedings. Failing an agreement, the arbitral tribunal shall determine the applicable language or languages.
II. The agreement on the language shall be deemed to apply to all submissions by the parties, the hearings, notifications, written proceedings, communications, award and other arbitral proceedings.
III. The arbitral tribunal may order that any documental evidence shall be accompanied by a translation into the language or languages agreed upon by the parties or determined by the arbitral tribunal, signed by an authorized expert.

4. Bulgaria – Law on International Commercial Arbitration, 1993

(Published in State Gazette No. 60 of 5 August 1988.
As amended by Law amending the Law on International Commercial Arbitration,
Published in State Gazette No. 93 of 2 November 1993)

Article 26
The parties are free to agree on the language or languages to be used in the arbitral proceedings. Failing such agreement, the arbitral tribunal shall determine the language or languages. It may order any written evidence to be accompanied by a translation into the language or languages agreed by the parties, or determined by the arbitral tribunal.

5. Canada – Commercial Arbitration Act, 2004

(In force 10 august 1986 and current to 21 October 2004)

Article 35 Recognition and Enforcement
(1) An arbitral award, irrespective of the country in which it was made, shall be recognized as binding and, upon application in writing to the competent court, shall be enforced subject to the provisions of this article and of article 36.
(2) The party relying on an award or applying for its enforcement shall supply the duly authenticated original award or a duly certified copy thereof, and the original arbitration agreement re-

ferred to in article 7 or a duly certified copy thereof. If the award or agreement is not made in an official language of Canada, the party shall supply a duly certified translation thereof into such language.

6. Canada – British Columbia International Commercial Arbitration Act, 2004
(Last amended 1998 and current to 21 October 2004)

Language
22
(1) The parties are free to agree on the language or languages to be used in the arbitral proceedings.
(2) Failing any agreement referred to in subsection (1), the arbitral tribunal must determine the language or languages to be used in the arbitral proceedings.
(3) The agreement or determination, unless otherwise specified, applies to any written statement by a party, any hearing and any arbitral award, decision or other communication by the arbitral tribunal.
(4) The arbitral tribunal may order that any documentary evidence must be accompanied by a translation into the language or languages agreed on by the parties or determined by the arbitral tribunal

Recognition and enforcement
35
(1) Subject to this section and section 36, an arbitral award, irrespective of the state in which it was made, must be recognized as binding and, on application to the Supreme Court, must be enforced
(2) Unless the court orders otherwise, the party relying on an arbitral award or applying for its enforcement must supply
the duly authenticated original arbitral award or a duly certified copy of it, and
the original arbitration agreement or a duly certified copy of it
(3) If the arbitral award or arbitration agreement is not made in an official language of Canada, the party must supply a duly certified translation of it into an official language.

7. Chile – International Commercial Arbitration Law, 2004

Article 22 Language
(1) The parties are free to agree on the language or languages to be used in the arbitral proceedings. Failing such agreement, the arbitral tribunal shall determine the language or languages to be used in the proceedings. This agreement or determination, unless otherwise specified therein, shall apply to any written statement by a party, any hearing and any award, decision or other communication by the arbitral tribunal.
(2) The arbitral tribunal may order that any documentary evidence shall be accompanied by a translation into the language or languages agreed upon by the parties or determined by the arbitral tribunal.

8. Costa Rica – Law on Alternative Resolution of Disputes and Promotion of Freedom from Social Unrest, 2000

Article 41 – Language
Arbitration shall be conducted in Spanish. Any writ or documentary evidence submitted in another language during the proceedings shall be accompanied by its translation.

Article 51 – Oral hearings

In the event of an oral hearing, the arbitral tribunal shall advise the parties at least fifteen days in advance as to the date, place, and time.

In the event the arbitral tribunal considers it advisable or if the parties have so agreed and requested of the tribunal at least five days prior to the hearing, the arbitral tribunal shall make the necessary arrangements to translate the testimonies of non Spanish-speaking witnesses

9. Croatia – Law on Arbitration, 2001

Language

Article 21

1. The parties are free to agree on the language or languages to be used in the arbitral proceedings. Failing such agreement, the arbitral tribunal shall determine the language or languages to be used in the proceedings. This agreement or determination by the arbitral tribunal, unless otherwise specified therein, shall apply to any written statement by a party, any hearing and any award, decision or other communication by the arbitral tribunal.
2. The arbitral tribunal may order that any documentary evidence shall be accompanied by translation into the language or languages agreed upon by the parties or determined by the arbitral tribunal.
3. Until the language of the proceedings had been determined, a claim, a defense and other deeds can be submitted in the language of the main contract, of the arbitration agreement or in the Croatian language.
4. If neither parties nor arbitrators can reach an agreement on the language of arbitration, the language of arbitration shall be the Croatian language.

Documents to be attached to a request for recognition and enforcement

Article 47

3. If the award or agreement referred to in paragraphs 1 and 2 of this article were not made in the Croatian language, the party shall also supply a duly certified translation thereof into the Croatian language.

10. Egypt – Law Concerning Arbitration in Civil and Commercial Matters, 2000

(Law No. 27/1994, as last amended by Law No. 8/2000. Official Gazette No. 13, 4 April 2000)

Article 29

1. The arbitration shall be conducted in Arabic, unless another language or languages are agreed upon by the two parties or determined by the arbitral panel. This agreement or determination shall apply to all written statements and briefs, to the oral hearings as well as to all awards, decisions or other communications by the arbitral panel, unless specified otherwise by the agreement of the two parties or by determination of the arbitral panel.
2. The arbitral panel may order that all or part of the documentary evidence submitted in the case shall be accompanied by a translation into the language or languages used in the arbitration. In the case of multiplicity of such languages, the arbitral panel may limit the translation to some languages to the exclusion of others.

Article 47

The party in whose favour the arbitral award has been made shall deposit, at the Secretariat of the court referred to in Article 9 of this Law, the original award or a copy thereof in the language in which it was rendered, or an Arabic translation thereof authenticated by a competent organism if it was rendered in a foreign language. The court's secretary shall evidence such deposit in a procès-verbal, and each of the two parties to arbitration may request a copy of the said procès-verbal.

11. Finland – Arbitration Act, 1992

(23 October 1992/967. In force 1 December 1992)

Section 26

1. The arbitral tribunal shall determine the language or languages to be used in the arbitral proceedings unless the parties have agreed thereupon.
2. The arbitral tribunal may order that any document submitted to the tribunal shall be accompanied by a translation into a language of the proceedings

Section 43

2. An application for the enforcement of an arbitral award, submitted to the court of first instance, shall be accompanied by the original arbitration agreement or the provision referred to in section 4 and by the original arbitral award, or certified copies thereof. A document drawn up in any other language than Finnish or Swedish shall, furthermore, be accompanied by a certified translation into either of these languages, unless the court grants an exemption.

Section 54

2. The application shall be accompanied by the original arbitration agreement or by a provision referred to in section 4 and by the original award, or certified copies thereof. A document drawn up in any other language than Finnish or Swedish shall, furthermore, be accompanied by a certified translation into either of these languages, unless the court grants an exemption.

12. Germany – Code of Civil Procedure, Book Ten on Arbitration Procedure, 1998

(Act on Reform of the Law relating to Arbitral Proceedings. In force 1 January 1998)

Section 1045. Language of proceedings

(1) The parties are free to agree on the language or languages to be used in the arbitral proceedings. Failing such agreement, the arbitral tribunal shall determine the language or languages to be used in the proceedings. This agreement or determination, unless otherwise specified therein, shall apply to any written statement by a party, any hearing and any award, decision or other communication by the arbitral tribunal.
(2) The arbitral tribunal may order that any documentary evidence shall be accompanied by a translation into the language or languages agreed upon by the parties or determined by the arbitral tribunal.

13. Greece – Law No. 2735 on International Commercial Arbitration, 1999

Article 22. Language

1. The parties are free to agree on the language or languages to be used in the arbitral proceedings. Failing such agreement, the arbitral tribunal shall determine the language or languages to be used in the proceedings. This agreement or determination, unless otherwise specified therein, shall apply to any written statement by a party, any hearing and any award, decision or other communication by the arbitral tribunal.
2. The arbitral tribunal may order that any documentary evidence shall be accompanied by a translation into the language or languages agreed upon by the parties or determined by the arbitral tribunal.

14. Guatemala – Decreto Numero 67 Ley de Arbitraje, 1995

Artículo 27. Idioma en el arbitraje internacional.
1. Las partes podrán acordar libremente el idioma o los idiomas que hayan de utilizarse en las actuaciones arbitrales de carácter internacional. A falta de tal acuerdo, el tribunal arbitral determinará el idioma o los idiomas que hayan de emplearse en las actuaciones. Este acuerdo o esta determinación será aplicable, salvo que en ellos mismos se haya especificado otra cosa, a todos los escritos de las partes, a todas las audiencias, y a cualquier laudo, decisión o comunicación de otra índole que emita el tribunal arbitral.

El tribunal arbitral podrá ordenar que cualquier prueba documental vaya acompañada de una traducción al idioma o los idiomas convenidos por las partes determinados por el tribunal arbitral

15. Hong Kong – Arbitration Ordinance, 1997

(Chapter 341. Effective 27 June 1997)

43. Evidence
The party seeking to enforce a Convention award must produce [...]
c) where the award or agreement is in a foreign language, a translation of it certified by an official or sworn translator or by a diplomatic or consular agent.

16. Hungary – Act LXXI on Arbitration, 1994

Language of the Proceedings
Section 30
(1) The parties are free to agree on the language to be used in the proceedings. Failing such agreement, the language of the proceedings is the Hungarian language.
(2) Unless otherwise agreed by the parties, the language specified in accordance with subsection (1) shall apply to any statements of the parties, any hearing, and any award, decision or other communication by the arbitral tribunal.

Chapter VI. International Arbitral Proceedings
Language of Proceedings
Section 48
(1) The parties may freely agree on the language or languages to be used in the course of the international arbitral proceedings. Failing such agreement, the language or languages to be used in the course of the proceedings shall be defined by the arbitral tribunal.
(2) The arbitral tribunal may order that a translation shall be attached to any written evidence in the language or languages defined by the parties or the arbitral tribunal.

Section 60
The party that makes a reference to an award of the arbitral tribunal, or applies for its enforcement, shall supply the original award or a certified copy thereof. If the award is not in the Hungarian language, the party shall also attach a certified Hungarian translation.

17. India – The Arbitration and Conciliation Act No. 26, 1996

(16th August 1996)

22. Language
(1) The parties are free to agree upon the language or languages to be used in the arbitral proceedings.

(2) Failing any agreement referred to in sub-section (1), the arbitral tribunal shall determine the language or languages to be used in the arbitral proceedings.
(3) The agreement or determination, unless otherwise specified, shall apply to any written statement by a party, any hearing and any arbitral award, decision or other communciation by the arbitral tribunal.
(4) The arbitral tribunal may order that any documentary evidence shall be accompanied by a translation into the language or languages agreed upon by the parties or determined by the arbitral tribunal.

Part II – Enforcement of certain foreign awards
Chapter I. New York Convention awards
47. Evidence
(2) If the award or agreement to be produced under sub-section (1) is in a foreign language, the party seeking to enforce the award shall produce a translation into English certified as correct by a diplomatic or consular agent of the country to which that party belongs or certified as correct in such other manner as may be sufficient according to the law in force in India.

Chapter II. Geneva Convention Awards
56. Evidence
(2) Where any document requiring to be produced under sub-section (1) is in a foreign language, the party seeking to enforce the award shall produce a translation into English certified as correct by a diplomatic or consular agent of the country to which that party belongs or certified as correct in such other manner as may be sufficient according to the law in force in India.

18. Indonesia – Law No. 30 Concerning Arbitration and Alternative Dispute Resolution, 1999

Article 28
The language to be used in all arbitration proceedings is Indonesian, except that the parties may choose another language to be used, subject to consent of the arbitrator or arbitration tribunal.

Article 35
The arbitrator or arbitration tribunal may order that any document or evidence be accompanied by a translation into such language as determined on by the arbitrator or arbitration tribunal.

19. Iran – The Law on International Commercial Arbitration, 1997

Article 21 – Language
The parties may agree on the language or languages to be used in the arbitral proceedings. Failing such agreement, the arbitrator shall determine the language or languages to be used in the proceedings. The agreement of the parties or the determination of the arbitrator in this respect, shall apply to any written statement, document or evidence of a party, record of hearings, communications by the arbitral tribunal and any awards.

20. Ireland – Arbitration Act No. 26, 1954

(As Amended by the Arbitration (International and Commercial) Act, 1998)

Part V. Enforcement of Certain Foreign Awards
57. Evidence
(2) In any case where any document required to be produced under subsection (1) of this section

is in a language, other than one of the official languages, it shall be the duty of the party seeking to enforce the award to produce a translation certified as correct by a diplomatic or consular agent of the country to which that party belongs, or certified as correct in such other manner as may be sufficient according to the law of the State.

21. Ireland – Arbitration (International Commercial) Act, 1998

Article 22. Language
(1) The parties are free to agree on the language or languages to be used in the arbitral proceedings. Failing such agreement, the arbitral tribunal shall determine the language or languages to be used in the proceedings. This agreement or determination, unless otherwise specified therein, shall apply to any written statement by a party, any hearing and any award, decision or other communication by the arbitral tribunal.
(2) The arbitral tribunal may order that any documentary evidence shall be accompanied by a translation into the language or languages agreed upon by the parties or determined by the arbitral tribunal.

Article 35. Recognition and enforcement
(2) The party relying on an award or applying for its enforcement shall supply the duly authenticated original award or a duly certified copy thereof, and the original arbitration agreement referred to in article 7 or a duly certified copy thereof. If the award or agreement is not made in an official language of this State, the party shall supply a duly certified translation thereof into such language.

22. Israel – Regulations For The Execution of The New York Convention (Foreign Arbitration), 1978

(5738- 1978)

3.
A party who applies to the court to confirm a foreign award shall attach to his application [...]
(b) a document referred to in sub-regulation (a) which was not made in Hebrew, Arabic, English or French, shall be accompanied by a translation into one of these languages; the translation shall be confirmed by a person who is authorized to authenticate translations according to the Israeli law or by a diplomatic or consular agent of the country in the language of which the document was made.

23. Italy – Code of Civil Procedure, Book Four, Title VIII Arbitration, 2000

(As amended by Legislative Decree No. 40 of February 2, 2006)

Article 816-bis (Course of the proceedings)
(1) The parties may establish in the arbitration agreement or in a separate document, prior in any case to the commencement of the arbitral proceedings, the rules that the arbitrators must apply in the proceedings and the language of the arbitration. In the absence of such rules, the arbitrators are free to regulate the course of the proceedings and to determine the language of the arbitration in the manner they deem most convenient. [...]

Article 839
Recognition and enforcement of foreign arbitral awards
(1) ...
(2) The petitioner shall supply the original award or a certified copy thereof, together with the

original arbitration agreement or an equivalent document, or a certified copy thereof.
(3) If the documents specified in the second paragraph are not written in Italian, the petitioner shall in addition produce a certified translation thereof.

24. Japan – Arbitration Law, 2003

Article 30 (Language)
(1) The parties are free to agree on the language or languages to be used in the arbitral proceedings and the proceedings to be conducted using that language or those languages.
(2) Failing such agreement as prescribed in the preceding paragraph, the arbitral tribunal shall determine the language or languages to be used in the arbitral proceedings and the proceedings to be conducted using that language or those languages.
(3) Failing any designation of proceedings to be conducted using the designated language or languages in the agreement prescribed in paragraph (1) or the determination prescribed in the preceding paragraph, the proceedings to be conducted using such language or languages are as follows:
i) any oral proceedings;
ii) any statement or notice in writing by a party; or
iii) any ruling (including an arbitral award) or notice in writing by the arbitral tribunal.
(4) The arbitral tribunal may order that any documentary evidence shall be accompanied by a translation into the language or languages designated in the agreement as prescribed in paragraph (1) or the determination prescribed in paragraph (2) (where designation has been made as to the language or languages to be used for translation, such language or languages).

25. Jordan – Loi Jordanienne No. 31, 2001
(du 14 juin 2001)

Article 28
a) L'arbitrage se déroule en langue arabe, à moins que les deux parties ne soient convenues, ou que le tribunal arbitral n'ait décidé, de l'usage d'une ou plusieurs autres langues. L'accord ou la décision sur ce sujet s'appliquera à la langue dans laquelle seront rédigés les exposés et mémoires écrits, aux plaidoiries orales et également à toute décision que le tribunal arbitral prendra, aux lettres qu'il enverra ou à la sentence qu'il rendra, à moins que l'accord des parties ou la décision du tribunal arbitral n'en ait disposé autrement.
b) Le tribunal arbitral peut décider que tout ou partie des documents écrits produits au cours de la procédure seront traduits dans une ou plusieurs des langues utilisées dans l'arbitrage. En cas de langues multiples, la traduction peut être limitée à certaines d'entre elles.

Article 53
a) La demande d'exécution de la sentence arbitrale est irrecevable tant que le délai pour agir en nullité n'est pas expiré.
b) La demande d'exécution doit être présentée à la juridiction compétente, accompagnée des documents suivants :
Copie de la convention d'arbitrage;
Original de la sentence ou copie certifiée de celle-ci;
Traduction en langue arabe de la sentence arbitrale, certifiée par une autorité agréée dans le cas où la sentence n'a pas été rendue en cette langue

26. Kenya – The Arbitration Act No. 4, 1995

(Date of Assent: 10 August 1995. Date of Commencement: 2 January 1996)

23. Language

(1) The parties are free to agree upon the language or languages to be used in the arbitral proceedings.
(2) Failing an agreement under subsection (1), the arbitral tribunal shall determine the language or languages to be used in the arbitral proceedings.
(3) The agreement or determination under subsection (1) or (2) shall, unless otherwise specified, apply to any written statement by a party, any hearing and any arbitral award, decision or other communication by the arbitral tribunal.
(4) The arbitral tribunal may order that any documentary evidence shall be accompanied by a translation into the language or languages agreed upon by the parties or determined by the arbitral tribunal.

36. Recognition and Enforcement of Award

(3) If the arbitral award or arbitration agreement is not made in the English language, the party shall furnish a duly certified translation of it into the English language.

27. (South) Korea – Arbitration Act, 1999

(Amended by Act No.6083 as of Dec. 31, 1999)

Article 23 (Language)

(1) The parties are free to agree on the language or languages to be used in the arbitral proceedings. Failing such agreement, the arbitral tribunal shall determine such language or languages, and otherwise the Korean language shall be used.
(2) The agreement or determination referred to in paragraph (1) shall, unless otherwise specified therein, apply to any written statement by a party, any hearing and any award, decision or other communication by the arbitral tribunal.
(3) The arbitral tribunal may, if considered necessary, order a party to submit any documentary evidence, accompanied by a translation into the language or languages referred to in paragraph (1).

28. Kuwait – The Civil and Commercial Procedure Code No. 38, 1980

(Effective 1 November 1980)

Article 183

The arbitrators' award shall be issued by majority, shall be in writing, shall include in particular a copy of the adversaries, the reasons for the award and its pronouncement, date and place of issue of the award and signatures of the arbitrators.
If one or more of the arbitrators refuse to sign the award the award shall mention the fact. It shall be valid if it is signed by the majority of arbitrators.
The award shall be written in Arabic, unless the adversaries otherwise agree, in which case there must be attached to it an official translation when the award is filed.
The award shall be deemed to be issued on the date it is signed by the arbitrators after writing it.

29. Lithuania – Law on Commercial Arbitration, 1996
(2 April 1996)

Article 25. Language of Arbitral Proceedings
1. In the event of national arbitration the case shall be tried in the Lithuanian language.
2. In the event of international arbitration the parties may agree on the language or languages to be used in the arbitral proceedings. Failing such agreement, the arbitral tribunal shall determine the language to be used in the proceedings. The agreement between the parties or the decree of the arbitral tribunal, unless otherwise specified therein, shall apply to any written statement by a party, any hearing and any award, decision or other documents adopted by the arbitral tribunal.
3. The arbitral tribunal may order that any documentary evidence shall be translated into the language or languages agreed upon by the parties or determined by the arbitral tribunal.

Article 39. Recognition and Enforcement of Foreign Arbitral Awards
2. The party applying the recognition and enforcement of a foreign arbitral award shall supply the Lithuanian Court of Appeal with the duly authenticated original award or a duly certified copy thereof, and the original arbitration agreement referred to in Article 9 or a duly certified copy thereof. If the arbitral award or arbitral agreement is not made in an official language of this State, the party shall supply a duly certified translation thereof into the Lithuanian language.

30. Lebanon – Nouveau Code de procédure civile libanais, 1993
(as amended by Law 440/2002)

2 – La reconnaissance des sentences arbitrales rendues à l'étranger ou en matière d'arbitrage international et leur exécution

Article 814:
Les sentences arbitrales sont reconnues et revêtues d'exequatur si la personne qui s'en prévaut établit leur existence et si elles ne sont pas manifestement contraires à l'ordre public international L'existence d'une sentence arbitrale est établie par la production, soit de son original accompagné de la convention d'arbitrage, soit des copies conformes de ces deux documents authentifiées par les arbitres ou par toute autorité compétente. Et si ces pièces sont rédigées en langue étrangère, il doit être procédé à leur traduction par un traducteur assermenté.

31. Madagascar – Loi No. 98-019 sur l'arbitrage, 1998
(11 Novembre 1998)

Article 459
1. Les parties sont libres de convenir de la langue ou des langues à utiliser dans la procédure arbitrale. Faute d'un tel accord, le tribunal arbitral décide de la langue ou des langues à utiliser dans la procédure. Cet accord ou cette décision, à moins qu'il n'en soit convenu ou décidé autrement, s'applique à toute déclaration écrite d'une partie, à toute procédure orale et à toute sentence, décision ou autre communication du tribunal arbitral.
2. Le tribunal arbitral peut ordonner que toute pièce soit accompagnée d'une traduction dans la langue ou les langues convenues par les parties ou choisies par le tribunal arbitral.

Article 464
1. La sentence arbitrale, quel que soit le pays où elle a été rendue, est reconnue comme ayant force obligatoire et, sur requête par écrit adres sée à la Cour d'appel d'Antananarivo, est exécutée sous réserve des dispositions du présent article et de l'article 464.1.

2. La partie qui invoque une sentence arbitrale ou qui en demande l'exécution doit en produire l'original dûment authentifié ou une copie certifiée conforme, ainsi que l'original de la convention d'arbitrage mentionnée à l'article 453 ou une copie certifiée conforme. Si ladite sentence ou ladite convention n'est pas rédigée en langue malgache ou en langue française, la partie en produit une traduction dûment certifiée par un traducteur inscrit sur la liste des experts.

32. Malta – Arbitration Act No. II, 1996

(Assented to 13 February 1996)

28. Language

(1) Subject to an agreement by the parties, the arbitral tribunal shall, promptly after its appointment, determine the language or languages to be used in the proceedings; unless the parties agree otherwise, the language chosen shall be Maltese. This determination shall apply to the statement of claim, the statement of defence, and any further written statements and, if oral hearings take place, to the language or languages to be used in such hearings.
(2) The arbitral tribunal may order that any documents annexed to the statement of claim or statement of defence, and any supplementary documents or exhibits submitted in the course of the proceedings, shall be delivered in their original language or languages agreed on by the parties or determined by the arbitral tribunal.

37. Oral hearing

(2) If the witnesses are to be heard, each party shall communicate to the arbitral tribunal and to the other party, at least fifteen days before the hearing, the names and addresses of the witnesses he intends to present, the subject upon which and the languages in which such witnesses will give their testimony.
(3) The arbitral tribunal shall make arrangements for the translation of oral statements made at a hearing and for a record of the hearing if either is deemed necessary by the arbitral tribunal in the circumstances of the case, or if the parties have agreed thereto and have communicated such agreement to the arbitral tribunal at least fifteen days before the hearing

77. Language of schedules

In case of any conflict between the Maltese and English text of any of the First, Second and Third Schedules to this Act, the English text shall prevail.

33. Mauritania – Loi No. 2000-06 portant code de l'arbitrage, 2000

Article 51 Langue

A défaut d'accord entre les parties, le tribunal arbitral détermine la ou les langues à utiliser dans la procédure arbitrale.
Les conclusions écrites d'une partie, les plaidoiries et toutes les décisions ou autres communications du tribunal arbitral sont rédigées dans la langue de choix des parties ou, à défaut d'accord entre les parties, dans la langue choisie par le tribunal.
Le tribunal arbitral peut ordonner que toute pièce soit accompagnée d'une traduction dans la ou les langues convenues entre les parties ou choisies par le tribunal arbitral.

Article 61

La sentence arbitrale, quel que soit le pays ou elle a été rendue, a l'autorité de la chose jugée prévue à l'article 30 du présent Code. Elle est exécutée sur requête écrite adressée au président du Tribunal de Wilaya et sous réserve des dispositions du présent article et des articles 62 et 63 du présent Code.

La partie qui invoque une sentence arbitrale ou qui en demande l'exécution doit fournir l'original dûment authentifié ou une copie certifiée conforme, ainsi que l'original de la convention d'arbitrage mentionnée à l'article 46 du présent Code, ou une copie certifiée conforme de cette convention. Les deux documents sus-indiqués seront accompagnés, le cas échéant, d'une traduction officielle en langue arabe.

34. Mexico – Federal Mexican Commercial Code, Title IV, Book V, Commercial Arbitration, 1993

(As amended by Decree of 22 July 1993)

Article 1438

1. The parties are free to agree on the language or languages to be used in the arbitral proceedings. Failing such agreement, the arbitral tribunal shall determine the language or languages to be used in the proceedings. This agreement or determination, unless otherwise specified therein, shall apply to any written statement by a party, any hearing and any award, decision or other communication issued by the arbitral tribunal.
2. The arbitral tribunal may order that any documentary evidence shall be accompanied by a translation into the language or languages agreed upon by the parties or determined by the arbitral tribunal.

Article 1461

2. The party relying on an award or applying for its enforcement shall supply the duly authenticated original award or a duly certified copy thereof, and the original arbitration agreement referred to in Articles 1416, section I and 1423 or a duly certified copy thereof. If the award or agreement is not made in Spanish, the party shall supply a duly certified translation thereof into such language.

35. New Zealand – Arbitration Act, 1996

(In force 1 July 1997)

Article 22 – Language

(1) The parties are free to agree on the language or languages to be used in the arbitral proceedings. Failing such agreement, the arbitral tribunal shall determine the language or languages to be used in the proceedings. This agreement or determination, unless otherwise specified, shall apply to any written statement by a party, any hearing, and any award, decision, or other communication by the arbitral tribunal.
(2) The arbitral tribunal may order that any documentary evidence shall be accompanied by a translation into the language or languages agreed upon by the parties or determined by the arbitral tribunal.

Article 35 – Recognition and enforcement

(2) The party relying on an award or applying for its enforcement shall supply the duly authenticated original award or a duly certified copy and, *if recorded in writing*, the original arbitration agreement or a duly certified copy. If the award or agreement is not made in *the English* language, the party shall supply a duly certified translation into *the English* language.

36. Nigeria – Arbitration And Conciliation Decree No. 11, 1988

(14 March 1988)

18. Language to be used in arbitral proceedings

(1) The parties may by agreement determine the language or languages to be used in the arbitral

proceedings, but where they do not do so, the arbitral tribunal shall determine the language or languages to be used bearing in mind the relevant circumstances of the case.
(2) Any language or languages agreed upon by the parties or determined by the arbitral tribunal under subsection (1) of this section, shall, unless a contrary intention is expressed by the parties or the arbitral tribunal, be the language or languages to be used in any written statements by the parties, in any hearing, award, decision or any other communication in the course of the arbitration.
(3) The arbitral tribunal may order that any documentary evidence shall be accompanied by a translation into the language or languages agreed upon by the parties or determined by the arbitral tribunal under subsection (1) of this section.

51. Recognition and enforcement of awards
(2) The party relying on an award or applying for its enforcement shall supply [...]
c) where the award or arbitration agreement is not made in the English language, a duly certified translation thereof into the English language.

Schedule 1 – Arbitration Rules
Article 17
1. Subject to an agreement by the parties, the arbitral tribunal shall, promptly after its appointment, determine the language or languages to be used in the proceedings. This determination shall apply to the statement of claim, the statement of defence, and any further written statements and, if oral hearings take place to the language or languages to be used at such hearings.
2. The arbitral tribunal may order that any documents annexed to the statement of claim or statement of defence, and any supplementary documents or exhibits submitted in the course of the proceedings, delivered in their original language, shall be accompanied by a translation into the language or languages agreed upon by the parties or determined by the arbitral tribunal.

Article 25
2. If witnesses are to be heard, at least 15 days before the hearing each party shall communicate to the arbitral tribunal and to the other party the names and addresses of the witnesses he intends to present, the subject upon and the languages in which such witnesses will give their testimony.
3. The arbitral tribunal shall make arrangements for the translation of oral statements made at a hearing and for a record of the hearing if either is deemed necessary by the tribunal under the circumstances of the case, or if the parties have agreed thereto and have communicated such agreement to the tribunal at least 15 days before the hearing.

37. Oman – The Law of Arbitration in Civil and Commercial Disputes, 1997

Article 29
1. The arbitration shall proceed in the Arabic language, unless the two parties agree, or the arbitral tribunal specifies, another language or languages. That which is laid down in the agreement or the decision shall also have effect in relation to the language of written statements and memoranda, and to oral submissions, and likewise to any decision such tribunal takes, any letter it sends, or any award it renders, unless the agreement of the two parties or a decision by the arbitral tribunal, provides otherwise.
2. The arbitral tribunal shall be at liberty to rule that all or part of the written documentation submitted in the case be accompanied by a translation into the language or languages used in the arbitration. In the event of there being a number of such languages, it shall be permissible to restrict the translation to certain of them.

Article 47

A person in whose favour an arbitral award is rendered shall deposit the original of the award, or a signed copy thereof in the language in which it was rendered, or a translation in the Arabic language certified by approved authority if it was rendered in a foreign language, with the registry of the court referred to in Article 9 of this Law.

Article 56

Competence to make an order enforcing an arbitrators' award shall lie with the President of the Commercial Court or the judge therein whom he delegates. An application for enforcement of the award shall be submitted with the following attached thereto.

3. A translation of the arbitral award into the Arabic language certified by approved authority, if it was not rendered in that language.

38. Paraguay – Law Nr. 1879 on Arbitration and Mediation, 2002

Article 25. Language

The parties are free to agree on the language or languages to be used in the arbitral proceedings. Failing such agreement, the arbitral tribunal shall determine the language or languages to be used in the proceedings. This agreement or determination, unless otherwise specified therein, shall apply to any written statement by a party, any hearing and any award, decision or other communication by the arbitral tribunal.

The arbitral tribunal may order that any documentary evidence shall be accompanied by a translation into the language or languages agreed upon by the parties or determined by the arbitral tribunal.

39. Peru – General Arbitration Law No. 26572, 1996

(In force since 6 January 1996)

Article 96. Formality of the document before the judicial authority

Each writing or writ addressed to a judicial authority of the Republic shall be drafted in the Spanish language. All documents issued outside the country shall be legalized in accordance with the laws of the country of origin and authenticated by a diplomatic agent or Peruvian consul, or someone serving in such stead, at the place of its issue. If the document was not drafted in Spanish it shall be translated into that language by a diplomatic agent or Peruvian Consul, or someone serving in such stead, at the place of its issue, or by an official translator.

Article 111. Language

The parties are free to agree on the language or languages to be used in the arbitral proceedings. Failing such agreement, the arbitral tribunal shall determine the language or languages to be used in the proceedings. This agreement or determination, unless otherwise specified therein, shall apply to any written statement by a party, any hearing and any award, decision or other communication by the arbitral tribunal.

The arbitral tribunal may order that any document shall be accompanied by a translation into the language or languages agreed upon by the parties or determined by the arbitral tribunal.

Article 124. Terms requirements and formalities

An application for setting aside must be made within fifteen days from the date on which the party making the application received the award or, if a request had been made under Articles 122, from the date on which that request had been resolved by the arbitral tribunal.

The requirements for admissibility set forth in Article 72 shall be applied. If the required documents are not in Spanish the party must present a translation thereof into such language, the provisions of Article 96 applying.

Article 127. Recognition and enforcement

An arbitral award, irrespective of the country in which it was made, shall be recognized as binding and, upon application in writing to the Civil Chamber of the Superior Court competent at the date of the filing at the place where the defendant is domiciled, or if the defendant is not domiciled within the territory of the Republic, the place where its property is located, and shall be enforced in accordance with the provisions of this Section.

The party relying on an award or applying for the recognition of an award shall supply the original award or a copy thereof, and the original arbitration agreement or a copy thereof. If the award or agreement is not made in Spanish, the party shall supply translation thereof into such language. In both cases the provisions of Article 96 shall apply.

40. Poland – Code of Civil Procedure Part Five, Arbitration, 2005

(Act of 17 November 1964, as amended on 17 October 2005)

Chapter V. Conduct of arbitral proceedings

Article 1187

§ 1. The parties are free to agree on the language or languages in which the proceedings will be conducted. Failing such agreement, the arbitral tribunal shall determine the language or languages of the proceedings. Agreement of the parties or determination by the arbitral tribunal shall, unless specified otherwise, apply to any written statements by the parties, any hearing and to any awards or other communications by the arbitral tribunal.

§ 2. The arbitral tribunal may order that any document shall be accompanied by a translation into the language or languages agreed upon by the parties or determined by the arbitral tribunal.

41. Romania – Code of Civil Procedure, Book IV on Arbitration, 1993

(As amended by Law No. 59 of 23 July 1993)

Article 369

The arbitral proceedings before the arbitral tribunal shall be in the language established by the arbitration agreement, or, if no provisions were made in this respect, and no subsequent agreement has been reached, they shall be in the language of the contract from which the dispute has arisen or in another language used in international communication established by the arbitral tribunal.

If a party is ignorant of the language in which the proceedings are carried on, the arbitral tribunal shall provide the services of a translator at the request and the expense of that party.

The parties may participate in the proceedings with their own translator.

42. Russian Federation – Law on International Commercial Arbitration, 1993

(In force 14 August 1993)

Article 22 – Language

1. The parties are free to agree on the language or languages to be used in the arbitral proceedings. Failing such agreement, the arbitral tribunal shall determine the language or languages to be used in the proceedings. This agreement or determination, unless otherwise specified therein, shall apply to any written statement by a party, any hearing and any award, decision or other communication by the arbitral tribunal.

2. The arbitral tribunal may order that any documentary evidence shall be accompanied by a translation into the language or languages agreed upon by the parties or determined by the arbitral tribunal.

Article 35 – Recognition and enforcement
1. An arbitral award, irrespective of the country in which it was made, shall be recognized as binding and, upon application in writing to the competent court, shall be enforced subject to the provisions of this article and of article 36.
2. The party relying on an award or applying for its enforcement shall supply the duly authenticated original award or a duly certified copy thereof, and the original arbitration agreement referred to in article 7 or a duly certified copy thereof. If the award or agreement is made in a foreign language, the party shall supply a duly certified translation thereof into the Russian language.

43. Saudi Arabia – Rules for the Implementation of the Arbitration Regulation, 1985

(27 May 1985)

Section 12
The summons or notice shall be written in the Arabic language and shall consist of two or more copies – according to the number of disputing parties – and shall contain the following:

Section 25
The Arabic language shall be the official language to be used before the arbitration panel, whether in the discussions or in correspondence. The arbitration panel and the parties may not speak other than the Arabic language and any party who does not speak Arabic shall be accompanied by an accredited translator, who shall sign with him the minutes of the hearing, approving the statements made.

44. Scotland – Law Reform (Miscellaneous Provisions) Act, 1991

(adopting the UNCITRAL Model Law, with certain modifications)

Article 22
Language
(1) The parties are free to agree on the language or languages to be used in the arbitral proceedings. Failing such agreement, the arbitral tribunal shall determine the language or languages to be used in the proceedings. This agreement or determination, unless otherwise specified therein, shall apply to any written statement by a party, any hearing and any award, decision or other communication by the arbitral tribunal.
(2) The arbitral tribunal may order that any documentary evidence shall be accompanied by a translation into the language or languages agreed upon by the parties or determined by the arbitral tribunal.

Article 35
Recognition and enforcement
(2) The party relying on an award or applying for its enforcement shall supply the duly authenticated original award or a duly certified copy thereof, and the original arbitration agreement referred to in article 7 or a duly certified copy thereof. If the award or agreement is not made in English, the party shall supply a duly certified translation thereof into English.

45. Serbia – Arbitration Act, 2006

(Published in the Official Gazette of Serbia No. 46/2006)

Article 35 – Language

The parties may agree on the language or languages in which the arbitration proceedings will be conducted. Failing such agreement, this will be decided by the arbitral tribunal, taking into consideration the place of arbitration, and the language used by the parties in their legal relationship.

Permanent arbitral institutions may regulate in their rules the question of the language of arbitral proceedings.

The language of arbitration applies to all written submissions of the parties, to the oral hearing, to the arbitral award, and to other acts of the arbitral tribunal, unless the parties agreed otherwise, or unless the arbitral tribunal decided otherwise in the absence of party agreement.

The arbitral tribunal may order that any documentary evidence shall be accompanied by translation into the language or languages agreed upon by the parties, or determined by the arbitral tribunal.

Until the language of the proceedings had been determined, the statement of claim, statement of defense and other submissions may be submitted in the language of the contract, or in the language of the arbitration agreement, or in Serbian.

46. Singapore – International Arbitration Act, 2002

(Chapter 143A. As amended and revised on 31 December 2002)

Part III. Foreign awards

Evidence

(1) In any proceedings in which a person seeks to enforce a foreign award by virtue of this Part, he shall produce to the court [...]

c) where the award or agreement is in a foreign language, a translation of it in the English language, duly certified in English as a correct translation by a sworn translator or by an official or by a diplomatic or consular agent of the country in which the award was made.

47. South Africa – Recognition and Enforcement of Foreign Arbitral Awards Act No. 40, 1977

(Assented to 25 March 1977. Date of Commencement: 13 April 1977)

3. Application for award to be made order of court

Application for an order of court mentioned in section 2(1) shall be made to any court and shall-

(a) be accompanied by- (i) the original foreign arbitral award concerned and the original arbitration agreement in terms of which that award was made, authenticated in the manner in which foreign documents may be authenticated to enable them to be produced in any court; or

(ii) a certified copy of that award and of that agreement; and

(b) if that award or agreement is in any language other than one of the official languages of the Republic, be accompanied by a sworn translation thereof into one of such official languages, authenticated in the manner in which foreign documents may be authenticated to enable them to be produced in any court.

48. Spain – Law on Arbitration, 2004
(Law 60 of 23 December 2003. In force 26 March 2004)

Article 28. Language of the Arbitration
1. The parties are free to agree on the language or languages to be used in the arbitration. Failing such agreement, the arbitrators shall determine the language, having regard to the circumstances of the case. Unless otherwise agreed by the parties or determined by the arbitrators, the language or languages established shall apply to any written statement by a party, any hearing, and any award, decision or other communication by the arbitrators.
2. The arbitrators, unless one of the parties objects, may order that, without need of translation, any documents be submitted or any proceedings be performed in a language different from that of the arbitration.

49. Sri Lanka – Arbitration Act No. 11, 1995
(Certified on 30 June 1995)

31. Application for filing and enforcement of award
(3) If a document or part of a document produced under subsection (2) is written in a language other than the official language of the court or other than in English, there shall be produced with the document a translation in such official language, or in the English language, of that document or that part, as the case may be, certified to be a correct translation.
(4) For the purposes of subsection (2), a translation shall be certified by an official or sworn translator or by a diplomatic or a consular agent in Sri Lanka of the country in which the award was made or otherwise to the satisfaction of the Court.

50. Sweden – Arbitration Act, 1999
(SFS 1999:116)

Section 56
An application for the enforcement of a foreign award shall be lodged with the Svea Court of Appeal.
The original award or a certified copy of the award must be appended to the application. Unless the Court of Appeal decides otherwise, a certified translation into the Swedish language of the entire award must also be submitted.

Section 58
Where the opposing party objects that an arbitration agreement was not entered into, the applicant must submit the arbitration agreement in an original or a certified copy and, unless otherwise decided by the Court of Appeal, must submit a certified translation into the Swedish language, or in some other manner prove that an arbitration agreement was entered into.

51. Switzerland – Intercantonal Arbitration Convention, 1969
(March 27/August 29, 1969)

Article 35 –Deposit and notification
The arbitral tribunal shall attend to the deposit of the award with the judicial authority provided for in Article 3.
The award shall be deposited together with as many copies of it as there are parties in cases where paragraph 4 of this article applies.

If the award is not drafted in one of the official languages of the Swiss Confederation, the authority with whom it is deposited may require an authenticated translation of the award.
Such authority shall notify the parties of the award, and shall inform them of the date of deposit.

52. Taiwan – Arbitration Act, 1998

Article 25

1. The parties are free to agree on the language or languages to be used in the arbitral proceedings. The arbitral tribunal may order that any documentary evidence shall be accompanied by a translation into the language or languages agreed upon by the parties or determined by the arbitral tribunal.
2. Interpreters may be employed if any party or arbitrator is a non-Chinese speaker.

Article 33

1. When it is deemed that the arbitration has proceeded to a point where a decision may appropriately be made, the arbitral tribunal shall declare the end of hearing and make a decision within ten days on the basis of the pleadings of the parties.
2. The award shall state the following information:
(3) the full names, nationalities and the places of domiciles or residences of the interpreters or translators, if any;

Article 48

1. The party relying on a foreign award or applying for its enforcement shall apply: ...
2. Where the documents are written in foreign language, the party shall supply a duly certified translation into Chinese.
3. The certified documents and their translation mentioned in sub-paragraphs 1 and 2 of paragraph 1 means those certified by the embassies, consulates or representative office of the Republic of China.
4. Copies of the application of enforcement of arbitral award shall be sent to the court in order to be delivered to the other parties.

53. Thailand – Arbitration Act, 2002

(Act BE 2545. As in force from 30 April 2002)

Section 28

The parties may agree on the language or languages to be used in the arbitration proceedings. Failing such agreement, the arbitral tribunal shall determine the language or the languages to be used in the proceedings. This agreement or determination, unless otherwise specified therein, shall apply to a claim, a defence, a written petition of the parties, a hearing, an award, a decision or other communication made by or to the arbitral tribunal.
The arbitral tribunal may order that any documentary evidence shall be accompanied by a translation into the language or languages agreed upon by the parties or determined by the arbitral tribunal.

Section 42

A party who wishes to enforce an arbitral award shall make a petition to the competent court within three years from the date of the enforceability of the award. Upon receipt of such petition, the court shall make an inquiry and render its judgment without delay.
The party petitioning for the enforcement of an award shall produce the following documents to the court:

3) the duly certified translation of the award and the arbitration agreement in Thai language with the translator having sworn or made oath before the court or before an official or person having such power, or with the certification by an official authorized to certify the translation, or by the Thai consulate in the country in which the award or the arbitration agreement was made.

54. Tunisia – Arbitration Code, 1993

(Promulgated by Law No. 93-42 of 26 April 1993. In force 27 October 1993)

Article 67

1. The parties are free to agree on the language or languages to be used in the arbitral proceedings. Failing such agreement, the arbitral tribunal shall determine the language or languages to be used in the proceedings. This agreement or determination, unless otherwise stipulated in the arbitral agreement, shall apply to any written statement by a party, any pleadings and any award decision or other communication by the arbitral tribunal.
2. The arbitral tribunal may order that any documentary evidence shall be accompanied by a translation into the language or languages agreed upon by the parties or determined by the arbitral tribunal.

55. Turkey – International Arbitration Law, 2001

(Law No. 4686 of 21 June 2001)

Article 10

Commencement, term and language of arbitration, statement of claim and defence, terms of reference

C) The language of the arbitration shall be Turkish or any other language, which is the formal language of a state that is recognized by the Republic of Turkey. The parties are free to agree on the language or languages to be used in the arbitral proceedings. Failing such agreement, the arbitral tribunal shall determine the language or languages. The agreement or determination, unless otherwise specified therein, shall apply to any written statement by a party, any hearing and any award, decision or other communication by the arbitral tribunal.

The arbitral tribunal may order that any documentary evidence shall be accompanied by a translation into the language or languages used in the arbitration proceedings.

56. Ukraine – Law on International Commercial Arbitration, 2003

Article 22 Language

1. The parties are free to agree on the language or languages to be used in the arbitral proceedings. Failing such agreement, the arbitral tribunal shall determine the language or languages to be used in the proceedings. This agreement or determination, unless otherwise specified therein, shall apply to any written statement by a party, any hearing and any award, decision or other communication by the arbitral tribunal.
2. The arbitral tribunal may order that any documentary evidence shall be accompanied by a translation into the language or languages agreed upon by the parties or determined by the arbitral tribunal.

Article 35 Recognition and enforcement

1. An arbitral award, irrespective of the country in which it was made, shall be recognized as binding and, upon application in writing to the competent court, shall be enforced subject to the provisions of this article and of article 36.
2. The party relying on an award or applying for its enforcement shall supply the duly authenti-

cated original award or a duly certified copy thereof, and the original arbitration agreement referred to in article 7 or a duly certified copy thereof. If the award or agreement is made in a foreign language, the party shall supply a duly certified translation thereof in the Ukrainian or Russian language.

57. United Arab Emirates – Loi sur la procédure civile des Émirats arabes unis Titre III: L'arbitrage, 1992

Article 212
6. La sentence doit être rédigée en langue arabe, à moins que les parties n'en conviennent autrement. Dans ce cas, une traduction officielle en langue arabe doit lui être jointe lors de son dépôt.

58. United Kingdom – Arbitration Act, 1996
(Chapter 23)

34. Procedural and evidential matters
(1) It shall be for the tribunal to decide all procedural and evidential matters, subject to the right of the parties to agree any matter.
(2) Procedural and evidential matters include-
b) the language or languages to be used in the proceedings and whether translations of any relevant documents are to be supplied

102. Evidence to be produced by party seeking recognition or enforcement
(1) A party seeking the recognition or enforcement of a New York Convention award must produce [...]
(2) If the award or agreement is in a foreign language, the party must also produce a translation of it certified by an official or sworn translator or by a diplomatic or consular agent.

59. Venezuela – Ley de Arbitraje Comercial, 1998

Artículo 10
Las partes podrán acordar libremente el idioma o los idiomas que hayan de utilizarse en las actuaciones arbitrales. A falta de tal acuerdo, el tribunal arbitral determinará el idioma o los idiomas que hayan de emplearse. Este acuerdo será aplicable, salvo que ellos mismos hayan acordado otra forma, a todos los escritos de las partes, a todas las audiencias y al laudo, decisión o comunicación de otra índole que emita el tribunal arbitral.
El tribunal arbitral podrá ordenar que los documentos presentados para su consideración estén acompañados de una traducción al idioma o los idiomas acordados por las partes o determinados por el tribunal arbitral.

60. Vietnam – Textes sur l'exécution des sentences arbitrales étrangères, 1995

Article 10. Demande de reconnaissance et d'exécution d'une sentence arbitrale étrangère que Vietnam
3. La demande en langue étrangère doit être traduite en vietnamien et la traduction devra être certifiée conformément aux stipulations de la loi vietnamienne

Article 11. Piéces à joindre à la demande
[...] Les pièces jointes en langue étrangère doivent être traduites en vietnamien et certifiées conformément aux dispositions de la loi vietnamienne

61. Yemen – Presidential Decree No. 22 Issuing The Arbitration Act, 1992

Article 7
Without prejudice to the provisions of this Act, the parties may, if one or all of them are not Yemeni, agree on the law applicable to the procedure and the substantive matters of the arbitration, as well as the language and the place of arbitration.

62. Zambia – Arbitration Act, 2000

(Government of Zambia Act No.19. Enacted by the Parliament of Zambia on 29 December 2000)

2. (1) In this Act, unless the context otherwise requires–
"Official language" means the English language;

18. (1) An arbitral award, irrespective of the country in which it was made, shall be recognised as binding and, upon application in writing to the competent court, shall be enforced subject to the provisions of this section and of section nineteen.
(2) The party relying on an award or applying for its enforcement shall supply the duly authenticated original award or a duly certified copy thereof, and the original arbitration agreement or duly certified copies thereof. If the award or agreement is not made in the official language, the party shall supply a duly certified translation thereof into the official language

63. Zimbabwe – Arbitration Act No. 6, 1996

(In force 13 September 1996)

Article 22. Language
(1) The parties are free to agree on the language or languages to be used in the arbitral proceedings. Failing such agreement, the arbitral tribunal shall determine the language or languages to be used in the proceedings. This agreement or determination, unless otherwise specified therein, shall apply to any written statement by a party, any hearing and any award, decision or other communication by the arbitral tribunal.
(2) The arbitral tribunal may order that any documentary evidence shall be accompanied by a translation into the language or languages agreed upon by the parties or determined by the arbitral tribunal.

Article 35. Recognition and enforcement
(1) An arbitral award, irrespective of the country in which it was made, shall be recognised as binding and, upon application in writing to the *High Court*, shall be enforced subject to the provisions of this article and of article 36.
(2) The party relying on an award or applying for its enforcement shall supply the duly authenticated original award or a duly certified copy thereof and the original arbitration agreement referred to in article 7 or a duly certified copy thereof. If the award or agreement is not made in *the English* language, the party shall supply a duly certified translation into *the English* language.

Annex III

Institutional Rules – Provisions Pertaining to Language and Translation

(Listed alphabetically by the name of the institution)

Table of Contents

21. China International Economic and Trade Arbitration Commission (CIETAC), Arbitration Rules, 2005
22. Commercial Arbitration and Mediation Center for the Americas (CAMCA), Arbitration Rules, 1996
23. Court of Arbitration for Sport (CAS), Code of Sports-related Arbitration, 1994
24. Court of Arbitration for Sport (CAS), Arbitration Rules for the Games of the XXVII Olympiad in Sydney, 2000
25. Croatian Chamber of Economy, Rules of Arbitration of the Permanent Arbitration Court (Zagreb Rules), 2002
26. Danish Institute of Arbitration, Rules of Procedure, 2004
27. Economic and Agricultural Chamber of the Czech Republic, Additional procedures for on-line arbitration (on-line Rules), 2004
28. Economic and Agricultural Chamber of the Czech Republic, Rules of the Arbitration Court (Prague Rules), 2002
29. Estonian Chamber of Commerce and Industry, Rules of the Arbitration Court, 1999
30. Euro-Arab Chambers of Commerce, Rules of Conciliation, Arbitration and Expertise, 1983
31. European Development Fund (EDF), Procedural Rules on Conciliation and Arbitration of Contracts Financed by the EDF, 1991
32. German Institution of Arbitration (DIS), Arbitration Rules, 1998
33. Hong Kong International Arbitration Centre, Domestic Arbitration Rules, 1993
34. Hong Kong International Arbitration Centre, Procedures for the Administration of International Arbitration, 2005
35. Hungarian Chamber of Commerce and Industry, Rules of Proceedings (Budapest Rules), 2005
36. Indian Council of Arbitration (ICA), Rules of Arbitration, 1998
37. Indonesian National Board of Arbitration (BANI), Procedural Rules, 2003
38. Inter-American Commercial Arbitration Commission (IACAC), Rules of Procedure, 2002
39. International Centre for Settlement of Investment Disputes (ICSID), Rules of Procedure for Arbitration Proceedings, 2003
40. International Centre for Settlement of Investment Disputes (ICSID), Schedule C. Arbitration (Additional Facility) Rules, 2003
41. International Chamber of Commerce (ICC), Rules of Arbitration, 1998
42. International Chamber of Commerce (ICC), International Centre for Expertise. Rules for Expertise, 2003
43. International Maritime Committee (CMI), International Maritime Arbitration Rules, 1978
44. Internet Corporation for Assigned Names and Numbers (ICANN), Rules for Uniform Domain Name Dispute Resolution Policy, 1999
45. Iran-US Claims Tribunal, Provisionally Adopted Tribunal Rules, 1983
46. Italian Arbitration Association (AIA), Arbitration Rules, 1985
47. Italian Arbitration Association (AIA), Rules For International Arbitration, 1994
48. Japan Commercial Arbitration Association (JCAA), Commercial Arbitration Rules, 2004
49. Korean Commercial Arbitration Board, Commercial Arbitration Rules, 2000
50. Lima Chamber of Commerce, Perú, National and International Conciliation and Arbitration Center, Procedural Arbitration Rules, 2004
51. London Court of International Arbitration (LCIA), Arbitration Rules, 1998
52. Multilateral Investment Guarantee Agency (MIGA), Rules of Arbitration For Disputes Under Contracts of Guarantee of MIGA, 1990
53. Netherlands Arbitration Institute (NAI), Arbitration Rules, 2001
54. Organisation pour l'Harmonisation en Afrique du Droit des Affaires (OHADA). Règlement d'arbitrage de la cour commune de justice et de l'arbitrage de l'OHADA, 1999

55. Permanent Court of Arbitration (PCA), Optional Rules For Arbitrating Disputes Between Two Parties Of Which Only One Is a State, 1993
56. Permanent Court of Arbitration (PCA), Optional Rules for Arbitration Involving International Organizations and States, 1996
57. Permanent Court of Arbitration (PCA), Optional Rules for Arbitration Between International Organizations and Private Parties, 1996
58. Permanent Court of Arbitration (PCA), Rules For Arbitration of Disputes Relating to Natural Resources and/or the Environment, 2001
59. Polish Chamber of Commerce in Warsaw, Rules of the Court of Arbitration, 2003
60. Santiago Arbitration and Mediation Center, Rules of Arbitration Procedure, 2002
61. Serbian Chamber of Commerce and Industry, Rules of the Foreign Trade Court of Arbitration (Belgrade Rules), 2001, as amended in 2004.
62. Singapore International Arbitration Centre (SIAC), Arbitration Rules, 1997
63. St. Petersburg International Commercial Arbitration Court, Rules
64. Stockholm Chamber of Commerce, Arbitration Rules of the Arbitration Institute (Stockholm Rules), 1999
65. Swiss Chamber of Commerce in Italy (CCSI), Regulations for CCSI Arbitration, 1995
66. Swiss Rules of International Arbitration (Swiss Rules), 2004
67. Tokyo Maritime Arbitration Commission (TOMAC), Rules of Arbitration, 2004
68. United States Center for Public Resources Institute for Dispute Resolution, Rules for Non-Administered Arbitration of International Disputes, 2000
69. Vancouver Maritime Arbitrators Association (VMAA), Arbitration Rules, 2005
70. Venice Court of National and International Arbitration (VENCA), Rules of Arbitration
71. Vietnam International Arbitration Centre, Arbitration Rules, 1993
72. World Intellectual Property Organization (WIPO), Arbitration Rules, 2002
73. World Intellectual Property Organization Arbitration and Mediation Center (WIPO), Supplemental Rules for Uniform Domain Name Dispute Resolution Policy, 1999

1. American Arbitration Association (AAA), International Centre for Dispute Resolution (ICDR), International Dispute Resolution Procedures (Including Mediation and Arbitration Rules), 2006

(Amended and effective 1 May 2006)

As the International Centre for Dispute Resolution (ICDR) is a division of the American Arbitration Association (AAA), parties can arbitrate future disputes under these rules by inserting either of the following clauses into their contracts
The parties may wish to consider adding:
c) 'The ***language***(s) of the arbitration shall be ________________'

Article 2 Notice of Arbitration and Statement of Claim
3. The notice of arbitration shall contain a statement of claim including the following
(g) may include proposals as to the means of designating and the number of arbitrators, the place of arbitration and the language*(s)* of the arbitration.

Article 3 Statement of Defense and Counterclaim
3. A respondent shall respond to the administrator, the claimant and other parties within 30 days after the commencement of the arbitration as to any proposals the claimant may have made as to the number of arbitrators, the place of the arbitration or the language*(s)* of the arbitration, except to the extent that the parties have previously agreed as to these matters.

Article 14 Language
If the parties have not agreed otherwise, the language(s) of the arbitration shall be that of the documents containing the arbitration agreement, subject to the power of the tribunal to determine otherwise based upon the contentions of the parties and the circumstances of the arbitration. The tribunal may order that any documents delivered in another language shall be accompanied by a translation into the language(s) of the arbitration.

Article 20 Hearings
2. At least 15 days before the hearings, each party shall give the tribunal and the other parties the names and addresses of any witnesses it intends to present, the subject of their testimony and the languages in which such witnesses will give their testimony.

2. Arbitration Chamber of Paris, Rules of Procedure, 2002

(5 June 2002)

Article 25
The parties must notify each other of their files (statements and evidences) and deposit with the Arbitration Chamber as many copies of the aforementioned files as there are Arbitrators sitting in First Degree or Second Degree Arbitral Tribunal, plus one for the Arbitration Chamber.
Dossiers filed with the Secretariat for the First Degree proceedings and still in the possession of the Secretariat may, should the occasion arise, be authenticated for Second Degree proceedings by any or all of the interested parties.
Documents in foreign languages must be accompanied by a French translation.
However, if the arbitration so requires, the Chairman of the Arbitration Chamber of Paris may decide to allow documents that are drafted or translated in English.

3. Australian Centre for International Commercial Arbitration (ACICA), Arbitration Rules, 2005

Model Clause
Any dispute, controversy or claim arising out of, relating to or in connection with this contract, including any question regarding its existence, validity or termination, shall be resolved by arbitration in accordance with the ACICA Arbitration Rules. The seat of arbitration shall be Sydney, Australia [or choose another city]. The language of the arbitration shall be English [or choose another language]. The number of arbitrators shall be one [or three, or delete this sentence and rely on Article 8 of the ACICA Arbitration Rules].

20. Language
20.1. Subject to an agreement by the parties, the Arbitral Tribunal shall, promptly after its appointment, determine the language or languages to be used in the proceedings. This determination shall apply to the Statement of Claim, the Statement of Defence, any further written statements and, if oral hearings take place, to the language or languages to be used in such hearings.
20.2. The Arbitral Tribunal may order that any submissions (written or oral), documents annexed to the Statement of Claim or Statement of Defence, and any supplementary documents or exhibits submitted in the course of the proceedings, delivered in their original language, shall be accompanied by a translation (or be translated) into the language or languages agreed upon by the parties or determined by the Arbitral Tribunal.

4. Austrian Federal Economic Chamber, International Arbitral Centre (Vienna International Arbitral Centre, VIAC), Rules of Arbitration and Conciliation (Vienna Rules), 2006

(Adopted by the Enlarged Presiding Committee of the Austrian Federal Economic Chamber on 3 May 2006, with effect from 1 July 2006)

Languages of correspondence
Article 6
Correspondence by the Parties with the Board and the Secretary General shall be conducted in German or English.

Conduct of the Proceedings
Article 20
2. Immediately after transmission of the files to the sole arbitrator (arbitral tribunal), the latter shall determine the language or languages of the proceedings, taking into consideration all circumstances, in particular, the language of the contract. In such matters, he (it) is bound by any agreement between the parties. The sole arbitrator (arbitral tribunal) can order that a translation be submitted of all documents that are not drafted in that language (those languages).

Further Costs of Procedure
Article 35
1. If the sole arbitrator (arbitral tribunal) considers certain action entailing costs, such as the appointment of experts, interpreters or translators, making verbatim records of the proceedings, a visual inspection, or relocation of the proceedings, to be necessary, he (it) must make arrangements to cover the expected costs and inform the Secretary General thereof.

5. Belarus Chamber of Commerce and Industry, Rules of the International Arbitration Court, 1999

Article 29.
The language to be used in the arbitral proceeding is determined by an agreement between the parties taking into account the language capabilities of the arbitrators. Unless otherwise agreed by the parties, the Belarusian language shall be used in the arbitral proceedings.
If one of the parties or its representative does not speak the language to be used in the arbitral proceedings the International Arbitration Court shall provide the services of an interpreter at the partys request and cost. There's no necessity to engage an interpreter in the proceedings if his functions to interpret the testimony of a single person may be fulfilled by a member of the arbitral tribunal or by the secretary of the arbitral proceedings.

Article 33.
The documents, mentioned in Article 32 of these Rules, except for written evidences, must be submitted in the language to be used in the arbitral proceedings or translated into this language at the expense of the party who is submitting them.
Written evidence shall be submitted in the original language. On its own initiative or up on the request of the other party the arbitral tribunal may order that written evidence shall be translated into the language to be used in the arbitral proceedings by the party submitting it or shall provide the translation at the expense of this party.

Exemplary texts of the arbitration clauses recommended for including in the contracts by the International Arbitration Court at the Belarusian Chamber of Commerce and Industry.
The arbitration clause or agreement may also include the indications to the applicable law (what country), a composition of the Arbitration Court (sole or panel of arbitrators), names of the arbitrators chosen by the parties, place of arbitration, the language to be used in the arbitral proceeding.

6. Belgian Centre for Mediation and Arbitration (CEPANI), Arbitration Rules, 2005

Clause:
The following provisions may be added to this clause:
The arbitration shall be conducted in the (.) language

Commencement of the Proceedings
Article 1 Request for Arbitration
1. A party wishing to have recourse to arbitration under the CEPANI rules shall submit its Request for Arbitration to the Secretariat.
The Request for Arbitration shall include, inter alia, the following information:
e) any comments as to the seat of the arbitration, the language of the arbitration and the applicable rules of law.

Article 2 Answer to the Request for Arbitration and filing of a counterclaim
1. Within one month from the date on which the Secretariat has received the Request for Arbitration and the annexes thereto, Respondent shall send its Answer to the Request for Arbitration to the Secretariat.
The Answer shall include, inter alia, the following information:
e) any comments as to the seat of the arbitration, the language of the arbitration and the applicable rules of law

Article 14 Language of the arbitration
1. The language of the arbitration shall be determined by mutual agreement between the parties. Failing such an agreement, the language or languages of the arbitration shall be determined by the Arbitral Tribunal, due regard being given to the circumstances of the case and, in particular, to the language of the contract.
2. The Arbitral Tribunal shall have full authority to decide which of the parties shall bear the translation costs, if any, and to what extent.

7. Belgian Institute of Arbitration, Rules of Arbitration, 2001
(As of 1 October 2001)

Article 5: Place and language of the procedure
The place of the reading of the award shall be considered the place of arbitration. The parties shall choose the language of the proceedings. The proceedings may take place in two languages. In the absence of an agreement, the language(s) of the proceedings is/are that/those of the country of the arbitration committee. All charges for translations, if any, are to be paid by the party remitting documents in another language. The verdict is written in the language of the procedure, in accordance with the place of enforcement.

8. British Columbia International Commercial Arbitration Centre (BCICAC), International Commercial Arbitration Rules and Fee Schedule, 2000

Article 21 Language
1. Unless the parties otherwise agree, until the arbitral tribunal has been constituted, the parties shall use the language(s) of the arbitration agreement in all communications related to the arbitration. A party shall provide a translation upon request of the Centre.
2. The arbitral tribunal shall determine the language to be used in the arbitral proceedings, having regard to the submissions of the parties and the language(s) of the arbitration agreement. Unless otherwise specified by the arbitral tribunal, that determination shall apply to any written statement by a party, any hearing and any arbitral award, decision or other communication by the arbitral tribunal. 3. The arbitral tribunal may order that documentary evidence be accompanied by a translation into the language determined by the arbitral tribunal under (2).
3. The arbitral tribunal may order that documentary evidence be accompanied by a translation into the language determined by the arbitral tribunal under (2).

Article 26 Hearings
4. If a party is giving evidence through witnesses, the party shall, within a period of time the arbitral tribunal determines, communicate to the tribunal and to the other party
a. the names and addresses of the witnesses it intends to present; and
b. the subject upon which, and the language in which, those witnesses will give their testimony.
5. The arbitral tribunal shall make arrangements for the translation of oral statements made at a hearing and for a record of the hearing if
a. either is deemed necessary by the tribunal under the circumstances of the case; or
b. the parties have agreed to it and have communicated such agreement to the tribunal at least 30 days before the hearing

9. Bulgarian Chamber of Commerce and Industry (BCCI), Rules of the Court of Arbitration (Bulgarian Rules), 2002

Language of the Hearings
Art. 23
The hearing of the case shall be conducted in the Bulgarian language but if one of the parties has seat or domicile abroad, the parties may agree on the use of another language, unless the dispute is of mandatory jurisdiction or the representative of the foreign party has a fair command of Bulgarian. The agreement on the language shall be reached before the composition of the Arbitral Tribunal. The latter shall appoint an interpreter for the party having no command of Bulgarian. The fee of the interpreter shall be for the account of that party, irrespective of the outcome of the case.

Evidence
Art. 29
(3) A party shall be free to submit written evidence in original or in a copy certified by it. The Arbitral Tribunal shall have the right to request a translation of these pieces of evidence into another language when it is necessary for the case. The written evidence submitted by one of the parties shall be served on the other party in due time.

Copies of the Award
Art. 41
(2) If the parties have not agreed upon the language in which the award is to be made, the party whose seat is abroad may be sent also a translation of the award for its own account, if requested.
(3) The copies and the translations shall be certified by the Secretary of the Court, bearing his / her signature and the seal of the Court of Arbitration.
(4) If the translation would require a certain time, the Secretary of the Court shall inform the foreign party by sending it excrepts from the award.

Arbitration Charges and Expenses
Art. 47
(4) The Arbitral Tribunal shall determine the remuneration for the interpreters, stenographer-secretary and experts, as well as their travel and other allowances.

10. Business Center for Conciliation and Arbitration (CEDCA), Venezuela, Rules of Conciliation and Arbitration, 2000

MODEL CLAUSES
2. Basic clause:
For disputes arising from a particular contract to be settled by arbitration, the arbitration agreement shall contain as a minimum the following declaration:
***
It should be noted that the use of the basic clause subjects the parties to certain parameters that apply in the absence of agreement, defined in CEDCA Rules, which is equivalent to the following clause:

> "Any dispute that arises in relation to this contract shall be resolved by arbitration ("*de jure*"), in conformity with the laws ("*that the parties may agree and failing that according to the law that the Arbitral Tribunal considers appropriate*"), in ("*the city and place that the parties determine and failing which in that indicated by the Arbitral Tribunal*"), in the language ("*that the parties agreed on and failing that in the language or languages determined by the*

Arbitral Tribunal"), in conformity with the rules of the Business Center for Conciliation and Arbitration (CEDCA), by an odd number of arbitrators freely determined by the parties and failing that of agreement by ("*three" arbitrators*) appointed pursuant to those Rules. The arbitrators may order conservatory measures, (even before the constitution of the Arbitral Tribunal which shall hear the merits of the dispute). The arbitral award (*shall be reasoned*) and (*shall be*) subject to the (prior presentation) provided for in said Rules. The summons to answer the request for arbitration shall be made at the address of the respondent indicated in this contract."

3. Integral clause:
The parties are reminded that they may select aspects in the arbitration agreement according to their interests or preferences, as follows:

"Any dispute that arises in relation to this contract shall be resolved through arbitration ("de jure") ("ex aequo et bono"), in conformity with the laws of _______ , in the city of (city/ country), in the place determined by the Arbitral Tribunal, in language (_____), in conformity with the rules of the Business Center for Conciliation and Arbitration (CEDCA), for ("one") ("three) arbitrator(s) appointed pursuant to those Rules. The arbitrators may (*not*) order conservatory measures, (even before the constitution of the Arbitral Tribunal that shall hear the merits of the dispute) . The arbitral award shall (*not*) be reasoned, and shall (not) be subject to the prior discussion provided for in said Rules. The summons for the answer to the request for arbitration shall be made to (the address of the respondent indicated in this contract)."

Article 5 Request for arbitration
5.3. The request shall, *inter alia*, contain the following information:
f) any comments as to the place of arbitration, the applicable rules of law and the language of the arbitration.

Article 6 Answer to the claim; counterclaim
The document shall contain, in particular:
e) any comments as to the place of arbitration, the applicable rules of law and the language of the arbitration.

Article 15 First hearing; terms of reference; procedural timetable
15.2. In the first hearing, the Arbitral Tribunal shall draw up, on the basis of the documents of the parties and taking into account their most recent submissions, a document that defining the terms of reference.
15.3. Said document shall contain:
g) language of the arbitration;

Article 17 Language of the arbitration
In the absence of an agreement between the parties, the Arbitral Tribunal shall determine the language or languages of the arbitration, taking into account any circumstances of the case, such as the language used in the contract, in the parties' correspondence and in any other relevant documents.

11. Cairo Regional Centre for International Commercial Arbitration (CRCICA), Arbitration Rules, 1998

(1 January 1998)

Language

Article (17)

1. Subject to an agreement by the parties, the arbitral tribunal shall, promptly after its appointment, determine the language or languages to be used in the proceedings. This determination shall apply to the statement of claim, the statement of defence, and any further written statements and, if oral hearings take place, to the language or languages to be used in such hearings.
2. The arbitral tribunal may order that any documents annexed to the statement of claim or statement of defence, and any supplementary documents or exhibits submitted in the course of the proceedings, delivered in their original language, shall be accompanied by a translation into the language or languages agreed upon by the parties or determined by the arbitral tribunal.

Article (25)

2. If witnesses are to be heard, at least fifteen days before the hearing, each party shall communicate to the arbitral tribunal and to the other party the names and addresses of the witnesses he intends to present, the subject upon and the languages in which such witnesses will give their testimony.
3. The arbitral tribunal shall make arrangements for the translation of oral statement made at a hearing and for a record of the hearing if either is deemed necessary by the tribunal under the circumstances of the case, or if the parties have agreed thereto and have communicated such agreement to the tribunal at least fifteen days before the hearing.

Costs (Articles 38 and 39)

Article (38)

7. The expenses of expertise and translation requested by either party or the arbitral tribunal shall be fixed separately according to its actual prices, and shall be paid according to the decision of the arbitral tribunal after deliberation with the Director of the Centre.

General Rules

3. Within the limits of the deposited sums, the Centre shall cover the administrative fees and expenses necessary to guarantee the right conduct of the arbitration proceedings, excluding the expenses or fees required for technical expertise or translation of documents presented to the arbitral tribunal which shall be estimated according to the Rules of the Centre and paid by the parties.

Model Arbitration Clause

Model Arbitration Clause: (i.e., the UNCITRAL Model Arbitration Clause): "Any dispute, controversy or claim arising out of or relating to this contract, or the breach, termination or invalidity thereof, shall be settled by arbitration in accordance with the Rules of Arbitration of the Cairo Regional Centre for International Commercial Arbitration ."
Note: Parties may wish to consider adding:
d) The language(s) to be used in the arbitral proceedings shall be...

12. Cámara de Comercio de Bilbao, Reglamento de Arbitraje del Tribunal Arbitral de Comercio de Bilbao, 2004

(26 March 2004)

Articulo 4°

Quienes litigan podrán dirigirse a la Corte de Arbitraje y a los/as Árbitros/as, en cualquiera de las lenguas oficiales de la Comunidad Autónoma del País Vasco, así como en otra lengua, siendo de su cuenta los gastos de traducción, si fueran precisos. .

13. Caracas Chamber of Commerce Arbitration Center, General Rules, 2000

(February 23, 2000)

Article 46. Language of the Arbitration.

Unless otherwise agreed by the parties, the Arbitration Tribunal shall determine the language(s) of the arbitration, proper regard being given to any relevant circumstances, including the language of the agreement. In the absence of special circumstances, the arbitration shall be conducted in the Spanish language.

14. Centre d'Arbitrage et de Médiation Rhônes-Alpes, Règlement d'arbitrage et médiation, 1993

(21 Décembre 1993)

E. Langue de l'arbitrage

Article 14 Langue

La langue de l'arbitrage est le français sauf convention contraire des parties ou autre décision de la Cour d'Arbitrage.

15. Centro de Arbitraje de Mexico, Arbitration Rules, 1997

(1 July 1997)

Article 6. Request for Arbitration

3. The Request shall, at least, contain the following information

e. a proposal as to the place of arbitration, the applicable rules of law and the language of the arbitration

Article 9. Answer to the Request for Arbitration

1. Within 30 days from the receipt of the Request from the Secretary General, the Respondent shall file an Answer, which shall contain, at least, the following information

d. its comments as to the place of arbitration, the applicable rules of law and the language of the arbitration.

Article 22. Language of the Arbitration

1. The arbitration procedure shall be held in the language agreed upon by the parties.
2. In the absence of an agreement between the parties, the Arbitral Tribunal shall determine the language of the arbitration, due regard being given to all relevant circumstances, and, in particular, the language of the contract. As long as the Arbitral Tribunal has not determined the language, the parties may present their submissions in the language of their choice, annexing a translation in Spanish or in English.

16. Chamber of Commerce and Industry of Romania and Bucharest, Rules of Arbitration, 2000

Art. 36.– (1) The Claimant shall submit to the Arbitral Tribunal an application in written form, called Request for Arbitration or arbitral claim, including the following information:

3) Where the Request for Arbitration or the documents in the file have been written in a foreign language, the Arbitral Tribunal may *ex officio* or upon request, order the involved party to submit a Romanian translation or, in case of international commercial arbitration, a translation into an international language. The parties may request the *Court of Arbitration* to provide for translation at their expense

Art. 48.– (1) The arbitral expenses include: the arbitral fee, expenses for producing evidence, expenses incurred by the translation of documents and of the proceedings, arbitrators', attorneys', experts' and advisers' fees, travel expenses of the parties, arbitrators, witnesses, experts and advisers as well as other expenditure relating to the settlement of the dispute.

Art. 49.– (1) The parties may participate at hearings either in person or through representatives and may be assisted by attorneys, advisers, interpreters or other persons.

Art. 64.– (1) Where the Arbitral Tribunal omits to decide in its award on an individual, main or accessory, claim or an a connected or incidental request the completion of the award may be requested within 15 days of its receipt
3) The provisions of this Article shall also apply where the Arbitral Tribunal failed to decide on requests made by witnesses, experts, translators, interpreters, or counsels, relative to their rights.

Special Provisions regarding International Commercial Arbitration

Art. 77.– (1) The hearings of the dispute before the Arbitral Tribunal shall be in the language established by the arbitral agreement or, unless otherwise provided or a subsequent convention intervenes, in an international language decided by the Arbitral Tribunal.
(2) Where a party is ignorant of the language in which the arbitration proceeds, the Arbitral Tribunal shall provide for the services of an interpreter upon the request and at the expense of that party.
(3) The parties may attend the hearings with their interpreter.

17. Chamber of Commerce and Industry of the Russian Federation, Rules of the International Commercial Arbitration Court (ICAC), 1995

(Approved on December 8, 1994, in force as of May 1, 1995)

§5. Reporters

2. The List of the Reporters shall be approved by the Presidium of the ICAC for a period of 5 years. Included in the List of the Reporters are persons with higher juridical education and knowing, as a rule, a foreign language.

§9. Presentation of Documents

1. All documents pertaining to the institution and carrying out of the arbitral proceedings shall be presented by the parties to the ICAC in five copies, or in three copies, if the case is to be considered by a sole arbitrator, unless otherwise determined, in case of necessity, by the Executive Secretary of the ICAC.

2. The documents mentioned in sub-paragraph 1 of this paragraph, excluding written evidence (para. 34, sub-para. 2), shall be presented in the language of the contract, or in the language of the correspondence conducted by the parties between themselves, or in the Russian language. The ICAC may, at its own discretion or at a party's request, direct the other party to translate into Russian the documents presented by him or to secure such translation at that other party's expense.

§10. Language of the Hearing

The hearing shall be conducted in the Russian language. With the consent of the parties the ICAC may conduct the hearing in another language. If a party does not know the language in which the hearing is conducted, the ICAC shall, at the party's request and expense, provide him with the services of an interpreter.

§34. Evidence

2. Either party may present written evidence in the original or in the form of copies certified by him. The arbitral tribunal may require translation of such evidence into another language where it is necessary in the interests of the examination of the case.

Appendix – to the Rules of the International Commercial Arbitration Court at the Chamber of Commerce and Industry of the Russian Federation

Schedule on Arbitration Fees and Costs

§1. Definitions

3. "Additional costs of the ICAC" shall mean specific expenses incurred by the ICAC in connection with examination of a particular case (particularly, expenses of conducting expert examination and preparing translations, remuneration of experts, interpreters, compensation of witnesses' expenses, reimbursement of travelling expenses, etc.).

§7. Covering of Additional Costs of the ICAC

4. If, in the course of arbitral proceedings the parties' explanations, statements, etc., as well as questions, commentaries and directions of the arbitral tribunal are, at a party's request, translated, the cost of translation shall be paid by that party. If the hearing, as agreed by the parties, is conducted in the language other than Russian, the likely costs of the translation may be charged on both parties in equal shares.

The ICAC may demand that the respective party or parties should deposit an advance sum to cover such costs. The same rule shall apply to translation of the awards of the ICAC.

18. Chamber of National and International Arbitration of Milan, Arbitration Rules (Milano Rules), 2004

(Entry into force 1 January 2004)

Clause for international arbitration

All disputes arising out of this contract shall be settled by arbitration under the Rules of the Chamber of National and International Arbitration of Milan. The Arbitral Tribunal shall consist of a sole arbitrator/three arbitrators appointed pursuant to those Rules.
The Arbitral Tribunal shall decide in accordance with the rules of law of.... (or: ex aequo et bono).
The seat of the arbitration shall be ....
The language of the arbitration shall be ....

Article 5 Language of the arbitration
1. The language of the arbitration shall be agreed upon by the parties in their arbitration agreement or subsequently until the Arbitral Tribunal is constituted.
2. In the absence of an agreement by the parties, the Arbitral Tribunal shall determine the language of the arbitration. The Secretariat shall indicate the language of acts precedent to that determination.
3. The Arbitral Tribunal may accept the submission of documents in a language other than the language of the arbitration and may order that they be translated into the language of the arbitration.

Art. 10 Request for arbitration
2. The request shall be signed by the party or by its counsel with power of attorney and shall contain or be accompanied by
e. all indications, if any, as to the rules applicable to the proceedings, the rules applicable to the merits of the dispute or the ex aequo et bono decision, the seat and the language of the arbitration

Art. 11 Statement of defence
2. The statement shall be signed by the party or by its counsel with power of attorney and shall contain or be accompanied by:
e. all indications, if any, as to the rules applicable to the proceedings, the rules applicable to the merits of the dispute or the ex aequo et bono decision, the seat and the language of the arbitration;

Art. 24 Constitution of the Arbitral Tribunal
3. The constitution of the Arbitral Tribunal shall be formalized in minutes dated and signed by the arbitrators, indicating the seat and language of the arbitration and establishing the modalities and time limits for further proceedings

19. Chambers of Commerce of the CMEA Countries, Uniform Rules of Procedure in the Arbitration Courts, 1974

§ 7. Presentation of Documents
2. The documents mentioned in sub-paragraph 1 of this paragraph, excluding written evidence (sub-paragraph 2 of § 27), shall be presented in the language of the contract, or in the language of the correspondence conducted by the parties between themselves, or in the language of the country of the Arbitration Court. The Arbitration Court can, at its own discretion or at a party's request, direct the other party to translate into the language of the country of the Arbitration Court the documents presented by it or to secure such translation at its own expense.

§ 8. The Language of the Case Examination
The examination of a case at the hearing shall be conducted in the language of the country of the Arbitration Court. With the consent of the parties concerned the Arbitration Court may conduct the examination in another language. If a party does not know the language in which the examination is conducted, the Arbitration Court shall, at the party's request and expense, provide it with the services of an interpreter.

§ 27. Evidence
2. A party can present written evidence in the original or in the form of copies certified by it. The Arbitration Court can require translation of such evidence into another language where it is necessary in the interests of the examination of the case.

Appendix to the Uniform Rules.
Rules on Arbitration Fees, Costs, and Expenses of the Parties

§ 6. Costs of the Arbitration Court
If in this course of the examination of the case, the parties' explanations, statements, etc., as well as the tribunal's questions, explanations, and directions are, at a party's request, translated into a language other than the language of the country of the Arbitration Court, the costs of translation shall be paid by that party.

20. Chambre officielle franco-allemande de commerce et d'industrie, Centre d'arbitrage, Règlement d'arbitrage

Article 4. Langue de l'arbitrage
4.1. La convention d'arbitrage visant un tribunal arbitral *ad hoc* peut librement stipuler la langue de l'arbitrage. En l'absence d'une telle stipulation, la langue de l'arbitrage est déterminée par le tribunal arbitral *ad hoc* en fonction des circonstances de l'afraire.
4.2. La convention d'arbitrage visant ou étant considérée comme visant l'arbitrage par le Tribunal arbitral permanent peut stipuler comme *langue* de l'arbitrage les *langues* allemande, française ou anglaise. En l'absence d'une telle stipulation, la *langue* de l'arbitrage est déterminée par le Tribunal arbitral permanent en fonction des circonstances de l'affaire. Toutefois, le Tribunal arbitral permanent pourra admettre pour la production de documents de toute nature ou l'audition de témoins et d'experts l'allemand, le français et l'anglais

Article 17. Règles applicables à la procédure
17.5. Sauf accord du tribunal arbitral et des parties, les audiences ne sont pas ouvertes aux personnes étrangères à la procédure. Les parties comparaissent soit en personne, soit par représentants, à moins que leur comparution personnelle ne soit ordonnée. Le tribunal arbitral peut admettre tous auxiliaires, tels que traducteurs et secrétaires, aux audiences après les avoir au préalable engagés au secret.

21. China International Economic and Trade Arbitration Commission (CIETAC), Arbitration Rules, 2005

(Revised and Adopted by the China Council for the Promotion of International Trade /China Chamber of International Commerce on January 11, 2005. Effective as from May 1, 2005)

Article 67 Language
1. Where the parties have agreed on the arbitration language, their agreement shall prevail. Absent such agreement, the Chinese language shall be the official language to be used in the arbitration proceedings.
2. At an oral hearing, if a party or its representative(s) or witness requires language interpretation, the Secretariat of the CIETAC or its Sub-Commission may provide an interpreter, or the party may bring its own interpreter.
3. The arbitral tribunal and/or the Secretariat of the CIETAC or its Sub-Commission may, if it considers necessary, request the parties to submit a corresponding version of the documents and evidence by the parties in Chinese or in other languages.

Article 69 Arbitration Fees and Actual Expenses
1. Apart from charging arbitration fees to the parties according to the Fee Schedule of the CIETAC, the CIETAC may collect from the parties other extra, reasonable and actual expenses including arbitrators' special remuneration and their travel and accommodation expenses incurred in deal-

ing with the case, as well as the costs and expenses of experts, appraisers and interpreters appointed by the arbitral tribunal, etc.

22. Commercial Arbitration and Mediation Center for the Americas (CAMCA), Arbitration Rules, 1996

Article 2 Notice of arbitration and statement of claim
3. The notice of arbitration shall include the following:
(g) may include proposals as to the number of arbitrators, the place of arbitration and the language(s) of the arbitration.

Article 3 Statement of defense and counterclaim
3. A respondent shall respond to the administrator, the claimant and other parties within thirty (30) days as to any proposals the claimant may have made as to the number of arbitrators, the place of the arbitration or the language(s) of the arbitration, except to the extent that the parties have previously agreed as to these matters

Article 15 Language
If the parties have not agreed otherwise, the language(s) of the arbitration shall be that of the documents containing the arbitration agreement, subject to the power of the tribunal to determine otherwise based upon the contentions of the parties and the circumstances of the arbitration. The tribunal may order that any documents delivered in another language shall be accompanied by a translation into such language or languages.

Article 22 Hearings
2. At least twenty (20) days before the hearings, each party shall give the tribunal and the other parties the names and addresses of any witnesses it intends to present, the subject of their testimony and the languages in which such witnesses will give their testimony.

23. Court of Arbitration for Sport (CAS), Code of Sports-related Arbitration, 1994

Procedural Rules
R 29 Language
The CAS working languages are French and English. In the absence of agreement between the parties, and taking into account all pertinent circumstances, the President of the Panel shall select one of these two languages as the language of the arbitration at the start of the proceedings before the Panel.
The parties may choose another language provided that the Arbitration Panel agrees. The parties shall advise the CAS of such a choice. In the event of such a choice, the Panel may order that the parties bear all or part of the translation and interpreting costs.

Costs of the proceedings
R 64 In general
R 64.3 Each party shall advance the cost of its own witnesses, experts and interpreters. If the Panel appoints an expert or an interpreter or orders the examination of a witness, it shall issue directions with respect to an advance of costs, if appropriate.

R 64.4 At the end of the proceedings, the Court Office shall determine the final amount of the cost of arbitration, which shall include the CAS Court Office fee, the costs and fees of the arbitrators computed in accordance with the CAS fee scale, the contribution towards the costs and expenses of the CAS, and the costs of witnesses, experts and interpreters.

R 64.5 The foregoing costs shall be stated in the arbitral award, which shall also determine which party shall bear such costs or in which portion the parties shall share them. As a general rule, the award shall grant the prevailing party a contribution towards its legal fees and other expenses incurred in connection with the proceedings and, in particular, the costs "858"of witnesses and interpreters. When granting such contribution, the Panel shall take into account the outcome of the proceedings, as well as the conduct and the financial resources of the parties.

24. Court of Arbitration for Sport (CAS), Arbitration Rules for the Games of the XXVII Olympiad in Sydney, 2000

Article 6 Language of Arbitration
The arbitration shall be conducted in English or French as determined by the President of the ad hoc Division.

25. Croatian Chamber of Economy, Rules of Arbitration of the Permanent Arbitration Court (Zagreb Rules), 2002

(Entered into force on 25 December 2002)

Evidence
Article 22
5. The Secretary of the Arbitration Court shall make the necessary arrangements to provide short-hand notes, sound recordings and minute taking in a foreign language on the presentation of evidence if one of the parties requests it or if the arbitral tribunal so orders and if a monetary deposit is given to meet the costs incurred.

Oral hearings
Article 25
2. If it is necessary to hear witnesses, each party shall furnish the arbitral tribunal and the other party with the names and addresses of witnesses they intend to propose at least fifteen days before the hearing, and communicate the subject of the testimony and the language in which the hearing of the witness will take place.
3. The arbitral tribunal shall be responsible for the interpretation of oral testimonies at the hearing and for keeping minutes of the hearing if it feels this is necessary in view of the circumstances of the case or if the parties have so agreed and informed the arbitration court of this at least fifteen days before the hearing is held.

26. Danish Institute of Arbitration, Rules of Procedure, 2004

Section 5
Par. 1: A request for arbitration shall be in writing and shall contain the following information:
5. Comments, if any, regarding the arbitration venue, the country whose law shall apply to the case, and the working language to be used in the proceedings

Section 9
Par. 1: The defendant's statement of defence shall contain the following information:
4. Comments, if any, regarding the arbitration venue; the country whose law shall apply to the case, and the working language to be used in the proceedings

Section 31
The parties shall decide the working language to be used in the arbitration case. If such agreement has not been made, the Arbitration Tribunal shall make the decision taking into account all

relevant circumstances, including the language in which the agreement between the parties is drafted.

Section 54
These Rules of Procedure of the Danish Institute of Arbitration (Danish Arbitration) have been prepared in Danish, English, German and French. In cases where the working language used in the proceedings is Danish, German or French, the Danish, German or French version, respectively, of these Rules of Procedure shall apply. In all other cases, the English version of these Rules of Procedure shall apply.

27. Economic and Agricultural Chamber of the Czech Republic, Additional procedures for on-line arbitration (on-line Rules), 2004

Section 10 Language of the arbitral proceedings
The proceedings shall be held and decisions shall be made in Czech (or Slovak) language. Upon an approval of the Arbitration Court, the proceedings may be held in other language than in Czech (or Slovak) under the conditions set by the Principles governing the Costs of arbitral proceedings (Section 41 of the Rules).

28. Economic and Agricultural Chamber of the Czech Republic, Rules of the Arbitration Court (Prague Rules), 2002

(Valid since 1st May 2002)

Sec. 6 Production of Documents
(1) All documents relating to the commencement and conduct of arbitration proceedings shall be produced in such number of copies that all parties and all members of the arbitral tribunal as well as the secretariat obtain one copy thereof.
(2) Save for written evidence, communications shall be produced in Czech (or in Slovak) language or in the language of the contract, or in the language used in the correspondence between the parties, as the case may be. If the Arbitration Court think it fit, or upon request of a party, the Arbitration Court may direct a party having produced the document to have it translated into Czech (or into Slovak) or may arrange for such a translation at the costs of such party.

Sec. 7 Language of the proceedings
(1) Oral hearings shall be held, and decisions shall be made, in Czech (or in Slovak) language; upon request of a party, the hearings and decisions will be translated into another language. Upon such request by a party, the Arbitration Court will arrange for an interpreter, or for the translation of the decisions or other writings, as the case may be.
(2) If necessary, the arbitral tribunal may, provided both parties agree, hold hearings and, as the case may be, pronounce the decision directly in another language.

Sec. 30 Minutes of Hearing
(1) At each hearing minutes of the proceedings in Czech (or in Slovak), or, upon agreement of the parties to the dispute in another language, shall be taken.
(3) A copy of the minutes shall be handed over or sent to the parties with translation, if any.

Sec. 31 Evidence
(2) Any party may produce written evidence in original or copy, to be authenticated by itself. The arbitral tribunal shall be free to request the original document or a translation thereof into another language, if necessary in the interest of the decision of the case

29. Estonian Chamber of Commerce and Industry, Rules of the Arbitration Court, 1999

Article 20. Language Used in the Proceedings
If the parties have not determined by mutual agreement the language of the arbitration proceedings, the Arbitration Court shall determine it, based, among other issues, on the language of the claim.

30. Euro-Arab Chambers of Commerce, Rules of Conciliation, Arbitration and Expertise, 1983

(10 January 1983)

Article 30 Languages
1. These Rules have been drawn up in three official languages – French, Arabic and English. The texts in all three languages are equally authentic.
2. In the event of any dispute regarding the interpretation of the different texts of the Rules, the Higher Arbitration Board to which the matter is referred either by the arbitrator(s) or the parties shall have absolute power to resolve it.
3. Translations in different working languages may be carried out at the instigation of one of the Arbitration Boards or of the Higher Arbitration Board. They shall be filed with the Secretariat/Registry and forwarded to the Higher Arbitration Board.
4. The Higher Arbitration Board may draw the attention of any Arbitration Board to differences in interpretation which may result from such translations

31. European Development Fund (EDF), Procedural Rules on Conciliation and Arbitration of Contracts Financed by the EDF, 1991

(1 June 1991)

Article 15 Language of the proceedings
15.1 Arbitration proceedings shall be conducted and the arbitration award made in the language of the Contract, the terms or execution of which gave rise to the dispute.
15.2 The Tribunal may order that any documents annexed to the statement of claim or statement of defence, and any other document or exhibit submitted in the course of the proceedings, and which are not drawn up in the language of the proceedings, shall be accompanied by a certified translation into the language of the proceedings.

Article 26 Oral proceedings
26.2 If witnesses are to be heard, each Party shall communicate to the Tribunal and to the other Party, at least 15 days before the hearing, the names and addresses of the witnesses he intends to call, the subjects upon and the languages in which such witnesses will give their testimony.
26.3 The Tribunal shall make arrangements for the translation of oral statements made at a hearing and for a record of the hearing if either is deemed necessary by the Tribunal under the circumstances of the case, or if the Parties have agreed thereto and have communicated such agreement to the Tribunal at least 15 days before the hearing.

32. German Institution of Arbitration (DIS), Arbitration Rules, 1998

(1 July 1998)

The German Institution of Arbitration advises all parties wishing to make reference to DIS Arbitration in their contracts to use the following arbitration clause:

It is recommended that the following provisions be added to the arbitration clause:
– The language of the arbitral proceedings is ....

Section 6 Commencement of arbitral proceedings
6.3. In addition, the statement of claim should contain:
(3) particulars regarding the place of arbitration, the language of the proceedings and the rules applicable to the substance of the dispute

Section 22 Language of proceedings
22.1. The parties are free to agree on the language or languages to be used in the arbitral proceedings. Failing such agreement, the arbitral tribunal shall determine the language or languages to be used in the proceedings. This agreement or determination, unless otherwise specified therein, shall apply to any written statement by a party, any hearing and any award, decision or other communication by the arbitral tribunal.
22.2. The arbitral tribunal may order that expert's reports and other documentary evidence shall be accompanied by a translation into the language or languages agreed upon by the parties or determined by the arbitral tribunal.

Appendix to Section 40 Sub. 5 of the Arbitration Rules
16) If a statement of claim, a counterclaim or any other written pleading is submitted to the DIS in any language other than German, English or French, the DIS may arrange for a translation. The costs for such translation may be added to the DIS administrative fee levied by the DIS pursuant to 15).

33. Hong Kong International Arbitration Centre, Domestic Arbitration Rules, 1993

(Adopted to take effect from 1 April 1993)

Article 14 Language
14.1 The language of the arbitration shall be English and all written communications and statements, and all hearings shall be conducted in the English language unless the parties and the Arbitrator otherwise agree.
14.2 The Arbitrator may order that any documents other than written statements which are produced in the course of the arbitration in their original language shall be accompanied by a translation into the language of the arbitration, such translation to be certified if not agreed.
14.3 Unless the Arbitrator otherwise orders, witnesses shall be entitled to give their evidence in the language of their choice and the Arbitrator may order the translation of that evidence into the language of the arbitration by a suitably qualified person.

34. Hong Kong International Arbitration Centre, Procedures for the Administration of International Arbitration, 2005

(Adopted to take effect from 31 March 2005)

15. Translation and Interpretation
Any necessary arrangements for live or written translation or interpretation services will be made by the HKIAC upon request of the parties. Although the HKIAC will make arrangements for such services, the cost of the services shall not be included in the administrative fee, but rather shall be paid by the parties to the HKIAC.

35. Hungarian Chamber of Commerce and Industry, Rules of Proceedings (Budapest Rules), 2005

(Effective as of October 1, 2005)

Standard Arbitration Clause

"The parties agree that all disputes arising from or in connection with the present contract, its breach, termination, validity or interpretation, shall be exclusively decided by the Court of Arbitration attached to the Hungarian Chamber of Commerce and Industry, Budapest in accordance with its own Rules of Proceedings."

Parties may wish to consider adding:

"The language(s) to be used in the arbitral proceedings shall be"

Art. 4. Arbitrators

(1) Any Hungarian or foreign national, whether or not listed in the roll of arbitrators, who:

- declares in writing to the Arbitration Court that he undertakes to perform the arbitrator's functions according to the present Rules of Proceedings;
- is independent and unprejudiced and declares these facts in writing to the Arbitration Court;
- commands the necessary level of legal, economic and other knowledge to enable him to resolve legal disputes falling under the jurisdiction of the Arbitration Court;
- possesses the required language skills; and
- does not fall under the limitations set forth in the provisions of § 12 of Act LXXI of 1994 on arbitration may be appointed an arbitrator.

(2) The Arbitration Court, for the purpose of informing the clients, shall compile a roll of arbitrators and make it public. The Assembly of the Delegates of the Hungarian Chamber of Commerce and Industry shall, upon the proposal of the Presidium of the Arbitration Court, select the arbitrators to be listed in the roll of arbitrators from among persons who command legal, economic and other knowledge necessary for the resolution of legal disputes by arbitration. The roll of arbitrators is drawn-up for a five-year period and shall include at least 25 and at most 120 persons. The arbitrators may be re-elected for further term(s) of five years each. The roll of arbitrators may include Hungarian and foreign nationals alike. The roll of arbitrators shall contain the given and family name, profession, qualification, degree, academic title and language skill of each arbitrator.

Art. 8. Filing of Documents

(1) All documents pertaining to the institution at the initiation or in the course of proceedings shall be submitted in that number of copies which enables each party and each interpleader to be provided with one copy and the Arbitration Court with four copies.

(2) The documents referred to in paragraph (1) shall be submitted in the language which the parties determined for the proceedings. (Paragraph (1) of Art. 9.)

(3) If no such determination was made, the documents shall, until the arbitral tribunal determines the language of the proceedings according to paragraph (3) of Art. 9., be submitted either in the Hungarian, the German or the English language depending on the decision of the Arbitration Court.

(4) The Secretariat of the Arbitration Court conducts its correspondence with the parties in one of the languages referred to in paragraph (3) until the arbitral tribunal determines the language of the proceedings.

(5) The parties shall send all documents submitted to the Arbitration Court simultaneously to the other party (parties), as well, in a way, proving the delivery (e.g. with notice of receipt).

Art. 9. The Language of Proceedings

(1) The parties may freely determine the language of the proceedings, provided the conditions for the proceedings conducted in such language may otherwise be ensured.
(2) If the parties fail to determine the language of the proceedings, the arbitral tribunal shall do so, taking into consideration all relevant factors in respect of the specific case, especially the language of the agreement entered into by the parties and the language of the correspondence.
(3) If the foreign party (parties) is (are) represented by a Hungarian attorney or a counsel (also), the proceedings shall be conducted in Hungarian, except in the case when the parties have stipulated a foreign language in accordance with paragraph (1) above.
(4) The minutes of the hearings and the resolutions adopted during the proceedings shall be in the language of the proceedings.
(5) At the request and expense of a party who is not familiar with the language of the proceedings, the Arbitration Court shall ensure the use of an interpreter. The Secretariat shall inform the affected parties about the terms and conditions relating to the use of such interpreter.
(6) If the foreign arbitrator is not familiar with the language of the proceedings, upon request, the Secretariat of the Arbitration Court shall provide an interpreter (translator).

Art. 19. Challenging the Arbitrators or the Presiding Arbitrator

(6) The provisions of the present Article shall also apply, where appropriate, to experts and interpreters

Art. 30. Interpleading in the Proceedings

(1) Any person having a legal interest in the outcome of the arbitral proceedings may submit an interpleader in order to assist the party having the same interest to win the case. A request concerning interpleading shall be submitted to the Arbitration Court at least fifteen days before the day of the first hearing in the language of the proceedings and in a number of copies enabling each party to be provided with one copy and the Arbitration Court with four copies.
(2) The admissibility of an interpleader shall be decided by the arbitral tribunal. An interpleader may only be admitted if all parties give their consent thereto

Art. 35. Evidence

(1) Each party must prove the circumstances on which he bases a claim or a defence. The arbitral tribunal may instruct a party to submit further evidence, order the presentation of expert opinion, obtain evidence from third persons and order the hearing of witnesses.
(2) The parties shall submit the original written evidence or a copy thereof, in such number of copies which enables each party to be provided with one copy and the Arbitration Court with four copies. If it becomes necessary for the determination of the case, the arbitral tribunal may request that the party submit the written evidence translated into the language of the contract or the language of the proceedings.

Regulation on the Arbitration Fees, Costs and Expenses of the Parties (Regulation on Fees)

Art. 1. Definitions

(3) "Arbitration Costs": Other costs incurred by the Arbitration Court in the course of the proceedings: experts' fees and additional costs of proceedings held in non Hungarian, English or German languages (see Art. 9 of the Rules of Proceedings, costs of other translations if any, fees of interpreters, experts and witnesses, travel and accommodation costs of arbitrators).

36. Indian Council of Arbitration (ICA), Rules of Arbitration, 1998
(1 March 1998)

Rule 56
The language of the arbitration proceedings shall be English unless otherwise agreed by the parties. If any documents filed by a party are in a language other than English, the party filing such documents shall simultaneously furnish an English translation of the documents. The Registrar may make arrangements for the service of an interpreter at the request of one or more of the parties and costs thereof shall form part of the costs of the reference.

37. Indonesian National Board of Arbitration (BANI), Procedural Rules, 2003
(1 March 2003)

Article 14 Language
1. Language of Proceedings
If the parties have not agreed otherwise, the process of case examination shall be conducted in the Indonesian language, unless the Tribunal, taking into consideration the situation (such as existence of foreign parties and/or foreign arbitrators who cannot speak Indonesian, and/or where the transaction arising from the dispute is conducted in another language), deems it appropriate to use the English language or another language.

2. Document Language
If the original documentation submitted or relied upon by the parties in the submission of the case in question is in a language other than the Indonesian language, then the Tribunal shall be empowered to determine whether or not the original documents must be accompanied by translation into the Indonesian language, or from the Indonesian language to another language. However, if the parties agree, or the Tribunal designates, that the language used in the case shall be a language other than the Indonesian language, then the Tribunal may request that the documents be submitted in the Indonesian language accompanied with authentic translation by a sworn translator in the English language or the other language to be used.

3. Interpreter
If the Tribunal and/or any party requires the assistance of an interpreter during the proceeding, such interpreter shall be provided by BANI at the request of the Tribunal, and the fee of the interpreter shall be borne by the parties as deemed appropriate by the Tribunal.

4. Award Language
The Award shall be prepared in the Indonesian language, and if requested by one party or otherwise deemed appropriate by the Tribunal, in the English language or another language. In case the original Award document is prepared in the English language or another language, an official translation shall be provided by BANI for registration purposes, and the cost for this shall be borne by the parties as instructed by the Tribunal.

38. Inter-American Commercial Arbitration Commission (IACAC), Rules of Procedure, 2002
(As in force from 1 April 2002)

Language
Article 14
1 Subject to an agreement by the parties, the arbitral tribunal shall, promptly after its appointment, determine the language or languages to be used in the proceedings. This determination

shall apply to the statement of claim, the statement of defense, and any further written statements and, if oral hearings take place, to the language or languages to be used in such hearings.
2 The arbitral tribunal may order that any documents annexed to the statement of claim or statement of defense, and any supplementary documents or exhibits submitted in the course of the proceedings, delivered in their original language, shall be accompanied by a translation into the language or languages agreed upon by the parties or determined by the arbitral tribunal.

Article 22
1 In the event of an oral hearing, the arbitral tribunal shall give the parties adequate advance notice of the date, time and place thereof.
2 If witnesses are to be heard, at least fifteen days before the hearing each party shall communicate to the arbitral tribunal and to the other party the names and addresses of the witnesses he intends to present, and the subject upon and the languages in which such witnesses will give their testimony.
3 The arbitral tribunal shall make arrangements for the translation of oral statements made at a hearing and for a record of the hearing if either is deemed necessary by the tribunal under the circumstances of the case, or if the parties have agreed thereto and have communicated such agreement to the tribunal at least fifteen days before the hearing.

39. International Centre for Settlement of Investment Disputes (ICSID), Rules of Procedure for Arbitration Proceedings, 2003

(1 January 2003)

Rule 1. The Request
(1) Any Contracting State or any national of a Contracting State wishing to institute conciliation or arbitration proceedings under the Convention shall address a request to that effect in writing to the Secretary-General at the seat of the Centre. The request shall indicate whether it relates to a conciliation or an arbitration proceeding. It shall be drawn up in an official language of the Centre, shall be dated, and shall be signed by the requesting party or its duly authorized representative

Rule 22. Procedural Languages
(1) The parties may agree on the use of one or two languages to be used in the proceeding, provided, that, if they agree on any language that is not an official language of the Centre, the Tribunal, after consultation with the Secretary-General, gives its approval. If the parties do not agree on any such procedural language, each of them may select one of the official languages (i.e., English, French and Spanish) for this purpose.
(2) If two procedural languages are selected by the parties, any instrument may be filed in either language. Either language may be used at the hearings, subject, if the Tribunal so requires, to translation and interpretation. The orders and the award of the Tribunal shall be rendered and the record kept in both procedural languages, both versions being equally authentic.

40. International Centre for Settlement of Investment Disputes (ICSID), Schedule C. Arbitration (Additional Facility) Rules, 2003

Article 2 The Request
(1) Any State or any national of a State wishing to institute arbitration proceedings shall send a request to that effect in writing to the Secretariat at the seat of the Centre. It shall be drawn up in an official language of the Centre, shall be dated and shall be signed by the requesting party or its duly authorized representative.

Article 28 Preliminary Procedural Consultation
(1) As early as possible after the constitution of a Tribunal, its President shall endeavor to ascertain the views of the parties regarding questions of procedure. For this purpose he may request the parties to meet him. He shall, in particular, seek their views on the following matters:
b) the language or languages to be used in the proceeding

Article 30 Procedural Languages
(1) The parties may agree on the use of one or two languages to be used in the proceeding, provided that if they agree on any language that is not an official language of the Centre, the Tribunal, after consultation with the Secretary-General, gives its approval. If the parties do not agree on any such procedural language, each of them may select one of the official languages (i.e., English, French and Spanish) for this purpose. Notwithstanding the foregoing, one of the official languages of the Centre shall be used for all communications to and from the Secretariat.
(2) If two procedural languages are selected by the parties, any instrument may be filed in either language. Either language may be used at the hearing subject, if the Tribunal so requires, to translation and interpretation. The orders and the award of the Tribunal shall be rendered and the record kept in both procedural languages, both versions being equally authentic.

41. International Chamber of Commerce (ICC), Rules of Arbitration, 1998

Article 4 Request for arbitration
3. The Request shall, *inter alia*, contain the following information:
(f) any comments as to the place of arbitration, the applicable rules of law and the language of the arbitration.

Article 5 Answer to the request; Counterclaims
1. Within 30 days from the receipt of the Request from the Secretariat, the Respondent shall file an Answer (the "Answer") which shall, *inter alia*, contain the following information:
(e) any comments as to the place of arbitration, the applicable rules of law and the language of the arbitration.

Article 16 Language of the arbitration
In the absence of an agreement by the parties, the Arbitral Tribunal shall determine the language or languages of the arbitration, due regard being given to all relevant circumstances, including the language of the contract.

42. International Chamber of Commerce (ICC), International Centre for Expertise. Rules for Expertise, 2003

Article 12 The Expert's Mission
1. The expert, after having consulted the parties, shall set out the expert's mission in a written document. That document shall not be inconsistent with anything in these Rules and shall be communicated to the parties and to the Centre. Such document shall include:
(e) a statement indicating the language in which the proceedings will be conducted

43. International Maritime Committee (CMI), International Maritime Arbitration Rules, 1978

8.) The arbitrator shall determine the language or languages of the arbitration, due regard being paid to all the relevant circumstances and in particular to the language of the contract.

44. Internet Corporation for Assigned Names and Numbers (ICANN), Rules for Uniform Domain Name Dispute Resolution Policy, 1999

(As approved 24 October 1999)

2. Communications

d) Communications shall be made in the language prescribed in Paragraph 11. E-mail communications should, if practicable, be sent in plain text.

11. Language of Proceedings

(a) Unless otherwise agreed by the Parties, or specified otherwise in the Registration Agreement, the language of the administrative proceeding shall be the language of the Registration Agreement, subject to the authority of the Panel to determine otherwise, having regard to the circumstances of the administrative proceeding.
(b) The Panel may order that any documents submitted in languages other than the language of the administrative proceeding be accompanied by a translation in whole or in part into the language of the administrative proceeding.

45. Iran-US Claims Tribunal, Provisionally Adopted Tribunal Rules, 1983

(9 March 1983)

Article 17 Language

1. Subject to an agreement by the parties, the arbitral tribunal shall, promptly after its appointment, determine the language or languages to be used in the proceedings. This determination shall apply to the statement of claim, the statement of defence, and any further written statements and, if oral hearings take place, to the language or languages to be used in such hearings.
2. The arbitral tribunal may order that any documents annexed to the statement of claim or statement of defence, and any supplementary documents or exhibits submitted in the course of the proceedings, delivered in their original language, shall be accompanied by a translation into the language or languages agreed upon by the parties or determined by the arbitral tribunal.

Notes to Article 17

2. In accordance with an agreement of the Agents, English and Farsi shall be the official languages to be used in the arbitration proceedings, and these languages shall be used for all oral hearings, decisions and awards.
3. In accordance with the provisions of Article 17 of the UNCITRAL Rules, the following documents filed with the Tribunal shall be submitted in both English and Farsi, unless otherwise agreed by the arbitrating parties
(a) The Statement of Claim and its annexes.
(b) The Statement of Defence, and any counter-claim, including any annexes.
(c) The reply (including any annexes) to any counter-claim.
(d) Any further written statement (e.g. reply, rejoinder, brief), including any annexes, which the arbitral tribunal may require or permit an arbitrating party to present.
(e) Any written request to the arbitral tribunal to take action or any objection thereto.
(f) Any challenge to a member.
4. The arbitral tribunal shall determine in each particular case what other documents, documentary exhibits and written evidence, or what parts thereof, shall be submitted in both English and Farsi.
5. Any disputes or difficulties regarding translations shall be resolved by the arbitral tribunal.

Article 25

1. In the event of an oral hearing, the arbitral tribunal shall give the parties adequate advance notice of the date, time and place thereof.
2. If witnesses are to be heard, at least *thirty* days before the hearing each party shall communicate to the arbitral tribunal and to the other party the names and addresses of the witnesses he intends to present, the subject upon and the languages in which such witnesses will give their testimony.
3. The arbitral tribunal shall make arrangements for the translation of oral statements made at a hearing and for a record of the hearing if either is deemed necessary by the tribunal under the circumstances of the case, or if the parties have agreed thereto and have communicated such agreement to the tribunal at least fifteen days before the hearing.

Texts Adopted as Internal Guidelines of the Tribunal

1. The arbitral tribunal may make such orders as it considers appropriate to co-ordinate and expedite cases which raise important issues, including, but not limited to, relinquishing cases to the Plenary Tribunal in accordance with Presidential Order No. 1, providing that such issues be heard separately and prior to hearing of the remaining issues, and co-ordinating scheduling of hearings. The arbitral tribunal may authorize arbitrating parties to give through a single designated representative, common expla 18 Inations on similar issues arising out of different cases, without resulting in consolidation or joinder. The following list is illustrative of the matters which may be considered at the pre-hearing conferences held pursuant to Note 4 to Article 15 of the Tribunal Rules, and the arbitral tribunal may in its discretion determine to consider additional, or fewer matters at the pre-hearing conference:

(i) determining what documentary evidence will require translation.

46. Italian Arbitration Association (AIA), Arbitration Rules, 1985

(19 June 1985)

Article 18 Language

If the parties fail to come to an agreement, within the period of time fixed for the answer to the request for arbitration, the arbitrator shall determine the language to be used in the arbitral proceedings, bearing in mind the circumstances of the case and, in particular, the language used in the contract, in relation to which the dispute arose, and in the correspondence between the parties. The arbitrator can authorize or request that translations be made or interpretation be provided by the party who has made them necessary and at that party's expense.

47. Italian Arbitration Association (AIA), Rules For International Arbitration, 1994

(Approved 15 April 1994. In force 30 September 1994)

Article 6 Request for arbitration

2. The request shall contain:

(d) the relevant information on the language of the arbitration, on the provisions applicable to the merits or the eventual request for a decision *ex aequo et bono* and on the modalities for the deliberation of the award;

Article 7 Answer to the request; Counterclaim and reply

2. The answer shall contain

(c) the relevant information on the language of the arbitration, on the provisions applicable to the merits or the eventual request for a decision *ex aequo et bono* and on the modalities for the deliberation of the award;

Article 21 Language of arbitration
1. Unless otherwise agreed by the parties, the request, the answer to same and the reply to the counterclaim shall be made in the language of the contract.
2. In the absence of an agreement between the parties within the period of time fixed for the answer to the request for arbitration, the arbitrator shall determine the language of the arbitration taking into account the circumstances and, in particular, the language used in the contract in relation to which the dispute has arisen and in the correspondence between the parties.
3. The arbitrator can authorize or request translations or interpretations, at the care and expense of the party who has justified same.

Article 23 The arbitrator's terms of reference
Before proceeding with the preparation of the case, the arbitrator, in accordance with the provisions of Article 24.3, shall draw up, on the basis of the documents submitted and, eventually, after having heard the parties, a document in writing which shall include:
(f) the indication of the seat and language of the arbitration

48. Japan Commercial Arbitration Association (JCAA), Commercial Arbitration Rules, 2004

(As amended and effective 1 March 2004)

Rule 11. Language
1. The language or languages to be used in arbitral proceedings shall be Japanese or English or both. The arbitral tribunal shall, except where the parties have agreed on one or both of such languages, determine, without delay, the language or languages to be used. The arbitral tribunal shall, in so determining, take into consideration whether interpreting or translating will be required and how the cost thereof should be allocated.
2. Arbitral proceedings conducted, prior to the determination of language or languages pursuant to the preceding paragraph, in a language other than the language or languages so determined shall remain valid. The Association may, if such language is one other than Japanese or English, require the submission of Japanese or English translations.
3. If it is determined that both Japanese and English are to be the languages used during arbitral proceedings, either Japanese or English may be, at a party's option, used during all arbitral proceedings, including hearings; provided that the arbitral award shall be written in Japanese and English, both versions of which shall be official, and if a discrepancy in interpretation arises between the two (2) versions, the interpretation of the Japanese version shall prevail.
4. The arbitral tribunal may request a party to attach to any documentary evidence its translation into the language or languages to be used in arbitral proceedings.

49. Korean Commercial Arbitration Board, Commercial Arbitration Rules, 2000

(As amended by the Supreme Court on April 17, 2000)

Article 29. Presentation of Translation
Parties shall, upon request, present to the Secretariat or the Tribunal, translations of the written statements and evidentiary documents and/or other written materials which are requested by the Secretariat or the Tribunal

Article 30. Interpretation or Translation
(1) The Secretariat shall make necessary arrangements for the services of interpretation or translation upon the request of one or both parties or by order of the Tribunal.
(2) The requesting party shall deposit an advance payment to the Secretariat of the expenses involved in such services described in Paragraph (1).

(3) The expenses involved in the services provided in Paragraph (1) herein by order of the Tribunal shall be paid from the deposits made in advance by the party under Article 65.

Article 50. Language
The Korean language shall be used in the arbitral proceedings unless otherwise agreed by the parties. In case there has been a request submitted by one of the parties or both, or there is among the arbitrators a person of nationality other than that of Korea, the arbitral award may be written in both Korean and English languages and both versions shall be the duly authenticated arbitral award. However, when a discrepancy in interpretation has arisen between the two versions, interpretation by the Korean language shall prevail.

Article 63. Expenses
(1) All the expenses required for arbitration including the expenses of the arbitrators and Clerk, the expenses of any proofs produced, the expenses of witness or expert witness, the expenses of inspection, interpretation or translation, tape record, stenographic record or all transcripts thereof shall be deposited in advance by the party ordering such services

50. Lima Chamber of Commerce, Perú, National and International Conciliation and Arbitration Center, Procedural Arbitration Rules, 2004

Artículo10 º. Idioma del arbitraje
Los procesos arbitrales se desarrollarán en idioma castellano, salvo pacto distinto de las partes. El Órgano Arbitral podrá ordenar que cualquier documento esté acompañado de una traducción al castella no o, en su caso, al idioma que rige el proceso.

51. London Court of International Arbitration (LCIA), Arbitration Rules, 1998

Article 1 The request for arbitration
1.1 Any party wishing to commence an arbitration under these Rules ("the Claimant") shall send to the Registrar of the LCIA Court ("the Registrar") a written request for arbitration ("the Request"), containing or accompanied by:
(d) a statement of any matters (such as the seat or language(s) of the arbitration, or the number of arbitrators, or their qualifications or identities) on which the parties have already agreed in writing for the arbitration or in respect of which the Claimant wishes to make a proposal;

Article 5 Formation of the arbitral tribunal
5.5 The LCIA Court alone is empowered to appoint arbitrators. The LCIA Court will appoint arbitrators with due regard for any particular method or criteria of selection agreed in writing by the parties. In selecting arbitrators consideration will be given to the nature of the transaction, the nature and circumstances of the dispute, the nationality, location and languages of the parties and (if more than two) the number of parties

Article 17 Language of arbitration
17.1 The initial language of the arbitration shall be the language of the Arbitration Agreement, unless the parties have agreed in writing otherwise and providing always that a non-participating or defaulting party shall have no cause for complaint if communications to and from the Registrar and the arbitration proceedings are conducted in English.
17.2 In the event that the Arbitration Agreement is written in more than one language, the LCIA Court may, unless the Arbitration Agreement provides that the arbitration proceedings shall be

conducted in more than one language, decide which of those languages shall be the initial language of the arbitration.
17.3 Upon the formation of the Arbitral Tribunal and unless the parties have agreed upon the language or languages of the arbitration, the Arbitration Tribunal shall decide upon the language(s) of the arbitration, after giving the parties an opportunity to make written comment and taking into account the initial language of the arbitration and any other matter it may consider appropriate in all the circumstances of the case.
17.4 If any document is expressed in a language other than the language(s) of the arbitration and no translation of such document is submitted by the party relying upon the document, the Arbitral Tribunal or (if the Arbitral Tribunal has not been formed) the LCIA Court may order that party to submit a translation in a form to be determined by the Arbitral Tribunal or the LCIA Court, as the case may be.

52. Multilateral Investment Guarantee Agency (MIGA), Rules of Arbitration For Disputes Under Contracts of Guarantee of MIGA, 1990

(January 1990)

Article 27 – Preliminary Procedural Consultation
As early as possible after the constitution of a Tribunal, its President shall endeavor to ascertain the views of the parties regarding questions of procedure. For this purpose he may request the parties to meet him. He shall, in particular, seek their views on the following matters:
(a) the number of members of the Tribunal required to constitute a quorum at its sittings;
(b) the language or languages to be used in the proceeding;

Article 29 – Procedural Languages
(1) The parties may agree on the use of one or two languages to be used in the proceeding or, in the absence of such agreement, each party may select a language for this purpose; provided always that the Tribunal, after consultation with the Secretary-General, gives its approval for the language or languages selected under this paragraph.
(2) If two procedural languages are approved for the proceeding, any instrument may be filed in either such language. Statements made before the Tribunal or by one of its members in one procedural language shall, unless the Tribunal decides to dispense therewith, be interpreted into the other procedural language. The orders and the award of the Tribunal shall be rendered and the minutes kept in both procedural languages, both versions being equally authentic.
(3) The Tribunal may authorize the use of a language other than a procedural language for a specified part of the proceeding. In such event it shall determine to what extent translation and interpretation into and from the procedural language or languages is required.

Article 32 – Supporting Documentation
(2) Each document which is not in a language approved for the proceeding shall, unless otherwise ordered by the Tribunal, be accompanied by a certified translation into such a language.

Article 60 – Other Assistance
(2) The Secretary-General shall provide such other assistance as may be required in connection with all meetings of the Tribunal, in particular in providing or arranging for translation and interpretation services.

Article 68 – Special Services to Parties
The Secretary-General shall only perform any special service for a party in connection with the proceeding (for example, the provision of translations or copies) if the party shall in advance have deposited an amount sufficient to cover the charge for such service.

53. Netherlands Arbitration Institute (NAI), Arbitration Rules, 2001

(in force as of 13 November 2001)

Recommended Text Arbitration Clause:
"All disputes arising in connection with the present contract, or further contracts resulting therefrom, shall be finally settled in accordance with the Arbitration Rules of the Netherlands Arbitration Institute (Nederlands Arbitrage Instituut)."
Additionally, Various Matters May be Provided for (see Introduction, §5):
"The arbitral procedure shall be conducted in the ... language."

Article 40 Language
1. The arbitral proceedings shall be conducted in the language or languages as agreed by the parties or, in the absence of such agreement, in the language or languages determined by the arbitral tribunal.
2. Until such time as the arbitral tribunal has determined the language or languages as referred to in paragraph (1), the Administrator may, at the request of the other party or on his own motion, require a party to provide translations of his submissions and documents in a language which the other party understands and in such form and within such period of time as the Administrator shall determine.
3. Without prejudice to the provisions of paragraphs (1) and (2), if any notice, submission or document is written in a language which the Administrator or the arbitral tribunal does not understand, the Adminstrator and, after its appointment, the arbitral tribunal may require the party from whom such notice, submission or document emanates to provide a translation in such language, in such form and within such period of time as the Administrator or the arbitral tribunal, as the case may be, shall determine.
4. At the request of the arbitral tribunal, the Administrator shall arrange for the presence of an interpreter at the hearing.

54. Organisation pour l'Harmonisation en Afrique du Droit des Affaires (OHADA). Règlement d'arbitrage de la cour commune de justice et de l'arbitrage de l'OHADA, 1999

(Adopté le 11 mars 1999)

Article 3 La désignation des arbitres
3.3 Pour nommer les arbitres, la Cour tient compte de la nationalité des parties, du lieu de résidence de celles-ci et du lieu de résidence de leur conseil et des arbitres, de la langue des parties, de la nature des questions en litige et, éventuellement, des lois choisies par les parties pour régir leurs relations.

Article 5 Demande d'arbitrage
Toute partie désirant avoir recours à l'arbitrage institué par l'article 2.1 ci-dessus (article 21 du Traité) et dont les modalités sont fixées par le présent règlement, adresse sa demande au Secrétaire général pour l'arbitrage de la Cour.
Cette demande doit contenir :
e) s'il en existe, les conventions intervenues entre les parties :
– sur le siège de l'arbitrage
– sur la langue de l'arbitrage

Article 15 Procès-verbal constatant l'objet de l'arbitrage et fixant le déroulement de la procédure arbitrale

15.1 Après réception du dossier par l'arbitre, celui-ci convoque les parties ou leurs représentants dûment habilités et leurs conseils, à une réunion qui doit se tenir aussi rapidement qu'il est possible, et au plus tard dans les soixante (60) jours de cette réception du dossier.

Cette réunion a pour objet :

b) de constater s'il existe ou non un accord des parties sur les points énumérés aux articles 5.e) et 6.b) et d) ci-dessus.

En l'absence d'un tel accord, l'arbitre constate que la sentence aura à se prononcer à ce sujet.

La langue de l'arbitrage fait, au cours de la réunion, l'objet d'une décision immédiate de l'arbitre au vu des dires des parties sur ce point, en tenant compte des circonstances.

En cas de besoin l'arbitre interroge les parties pour savoir si celles-ci entendent lui attribuer les pouvoirs d'amiable compositeur. Il est fait mention de la réponse des parties.

55. Permanent Court of Arbitration (PCA), Optional Rules For Arbitrating Disputes Between Two Parties Of Which Only One Is a State, 1993

(Effective 6 July 1993)

Language Article 17

1. Subject to an agreement by the parties, the arbitral tribunal shall, promptly after its appointment, determine the language or languages to be used in the proceedings. This determination shall apply to the statement of claim, the statement of defence, and any further written statements and, if oral hearings take place, to the language or languages to be used in such hearings.

2. The arbitral tribunal may order that any documents annexed to the statement of claim or statement of defence, and any supplementary documents or exhibits submitted in the course of the proceedings, delivered in their original language, shall be accompanied by a translation into the language or languages agreed upon by the parties or determined by the arbitral tribunal.

Article 25

1. In the event of an oral hearing, the arbitral tribunal shall give the parties adequate advance notice of the date, time and place thereof.

2. If witnesses are to be heard, at least thirty days before the hearing each party shall communicate to the arbitral tribunal and to the other party the names and addresses of the witnesses it intends to present, the subject upon and the languages in which such witnesses will give their testimony

Future Disputes

Where a State and a private entity are parties to a contract and wish to have any dispute referred to arbitration under these Rules, they may insert in the contract an arbitration clause in the following form:

1. If any dispute arises between the parties as to the interpretation, application or performance of this contract, including its existence, validity or termination, either party may submit the dispute to final and binding arbitration in accordance with the Permanent Court of Arbitration Optional Rules for Arbitrating Disputes Between Two Parties of which only one is a State, as in effect on the date of this contract

Parties may wish to consider adding:

2. *The number of arbitrators shall be...* [insert "one" or "three"]

3. *The* language*(s) to be used in the arbitral proceedings shall be...* [insert choice of one or more languages]

(3 If the parties do not agree on the language, or languages, to be used in the arbitral proceedings, this shall be determined by the arbitral tribunal in accordance with article 17 of the Rules.)

56. Permanent Court of Arbitration (PCA), Optional Rules for Arbitration Involving International Organizations and States, 1996

(1 July 1996)

Article 17 Language

1. Subject to an agreement by the parties, the arbitral tribunal shall, promptly after its appointment, determine the language or languages to be used in the proceedings. This determination shall apply to the statement of claim, the statement of defence, and any further written statements and, if oral hearings take place, to the language or languages to be used in such hearings.
2. The arbitral tribunal may order that any documents annexed to the statement of claim or statement of defence, and any supplementary documents or exhibits submitted in the course of the proceedings, delivered in their original language, shall be accompanied by a translation into the language or languages agreed upon by the parties or determined by the arbitral tribunal.

Article 25

2. If witnesses are to be heard, at least thirty days before the hearing each party shall communicate to the arbitral tribunal and to the other party the names and addresses of the witnesses it intends to present, the subject upon and the languages in which such witnesses will give their testimony.
3. The International Bureau shall make arrangements for the translation of oral statements made at a hearing and for a record of the hearing if either is deemed necessary by the tribunal under the circumstances of the case, or if the parties have agreed thereto and have communicated such agreement to the tribunal and the International Bureau at least thirty days before the hearing or such longer period before the hearing as the arbitral tribunal may determine.

Future Disputes

Where an international organization, and a State or an international organization are parties to an agreement and wish to have any disputes referred to arbitration under these Rules, they may insert in the agreement an arbitration clause in the following form:

1. "Any dispute, controversy or claim arising out of or relating to the interpretation, application or performance of this agreement, including its existence, validity or termination, shall be settled by final and binding arbitration in accordance with the Permanent Court of Arbitration Optional Rules for Arbitration involving International Organizations and States, as in effect on the date of this agreement."

Parties may wish to consider adding:

2. "The number of arbitrators shall be ..." [insert "one", "three" or "five"]
3. "The language(s) to be used in the arbitral proceedings shall be ..." [insert choice of one or more languages].

(3 If the parties do not agree on the language, or languages, to be used in the arbitral proceedings, this shall be determined by the arbitral tribunal in accordance with article 17 of the Rules

57. Permanent Court of Arbitration (PCA), Optional Rules for Arbitration Between International Organizations and Private Parties, 1996

(1 July 1996)

Article 17 Language

1. Subject to an agreement by the parties, the arbitral tribunal shall, promptly after its appointment, determine the language or languages to be used in the proceedings. This determination shall apply to the statement of claim, the statement of defence, and any further written statements and, if oral hearings take place, to the language or languages to be used in such hearings.

2. The arbitral tribunal may order that any documents annexed to the statement of claim or statement of defence, and any supplementary documents or exhibits submitted in the course of the proceedings, delivered in their original language, shall be accompanied by a translation into the language or languages agreed upon by the parties or determined by the arbitral tribunal.

Article 25

2. If witnesses are to be heard, at least thirty days before the hearing each party shall communicate to the arbitral tribunal and to the other party the names and addresses of the witnesses it intends to present, the subject upon and the languages in which such witnesses will give their testimony.

3. The International Bureau shall make arrangements for the translation of oral statements made at a hearing and for a record of the hearing if either is deemed necessary by the tribunal under the circumstances of the case, or if the parties have agreed thereto and have communicated such agreement to the tribunal and the International Bureau at least thirty days before the hearing or such longer period before the hearing as the arbitral tribunal may determine.

58. Permanent Court of Arbitration (PCA), Rules For Arbitration of Disputes Relating to Natural Resources and/or the Environment, 2001

(19 June 2001)

Article 17 Language

1. Subject to an agreement by the parties, the arbitral tribunal shall, promptly after its appointment, determine the language or languages to be used in the proceedings. This determination shall apply to the statement of claim, the statement of defence, and any further written statements and, if oral hearings take place, to the language or languages to be used in such hearings.

2. The arbitral tribunal may order that any documents annexed to the statement of claim or statement of defence, and any supplementary documents or exhibits submitted in the course of the proceedings, delivered in their original language, shall be accompanied by a translation into the language or languages agreed upon by the parties or determined by the arbitral tribunal.

Article 25

1. In the event of an oral hearing, the arbitral tribunal shall give the parties adequate advance notice of the date, time and place thereof.

2. If witnesses are to be heard, at least thirty days before the hearing each party shall communicate to the arbitral tribunal and to the other party the names and addresses of the witnesses it intends to present, the subject upon and the languages in which such witnesses will give their testimony.

3. The International Bureau shall make arrangements in consultation with the parties for the translation of oral statements made at a hearing and for a record of the hearing if either is deemed necessary by the tribunal under the circumstances of the case, or if the parties have agreed thereto and have communicated such agreement to the tribunal and the International Bureau at least thirty days before the hearing or such other period before the hearing as the arbitral tribunal may determine.

59. Polish Chamber of Commerce in Warsaw, Rules of the Court of Arbitration, 2003

Proceedings before the Arbitration Court

§ 20 Language of the proceedings before the Court

1. The parties may freely agree upon the language of arbitration proceedings: Polish, English, French, German or Russian. In the event that they do not agree upon a specific language, the

proceedings shall be conducted in Polish *[unless the Arbitral Tribunal decides otherwise]*. The language agreed by the parties or decided by the Arbitral Tribunal shall be applied to hearings and any written statements in arbitration proceedings.
2. The president of the Arbitral Tribunal shall appoint an expert translator for the entire hearing that is conducted in the language other than Polish.
3. Records of hearings shall be prepared in polish and translated into the language of the proceedings.
4. Written statements filed by the parties or made by the Arbitral Tribunal in a foreign language shall be translated into Polish by a translator accepted by the Court or by parties.
5. The costs of the participation of a translator in a hearing and for the translation of documents shall be borne by the parties in accordance with principles set out by the Arbitral Tribunal.

60. Santiago Arbitration and Mediation Center, Rules of Arbitration Procedure, 2002
(Version in effect beginning November 1, 2000, published in Official Gazette May 8, 2002)

Article # 28
The arbitration tribunal shall give sufficient notice to the parties of any hearing.
If witnesses are to testify, each party shall advise the arbitration tribunal and, through the intermediary thereof, the other party ten days in advance of the hearing, indicating the name and address of the witnesses who will testify, the subject and language in which they will do it. The notice to the tribunal should be given during the probatory period.

61. Serbian Chamber of Commerce and Industry, Rules of the Foreign Trade Court of Arbitration (Belgrade Rules), 2001, as amended on June 15, 2004

2. Institution of Arbitral Proceedings
2.1. Submitting of the claim
Article 20
(3) The claim and evidence are submitted in the Serbian language and in the language of the contract that exists between the parties.

4.4. The language
Article 37
The arbitral proceedings are conducted in the Serbian Language.
The parties may agree that the proceedings be conducted in some other (foreign) language, provided that they pay all the additional costs (translation of documents, evidence and hearings).
If the members of the Arbitral Tribunal or the sole arbitrator are foreign citizens appointed by the parties, the party that appointed the arbitrator shall bear the costs of translation of the documents, evidence, the hearings and the in camera deliberations of the Arbitral tribunal.
The written correspondence of the Secretariat with the foreign party that is not represented by a domestic person, and that clearly has no knowledge of the Serbian language, is conducted in English or in some other foreign language.

62. Singapore International Arbitration Centre (SIAC), Arbitration Rules, 1997
(22 October 1997)

In drawing up contracts, parties are recommended to include the following arbitration clause. Parties may add: "The language of the arbitration shall be ...."

Rule 20 Language of arbitration

20.1 Subject to any agreement by the parties, the Tribunal shall, promptly after its appointment, determine the language or languages to be used in the proceedings. This determination shall apply to the Statement of Case, the Statement of Defence, and any further written statements or other communications and, if oral hearings take place, to the language or languages to be used in such hearings.

20.2 If a document is drawn up in a language other than the language(s) of the arbitration, and no translation of such document is submitted by the party producing the document, the Tribunal, or if the Tribunal has not been established, the Registrar, may order that party to submit a translation in a form to be determined by the Tribunal or the Registrar.

63. St. Petersburg International Commercial Arbitration Court, Rules

Article 17. Language

1. Subject to an agreement by the parties, the arbitral tribunal shall, promptly after its appointment, determine the language or languages to be used in the proceedings. This determination shall apply to the statement of claim, the statement of defense, and any further written statements and, if oral hearings take place, to the language or languages to be used in such hearings.
2. The arbitral tribunal may order that any documents annexed to the statement of claim or the statement of defense, and any supplementary documents or exhibits submitted in the course of the proceedings, which are delivered in their original language, shall be accompanied by a translation into the language or languages agreed upon by the parties or determined by the arbitral tribunal.

Article 25. Hearings

1. In the event of an oral hearing, the arbitral tribunal shall give the parties adequate notice of the date, time and place thereof.
2. If witnesses are to be heard, at least 15 days before the hearing each party shall communicate to the arbitral tribunal and to the other party the names and addresses of the witnesses whom it intends to present, as well as the subject upon and the languages in which the witnesses will give their testimony.
3. The arbitral tribunal shall make arrangements for the translation of oral statements made during the proceedings and for a record of the hearing if either is deemed necessary by the arbitral tribunal under the circumstances of the case, or if the parties have agreed thereto and have communicated such agreement to the tribunal at least 15 days before the hearing.

64. Stockholm Chamber of Commerce, Arbitration Rules of the Arbitration Institute (Stockholm Rules), 1999

Article 23 Language

Unless the parties have agreed in the arbitration agreement on the language or languages to be used in the proceedings, the Arbitral Tribunal shall, after consultation with the parties, make such decision.

65. Swiss Chamber of Commerce in Italy (CCSI), Regulations for CCSI Arbitration, 1995

Art. 10: Language of the Proceedings

The languages of the proceedings are Italian, French, German and English. Failing an agreement between the parties, the Arbitrators will decide wich of these four languages is the most suitable

for the Arbitration Proceedings, bearing in mind the nature of the controversy and the language of the contract.
In any case they shall proceed in such a way as to ensure the protection of the parties' rights and a speedy conclusion.

66. Swiss Rules of International Arbitration (Swiss Rules), 2004
(1 January 2004)

Any dispute, controversy or claim arising out of or in relation to this contract, including the validity, invalidity, breach or termination thereof, shall be resolved by arbitration in accordance with the Swiss Rules of International Arbitration of the Swiss Chambers of Commerce in force on the date when the Notice of Arbitration is submitted in accordance with these Rules.
The number of arbitrators shall be ... (one or three);
The seat of the arbitration shall be ... (city in Switzerland);
The arbitral proceedings shall be conducted in ... (insert desired language).

Article 3
5. If the Notice of Arbitration is incomplete or if the copies or attachments are not submitted in the required number, or if the Registration Fee is not paid, the Chambers may request the Claimant to remedy the defect within an appropriate period of time. The Chambers may also request within such time-limit a translation of the Notice of Arbitration if it is not submitted in English, German, French or Italian. If the Claimant complies with such directions within the applicable time-limit, the Notice of Arbitration shall be deemed to have been validly filed on the date when the initial version was received by the Chambers.

Language
Article 17
1. Subject to an agreement by the parties, the arbitral tribunal shall, promptly after its appointment, determine the language or languages to be used in the proceedings. This determination shall apply to the Statement of Claim, the Statement of Defence, and any further written statements and, if oral hearings take place, to the language or languages to be used in such hearings.
2. The arbitral tribunal may order that any documents annexed to the Statement of Claim or Statement of Defence, and any supplementary documents or exhibits submitted in the course of the proceedings, delivered in their original language, shall be accompanied by a translation into the language or languages agreed upon by the parties or determined by the arbitral tribunal.

Evidence and Hearings (Articles 24 and 25)
Article 25
2. Any person may be a witness or an expert witness. If witnesses or expert witnesses are to be heard, at least fifteen days before the hearing each party shall communicate to the arbitral tribunal and to the other party the names and addresses of the witnesses or expert witnesses it intends to present, the subject upon and the languages in which such witnesses or expert witnesses will give their testimony.
3. The arbitral tribunal shall make arrangements for the translation of oral statements made at a hearing and for a record of the hearing if either is deemed necessary by the tribunal under the circumstances of the case, or if the parties have agreed thereto and have communicated such agreement to the tribunal at least fifteen days before the hearing.

67. Tokyo Maritime Arbitration Commission (TOMAC), Rules of Arbitration, 2004

(In force 1 March 2004)

Article 30 Language

The language employed in the Statement of Claim, the Defense, the Supplementary Statements, the hearings and the arbitral award in domestic arbitrations shall be the Japanese language, and that in international arbitrations shall, in principle, be the English language. However, except where the Tribunal has specified otherwise, it is not necessary to translate documentary evidence.

Article 31 Interpreting

The parties who will need interpreters at the oral hearings may, at their own expense, arrange for interpreters to be present at the hearings

68. United States Center for Public Resources Institute for Dispute Resolution, Rules for Non-Administered Arbitration of International Disputes, 2000

(15 September 2000)

C. Rules with Respect to the Conduct of the Arbitral Proceedings

Rule 9 – General Provisions

9.3 The Tribunal shall hold an initial pre-hearing conference for the planning and scheduling of the proceeding. Such conference shall be held promptly after the constitution of the Tribunal, unless the Tribunal is of the view that further submissions from the parties are appropriate prior to such conference. The objective of this conference shall be to discuss all elements of the arbitration with a view to planning for its future conduct. Matters to be considered in the initial pre-hearing conference may include, inter alia, the following:

a) procedural matters (such as the timing and manner of any required disclosure; the desirability of bifurcation or other separation of the issues in the arbitration; the desirability and practicability of consolidating the arbitration with any other proceeding; the scheduling of conferences and hearings; the need for and costs of translations; the scheduling of pre-hearing memoranda; the need for and type of record of conferences and hearings, including the need for transcripts; the amount of time allotted to each party for presentation of its case and for rebuttal; the mode, manner and order for presenting proof; the need for expert witnesses and how expert testimony should be presented; and the necessity for any on-site inspection by the Tribunal);

9.6 If the parties have not agreed otherwise, the language(s) of the arbitration shall be that of the documents containing the arbitration agreement, subject to the power of the Tribunal to determine otherwise based upon the contentions of the parties and the circumstances of the arbitration. The Tribunal may order that any documents submitted in other languages shall be accompanied by a translation into such language or languages.

Rule 12 – Evidence and Hearings

12.1 The Tribunal shall determine the manner in which the parties shall present their cases. Unless otherwise determined by the Tribunal or agreed by the parties, the presentation of a party's case shall include the submission of a pre-hearing memorandum including the following elements:

e. the evidence to be presented, including documents relied upon and the name, capacity and subject of testimony of any witnesses to be called, the language in which each witness will testify, and an estimate of the amount of time required for the party's examination of the witness.

12.4 The Tribunal shall determine the manner in which witnesses are to be examined, including the need and arrangements for translation of any witness testimony in a language other than the language of the arbitration. The Tribunal shall have the right to exclude witnesses from hearings during the testimony of other witnesses.

69. Vancouver Maritime Arbitrators Association (VMAA), Arbitration Rules, 2005

(Amended as of February 24th, 2005)

Appendix A Oaths

3. Oath to be taken by interpreter:
Do you solemnly swear that you will faithfully and fairly translate in a verbatim and objective manner from the language or vice versa the oral or written communications you will be called upon to interpret?

Code of Ethics

Code of Ethics for Vancouver Maritime Arbitrators Association

1. A prospective arbitrator shall accept an appointment only if he is fully satisfied that he is able to discharge his duties without bias, he is competent to determine the issues in dispute, he has an adequate knowledge of the language of the arbitration, and he is able to give to the arbitration the time and attention which the parties are reasonably entitled to expect.

70. Venice Court of National and International Arbitration (VENCA), Rules of Arbitration[1]

Art. 39 – Language of the arbitration

1. The parties shall indicate the language of the arbitration in the request for arbitration and the answer to the request. The parties failing to do so, the language of the arbitration shall be indicated by the arbitrator, having regard to the language of the contract concluded by the parties in dispute and used by the parties in the course of their relationship, with particular reference to the correspondence exchanged between them.

2. The arbitrator may authorize the submission of documents in a language other than the language of the arbitration, and may order that the documents be translated in the language of the arbitration

71. Vietnam International Arbitration Centre, Arbitration Rules, 1993

Article 5

The Request for arbitration must be written in the Vietnamese language or in a foreign language widely used in international transactions (English, French, Russian).

Article 22

The arbitral tribunal shall conduct the hearing in the Vietnamese language.
The parties may request the Centre to provide interpreters at their own expenses.

---

[1] According to the Transitional Provisions contained in Art. 50, "*These Rules substitute the VENCA Rules of Arbitration, adopted by the Court of Arbitration of the VENCA Foundation on July 2, 1998.*" The date of the present new Rules is not indicated in the text of the Rules, available on the web site of VENCA at www.venca.it .

72. World Intellectual Property Organization (WIPO), Arbitration Rules, 2002
(Effective from October 1, 2002)

Language of Arbitration
Article 40
(a) Unless otherwise agreed by the parties, the language of the arbitration shall be the language of the Arbitration Agreement, subject to the power of the Tribunal to determine otherwise, having regard to any observations of the parties and the circumstances of the arbitration.
(b) The Tribunal may order that any documents submitted in languages other than the language of arbitration be accompanied by a translation in whole or in part into the language of arbitration.

73. World Intellectual Property Organization Arbitration and Mediation Center (WIPO), Supplemental Rules for Uniform Domain Name Dispute Resolution Policy, 1999
(In effect as of 1 December 1999)

4. Submission of Complaint
(a) Complaint Transmittal Coversheet. In accordance with Paragraph 3(b)(xii) of the Rules, the Complainant shall be required to send or transmit its complaint under cover of the Complaint Transmittal Coversheet set out in Annex A hereto and posted on the Center's web site. Where available, the Complainant shall use the version that is in the same language(s) as the registration agreement(s) for the domain name(s) that is/are the subject of the complaint.

Table of Cases

Arbitration Cases

(cases without references are unpublished cases)

Budapest Court of Arbitration

- *Case No. Vb/01089* – Procedural Order of September 23, 2002
- *Case No. Vb/01181* – Award of 21 May 2002, Award of May 22, 2002
- *Case No. Vb/03501*
- *Case No. Vb/04362*

GAFTA

- *Romak S. A. Geneva v. FTC Uzdon Tashkent*, in 16-10 *Mealey's International Arbitration Report* (2001)

ICC

- *Case No. 13798/AVH*
- *Procedural Order No. 7170, 1993*, in *Collection of Procedural Decisions in ICC Arbitration 1993-1996*, 2nd edn. (Kluwer, ICC Publishing 1998) p. 55
- *Seller (Central Europe) v. Buyer (Western Europe),* Final award in case No. 8790/2000, in *Yearbook Commercial Arbitration*, Vol. XXIX (2004), p 13
- *Case No. 5926* – Procedural Order of September 26, 1988, in Collection of Procedural Decisions in *ICC Arbitration 1993-1996*, 2nd edn. (Kluwer, ICC Publishing 1998) p. 105

ICSID

- *MTD Equity (Malaysia), MTD Chile (Chile) v. the Republic of Chile* – Award of May 25, 2004, in *International Law in Brief*, prepared by the Editorial Staff of the ASIL International Legal Materials, August 13, 2004

Iran-US Claims Tribunal

- *Harza v. Iran* – Presidential Order 120-2, in 1 *Iran-U.S. C.T.R.* at 234
- *The Islamic Republic of Iran v. The United States of America, Case No. A18* – Full Tribunal Decision No. DEC 32-A18-FT of Apr. 6, 1984, in 5 *Iran-U.S. C.T.R.* 251
- *Sylvania Technical Systems Inv. v Iran* – Award No. 180-64-1, in 8 *Iran-U.S. C.T.R.* at 300
- *Houston Contracting Company v. National Iranian Oil Company, National Iranian Gas Company and the Islamic Republic of Iran, Case No. 173, Chamber Three* – Order 173-3 of January 19, 1987, in 14 *Iran-U.S. C.T.R.* at 18
- *Watkins-Johnson company, Watkins-Johnson Ltd. v. Islamic Republic of Iran, Bank Saderat Iran* – Award No. 429-370-1 of July 27, 1989, in *22 Iran-US C.T.R.* at 218
- *Juliette Allen v. The Government of the Islamic Republic of Iran, Case No. 930, Chamber Three* – Award No. 541-930-3 of December 11, 1992, in 28 *Iran-US C.T.R.* at 384
- *Vera-Jo Miller Aryeh, et al. v. The Islamic Republic of Iran* – Award No. 581-842/843/844-1, of May 22, 1997, in 33 *Iran-US C.T.R.* at 278

Stockholm Court of Arbitration

- *Swedish claimant v. Chinese respondent* – Interim award of 17 July 1992, Final award of July 13, 1993, in *Yearbook Commercial Arbitration,* Vol. XXII (1997) p. 197

Vienna Court of Arbitration

- *Case SCH-4480,* decided in 1997
- *Case SCH-4502,* decided in 1997

WIPO

- *Citizens Watch (China) Co. Ltd. v. Cheng Zhi Zang, Case No. D2001-1305* – Administrative Panel Decision of January 1, 2002, available at http://www.arbiter.wipo.int.domains/decisions/html/2001/d2001-1305.html.

Court Cases

Austria

- Oberster Gerichtshof (Supreme Court), decision of 17 November 1965, in 9 *Zeitschrift für Rechtsvergleichung* (1968) 123
- *Plaintiff: Respondent in the arbitral proceedings v. Defendant: Arbitral tribunal, 4 Ob 1542/94* Oberster Gerichtshof (Supreme Court), Decision of 4 December 1994, in *Yearbook Commercial Arbitration,* Vol. XXII (1997) pp. 263-265
- *H. GmbH v. Hans-Otto S.* decision No. 1 Ob 253/97 of April 28, 1998 of the Oberster Gerichtshof (Supreme Court), in Entscheidungen des Österreichischer Obersten Gerichtshofes in Zivil – (und Justizverwaltungs) – sachen, (SZ) 71/76 pp. 446-455; English text in *Yearbook Commercial Arbitration,* Vol. XXVI (2001), p. 221-229; French text in *Revue de l'arbitrage* (1999) p. 392-400
- *S*** (United States) v. A***, H***, Andre H*** and Stefan S****, Oberster Gerichtshof (Supreme Court) decision No. 30b347/99x of June 20, 2000, at http://www.ris.bka.gv.at/jus/

Bulgaria

- *Continental Export-Import (Macedonia) v. Pharmachim (Bulgaria)*, Decision No. 168 of July 22, 1994 of the Sofia City Court; Decision No. 141 of February 20, 1995 of the Supreme Court of Bulgaria, Third Civil Law Chamber (case not published)

Canada

- *Kanto Yakin Kogyo Kabushiki-Kaisha v. Can-Eng Manufacturing Limited*, Ontario Court of Justice, Judgment of January 30, 1992, 4 B.L.R. (2d) 108, 40 C.P.R. (3d) 451

China

- *Zhejiang Province Garment Import and Export Company (China) v. Siemssen & Co. (Hong Kong),* Supreme Court of Hong Kong, decision of June 2, 1992, in 1992 *HK Law Digest* F8
- *China Nanhai Oil Joint Service Corporation, Shenzen Branch v. Gee Tai Holdings*, Supreme Court of Hong Kong, High Court, 1994, in *Yearbook Commercial Arbitration*, Vol. XX (1995) p. 671
- *To Kan Chi and others v. Pui Man Yau and others*, Judgment of November 26, 1998 of the High Court of the Hong Kong Special Administrative Region, Court of First Instance, HCMP 002084/1994
- *Medson Co. Ltd. v. Viktor (Far East) Ltd*, High Court of the Hong Kong Special Administrative Region, Court of First Instance, decision of 8 April 2000, in *Yearbook Commercial Arbitration,* Vol. XXVIII (2003) p. 270-271

England

- *Margulies Brothers Ltd. v. Dafnis Thomaides & Co. (UK) Ltd.*, Court of Appeal, 1 *Lloyd's Rep.* (1958) 205
- *E. Rotheray & Soons Ltd v. Carlo Bedarida & Co.*, Queens Bench Division, decision of February 22, 1961, 1 *Lloyd's Rep.* (1961) 220
- *Tongyuan (USA) International Trading Group (China) v. Uni-Clan Ltd.*, decision of January 19, 2001 of the High Court of Justice, *Queen's Bench Division* Commercial Court, 2001 WL 98036 (QBD – Comm.Ct.)

France

- *Société La Belle Créole v. Société The Gemtel Partnership*, decision of July 12, 1989 of the President of the Tribunal de grande instance, *Revue de l'arbitrage* (1990) p. 176
- *Compagnie Honeywell Bull (France) v. Computacion Bull (Venezuela)*, Cour d'appel de Paris, 1re Ch. suppl., Decision of June 21, 1990, *Revue de l'arbitrage* (1991) p. 96
- *Société Campenon Bernard v. Eurodisneyland SCA*, Tribunal de grande instance in 1991, *Revue de l'arbitrage* (1996) (3) p. 516
- *Cubic Defense Systems Inc. v. ICC*, Court of Appeal of Paris, First Chamber, section A, Judgment of September 15, 1998, corrected by a Judgment on Rectification of Material Errors Discovered by the Court» of October 7, in *Revue de l'arbitrage*, 2001; English translation in *Mealey's International Arbitration Report* (1998) Document #05–990426–109
- *JDA Software France and JDA Worldwide v. SA Kiabi*, Paris Cour d'appel, decision of April 11, 2002, 4 *Revue de l'arbitrage* (2003) p. 1252
- *Société Comecim v. Société Theobroma*, Cour d'appel de Paris, decision of June 27, 2002, *Revue de l'arbitrage* (2003) p. 427-434
- *S.A.R.L. Synergie v. Société SC Connect SA*, decision of the Paris Cour d'appel of March 18, 2004, *Revue de l'arbitrage* (2004) p. 454-455
- *Bargues Agro Industrie v. Young Pecan*, Paris Cour d'appel, in *Yearbook Commercial Arbitration*, Vol. XXX (2005) p. 499

Germany

- *Danish claimant v. German respondent*, Cologne Court of Appeal (Oberlandesgericht Köln), 16 December 1992, in *Yearbook Commercial Arbitration*, Vol. XXI (1996) p. 535
- Dresden Court of Appeal (Oberlandesgericht Dresden), Decision No. 11 Sch.04/98 of October 20, 1998, in *Yearbook Commercial Arbitration*, Vol. XXIX (2004) p. 673
- *Company X (Russian Federation) v. Company Y (Germany),* decision No. 4 Z Sch H5/00 of the Court of Appeal of Bavaria (Bayern Oberlandesgericht) of August 11, 2000, in *Yearbook Commercial Arbitration*, Vol. XXVII (2002) p. 451
- Bundesgerichtshof (Supreme Court of Germany), Beschluss vom 17 August 2000, in III ZB 43/99, and at www.bundesgerichtshof.de
- Bundesgerichtshof (Supreme Court of Germany), Urteil, February 1, 2001, in III ZR 332/99, at www.bundesgerichtshof.de; and also in 19 *ASA Bulletin* (2001) p. 325-334
- *Trading company (Israel) v. Buyer (Germany),* decision No. 9 Sch 01-03 of the Cologne Court of Appeal (Oberlandesgerict Köln) of April 23, 2004, in *Yearbook Commercial Arbitration*, Vol. XXX (2005) p. 557, and SchiedsVZ 2005, p. 163
- *Claimant: Lawyer (Austria) v. Defendant: Client (Germany),* decision No. 4 Z Sch 09/04 of the Higher Court of Appeal of Bavaria (Bayerisches Oberstes Landesgericht) of July 5, 2004, in *Yearbook Commercial Arbitration*, Vol. XXX (2005) p. 563
- *K. Trading Comp. (Syria) v. Bayerische Motoren Werke A.G. (Germany),* decision No. 4Z Sch 005-4 of the Higher Court of Appeal of Bavaria (Bayerisches Oberstes Landesgericht) of September 23, 2004, in *Yearbook Commercial Arbitration*, Vol. XXX (2005) 568, at p. 571

Italy

- *S.a.S. Wieland K.G. (Austria) v. Società Industriale Meridionale (S.I.M.) (Italy),* Corte de Appello di Messina, decision of May 19, 1976, in *Yearbook Commercial Arbitration*, Vol. V (1980) p. 266
- Corte di Cassazione (Supreme Court of Italy), 1981, 21 *Rassegna dell'Arbitrato* (1981) p. 134
- *Campomarzio Impianti srl. (Italy) v. Lampart Vegyipari Gépgyár (Hungary),* Corte di Cassazione (Supreme Court of Italy), 20 September 1995, in *Yearbook Commercial Arbitration*, Vol. XXIV (1999) p. 698-702

Japan

- *Plaintiff: Seller (P.R. China) v. Defendant: Buyer (Japan),* District Court of Yokohama, 25 August 1999 (Docket: Heisei 10/wa/3851), in *Yearbook Commercial Arbitration,* Vol. XXVII (2002) p. 515-518

Korea (South)

- *Adviso N.V. (Neth. Ant) v. Korea Overseas Construction Corp. (South Korea),* decision No. 93Da53054 of the Supreme Court of Korea of February 14, 1995, in *Yearbook Commercial Arbitration* Vol. XXI (1996) p. 612-616

Netherlands

- *Southern Pacific Properties (Middle East) Ltd. V. the Arab Republic of Egypt*; District Court of Amsterdam, decision of July 12, 1984, in 24 *International Legal Materials* (1985) 1040
- *China Packing Design Corporation v. SCA Recycling Reukema Trading B.V.*, Arrondissements-rechtbank in Zutphen, decision of November 11, 1998, in *Yearbook Commercial Arbitration*, Vol. XXIV (1999) p. 724

Norway

- *Pulsarr Industrial Research B.V. (Netherlands) v. Nils H. Nilsen A.S. (Norway),* Judgment of 10 July 2002 of the Enforcement Court in Vardø, in *Yearbook Commercial Arbitration,* Vol. XXVIII (2003) p. 821

Spain

- *Pastrederiet m/v Jytte Dania v. Más S.A.*, Spanish Supreme Court 1985, in *Yearbook Commercial Arbitration*, Vol. XIV (1989) p. 704; also published in 2 *Revista de la corte española de arbitraje* (1985) p. 223-224

Switzerland

- *Apellant: N.Z. (nationality not indicated) v. Apellee: I. (Romania),* Basel Court of Appeal, in *Yearbook Commercial Arbitration,* Vol. XVII (1992) p. 581
- *Inter Maritime Management S.A. v. Russin & Vecchi*, Swiss Federal Tribunal, decision of January 9, 1995, 10 *International Arbitration Report* (1995) pp. D-1-D-13
- *Transport en Handelsmaatschappij "Vekoma" B.V. v. Maran Coal Corp*, decision of the Swiss Federal Tribunal of August 17, 1995, German and French text in 14(4) *ASA Bulletin* (1996) p. 673, English excerpts in Várady-Barcelo and Von Mehren, *International Commercial Arbitration*, 3rd edn. (Thomson & West 2006) pp. 758-761
- Obergericht Zug, decision of February 27, 1998, reported in 18 *ASA Bulletin* (2000) p. 363
- *R. SA v. A. Ltd.,* Cour de Justice, Genève, arrêt du 15 avril 1999, 18 *ASA Bulletin* (2000) p 786
- *Italian party v. Swiss company*, decision of February 14, 2003 of the Court of First Instance (Bezirksgericht) of Zurich, confirmed by a decision of the Obergericht (Court of Appeal) of Zurich of July 17, 2003, in *Yearbook Commercial Arbitration,* Vol. XXIX (2004) p. 819-833

- Basel-Stadt, Appelationsgericht, decision of November 5, 2003, 24 *ASA Bulletin* (2006) p. 125
- *A. Ltd v. Republic of Turkey*, Swiss Federal Tribunal, First Civil Chamber, Judgment of October 18, 2004, 23 *ASA Bulletin* (2005) pp. 164-174

United States

- *Wilko v. Swan*, 346 U.S. Supreme Court, U.S. 427, 436-7 (1953)
- *Electronics Corp. of America v. International Elec., Radio and Machine Workers*, AFL-CIO Local 272, U.S. Court of Appeals, First Circuit, 494 F.2d 1255 (1st Cir. 1974)
- *National Post Office Mailhandlers, Watchmen, Messengers and Group Leaders Division v. United States Postal Service*, U.S. Court of Appeals, Sixth Circuit, judgment of January 3, 1985, 751 F.2d 834 at 843
- *Wimber v. Timpe*, Court of Appeals of Oregon, 109 Ore.App.139, 146 (1991)
- *Compagnie des Bauxites de Guinée v. Hammermills*; U.S. District Court of the District of Columbia, Memorandum Opinion of May 29, 1992, 1992 WL 122712 (D.D.C.)
- *Chicago v. Kaplan*, U.S. Supreme Court, 514 U.S. 938, 115 S.Ct. 1920, 1923 (1995)
- *Conlux USA Corporation v. Dixie-Narco Inc. and Maytag Corporation,* United States District Court, N.D. Ohio, Eastern Division, decision of January 25, 1996, 929 F. Supp. 269
- *The People of the State of New York v. G. Smith*, Supreme Court of Bronx County, New York, decision of April 4, 2003, 195 Misc.2d 434, 759 N.Y.S-2d 315,
- *Marzieh Geranghadr v. Abdolreza Entagh,* Court of Appeals of Oregon, decision of July 30, 2003, 189 Ore.App.567; 2003 Ore.App.Lexis 1333
- *Pacific Reliance Inc. v. Transmoreprodukt (Russia),* decision of the Superior Court of Kin County, 128 Wn.App.1007, and the Decision of the Court of Appeals of Washington, Division One, June 13, 2005, 2005 Wash. App. LEXIS 1367

International Criminal Tribunal for the former Yugoslavia (ICTY)

- *Prosecutor v Vojislav Šešelj*, Case No. IT-03-67-PT, ICTY, Trial Chamber II, Order on Translation of Documents of March 6, 2003

Bibliography

ARNOLD, TOM, *Checklist of Arbitration Considerations, in Patents, Copyrights, Trademarks, and Literary Property,* Course Handbook Series (Practising Law Institute 2000).

BORN, GARY B., *International Commercial Arbitration in the United States* (Kluwer, 1994).

CACHARD OLIVIER, 'Translating the French Civil Code: Politics, Linguistics and Legislation', 21 *Connecticut Journal of International Law* (2005) p. 41.

CROOK, JONATHON, 'Leading Arbitration Seats in the Far East: A Comparative View', in S. Frommel and B. Rider, eds., *Conflicting Legal Cultures in Commercial Arbitration* (Kluwer 1999) p. 63.

DELVOLVÉ, JEAN-LOUIS, 'Note (Compagnie Honeywell Bull S.A. c/ Computacion Bull de Venezuela, Cour d'appel de Paris (1re Ch. suppl., Decision of June 21, 1990)', *Revue de l'arbitrage* (1991) pp. 103-109.

DERAINS, YVES and SCHWARTZ, ERIK A., *A Guide to the New ICC Rules of Arbitration* (Kluwer 1998).

DUFF MCCONNEL, ALAN, *The Third Language – Recurrent Problems of Translation into English* (Pergamon Press 1981).

DUFF MCCONNELL, ALAN, *Into English – Writing and Translating into English as a Second Language* (Ljubljana 2000).

FOUCHARD, PHILIPPE, 'Note (Société Campenon Bernard v. Eurodisneyland SCA, decision of December 12, 1991, second decision of December 20, 1991)', *Revue de l'arbitrage* (1996) p. 523.

FOUCHARD, PHILIPPE, GAILLARD, EMMANUEL AND GOLDMAN, BERTHOLD, *On International Commercial Arbitration* (Kluwer 1999).

GARZONE, GIULIANA, 'Arbitration Rules across Legal Cultures: An Intercultural Approach,' in V. Bhatia, Ch. Candlin and M. Gotti, eds., *Legal Discourse in Multilingual and Multicultural Contexts: Arbitration Texts in Europe* (Bern, Peter Lang Publishers 2003) pp. 177-220.

HOLTZMANN, HOWARD M. and NEUHAUS, JOSEPH E., *A Guide to the UNCITRAL Model Law on International Commercial Arbitration: Legislative History and Commentary*, (The Hague, Kluwer 1989).

JANEVSKI, ARSEN, 'Language of Arbitration as a Ground for Non-Enforcement and Setting Aside: Tracing a Bulgarian Case', 5 *Croatian Arbitration Yearbook* (1998) p. 101.

JARVIN, SIGVARD, 'To What Extent Are Procedural Decisions of Arbitrators Subject to Court Review?', in *Improving the Efficiency of Arbitration Agreements and Awards: 40 Years of Application of the New York Convention* (ICCA, Kluwer 1999) pp. 366-382.

KAHN, PHILIPPE, 'Note (Société La Belle Créole v. Société The Gemtel Partnership, decision of July 12, 1989)', *Revue de l'arbitrage* (1990) p. 194.

KARRER, PIERRE, 'Arbitration and Language, Look for the Purpose', 11 *Croatian Arbitration Yearbook* (2004) p. 7.

KARRER, PIERRE, 'Unbestimmtheit und Unvollständigkeit in Vereinbarungstexten', in V. Bharia et al., eds., *Vagueness in Normative Texts* (Bern, Peter Lang Publishers 2005) pp. 97-108.

LAZAREFF, SERGE, 'The Language of Institutional Arbitration', 8(1) *The ICC International Court of Arbitration Bulletin* (May 1997) p. 18.

LEW, JULIAN D., MISTELIS, LOUKAS A. AND KRÖLL STEAN M., *Comparative International Commercial Arbitration* (Kluwer 2003).

LIEBSCHER, CHRISTOPH M., 'Note (Decision No. 1 Ob 253/97 of April 28, 1998 of the Supreme Court of Austria)', *Revue de l'arbitrage* (1999) pp. 392-400.

MACARTNEY, CARLILE AYLMER, *National States and National Minorities* (New York, Russel and Russel 1986).

MELIS, WERNER, 'Note (Oberster Gerichtshof, Decision of 4 December 1994, 4 Ob 1542/94) *Yearbook Commercial Arbitration*, Vol. XXII (1997) p. 264.

MELLINKOFF, DAVID, *The Language of the Law* (Boston-Toronto, Little, Brown and Comp. 1963).

POLLOCK, FREDERICK and MAITLAND, FREDERIC WILLIAM, *The History of English Law*, 2nd edn. (1898).

RAESCHKE-KESSLER, HILMAR and BERGER, KLAUS PETER, *Recht und Praxis des Schiedsverfahrens* (Köln 1999).

REDFERN, ALAN and HUNTER, MARTIN, *Law and Practice of International Commercial Arbitration*, 3rd edn., (London 1999).

REDFERN, ALAN and HUNTER, MARTIN, *Law and Practice of International Commercial Arbitration*, 4th edn., Student Version (London 2004).

RUBINSTEIN, ARIEL, *Economics and Language, Five essays* (Cambridge, Cambridge University Press 2000).

SAINT JEROME, 'To Pammachius on the Best Method of Translating – Letter LVII', available on the web: http://www.newadvent.org/fathers/3001057.htm.

SCHÄFER, VERBIST IMHOOF, *Die ICC Schiedsgerichtsordnung in der Praxis* (Bonn 2000).

SONTAG, SUSAN, 'On Being Translated', in *Where the Stress Falls – Essays* (Vintage 2003) p. 334.

VAN DEN BERG, ALBERT JAN, *The New York Arbitration Convention of 1958*, 1981 edn. (Kluwer, reprint of 1994).

VAN HOF, JACOMIJN J., *Commentary on the UNCITRAL Arbitration Rules, The Application by the Iran-U.S. Claims Tribunal* (Kluwer 1991).

VÁRADY, TIBOR, 'Arbitration Despite of the Parties?', in M. Sumampouw et al., eds., *Law and Reality*, (in Honour of C.C.A. Voskuil) (Martinus Nijhoff Publishers 1992) pp. 351-376.

VÁRADY, TIBOR, 'O jeziku arbitraže – Opaske i sugestije povodom člana 37 Pravilnika Spoljnotrgovinske arbitraže pri Privrednoj komori Srbije', in *Arbitraža* (Belgrade 2003) pp. 11-27.

VÁRADY, TIBOR, 'Challenge of Arbitral Awards in Recognition Proceedings on Grounds of Shortcomings Pertaining to Language', in *Balancing of Interests, Liber Amicorum Peter Hay* (Frankfurt, Verlag Recht und Wirtschaft 2005) pp. 435-449.

VÁRADY, TIBOR, 'The Language Issue in International Commercial Arbitration – Notions and Questions', in Prawo *Priwatne Czasu Przemian (Festschrift Soltysinski)* (Poznan 2005) pp. 923-954.

VÁRADY, TIBOR, BARCELO, JOHN J. and VON MEHREN, ARTHUR T., *International Commercial Arbitration – A Transnational Perspective*, 3rd edn. (Thomson & West 2006).

VON BREITENSTEIN, DETLEV, 'La language de l'arbitrage – une language arbitraire?', XIII *ASA Bulletin* (1995) pp. 18-21.

VON SCHLECHTRIEM, PETER, 'Das "Sprachrisiko" – ein neues Problem', in Horst Ehmann, Wolfgang Hefermehl and Adolf Laufs, eds., *Privatautonomie, Eigentum und Verantwortung, Festgabe für Hermann Weitnauer* (Berlin 1980).

WESTON, MARTIN, 'Problems and Principles in Legal Translation', 22(4) *The Incorporated Linguist* (Autumn 1983) p. 207.

WILKEY, MALCOLM, 'The Practicalities of Cross-Cultural Arbitration', in S. Frommel and B. Rider, eds., *Conflicting Legal Cultures in Commercial Arbitration* (Kluwer 1999) p. 79.

YOON, BYUNG-CHOL, SUH, JUNG-KEOL, KIM, DAI-HYUN and KIM, GRANT L., 'Arbitration in Korea', in Ph. McConnaughay and Th. Ginsburg, eds., *International Commercial Arbitration in Asia* (JurisNet Publ. 2006).

INDEX